Women and Religion in the African Diaspora

LIVED RELIGIONS

Series Editors: David D. Hall and Robert A. Orsi

Women and Religion
in the African Diaspora

Knowledge, Power, and Performance

Edited by

R. MARIE GRIFFITH

BARBARA DIANNE SAVAGE

The Johns Hopkins University Press
Baltimore

© 2006 The Johns Hopkins University Press
All rights reserved. Published 2006
Printed in the United States of America on acid-free paper
2 4 6 8 9 7 5 3 1

The Johns Hopkins University Press
2715 North Charles Street
Baltimore, Maryland 21218-4363
www.press.jhu.edu

Library of Congress Cataloging-in-Publication Data
Women and religion in the African diaspora : knowledge, power, and
performance / edited by R. Marie Griffith and Barbara Dianne Savage.
p.   cm.
Includes bibliographical references and index.
ISBN 0-8018-8369-5 (hardcover : alk. paper)
ISBN 0-8018-8370-9 (pbk. : alk. paper)
1. Women and religion.   I. Griffith, R. Marie (Ruth Marie), 1967–
II. Savage, Barbara Dianne.
BL458.W56375 2006
200.89′96—dc22
2005032618

A catalog record for this book is available from the British Library.

CONTENTS

This volume is part of a larger project on Women and Religion in the African Diaspora, generously funded by the Ford Foundation and sponsored by the Center for the Study of Religion at Princeton University. We are grateful to Ford and to our visionary program officer Constance Buchanan for helping shape the project from the beginning and supporting it thereafter. We also wish to thank Robert Wuthnow, the Director of the Center for the Study of Religion, for his thoroughgoing support of this project and for first suggesting the idea of this volume with the two of us as co-editors.

William B. Hart, Melani McAlister, and Judith Weisenfeld served actively as project advisers during the initial planning phase in 2000–2001. Anita Kline, Barbara Bermel, Wendy Cadge, and Tisa Wenger provided vital administrative and event-planning support throughout this project's duration into 2005. The center also sponsored several Ford-funded visiting research fellows whose work appears in this collection. Scholars too numerous to name provided crucial advice to us throughout the project; we are grateful to all of them, particularly Jualynne Dodson, Frances Smith Foster, Evelyn Brooks Higginbotham, Jacob K. Olupona, Peter J. Paris, Martha Saavedra, Patrick Taylor, Joe William Trotter, and David Wills.

The Program in African American Studies at Princeton University collaborated with the Women and Religion in the African Diaspora Project in sponsoring numerous public events. Many thanks to Nell Irvin Painter, Noliwe Rooks, and Valerie A. Smith for their enthusiastic support and assistance. Several scholars delivered public lectures or served as respondents under the auspices of this project and also gave crucial feedback to it; these include Joan Dayan, Jacquelyn Grant, Darlene Clark Hine, Laurie Maffly-Kipp, Elizabeth McAlister, Joycelyn Moody, Jacob Olupona, Mercy Amba Oduyoye, Oyèrónké Oyěwùmí, and Peter Paris.

The core of the Women and Religion in the African Diaspora project was the collaborative research group of scholars whose work is featured in this volume. We could not have put together a more extraordinary nor a more collegial assembly. The group met three times over three years, culminating in a three-day public conference in April 2004. Conference participants benefited from the keynote address by Brent Hayes Edwards, the final commentaries by Farah Jasmine Griffin and Eddie S. Glaude Jr., and the insightful comments delivered by a broad range of discussants: Mia Bay, Kim D. Butler, Leslie Callahan, Bettye Collier-Thomas, Yvonne Chireau, Sandra Greene, Nancy A. Hewitt, Lawrence Little, Elizabeth McAlister, Cecilia Moore, Diane Batts Morrow, Albert J. Raboteau, Valerie A. Smith, Margaret Rose Vendryes, Nicole von Germeten, and Timothy P. Watson.

Artist Bill Gaskins provided our logo and did a marvelous job with the project's printed materials and website. Heather White provided skilled assistance during the conference itself. Grey Osterud meticulously edited the conference papers and the volume's introduction during the summer of 2004. Her fine eye has improved all of our work. Peter Agree of the University of Pennsylvania Press generously provided us with indispensable early advice on the shaping of this volume.

It has been a great pleasure to guide these essays into publication. We are grateful to Catherine Brekus for her cogent comments on each and every piece that appears here, and for her judicious support of this venture. Henry Tom, our editor at Johns Hopkins University Press, ably directed the collection into print, with assistance from Clare McCabe and copyeditor Julia R. Smith. We are grateful, finally, to David D. Hall and Robert A. Orsi for supporting this volume as a valuable addition to their new series on Lived Religions.

Gwendolyn Brooks's poem "To the Diaspora" evokes a journey from some un-named point of departure to "Afrika," a double movement that opens possibili-ties for dialogue and reflection. It is a voyage of personal discovery and under-standing that circles back to the self.

> You did not know you were Afrika
> When you set out for Afrika
> You did not know you were going.
> Because
> You did not know you were Afrika.
> You did not know the Black continent
> that had to be reached
> was you.

Africa becomes an imagined place within this diasporic view and thus returns readers to themselves in a more integral way than any literal journey to places of ancestral origin.

Brooks's hopeful vision builds a bridge to possibilities beyond suffering, a search that comes only through something as fragile and necessary as belief. This creative task is only possible, after all, for those who believe it to be so. "You would not have believed my mouth," writes the poet.

> When I told you, meeting you somewhere close
> To the heat and youth of the road,
> liking my loyalty, liking belief,
> you smiled and you thanked me but very little believed me.

The poem closes with a call to venture forth into the uncertain, partly lit terrain of diasporic identities in new lands.

Here is some sun. Some.

Now off into the places rough to reach.

Though dry, though drowsy, all unwillingly a-wobble,

into the dissonant and dangerous crescendo.

Your work, that was done, to be done to be done to be done.

To embark on this journey is to believe in the possibility of creating new knowl-edge, altering perception in order to confront loss, traversing "places rough to reach," and doing what needs to be done. The substance of "your work" remains only loosely named, a matter of personal vocation and design.

Crossing between the concrete and the metaphoric, joining uncertainty to an-ticipation, "To the Diaspora" offers an evocative entrée to the collection presented here. These thirteen new essays journey into diasporas at different times and places. They illuminate some ways in which diverse women of African descent have practiced religion as part of the work of their ordinary and sometimes extraordinary lives. In pursuing this subject comparatively, through studies of various geographical locations in the present and the past, the volume maps new approaches to this fresh field of inquiry.

The book's genesis is a three-year collaborative research project on Women and Religion in the African Diaspora, a broad rubric that suggests the wide range of essays written especially for this interdisciplinary collection and featured at a spring 2004 public conference at Princeton University. While scholars have long grappled with the categories of women, religion, and diaspora, this is the first body of work to bring them together deliberately and in a cross-disciplinary way. In undertaking this venture, we have sought to explore the patterns that emerge when we consider how these subjects intersect, influence, and reshape one an-other in particular locations. What happens to our ideas about religion when black women surface as central protagonists in American, Caribbean, or post-colonial African settings? How does attention to gendered forms of religious ex-perience shift our understandings of diaspora, a concept that is still evolving through varied imaginings and reinventions? And when we focus on the com-plexities of African diasporic crossings in particular, what do we learn by study-ing women's resourceful uses of religious ideas, idioms, and practices?

These essays address such complex questions in rich and diverse ways that suggest emergent models for studying women, religions, and diasporic shifts across time and space. The collection gathers these approaches without seeking to synthesize them or erase their disparities. The first section focuses upon the much-contested matters of history, tradition, and the authenticity of African-derived spiritual practices in a variety of contexts where memories of suffering remain starkly felt. The second section focuses on matters of power and leadership, looking especially at African American women who have insisted upon their own authority even within institutional settings that have traditionally sought to limit it. The third section turns to religious expressions that take place outside institutional settings—in the arts, in media and consumer culture, and in domestic spaces—in order to illustrate their complicated interactions in modern everyday practice. Although these essays echo one another in their attention to power, no single narrative dominates. A recurrent refrain recounts the yearning of these female subjects to claim redemption amid suffering, to forge an integral sense of self, and to preserve faith in the future. To thematize these needs is to open a conversation about the contours, complexity, and specificity of women's religious lives in distinct settings. The stance taken here is not wholly celebratory, as if women's engagement with religion were always and everywhere liberating, nor is it entirely critical, as if religion tended uniformly to reinforce women's oppression. The book sidesteps such false dichotomies to examine what meanings women themselves have made of their religious lives.

One of the revelations of this volume is that fruitful engagement with the questions raised here necessitates cross-disciplinary work and the productive dissonance that comes from collaboration. Only through a variegated approach can the richness of practices, beliefs, and processes in lived religion be revealed, interrogated, and interpreted. In addition to religious studies, the work in this volume spans the disciplines of history, anthropology, sociology, and art history. Professionally trained to think in plainly dissimilar ways about their subject matter, researchers readily aired contrasting perspectives during each of our working group meetings, obliging one another to respond to questions raised outside his or her discipline. That methodological multiplicity is apparent here. The geographic scope of the individual essays is equally diverse, including Africa, Brazil, the Caribbean, and the United States during the nineteenth and twentieth centuries. We have, however, been less concerned about breadth of coverage or territorial and temporal balance than about analytic depth around a common set of interrelated themes.

The aim of this endeavor, from its inception to this culmination, has been to encourage experimental ways of posing questions about women and lived religion in specific periods and places that are rarely considered in proximity to one another. By taking differences across times and spaces as seriously as crosscultural religious convergences, this volume's transnational mixture complicates existing paradigms for teaching and studying women and religion, particularly concerning women of African descent in the Americas and those in Africa. No longer can we conceive of a simple, invariant, and timeless relationship between religious participation and transformational political struggle, for the dynamic patterns that become apparent in these contributions represent dramatically different modes of black female expression and identity. To underscore these variances is to take seriously the shifting power relationships, complex cosmologies, and ambivalent encounters that have shaped the women whose religious lives are analyzed here. Doing so suggests new ways of configuring the conceptual significance of lived religion to the worlds in which we dwell.

We begin by highlighting the ineluctable differences and dissonances within the conceptual framework of the African diaspora itself. Like the symbol "Africa," which contributor Tracey Hucks reminds us might fruitfully be recast as "an elastic category of religious analysis," *diaspora* as an analytic category is still in the process of development, marked by its own controversies and tensions. In its most general and imprecise usages, the term rested on notions of imagined communities (Benedict Anderson's term for nationalism that is based not on the concrete, experiential entity of the nation as much as ideas of commonality and connection, or an imagined homeland); cultural hybridity (metaphorically, the cross-fertilization of different peoples and cultures that takes place in situations of communication, contact, or displacement); and timeless connections to a monolithic and primordial continent. Recently, more refined definitions have acknowledged the diverse, complex, and shifting nature of historical and contemporary migrations of people of African descent. The search for a unifying concept of diaspora has turned toward political constructions: ideas of shared suffering under racist regimes, of parallel subjugation by slavery and colonialism and of common modes of resistance to oppression. Although many scholars—Hortense Spillers, Kwame Anthony Appiah, Paul Gilroy, Katherine Clay Bassard, and Brent Hayes Edwards, among others—have worked to complicate our understanding of this term, the risk of invoking *diaspora* as a unified or ontological category remains ever present.[1]

In particular, Edwards's recent work challenges us to recall that dissonance is central to any practice or theory of diaspora—no less, we hasten to add, than to any practice or theory of religion. Analyzing the politics of diaspora in black historiography and cultural criticism, Edwards remarks that its continued utility "is not that it offers the comfort of abstraction, an easy recourse to origins, but that it forces us to consider discourses of cultural and political linkage only through and across difference." Bassard, too, views diasporic figurations as "structures of vision" that challenge rather than reinforce common presuppositions about African collective identity. Keeping in mind these salutary warnings, we now regard *diaspora* as an analytic tool for investigating the place of women in questions about religious authenticity and the transmission of historical memory.[2]

Earlier theoretical formulations of diaspora are both too porous and too blunt to help us understand the variety of religious practices that exist among the women represented in this collection. The essays in part 1 clarify this point with perspicuity and precision. According to Rachel Harding's study of the Afro-Brazilian religion of Candomblé, inherited memories of slavery evoke deep suffering and loss, and this embodied knowledge shapes women's religious practice in ways that differ profoundly from how U.S. women's religious lives (documented in later chapters) are formed. Isabel Mukonyora finds a link between the afflictions of barren, excluded, or dispossessed women who participate in a contemporary Zimbabwean Christian movement and the wilderness imagery its leaders invoke. This discovery leads her to a riveting conceptualization of the innovative prophetic dimensions of a "Diaspora within" continental Africa marked by wandering, homelessness, and the reclamation of sacred spaces on the margins of the social landscape. In this contemporary setting, as in Hucks's investigation of Trinidad and Deidre Crumbley's essay on Nigeria, disputes repeatedly emerge over the parameters of orthodoxy, including the meanings attributed to indigenous African and Christian symbols and their relative weight in postcolonial contexts. Paul Christopher Johnson explores the powerful ways in which diaspora works as "sentiment and subjectivity" for the Garífuna people of Honduras and New York, becoming a potent yet highly contested symbol of historical, political, and religious legitimacy in the course of repeated migrations. What matters, Johnson and other contributors emphasize, is not the facticity of claims to authentic African origins but rather how those claims function to define and validate a diasporic identity and consciousness. Traveling "to the diaspora," we are reminded, is a creative venture requiring repetitive, commemorative work in shifting cultural locations and relocations. Little wonder, then, that these journeys are highly fraught with risk and instability.

What then of the category *women* and the attention to gender at the core of this project? The field is surely ripe for such a focus: as Sandra Gunning, Tera W. Hunter, and Michele Mitchell have recently noted, "the use of gender as a category of analysis remains something of a challenge for African Diaspora studies."[3] There has been a dearth of scholarly attention to black women's religious lives more generally, with only a handful of scholars pursuing historical, sociological, or anthropological research on this subject.[4] Recentering women in a study of diasporic religions reveals the extensive cultural and political work of black women in transnational settings. Predictably, we find women keeping faith alive and sustaining ritual and spiritual communities in concrete, daily acts. Readers will find many commonalties among these case studies, even as they move across time and space. Yet looking at this subject from the positions and perspectives of women and listening to women's voices and visions ultimately discloses more dissonances than resonances, revealing specific ways of living religion that are not coterminous with one another. Diverse places of origin, different experiences of displacement, and disparate living conditions are connected in women's religious lives to equally distinctive modes of spiritual expression and ritual action, dynamics of adaptation and innovation, and strategies that maneuver within and across religious and social settings. Just as Africanness is not a single point of origin and diaspora is not a single geographic or ontological destination, so black womanhood in this transnational context signifies patterns of divergences and convergences.

If we embark on the project of constructing a feminist theory of diaspora, as Edwards and others have urged, this book offers a rich and variegated archive that records and reconstructs the theological work and religious labors of women, whether or not they aspired to leadership. Although scholarship has recently been shifting from looking at women toward taking on gender as a category of analysis, this move works better in fields where women's positions and perspectives have been more fully registered than has been the case in African diasporic studies. As the research presented here demonstrates, exciting moments of discovery and recovery still await those who explore this relatively uncharted terrain, and placing women at the center of our inquiry transforms our conceptual map of lived religion. The variations in women's voices and viewpoints and in patterns of continuity and change suggest the need for more inclusive and dynamic models of diaspora. Studying women in the African diasporic context enables us to return to time-honored questions about authority, leadership, and power and to perceive and conceive them in new ways.

Part 2 focuses especial attention on these questions, noting that while women everywhere play essential roles in the creation, maintenance, and transfer of religious culture and practice, those roles do not look the same even within a specific national context. In the United States, for example, the politely assertive public culture forged by activist northern Methodist women whom Martha Jones studies is manifestly distinct from the fiery Pentecostal arena inhabited by the sexually ambiguous preaching women whose self-presentation Wallace Best examines. Neither of these groups operates with the same assumptions about gender roles and relationships—and, more subtly and subversively, strategies for destabilizing them—as do the Bible Bands whose history Anthea Butler traces or the black community activists whose life stories Cheryl Townsend Gilkes analyzes. These essays define and explore matters of power and authority in several dimensions. Jones pays close attention to the intellectual foundations and implications of women's religious experience, Best scrutinizes women's divergent strategies for subverting gender expectations, Butler explicates devotional readings of scripture that create a "new sense of self and sense of duty to God," and Gilkes traces the "inextricable connection" between women's faith and their work for social change. Taken together, these essays lift up the disparities more than the continuities in the religious worlds of African American women in the nineteenth and twentieth centuries.

Finally, what can readers make of *religion*, the third category that is central to this project? We believe that research on religion offers a particularly intriguing and less well-traveled route for transnational and diasporic studies, historical and contemporary. Like *diaspora* and *women*, the category *religion* is easily romanticized—especially as a source of female authority, agency, and solidarity. Indeed, women's narratives of their own religious experiences frequently uphold such a view, invested as they are in demonstrating the redemptive potential of their own practices or even converting outsiders to their worldview. Some analysts of religion continue to write in this vein out of a desire to topple old paradigms (such as those influenced by the writings of Marx, Freud, Daly, and Foucault) that presume religion to be a source of oppression, most particularly for women. The essays in this collection defeat the narrow, dichotomous view that religious participation signifies either gullible capitulation to structures of oppression or an emancipatory overthrow of them. They suggest an alternative, namely, that women's accounts of their religious experiences may demonstrate multiple shifting claims to power that are sometimes built on and sometimes defiant of their understandings of womanhood.

Consider the artists who elaborate the "arts of enchantment" documented in Lisa Gail Collins's essay. These visionaries confound ordinary descriptions of religion through their commitment to what Collins terms a "black diasporic premise" about material objects, desire, and emotional control. This reliance on "cross-cultural artistic experimentation" surfaces as well in Judith Weisenfeld's analysis of how black female composers such as Eva Jessye have used art to do theological work and to present their theologies as liturgical performances in public, even secular arenas. Jessye's insistence upon her stylistically hybrid musical art being what Weisenfeld terms "religious praxis" reminds us of the expansive possibilities for religious expression outside formal institutional contexts. Exploring the seemingly secular realm of shopping, Carolyn Rouse analyzes the religious dimensions of consumption practices and performances of self. Black Muslim women like Sister Zubayda make meaning by participating in popular American culture (eating at McDonalds, buying Barbie dolls, and attending fashion shows) and by subverting select conventions by making religiously informed choices and interpretations (ordering *halal* meat or eschewing cheeseburgers, sewing modest clothing and head coverings for dolls, and purchasing garments with hybrid fabric and design) in order to "cross a number of different domains: Muslim, African American, woman, Los Angelina, mother, wife." Marla Frederick-McGlathery accentuates women's negotiation of televangelism as part of a "sifting process," a "renegotiation of self" that proclaims personal liberation from suffering and oppression but may also dissent from televangelists' silence about larger questions of social justice or their explicit political conservatism. All of these women are shown in these essays to live their religion through strategies of improvisation and compromise that help them attain a sense of purpose and "make peace" (Rouse's term) with those realities of their lives over which they have little or no control.

Exploring religion's meanings for women does not lead to fatuous declarations of religion's universal, unequivocal benefits for its female adherents any more than it commands sweeping condemnations of religion's overwhelmingly oppressive and patriarchal power. Shifting our stance to examine what women themselves make of religion emancipates us from such false generalizations and polarizations. At times, religion is prophetic and empowering. The community organizers Gilkes interviewed testified that faith enabled them to cultivate voices that were "loud, disruptive, and fearsome" to the injustices surrounding them, amplifying and sharpening their forceful response to oppressive conditions and facilitating their work with male allies. At other times, as in Mukonyora's study of the Masowe Apostles movement, women must struggle against theological and cultural assumptions, such as those linking women and nature as resources that men "dominate and exploit" even while "yield[ing] to them ritual power." Everywhere in these essays, lived religion is marked by conflict, contradiction, ambiguity, and the potential for manipulation.

The rubric of *lived religion* is exceptionally useful for the work included here. Since its inception in the early 1990s, lived religion has served as a conceptual signpost for particular approaches to the study of religion that concentrate on negotiations of power and identity in ordinary life, within ecclesial structures (church, synagogue, mosque, etc.) and outside them in domestic life and in a wide variety of so-called public spheres (voluntary organizations, the media, or self-help groups, for instance). Researchers in the field, influenced by studies of culture in anthropology, history, and literature, have sought to understand how diverse peoples have strategically utilized religious practices to maneuver in every-day encounters and thereby have reshaped their own participation in society and culture. Through this work, scholars have sought to supplant old hierarchies in the study of religion that have long distinguished matters of belief, theology, and intellectual life from behaviors, habits, and material practices such as ritual activity. Theorists of lived religion have challenged timeworn distinctions between public and private realms, elite and popular forms of religion, and the very division between religious and social domains, as scholars have illuminated the creative ways people mediate these arenas and negotiate culture with the tools at hand. The implications of this ongoing methodological and theoretical shift are vast, not least because it lends itself to more inventive renderings of "religion" itself than were once considered appropriate.

The study of lived religion has attended with particular care to moments of conflict, dissonance, and displacement. Scholars have perceived such moments, whether occurring at the level of the family, local community, or even nation, to be meaningful and productive, generating the need for new narratives of identity that justify particular forms of religious participation in a specific historical setting. Like other interdisciplinary academic fields to which it is kin—cultural studies, postcolonial studies, and subaltern studies—lived religion has focused chiefly on people whose lives have been ruptured by social, political, and historical circumstances, and such work highlights multiple creative uses of religion in the midst as well as the aftermath of these dynamic changes. Women have risen to the fore as protagonists in studies of lived religion, and scholars have keenly sought to understand how women in male-led religious groups have maneuvered among the religious repertoires available to them in "making peace," or coming to terms, with what some perceive as enforced subordination.

Very little of the scholarship on lived religion has focused specifically on black women, despite its concern with women and gendered negotiations of power. Similarly, although a number of studies under this rubric have emphasized transnational alliances and conflicts, these have largely focused on Anglo-American and white European groups. Centering women of African descent in the analytic space opened up by lived religion sheds new light on this subject and enables us to stretch the lived religion rubric itself. In this volume, we attend not only to recognized topics and approaches, such as ritual, healing, memory, and identity formation, but also to themes and questions that remain untapped or nascent in the current literature. Here we see diverse ways in which women serve as sources of embodied knowledge, quite apart from visible indicators of social headship, and we observe vital instances of women's ritual bilingualism (Hucks's phrase) across cultures. Movement emerges as a theme again and again: dispossession and loss generate forced exile as people are driven from their land, yet dancing, traveling, migrating, and wandering in the wilderness are modes through which new religious practices and peoples are created. Space, mythic and real, arises thematically in many of these essays, as women work to envisage sites such as Africa, the slave quarters, the wilderness, or the geography of an art gallery. The essays pay attention to elaborate rituals of fashion and adornment in female religious settings, along with the sundry prohibitions against ornamentation. And they speak of a hoped-for solidarity generated through intertwined albeit distinct histories of struggle and suffering.

Studying women in diverse religious contexts through the lens of lived religion offers a unique and fruitful way of marking clearly the very dissonances that are the heart of notions of diaspora—often within the same religious tradition. Many of the essays in this volume focus on women in Christian traditions, but they show women engaging those traditions in radically different ways. We find neither representations of an identical belief system across time and space nor much evidence of easily transferable modes of behavior and religious worship; rather, we find a fascinating series of distinct yet highly visible subversions of dominant theological strands and ritual practices. In the essays by Jones and Crumbley, women struggle over rights to ministry; in the late nineteenth-century United States, women created a public culture within which they could assert their claims to spiritual authority; and in contemporary Africa women make a place for themselves as preachers and elders. Best's subjects clash over female inversions of sexual convention and gendered authority; Mukonyora's enact complicated forms of spiritual ecstasy and establish unmediated relationships with God. These are some of the most vivid challenges to earthly authorities and spiritual hierarchies that are elaborated in this collection. Yet it is important to recognize, as the African cases strongly remind us, that these subversions do not all take place in reaction to the legacy of slavery. African American religious historians have long organized their analysis around an axis of oppression and liberation based on the specific brutal realities of slavery in American history. It has been all too easy and it is still tempting to extrapolate that axial narrative *tout court* onto other geographical contexts, including the African continent itself. In these case studies, other political models of analysis emerge that encompass the legacies of colonialism and are more particular to settings outside of the United States. These approaches, in turn, may enable scholars to escape the limitations of a polarized model of subordination and resistance and explore other axes along which black women have lived their religion.

In promoting these and other reconceptualizations, this new work on religious women of African descent in the Afro-Atlantic world and women in Africa helps us to understand how women's religious labors embody historical knowledge. Harding's essay on Brazilian Candomblé wondrously evokes the performative meanings and memories of slavery conveyed by the body through dance, physical labor, and clothing, along with other forms of decorative art. Collins's article on the religiously inspired, erotic art of Alison Saar focuses on the sexual and medicinal uses of natural and found objects as especially expressive forms of religious power. Rouse's analysis of shopping and consumption in the lives of black Sunni Muslim women living in Los Angeles points us to other ways of considering what is all too frequently invisible about women's mundane religious work. Bodily experience, these and other essays recurrently reveal, is inseparable from the spiritual work performed by women; religious knowledge is itself carried in and enacted through the body. Moreover, the gendering of bodily experiences takes fascinating forms that are not always easily mapped upon ordinary definitions of male and female, masculine and feminine. Theorists of religion have long been fascinated by this performative dimension of the body, and this collection points to some emergent ways of conceiving the body's religious exercise across a set of diasporic contexts.

Recognizing how these women's religious labors embody historical knowledge opens the way for us to see, in turn, how religion also works to link the prophetic with the political and the practical in the lives of women. Frederick-McGlathery's essay on women's responses to televangelism and Gilkes's analysis of black female activists motivated by religious faith make these connections most apparent. We can also discern such lines of connection in the public life of the American composer and conductor Eva Jessye, limned carefully here by Weisenfeld. As separated as these and other women may be by space and time and concrete beliefs, their life's work in religious worlds is motivated by an intertwining of the political and the prophetic. That prophetic potential may not always flourish consistently or be realized wholly over time, but even its frail and partial manifestations counter stale but persistent notions of religion as wholly manipulative, compensatory, or oppressive.

Women have played prominent roles in many diasporic religious settings as official leaders, unofficial mediators of spiritual power, and active participants whose presence legitimizes the religious messages of others. Some black women in the New World have embraced Islam, while others have adopted African-derived religions such as Yoruba *vodou* or Candomblé, even while crafting forms of religious engagement whose relation to orthodox Muslim or indigenous African spiritual practices remains contested. Other women of African descent have remained within the Protestant traditions once shared with their enslavers, while continuing to alter those traditions to suit their own needs as they inhabit new places and encounter new problems. Meanwhile, many women living in Africa have converted to innovative forms of Christianity that subtly or explicitly subvert the legacy of European colonialism and draw upon local spiritual practices to forge a prophecy and practice of redemption.

Although some of the women studied here are acutely conscious of a diasporic history of movement or displacement linking them to diverse geographic peoples and religious configurations, that awareness plays less of a formative role in the lives of many others. Women in contemporary African settings who are reckoning with relocations on the continent rather than international displacements envision diaspora differently from women of African descent in the Americas. Yet migrations within the American hemisphere often give rise to a diasporic consciousness that was not salient until women left the places they knew as home, venturing from the Caribbean or the U.S. South into multicultural northern cities.

Such is the multiplicity of women's religious experiences preserved and presented in this book. These writings represent the labors of a group of scholars striving to better understand and interpret those experiences and to find concrete new ways of theorizing about race, gender, religion, and power in the modern world. Taken together, their scholarship opens up new points of departure for others willing to join in the challenge of doing more of this work, even though, as Brooks warns, it will take them and us "off into the places rough to reach."

PART I

DIASPORIC KNOWLEDGE

CHAPTER ONE

É a Senzala

Slavery, Women, and Embodied Knowledge in Afro-Brazilian Candomblé

RACHEL ELIZABETH HARDING

For the religions of the Afro-Atlantic diaspora, whose roots are in the trials and traumas of the creation of the New World, the experience of slavery is a foundational element, embedded in the structure and meaning of these traditions and present in their contemporary expressions. The examples are myriad, from the continuing power of spirituals and the Old Testament stories of the Israelites' deliverance in the black Protestantism of North America to the cultivation of the vigorous and vehement Petro[1] deities of Vodou whose righteous anger registers a stance of resistance to slavery and French colonial domination. In so many ways, the experience and memory of slavery continue to inform the practice and meaning of black religion in the Americas.

One of the major religions of the Afro-Atlantic diaspora is Candomblé, a rich, poetic tradition of reciprocity and engagement among living human beings and ancestral energies, the natural world, and the world of the spirits. Candomblé emerged in the cities and *senzalas* (slave quarters) of nineteenth-century northeastern Brazil out of the lives and struggles of African women and men and their Brazilian-born descendants. The religion combines cosmologies and ritual practices from West and Central African sources with elements developed in the New World matrix of slavery, interactions with Native Americans and Europeans, and reconstructed meanings of identity and lineage. At the heart of Candomblé is the ritual cultivation of connection between the children of the African diaspora and the spiritual energies (*orixás, nkisis, voduns*) they inherit from their ancestors. Mãe Stella de Oxôssi, *iyalorixá* (chief priestess) of the Ilê Axé Opô Afonjá Candomblé community, believes "Todo negro tem herança de orixá" (All blacks have an *orixá* inheritance).[2]

Like Haitian Vodou, Cuban Santeria, Surinamese Winti, African American Christianity, and many other religions of the Afro-Atlantic world, Candomblé developed as a central element in the effort of enslaved and subordinated people to make sense of an experience of extraordinary disjunction and to hold fast to the deepest sources of their own humanity in the midst of great personal and collective trauma.

Through the nineteenth and twentieth centuries, Candomblé developed into one of Brazil's most important indigenous religious practices, with marked participation and leadership by black women. While the earliest leaders of Afro-Brazilian religious communities in Bahia were African-born men, for most of the nineteenth century, black women—African and Brazilian born—predominated among participants. When slavery was abolished in 1888, observers noted that the children and grandchildren of Africans were increasingly assuming leadership of Candomblé *terreiros* (ritual communities) and many of the new leaders were female. Among these Brazilian-born leaders were women who founded the oldest continually recognized *terreiros* in the city of Salvador, capital of the northeastern state of Bahia. Ilê Axé Iyá Nassô Oká, popularly known as Casa Branca; Ilê Axé Opô Afonjá; Ilê Maroiá Láji, or Alaketu; and Axé Iaomin Iamassê, also known as Gantois—all were organized by black women and, like many other *terreiros* in the city and its environs, have maintained a tradition of Afro-Brazilian, female leadership in ensuing generations.[3]

This chapter briefly examines the historical development of the religion and the role of women as leaders and devotees. It then explores the orientation to history embodied in Candomblé tradition—specifically, how the legacy of slavery informs the contemporary experience, meaning, and resources of the religion.

Historian of religions Charles H. Long provides an important framework for understanding the relationship of the history of slavery to the development of religions of the Afro-Atlantic diaspora. A central impulse for most of these religions was and remains that of (re)claiming identities of wholeness and transformative possibility for devotees who are besieged and subjected peoples. Slaves "had to experience the truth of [their] negativity and at the same time transform and create *an-other* reality." For Long, the religious consciousness of enslaved people was the context in which that *other* reality emerged, was nurtured, and became the source of deeply sustaining cultural forms and historical meanings.[4]

My intention here is to describe and explore connections to a meaning of historical experience operative in the lives, gestures, and orientations of Candomblé devotees, especially the women. I suggest that these connections, and their creative and transformative possibilities, exist at the level of religious consciousness in *terreiro* communities and that the orientation to the historical past is so deeply imbued in daily ritual life that it becomes a past, experienced, in some sense, in the present.

Slavery and the Reshaping of African Tradition

Over the more than three hundred years that slavery existed in Brazil, that nation maintained the dubious distinction of consuming the labor and lives of more Africans than any other New World society. By the conservative estimates of Phillip Curtin, close to four million Africans arrived in the slave markets of Brazil from the mid-sixteenth through the mid-nineteenth centuries. Of that number, almost one-and-a-half million landed at Salvador and were made to work in the houses, small commerce, and streets of that city as well as in the towns and agricultural estates of the surrounding *recôncavo* (the plantation region surrounding Salvador and the Bay of All Saints). Most of these individuals were men. Most were young, between the ages of sixteen and thirty. And most did not live to be old. From the late eighteenth century until the effective end of the slave trade in 1850, the majority of those enslaved in Brazil was transported from Yoruba- and Fon-speaking areas of West Africa, particularly around the Bight of Benin.

The ethnic and regional origin of enslaved Africans in nineteenth-century Bahia is an important element in the history of Candomblé because Yoruba-speaking people (called *Nagôs* in Brazil) and Ewes or Fon-speaking people (called *Jêjes* in Brazil) gave Candomblé much of its linguistic and liturgical structure. Cabindas, Benguelas, and other peoples from central and southwestern Africa were also important to the emerging religion; they created some of its New World precursors, such as the eighteenth-century Afro-Brazilian tradition known as *Calundu*. The influence of West African Muslims and of several other less-well-represented ethnic groups like the Gruncis and Tapas also was marked, though less strongly, in the language and ritual of candomblé *terreiros*.[5]

The work that enslaved men and women performed in Brazil was remarkably varied. In the cold and damp of the mines, they dug for gold and diamonds. On the plantations of the northeast and central south, they planted and chopped cotton, turned sugar cane into molasses, and harvested coffee beans, tobacco, and cacao. Their presence was ubiquitous in the cities, especially the ports of Rio and Salvador. There they worked as stevedores, carrying everything from bales of cotton and barrels of rum to people and pianos on their shoulders, backs, and heads. They washed other people's clothes. They nursed other people's children. They cooked other people's food and kept other people's houses clean. Many urban slaves sold sundries in the markets and through the streets: fruits, vegetables, cooked foods, lace, buttons, candles, almost anything that could be manufactured by hand.

The experience of slavery in late colonial and imperial Brazil (that is, from the late eighteenth through the late nineteenth centuries) was distinguished by an extraordinary variety of labors; by regular, grim punishments for acts of resistance; by the prevalence of chronic and epidemic diseases; by often inadequate food, clothing, and shelter; and by a consistent excess of deaths over births. However, especially in the urban areas of the country, such as Salvador, slavery was also characterized by conscious ethnic identification among slaves and freedpeople, by a task-based form of slave labor that enabled some men and women to work toward their freedom when they had finished the duties their owners required of them, and by close living and working relations between slaves and the growing class of free or freed black poor. These specific circumstances of urban Brazilian slavery allowed some enslaved people to wrest from within its constrictions a measure of autonomy sufficient to create and sustain a variety of Afro-Brazilian cultural/ritual communities.

The *ganho* or "earning" system was the major configuration of black labor in the city of Salvador during the nineteenth century. The *escravos de ganho* (slaves) and *negros de ganho* (freedpeople), as blacks who worked under this arrangement were called, commonly worked in the street, selling either homemade manufactured items or their own labor as carriers of water, cargo, and human beings. Slaves who did this work were obliged to return a daily or weekly portion of their earnings to the master or mistress. They were also often required to pay for their own upkeep—food, clothing, and shelter—out of the funds remaining. Women who worked under the *ganho* system, called *ganhadeiras*, were involved in a variety of forms of ambulatory commerce, especially selling foodstuffs: produce, fish, and prepared dishes. They also worked as washerwomen, lace makers, seamstresses, and embroiderers. Women were used in heavy manual labor in Salvador; until 1850, female slaves did construction work. Working as water carriers, women balanced full buckets and heavy barrels on their heads and backs as they supplied their owners' homes and businesses or sold portions to customers along the roads.[6]

While *ganhadeiras* were a visible and important aspect of Bahian daily life, street vending was not the primary task of the majority of urban female slaves. Most enslaved women and girls in Salvador were domestic workers. In the city's households they were maids, cooks, wet nurses, laundresses, starchers, seamstresses, and personal attendants. House slaves generally lived with greater restrictions on their movements than did the *escravos de ganho*. They were usually *crioulas* or *pardas* (black and brown-skinned Brazilian-born women) because slave owners generally preferred Brazilian-born slaves to Africans for household work. Domestic slaves had little or no access to money and were more dependent on personal relations with their owners. But the categories of house slaves and *escravos de ganho* were sufficiently permeable that a domestic slave might be sent to work in the streets or rented to another person when not engaged in the owner's house, particularly if she or he had desirable skills.[7]

Because of the relative mobility it allowed, the *ganho* system was very important in the formation of Candomblé. Street workers circulated more or less freely among communities of Afro-Brazilians in Salvador. Some even traveled to surrounding towns, becoming conduits for information, materials, and connections among groups of people in different parts of the *recôncavo*. Because of the relative lack of *senhorial* supervision, these women and men were able to build networks of social, economic, and spiritual support that they drew upon in the formation of early Candomblé communities.

Black street workers—slave and freed—organized into groups to share their labors and keep one another company. They often lived in close proximity, sometimes in the same dwelling. Among African men, these occupational affinity groups, called *cantos*, were usually organized by ethnicity and associated with a location of substantial traffic—a plaza, a fountain, the lower docks of the city— where the *cantos'* members could wait for and solicit customers. When not selling merchandise or performing labor for hire, they did craft work: braiding mats and hats of straw, making leather and shell bracelets, fashioning birdcages, or stringing rosaries. The places where these *cantos* met became informal centers of black cultural interaction; ambulatory barbers and food vendors would set up shop nearby, and other workers were attracted by the makeshift stoves and large pots of porridges, stews, and African-inspired meat, fish, and vegetable dishes.[8]

The food vendors were generally women, and although they also worked in proximity to friends, one contemporary observer noted that the women's *cantos* were not so strongly distinguished by ethnicity as those of men.[9] They were more apt to include members of several ethnic groups. Women's affinity workgroups likely included gatherings of washerwomen who met together at a particular fountain or riverbank, market women who set up their wares in stalls near each other, and food vendors who shared a plaza corner. These women, who made their living and that of their owners in the small-scale commerce of the capital city of Bahia, were known for business savvy and good communication skills.[10]

In Salvador, the *ganhadeiras* were intimately associated with Candomblé. Police documents and oral histories of many of the older *terreiros* suggest that

African- and Brazilian-born black women who worked in the city's streets were among the major participants and leaders of Afro-Brazilian religious communities in the area.[11] That women's *cantos* appear to have been more inclusive than those of their male counterparts suggests a connection between multiethnic work and friendship associations and the developing pan-African character of Candomblé *terreiros* during the second half of the nineteenth century.

Several documents from the historical record support the significance of *ganhadeiras* and pan-black alliances in the development of Candomblé. Two reports from the 1860s are particularly instructive. In 1862, the Salvador chief of police ordered a local subdelegate (police officer) to raid the house at number 7 Santa Theresa Hill in the neighborhood of São Pedro. The house was the location of twice-weekly meetings of slaves and others organized by the owner, Domingos Sodré (known as Papai Domingos), a freed African. Theodolinda, a Yoruba slave, was a frequent visitor to the house, and her owner, José Egydio Nabuco, a customs clerk, complained to police that the woman stole items and money from him and carried them to Sodré's residence "under the pretext of obtaining freedom by means of sorcery." According to the police reports, Sodré worked in cooperation with two freed African women identified as *ganhadeiras*. These three freedpeople acted as mediums and "luck changers," counseling slaves to make offerings to modify the behavior of the people who owned them and to use magico-pharmacopoeic and ritual means to free themselves from bondage. During the raid, altars and various Candomblé ceremonial items were discovered. Slaves had also brought jewelry and other valuable objects to the house as gifts or payment in exchange for "drinks and mixtures," which they gave to their masters and mistresses in order to mollify them. The police authorities blamed Sodré and the unnamed African women for the loss of the labor of many Africans and recommended an "urgent and proficient remedy" to rid Bahia of such individuals "so harmful in our country, the larger part of whose fortune is completely in the possession of slaves."[12]

Two years later, in 1864, the journal *O Alabama* described the leadership of the Dendezeiro *terreiro* in Salvador: an Angolan-born *mãe-de-santo* (*terreiro* leader or priestess) Ana Maria; a freedwoman named Antonia Fernandes da Silva, who was "responsible for the altar; the place where the saints [*orixás*] are present"; and Maria, a *parda* who was the seamstress of the house. Antonia was described as the "secretary" of the Candomblé house, although her ritual duties mark her as an *iylaxé,* the person responsible for feeding and maintaining the spiritual energy of the *terreiro* and its *orixás* or *nkisis*. As a slave, she had been sold from Salvador to Rio de Janeiro but had returned to Bahia after securing her manumission. Two other women were identified as Balbina, who ironed the ritual garments of the *terreiro* community, and Maria dos Santos, who headed "a group which informs the people in the city" about the activities of the Candomblé.[13] The work of Maria, the seamstress, and Balbina, the ironer, are reminders of the continuum of labor black women performed in the Bahian economy and the skills they brought to the maintenance of Candomblé communities. Maria dos Santos, the leader of the *terreiro*'s information network, was likely a *ganhadeira,* serving a similar role in her perambulations as that of the women who worked with Domingos Sodré.

While the records do not tell us the specific ethnic identification of Sodré and the *ganhadeiras* who were his coworkers in the São Pedro Candomblé house, the women's access to communities of enslaved people through their regular presence in the city's streets surely contributed to the *terreiro*'s ability to attract clients and participants to its ritual work. Some of the items discovered in the house suggest that the *ganhadeiras,* or other women, may have actually lived there, which correlates with *terreiro* members' practice of spending significant periods of time at their spiritual homes and in some instances more or less permanently residing on the grounds. The presence of the items may also suggest that women, in particular, sought community, assistance, and recognition of their leadership capacities in places like the house on Santa Theresa Hill.

The description of the Dendezeiro Candomblé community does not give a complete accounting of the ethnic and racial identifications of the participants. However, it is apparent that this *terreiro* represented the increasingly pan-black character of Candomblé in the city. African- and Brazilian-born blacks; slaves, freed, and free people; women and men—all shared ritual responsibilities in that religious community.[14] The leadership of the Angolan-born *mãe-de-santo,* Ana Maria, also illustrates the growing trend toward women's leadership in *terreiros* during the second half of the nineteenth century.

For many of the individuals who were kept in bondage in Bahia, family and lineage relations that were ruptured in the Middle Passage and through the sale of relatives away from one another were reconfigured by means of ethnicity. For Yoruba-speaking people from Oyo or Ketu, for example, the connections they established with others from their homelands were among the most significant ways they had to remember who and what they were prior to the holocaust of their enslavement. However, as African religiosity in Bahia was transformed by New World exigencies, its Afro-Brazilian manifestations were increasingly interethnic, based on commonalties of symbolic, ritual, and philosophical meaning which were shared by Africans from a variety of points on the continent. Women, through their multiethnic work and ritual alliances, must have played a particularly important role in this transformation and in the developing pan-black experience of Candomblé.

As individuals from various regions and ethnicities were scattered throughout Brazil's plantations, mines, and cities, their original ethnic and spiritual affiliations were eventually fragmented, and they created new gatherings for the reconstruction of religion and identity. The physical organization of Candomblé *terreiros* became a reflection and a representation of the pan-Africanizing impulse in the religion's development.

Although the earliest *terreiros* were established during the first half of the nineteenth century by more or less ethnically homogeneous groups of individuals, relatively quickly, the community of devotees in *Nagô, Jêje,* or *Angola* candomblés began to manifest a decidedly multiethnic, pan-African character. By the end of the nineteenth century, Afro-Brazilian devotees of Candomblé were identifying themselves by the ethnic "nation" of their *terreiro,* with the understanding that the designation referred to the spiritual lineage in which they had been initiated and not necessarily to their blood ancestry. As leaders and participants in these ritual communities, black women helped transform the meanings of family, ethnicity, and ancestry in the Afro-Brazilian context. For example, Eugênia Anna dos Santos (Mãe Aninha), founder of Ilê Axé Opô Afonjá and one of the legendary forces in Bahian Candomblé, was the daughter of Africans of Grunci ethnicity. She was initiated into Candomblé, however, by a Yoruba (*Nagô*) priestess, a daughter of the famous Iyá Nassô, founder of the Barroquinha *terreiro,* which later moved to Engenho Velho and became known as Casa Branca. Mãe Aninha was proud to proclaim that the *terreiro* she formed and led for many years was "pure *Nagô,*" emphasizing an understanding of ethnic genealogy that was more spiritual than consanguineous.[15]

As Africans and their descendants reorganized the structures of ritual cultivation of African (and soon also Amerindian) spiritual energies in Brazil, they brought together various deities under the collective care of a single community. Each *orixá* was accorded a specific, delimited space—often a room, a portion of a room, or a one-room "house"—in which the divinity is said to reside.[16] This is the place where the *orixá*'s energy is ritually cultivated and where various rites for devotees are conducted.

In most of the West and Central African traditions from which Candomblé derives, deities were associated with and venerated by particular families, ethnic groups, and geopolitical entities. In the collectivizing experience of Candomblé— in the circle-dance ceremonies in honor of multiple *orixás,* as well as in the structure and organization of altar space in the religious communities—deities of various ethnic and subethnic groups were brought together in a single ritual space. At the same time, a sense of each god's particular origins and the relationships among groups of deities was maintained through myths, language, alimentary preferences, dance, and music rhythms. This process modeled the experience of the Africans and Afro-Brazilians themselves and perhaps stimulated the growth of pan-African consciousness.[17]

Another characteristic that distinguishes Afro-Brazilian Candomblé from its African origins is the increased number of individuals "chosen" by the *orixá* to host and manifest the divine energies in their bodies. African slaves and freedpeople living in Bahia during the late nineteenth century who were interviewed by the forensic physician Raimundo Nina Rodrigues noted that blacks in Brazil had a greater propensity to *cair no santo*—"fall in the saint"; go into trance, become possessed by an *orixá*—than their counterparts on the African continent.[18] Pierre Verger, a French scholar of African and Afro-Brazilian religion, wrote in the mid-twentieth century that one of the principal distinctions between the practice of Yoruba religion in Africa and Candomblé was the greater obligation of members of Brazilian ritual communities to attend to the needs and requirements of the *orixás* they served. This situation highlighted an especially intense connection between devotees and spirits in the New World community.[19]

A scholar of Haitian Vodou, Karen McCarthy Brown, contributes an important insight into the phenomenon of increased intimacy among African spirits and their human devotees in the Americas. She describes the experience of some Haitian children who arrived in the United States as refugees during the 1980s. In the island nation itself, children are rarely possessed by the *lwas* (gods, orixás); the experience is perceived as too dangerous for them. Upon arriving at the Florida coast, many of the young boys and girls who had made the perilous journey were separated by the U.S. Immigration and Naturalization Service from the adults they knew and trusted and with whom they had traveled. These children, writes Brown, "responded to their fear by going into possession."[20] It was as if, in the midst of what was surely a terrifying situation for the children, the closeness and assurance of the presence of the *lwas* was an urgency. Brown reflects that the experience of contemporary Haitian children may have some similarities to that of individuals arriving in eighteenth-century Haiti from Africa.

In Afro-Atlantic traditions where the proximity of divine protectors and guides is an important dimension of religious experience, it appears that the pressing need for the nearness of God in tragic and traumatic circumstances has intensified the force of connection and mutual responsibility between devotees and deities. I suggest that the central paradigm for this response—in Candomblé as well as in Vodou, Santeria, Winti, African American Protestantism, and many other religions of the diaspora—is the embodied, embedded memory of slavery.

Terreiro Organization and Embodied Knowledge

In Candomblé, women are a primary link to that memory of slavery and to the engagement of its continuing meaning for the present: the *mães-de-santo* who founded and led many of the oldest extant *terreiros,* their successors, and the initiates and devotees who form the rising generation of caretakers of the religion. These women absorb, carry, wrestle with, and yield to the history and its ghosts, the experience of slavery and survival that created and sustains an ancestral connection to Africa at the heart of Candomblé.

Most *terreiros* follow a fairly strict organization of ritual responsibilities according to gender and length of initiation. At the pinnacle of the *terreiro* leadership is the *mãe-* or *pai-de-santo*—the head priestess or priest—whose authority is supreme within the ritual community. Outside of the ritual context, these religious leaders are usually well respected, and those connected with long-established houses are eagerly and publicly identified with the African heritage of the city, the state, and even the nation.[21] In some houses, the line of succession is consanguineous and new leaders are chosen from initiated members in the natural family of the *terreiro*'s founder. In other cases, a leader is selected from the circle of older initiates (*ebomis*) who have years of experience and familiarity with the practical and mystic demands of priesthood. Whatever the custom, the final decision is made by the *orixás* themselves, through divination. The new *iyalorixá* or *babalorixá* (female or male spiritual leader)[22] always must come from the ranks of initiated members who have a minimum of seven years of experience.

In Bahia, because the majority of initiates are women, the pool of candidates for the leadership of Candomblé communities is predominately female. Some of the most eminent *terreiros* in the country, such as Casa Branca, Gantois, and Ilê Axé Opô Afonjá, have a long-standing tradition of exclusively consecrating women as supreme leaders of the community. Every Candomblé *terreiro* constitutes its own ritual family. Mãe Stella suggests that women make better leaders in Candomblé because of their natural "mothering" qualities, as well as their ability to be responsive to the demands of the *orixá*.[23] The skills required to manage and sustain the *terreiro*'s intricate dynamics of interpersonal relations, hierarchy, and spiritual powers are perhaps cultivated more consistently and effectively among female leaders. Whatever the cause, the place of women as supreme ritual authorities in many individual *terreiros* (and particularly those that serve as exemplars for so many others) is a distinguishing characteristic of the religion, and Candomblé communities have often been recognized as "privileged" women's spaces in Brazilian society.

In her collection of interviews with priestesses of Candomblé *terreiros* in Bahia, the social psychologist Maria Salete Joaquim quotes Cleo de Oliveira Martins, Agbeni Xangô of Ilê Axe Opô Afonjá: "In the spiritual sense [the *mãe-de-santo*] is the one who transmits, by words and actions, the culture of the ancestors. Candomblé is very much a lived culture."[24] By and large, *mães-de-santo* are very conscious of their responsibility as religious leaders to teach and maintain Afro-Brazilian cultural and spiritual traditions. Angenora Ana Brito (Mãe Pastora), *iyalorixá* of Terreiro Maroketo, says that this is indeed the role of the chief priestess of a Candomblé community. A *mãe-de-santo* "transmits from one generation that which will be passed on to the following ones."[25]

Not all *terreiros* have gender specifications for the chief sacerdotal positions. In general, though, ritual roles are explicitly designated for males or females. In Yoruba-based Candomblé communities, the posts most commonly held by women include *iyakekere* or *mãe pequena*, "small mother," the second-highest leadership role, assistant to the high priestess or priest; *ekedis*, initiated women who do not receive the *orixás* but assist those who do in a variety of ritual circumstances; and *ebomis*, a general term for initiates who have completed seven years or more of consecration to the *orixá*. *Iawôs*, literally, "wives" of the *orixá*, are devotees specifically consecrated to receive the deities in their bodies and become their vessels in the human community, undergoing an obligatory seven-year process of training. *Iawôs* can be male or female, although in Bahia they are overwhelmingly women. These are the individuals from among whom, eventually, succeeding leaders are selected. *Abiãs*, the most junior members of the community, are being prepared for initiation and have undergone one or more fairly simple rituals of spiritual fortification, the *obi* or *bori*. *Abiãs* can be male or female, but most are women and girls. Specifically male roles include *babalorixá*, or chief priest, in *terreiros* headed by a male rather than a female; *ogãs*, initiated men who do not receive the *orixá* but assist the *terreiro* community in a variety of ways, from physical maintenance to financial assistance and political influence; *axogún*, ritual slaughterer of votive animals; and *alabês*, drummers. Finally, all members of the community are considered *filhos-de-santo*, "children" of the *mãe-* or *pai-de-santo*, and they are expected to relate to each other as family.

Just as for nineteenth-century devotees of Candomblé, black women in the contemporary practice of the religion in Bahia are the main resource of devotional labor. Although the demographics of the religion have been changing over the past fifty years, in Salvador the majority of Candomblé participants are not wealthy, and many are irregularly employed.[26] The *terreiro* community in some ways functions as a kind of mutual-aid association where those in greatest need can find assistance from the *terreiro* leadership and fellow devotees. The absence of a clear distinction between "work" and "worship" in Candomblé exemplifies how the history of the tradition and the history of Afro-Brazilians are embodied in the contemporary experience of *terreiro* communities.

Candomblé is an extremely labor-intensive religion, and the work of devotees involves a major commitment of time, effort, and resources. Regular tasks include cleaning and maintaining the *terreiro* grounds, altars, and sacramental vestments; preparing meals for community members and guests; caring for children and older people who live at the *terreiro;* helping community members in need of financial or other assistance; and making daily, weekly, or other periodic offerings of food, flowers, candles, prayers, water, and votive sacrifices to the *orixás*. Much of this work is done manually, without the aid of electric labor-saving devices. In addition, *terreiro* members are responsible for assisting with initiatory rites and organizing and participating in the annual cycle of major ceremonial feasts that most Candomblé communities host in honor of the *orixás*.

Some contemporary adherents recognize connections between devotional labor in Candomblé and the work of enslaved ancestors who preceded them in the trials of black life in the New World. Valnizia de Xangô Airá, the *iyalorixá* of the Terreiro do Cobre, explains that the tremendously physical and exhausting collective labor involved in maintaining present-day Candomblé communities is a connection to the unremunerated, distressed labor of the enslaved ancestors of the participants.[27] Not only are the physical tasks similar but the vulnerabilities of the economic, political, and social lives of many devotees echo the stresses of the lives of their forebears. Candomblé is not easy. But neither are the lives of its adherents. As Mãe Val says, "It is the religion of slaves and everything about the slaves' lives was hard. Even their religion was difficult, tiring. And imagine if it's hard work for us now—for them, trying to cultivate the *orixás* in the slave quarters, in the hidden places in the forests, where they went to hold their ceremonies. But in compensation, after long days of backbreaking labor, they had their *orixás* and the joy of celebrating them. We know that joy." Then, in a pensive moment as she swept the large, clay-tiled room used for public ceremonies, Mãe Val added, "We've only gotten free of the stocks, but we're still in the slave quarters."[28]

One particularly hot afternoon a few years ago, while a group of devotees at the Terreiro do Cobre were hand washing mounds of laundry in the sun, one exclaimed to me in laughter and exasperation, *"É a senzala, Raquel, acredite!"* (It's the slave quarters, Rachel, believe it!).[29] While the comment was meant to be humorous, it was also an illuminating response to the intensity and manual nature of the work, to its history, and to the tiredness it engenders. The quarters. And even if the fatigue is mitigated by the company of comrades and the comfort and confidence of directing one's efforts toward the well-being of the community and the *orixás*, the connection to the *senzala*, the slave quarters, remains—as memory, as referent, but also as resource. The memory of the hardships experienced by earlier generations is somehow a guide, a support, and even a responsibility for those who are the current caretakers of that legacy.

There are other resources, other referents to the memory of slavery in Candomblé: clothing, food, music and dance, and a wide range of material objects, from straw mats and clay water vessels to ritual drums and raffia palm window coverings. The workaday dress in contemporary Candomblé is the traditional dress of slaves. Women wear a long, wide, Iberian-style calico skirt in white or simple prints, secured with a cord; a white short-sleeved blouse with attached slip; a rectangular pane of cloth wrapped around the upper torso; beaded necklaces; a head wrap and bare feet. Men wear simple lightweight cotton pants and shirt and are also barefoot. The festive dress that female devotees wear during annual public celebrations for the *orixás* matches a nineteenth-century description of the gala dress of well-to-do *crioulas* and freedwomen or slaves of wealthy masters: a voluminous, wide skirt with lace embellishment at the hem and a lace underskirt that emphasized the garment's circular shape; a muslin blouse; an elegant, African-style rectangular cloth worn over the shoulder; dainty, heeled sandals; and elaborate jewelry, often of coral, gold, and multicolored West African trade beads.[30]

Alimentary traditions are another place where the influence and memory of slavery is strongly marked in Candomblé. Each *orixá* cultivated in a particular *terreiro* requires specific ritual foods. *Acarajé* (black-eyed pea patties deep-fried in palm oil) for *Iansã*, *amalá* (okra and dried shrimp stew) for *Xangô*, white corn for *Oxalá* and *Iemanjá*, yellow corn and squash for *Oxóssi*, popcorn for *Omolú*—the list is considerable. These culinary traditions were brought from Africa or, in some cases, borrowed from the Amerindians in Brazil, and practiced, whenever possible, under slavery.

Women are at the center of these continuities. They sew the sacramental clothing and prepare the ritual cuisine, and many have maintained the tradition of selling Afro-Brazilian "soul food" snacks, most famously *acarajé*, in the plazas and street corners of Salvador as a primary source of income for themselves and their families. Not all the black women who sell *acarajé* to the public are members of Candomblé *terreiros*, but the association of that work with Candomblé is so strong that even those who are not devotees dress as if they were, conforming to what has become a highly recognizable, iconic, and touristic image of black Bahian women.

Another element of connection to the past in Candomblé is the role of dance. European and North American visitors in the eighteenth and nineteenth centuries commonly remarked at the "spirit" of black Brazilian dance, particularly its transformational capacities. Although observers discussed the metamorphosis that occurred in the dancers when they moved, most failed to ascribe it to anything other than an uncontrollable or even demonic urge, which fascinated them and evoked a certain wariness. Some described the movements as "savage enthusiasm," others as "delirium" or "enchantment."[31] Whatever the descriptions, people of African descent in Brazil used dance and music to transform space and meaning in their lives. The music, especially the rhythms associated with their homelands and the cultivation of their deities, afforded people another way of knowing themselves and engaging their situation. Muniz Sodré, a scholar of Afro-Brazilian religion and culture, writes: "Dance is a decentering movement, a symbolic re-elaboration of space. Consider the dance of the slave. Moving himself in the master's space, he momentarily stops perceiving himself purely as a slave and remakes the surrounding space in terms of another orientation; one which has to do with a symbolic system different from that managed by the master and which breaks the boundaries fixed by the dominant territorialization."[32] What Sodré puts in the generic masculine certainly applies to devotees of the feminine gender as well.

Using specific movements, percussive rhythms, and songs to call the *orixá* into devotees' bodies, dance in Candomblé is a privileged form of communication with the spirit. As Luc de Huesch notes for the religions of West Africa from which Candomblé derives, "dialogue with the gods calls for specific corporal techniques."[33] Feet bared; shoulders and arms imitating the whirling wind or the undulating sea; swift wrists slicing the air as if swords or lances; curved, hunched backs and the slow, bent knees of great age—in Candomblé dance the bodies of devotees echo and beckon the gods. Women are the primary source of this embodied engagement with the forces of the universe. As the dance anthropologist Rosamaria Susanna Barbara explains, "the body of the dancer-priestess [in Candomblé, is] a microcosm, in which are found all of the energies of nature in a balance unique and specific to each individual; a mirror of the energies of the macrocosm."[34]

In African and diasporan traditions, beyond its central role of invoking communion among the human beings and the divinities, dance is a means of experiencing a knowledge that is not otherwise conveyable. For Africans as for the ancient Greeks, according to Sodré, dance "is manifestly pedagogical or 'philosophical', in the sense that it exposes or communicates a knowledge of which present and future generations should be aware. Inciting the vibration of the body to the rhythm of the cosmos, provoking an opening for the advent of the divinity, dance occasions a meditation . . . [and transmits a knowledge] glued to the experience of the body itself."[35]

Embodied knowledge. A way of experiencing a relationship to history, to divinity, to ancestry from within the movements of one's own body, from within the deepest memories of one's own cells. What is perhaps most striking and fundamentally remarkable about Candomblé is this relationship to history. It is a transformational relationship in which devotees take the straw mats, the wide meters of swirling cloth, the foods stained red with palm oil, their own danced communion with the *orixás* and use them to transform the pain and trauma of their historical and contemporary experience. The effort is neither to ignore nor run from the history (which would, in any case, be impossible; Candomblé is saturated with historical memory)[36] but to enter into it, with humility and grace—on its own terms, with great respect for what those who have gone before witnessed and lived. Indeed, to take on some of their burden because that is, ultimately, where their (and our) strength lies.

In the late 1930s, one of the most highly respected *babalawos* (Ifá divination specialists) of Bahian Candomblé, Martiniano Eliseu de Bomfim, shared information with North American anthropologist Ruth Landes as she was researching her book, *The City of Women*.[37] Seu Martiniano, as he was respectfully called, was close to eighty years old at the time he and Landes met. The babalawo kept in a section of his house an altar room, which he allowed Landes and a companion to see during one of their last visits. There he maintained the shrines his African-born parents had kept for the *orixás*.[38] Landes describes a formidable array of sacred items—carved statues, beads, fans, swords, plates of ritual food, and stones drenched in the liquid substances of sacramental offering—oil, blood, and alcohol. The room was close and windowless, and Seu Martiniano generally allowed no one entrance.

Lifting up a statue of Iansã for Landes to see,[39] the older man explained that it had belonged to his father and that the *orixá* had been his father's protector. "So I still make sacrifices to her," he said. Seu Martiniano remarked on the discomfiting responsibility of caring for the altar room. "You have to know how to move around in there or something bad will happen. I wish I didn't have to take care of it, but my parents left it."[40] Elsewhere, the ritual elder is quoted in a newspaper interview recalling his parents' experience in slavery—"My mother, I remember well, had a scar on her buttocks from a beating they gave her as punishment." He said, "All this must be studied."[41]

Seu Martiniano's mother's scar, his father's Iansã, and his own sense of responsibility for maintaining connection to the spirits that aided his parents through their ordeals are another suggestion of the way that Candomblé devotees have oriented themselves toward a meaning of history embodied and embedded in their relationship to the divine. That is to say, one feeds the meaning of the other. For Seu Martiniano, his mother's punishment and marks were essential to understanding the meaning of slavery. And the fact of that history was essential to understanding his own relationship to the *orixás* he continued to cultivate in his parents' altar room. Indeed, knowing "how to move around in there"—in the spaces between the trauma and the transformation—remains a key resource of Afro-Atlantic religiosity in general and of Candomblé in particular. As Charles Long writes, in the context of their struggles in this hemisphere, black people often discovered "a modality of experiencing and knowing that expressed a unique manner of coming to terms with what is the case by transforming negative situations into creative possibilities."[42]

In Salvador, Bahia, since the early twentieth century, black women have been the majority in leadership of Candomblé *terreiros* as well as among initiates who receive the *orixá*. They carry the burdens, resonances, and responsibilities of the religion in their bodies. The history of those who preceded them is annealed to their sacred and secular identities. These women are uniquely equipped to offer new approaches to understanding and indeed transforming the meaning of the historical experience of the formation (and continuation) of New World societies. Makota Valdina Pinto, a priestess of the Tanuri Junçara *terreiro* in Salvador, reminds us: "The suffering of our ancestors, the great suffering we share only in glimpses, only in traces, the suffering we have difficulty even imagining, has gifted us an understanding, a creativity, a joy, a transformational capacity, a solidarity with those in pain and struggle that is much needed in the world today."[43]

CHAPTER TWO

"I Smoothed the Way, I Opened Doors"

Women in the Yoruba-Orisha Tradition of Trinidad

TRACEY E. HUCKS

In June 1981, Iyalorisha Molly Ahye publicly defended the legitimacy of Trinidad's Orisha practice to an international audience attending the First World Congress of Orisha Tradition and Culture in Ile-Ife, Nigeria. At the conference, a Nigerian priest of the Yoruba tradition expressed his delight in the number of representatives from African diasporic communities in the Americas and the Caribbean who returned "home" to Africa in order to "correct a few points" concerning their local religious practices. Molly Ahye, a native-born Trinidadian, boldly responded to the Nigerian priest's assertion. "I would like to say that we shouldn't be 'corrected.' We should leave to ourself the way we worship because I'm not sure that 'you' are correct or 'we' are correct." Because both African and African-diasporic practitioners represent the various local trajectories that constitute the global Yoruba community, Ahye concluded, the goal of the conference should not be "a matter of correction, but to exchange ideas."

Mediating moments of "correction" and "exchange" have been at the center of emerging discourses on African-derived traditions in black diasporic communities. On the Caribbean island of Trinidad, female practitioners like Ahye have been at the forefront of fostering cross-national discussions with Nigerians and intranational discussions with other Trinidadians on the nature of Yoruba religious identity. Underlying these discussions has been the negotiation of new vocabularies of transnationalism, transculturalism, and religious authority, as well as the formulation of new conceptions of local orthodoxy and religious hybridity.

In examining the public religious activities of Trinidadian women, we are dually challenged to recast the symbolic significance of Africa as an elastic category of religious analysis, as well as to rethink gendered notions of empowerment and authority within the complex religious world of Trinidad Orisha. As agents of history and memory, public religious advocacy, and political activism, women such as Molly Ahye, Melvina Rodney, Patricia Sangowunmi, and poet laureate Eintou Pearl Springer represent multiple ways in which Africa has been religiously revalued within Caribbean Atlantic contexts. More significantly, these women of the Trinidad Orisha tradition function as important models for how diaspora communities theorize broader issues of religious authenticity, global legitimacy, and local meaning.

African Origins and Trinidadian Traditions

African-derived religions (African in historical origin and diasporic in innovation) were primarily furthered in the New World by displaced Africans who struggled to maintain their religious practices in disparate diasporic contexts. Religions such as Candomblé, Vodou, and Santería were largely promulgated through slave communities in Brazil, Haiti, and Cuba. Throughout the diaspora, these traditions shared broad religious attributes that emphasized service to spiritual deities; engaged in the veneration of their forbears or ancestors; appeased spirits with offerings of food and animals; performed rituals of divination; healed with herbal pharmacopoeia; ritualized with song, chant, and dance; and ritually embodied spirits through manifestation and possession.[1] These common features were especially visible in the Caribbean, given its distinctive historical development in the early transplantation of enslaved Africans, which continued unabated through the nineteenth century and reinforced the African elements of culture amid a Creole population.

The case of Trinidad was somewhat unique in that the Yoruba ethnocultural group most associated with African Orisha rites derived primarily from a post-slavery indentured labor force. Following the emancipation of slaves in British West Indian colonies in 1838, the system of plantation agriculture generated a continued demand for labor. This void was filled by African indentured labor groups like the Yoruba who resettled in close-knit communities and asserted a powerful influence on African-descended people of other ethnocultural origins. According to David Trotman,

> The Yoruba who settled in British Guiana and Trinidad between 1838 [and] 1870 came not as slaves but as immigrants. They were recruited from the large number of Africans who had been liberated by the Royal Navy from slave ships bound for Cuba, Brazil, and the United States and settled in Sierra Leone and Saint Helena. These Africans were offered the choice between apprenticeship in Sierra Leone or

St. Helena, enlistment in the West India Regiment, or service in the Royal Navy. After 1838, the option of emigrating to the West Indies as plantation labor was another available alternative.[2]

In nineteenth-century Trinidad, Yoruba-dominated villages were formed in numerous sections of the island, including Montserrat and Yarraba Village, Oropuche, Princes Town, St. Joseph, Third and Fifth Company Villages, Couva, Carenage, and Sierra Leone Village in Diego Martin.[3] Subsequently, Yoruba-Orisha practices became heavily concentrated in these geographical regions.[4] Trinidadian scholar Maureen Warner-Lewis quotes an 1856 observer of these early Yoruba communities in colonial Trinidad: "they are . . . guided, in a marked degree, by the sense of association; and the principle [of] combination for the common weal has been fully sustained wherever they have settled in any numbers; in fact, the whole Yaraba race of the colony may be said to form a sort of social league for mutual support and protection."[5] Warner-Lewis, a linguist by training, concluded that many Yoruba immigrants to Trinidad settled in language enclaves that allowed the reconstitution of Yoruba language in local folktale, music, secular activities, and religion.[6] They were characterized by nineteenth-century Europeans as "industrious and laborious, but avaricious, passionate, prejudiced, suspicious, and many of them still adhering to heathenish practices."[7]

Colonial laws were enacted to restrict the "heathenish practices" that threatened Christian religious sovereignty in Trinidad. All distinctions among African-derived religions in Trinidad were collapsed in the colonial literature and legislature. A wide variety of religious practices were subsumed under the term *Obeah*, which was based on analogies between witchcraft, sorcery, and fortune-telling. Colonial governments throughout the British Caribbean eventually instituted laws prohibiting the "assumption of supernatural power or knowledge" or the use of "superstitious devices."[8]

In part, Obeah was a creation of the colonial imagination made incarnate in legal code. Nearly three decades after emancipation, legislation against the practice of Obeah became inscribed in Trinidad as a legal instrument of black social control. According to the Summary Offences of the Laws of Trinidad and Tobago of 1868, "Any person who, by the practice of obeah or by any occult means or by any assumption of supernatural power or knowledge, intimidates or attempts to intimidate any person, or . . . pretends to discover any treasure or any lost or stolen goods, or the person who stole the same, or to inflict any disease, loss damage, or personal injury to or upon any other person, . . . is liable to imprisonment for six months, and . . . may be sentenced to undergo corporal punishment."[9]

Nineteenth-century colonial laws in Trinidad restricted specific practices vital to the ritual life of African-derived religions, such as the "beating of any drum" or "any dance or procession," and found public assemblies of Africans a threat to colonial social order.[10] Given the existence of these laws and the sporadic or systematic attempts to enforce them, practitioners of African-derived traditions in Trinidad often found themselves under state surveillance and vulnerable to religious repression. Their autonomous gatherings could be stopped by colonial authorities at any time. From 1868 to 1899, approximately fifty-three Afro-Trinidadians were convicted and punished under the jurisdiction of these laws.[11] Close to a century later, in 1962 when Trinidad gained its independence, the laws restricting these practices, though often challenged by Afro-Trinidadians, remained largely intact.

Trinidad's long history of public castigation of Orisha practitioners left them vulnerable to social disparagement. As devotees of the Orisha deity, they were often forced to mediate their religious lives through public prisms of disdain and collective repression. Outward identification with the Orisha religion severely undermined social prestige and respectability for men and women in Trinidad. Yet within the complex clandestine world of the Orisha tradition, women were especially able to access alternative avenues of empowerment. Christian, primarily Catholic, institutions were governed under strict male authority. Orisha shrines, however, afforded women alternative means of religious authority and empowerment. According to theologian Dianne M. Stewart, "a number of African-derived Caribbean religions offer sacrosanct countertraditions of female authority, agency, and empowerment not readily found in most Christian traditions."[12] Although publicly maligned, these religious structures allowed women access to esteemed leadership positions as heads of shrines and ritual specialists.

Spiritual authority asserted through age, initiation, or experience subverted the patriarchal norms of society while leveling gendered access to positions of power. In other words, within the Orisha tradition leadership was not wholly male. This directly countered conventional gender hierarchies in Trinidad society that excluded women from positions of religious authority. Women's power, therefore, was reconfigured and reinscribed within the Orisha tradition, not through rigidly held conceptions of gender but through their status as elders within the tradition, their roles as public advocates on behalf of the religion, or their positions as prominent leaders of shrines. Currently, of the 80 to 150 Trinidadian Orisha shrines servicing several thousand devotees, supporters, and divination clients, more than half are led by women.[13] In comparison to Africa, scholars of Trinidad Orisha such as Rawle Gibbons and Funso Aiyejina postulate that "the centrality of women as followers, as the leading performers of Orisa rituals, as owners of shrines, and as the leading organizers of shrine activities are some of the other areas in which the Trinidad/New World practice of the Orisa tradition has been altered in line with the reality of the New World where the African woman has been in the vanguard of the struggle for survival."[14] Within Orisha shrines in Trinidad, women function in their capacities as Iyalorishas (Iyas) or initiated spiritual mothers to a body of male and female practitioners who maintain their normal kinship ties but, in effect, are reconstituted into larger spiritual family networks within the shrine. The following narratives illustrate how women's efforts have been integral to the sustaining power and presence of the Trinidad Orisha tradition, the reshaping and refashioning of its public image, and the translating and decoding of its often clandestine sources of meaning and empowerment.

African Purity and Diaspora Hybridity: Contested Notions of Religious Authority in Trinidad Orisha

Trinidad's most senior priestess of Orisha, Iya Rodney, has been a practitioner for over eighty-five years since her initiation in the 1920s.[15] Iya Rodney's spiritual godfather was the shrine leader Ebenezer Eliot, who traced his own spiritual lineage to an African-born woman, Ma Diamond. Through subsequent initiations of numerous "spiritual children" over several decades, Iya Rodney has expanded the spiritual family of Orisha throughout Trinidad. As a leader of the *palais,* or spiritual shrine, incorporated as *Egbe Orisa Ile Wa,* Iya Rodney is responsible for priestly initiations, divinations, offerings, sacrifices, and Orisha-related rituals and feasts. As a result of her religious status and ritual activities throughout Trinidad, Iya Rodney has been fundamental in legitimizing and concretizing the local authority of the religion.

Within the Orisha Council of Elders incorporated in 1998, authority is apportioned not by gender but according to age, experience, and seniority. Therefore, as the oldest living priestess on the island, Iya Rodney is the spiritual head of the Orisha Council of Elders, and as such her governance extends over an organized body of Trinidad's male and female Orisha priesthood. Iya Rodney's authority has not gone unchallenged. Many of these challenges are levied by younger practitioners, female and male, who eschew Rodney's ritual alliances with Catholicism. Understanding the development of this recent debate and what it means in terms of the authenticity of diasporic forms of Orisha, as well as unpacking its gender and generational dynamics, requires a brief exploration of the complex relationship between Orisha and the dominance of Catholicism on the island.

Elders of Iya Rodney's generation are now being criticized for adding Christian elements—ranging from symbolic objects to the use of saints—within the Orisha ritual complex. Many elders counter such critiques by explaining that they lived through a period in Trinidad's history when restrictive ordinances, legal persecution, and physical threats jeopardized the individual survival of practitioners and the institutional survival of the religion. Orisha rituals were maintained despite severe legal pressure and in defiance of dominant social norms. According to Iya Rodney, "When I get involve in this Orisa movement, we could not have beat drums until 10:00 o'clock or if not the police will come. I passed through all that."[16] In other words, Orisha practitioners who wanted to hold a public religious ceremony involving the beating of drums were required to obtain a license from the local police station in order to avoid intervention and legal prosecution.[17] Devotees like Iya Rodney negotiated adverse social and legal terrains in the early 1930s, 1940s, and 1950s in order to preserve Orisha practice. At times, they found that assuming a visible Christian identity often provided significant measures of social protection. Today, younger generations initiated into the Orisha tradition in less hostile environs often overlook the complex social and religious dynamics traversed by earlier generations. As a result, they often devalue religious hybridity and diasporic innovations upon the tradition while imposing standards of African purity as the proper measure of authenticity.

These dichotomous notions of hybridity versus purity are not universally accepted among the spiritual leaders of Trinidadian Orisha, particularly those who accommodate Catholic elements. According to Caribbean scholar Rex Nettleford, "Orishas grapple with Christian saints to find a central place in the ontology of African-Trinidadian existence."[18] In spiritual spaces headed by women like Iya Rodney, the Orishas and the saints are allowed to inhabit the same sacred landscape. Catholic iconography and symbols, as well as such ritual actions as reciting Catholic prayers and Hail Marys, are not uncommon among elder practitioners. Scholars previously problematized this phenomenon as "syncretism," portraying it as a process by which the religion of a dominant culture was imposed upon and absorbed by the religion of a subordinated group—a social-historical narrative that was closely related to assimilationist models of cultural change. More recently, however, scholars recognize practitioners as authors and shapers of their own spiritual beliefs and ritual acts. What previously was regarded as syncretism is now seen as a deliberate form of "masking"[19] or "contextual convenience"[20] aimed at securing the survival of a religion under conditions of oppression. Given Trinidad's history of formal legal persecution and informal social castigation of Orisha, many practitioners in the past strategically assumed respectable public Christian identities while concealing their allegiances to African traditions. Visible displays of Christian material culture garnered social protection and ensured access to social privileges such as private Christian schools. Elders themselves sometimes portrayed their outward appearance of embracing Catholicism as a façade that enabled them to continue secretly practicing Orisha. Despite the recognition that spiritual leaders adopted such strategies in a challenging historical context, the inclusion of Catholic iconographic references in ritual has emerged as a major source of religious contestation within the Trinidad Orisha tradition.

Since the nineteenth century, Yoruba-Orisha practices have been affected by a myriad of influences. In addition to the legal repression that forced practitioners to perform rituals in secret, the content and context of their ritual observance was modified by interaction with other cultural and religious traditions. The influence of Trinidad's dominant Catholic presence as well as interethnic exchange of Trinidad Yoruba with other ethnocultural groups originating in West and Central Africa led to inevitable shifts in the system of beliefs, set of deities, and forms of ritual devotion. The religious practices of present-day Trinidad Orisha reflect the compound influences that have shaped it and the multicultural mix that surrounds it. Elder practitioners like Iya Rodney who are commonly known in Trinidadian vernacular as "Old Heads," continue to deny that the use of Catholic and other elements are totally incongruous with African-derived ritual expression. They validate continuity with African origins and Trinidadian innovations. However, a newer generation of practitioners has sought to both "de-Christianize" and "Africanize" the Orisha tradition in Trinidad as a way of authenticating the religion's primordial source, inevitably privileging African origins over diasporic developments.[21]

Embedded in these proposals for change are perspectives on broader questions of experiential knowledge, ritual orthodoxy, and the location of religious authority. These debates involve disputes over such foundational matters as the source of the authority of the elder priesthood, the relationship between Christian influences and ritual purity, and the geographic primacy of Trinidad or Africa. According to one of Iya Rodney's spiritual children, Rawle Gibbons:

The authority is the practice as it has taken place here [in Trinidad] . . . The Elders are the people who have carried the tradition . . . They go back to the thirties. They go back to when the police used to raid and used to beat you. They had to go and humble themselves before the law in order to get a license. They carried it. It had nothing to do with Africa . . . The Elders will tell you that the experiences and the hardships they have gone through, *that* is the authority and they don't make any bones about it. They will tell you, "We are the ones who, when they were cuttin' people's tails for beating drums and when they were jailing you, we were a part of that, not you, and nobody in Africa."[22]

This defense of local practices and the power of the elders is based on the premise that those who "carried" the Orisha tradition in Trinidad are a legitimate source of spiritual authority. Therefore, this recent history, not a remote originary site, is the foundation of religious authenticity.

The proponents of de-Christianization seem to challenge the local authority of traditional elders and the validity of the ritual practices they have maintained. Supporters of Trinidad's local religious authority assert that the elders "are the ones who carried it and that gives them the authority to say how it is to be practiced. Nobody is going to tell them that. It has been handed down to them in a particular way according to certain traditions and practices and they are keeping that. They have said their prayers in English. They said Christian prayers because that is what they know and those prayers have worked for them as far as they are concerned . . . So on [the] strength of their experience rests their authority."

This defense of the elders situates the older generation of Orisha leaders in an unbroken chain of local tradition, which itself validates their authority and the legitimacy of their ritual practices. Keeping what has been handed down to them and passing it on to their spiritual children is a significant act, constituting them as authentic spiritual leaders. The Christian prayers they say in English have demonstrated spiritual power and are thus not ontologically different from the phonetically African prayers they also perform in this ritual context. This perspective maintains that experiential knowledge defines religious orthodoxy. Ultimately, those, like Gibbons, who sympathize with this position argue that "you can't come now and tell them [the elders] about the practice, that what they are doing is wrong or that they have too much [Christianity] in what they are doing . . . You cannot invalidate the experiences of the Elders and the people who still want to hold on to that tradition. I can't say that it doesn't have spiritual meaning for them . . . *They* kept it. It worked for them and *they* fought for it and however it was kept, it was kept. They are very clear on that."

Women figure prominently on both sides of this controversy. While Iyalorisha Melvina Rodney leads the elders who represent Trinidadian traditions, Iyalorisha Patricia Sangowunmi represents the position articulated by younger initiates who seek to re-Africanize Orisha rituals. Iya Sangowunmi leads an important shrine, *Ile Sango Osun Milosa*, and has played a key role in bringing Orisha into public view as a legitimate part of Trinidadian culture. Iya Sangowunmi is the first female practitioner licensed to perform legal Orisha marriages in Trinidad and Tobago. She also seeks to foster the Orisha tradition in Trinidad through the education of children. The accredited Abiadama School in the Woodbrook section of Trinidad, which Iya Sangowunmi founded, provides children with a rigorous academic environment and instills within them a positive respect for and understanding of the Orisha tradition.

Iya Sangowunmi and the more senior priestess, Iya Rodney, have each traveled to Ile-Ife in Nigeria, the commonly recognized source of Yoruba religious development, and both recognize the preeminence of Nigeria's appointed spiritual monarch, the *Oni* of Ife. They share a desire to honor the Orisha and the ancestors with spiritual and ritual integrity. The difference between them lies in their ritual and ceremonial approaches to these goals and in what they posit as the proper relationship between African and Trinidadian practices.

Iya Sangowunmi, whose priestly initiation was performed in Nigeria, represents a growing philosophical trajectory that privileges African models of religious ritualization and avoids the use of Catholic emblems and material culture. Iya Sangowunmi's spiritual descendant is linked to that of the noted Nigerian scholar and Nigerian Yoruba priest Dr. Wande Abimbola. Her public ritual life as instituted through her shrine presents ceremonies patterned in their content and theology after Nigerian Yoruba. According to Sangowunmi, "I feel that the Yoruba way gives you form. It gives you strength. It gives you a theology and a philosophy. It gives you a sense of self where you can really understand yourself in this universe."[23] Distinctly and deliberately absent from the ritual performances of Iya Sangowunmi are many of the spiritual ingredients that entered into local Trinidadian Orisha identity over time through non-African channels.

Commenting on this new impulse, Rawle Gibbons observes that "there is a revived, rejuvenation of interest in Africa and more contact with Africa. That has become the basis now for validating a lot of what we do [in Trinidad] . . . Their *ashe* has been taken from Africa. So their point of reference is not really Trinidad." He categorizes as "new Africanist" or "neo-Africanist" those whose *ashe* or spiritual energy has been ritually passed on through initiation in Africa (not Trinidad) and those supporters who embrace this emerging perspective. His concern with this perspective is not that it involves change, for he asserts that local Trinidadian Orisha elders are "not resistant to the notion of their religion being more African-ized in that sense." However, Gibbons makes a clear distinction between changes or variations in religious practice, which he accepts, and notions of religious or-thodoxy, which he rejects. What local elders "resent and what they resist is the in-validation of their experiences." In his view,

> There is no pure form. No African talks about the tradition in any pure way. There are many diverse forms that you will find on the Continent. Maybe not in form, but they have different ways of practicing . . . You cannot invalidate it because the rock of the thing is not in Africa, it's here [in Trinidad] . . . I don't think we have to change the rhythms of the things that we play because you might not hear it in that way in Africa, because you will hear it differently in Cuba and Brazil . . . We have to retain our sense of who it is we are . . . It's valid because people who have been using it have found it efficacious . . . But you cannot invalidate the experiences of the Elders and people who still want to hold to that tradition.[24]

Gibbons and those who share this view believe that all religious traditions develop over time and across space. Variations in ritual are signs of spiritual vitality, not marks of deviation from some authentic, static form; they are to be appreciated as creative and effective modes of spiritual practice rather than "corrected" by the imposition of some supposedly original orthodoxy. This perspective validates the move to introduce certain Yoruba ritual practices recently learned from Africa, but it denies that Trinidadian practices are thereby invalidated.

Scholarly debates on syncretism premise their theories on the fusion of for-eign images and symbols with local religious practices, and consideration of the deeper theological content of such ritual differences is often sacrificed. In the case of Trinidad, it would be shortsighted to conclude that "Old Heads" like Iya Rod-ney are spiritually invested in the actual physical icons and prayers of Christian-ity. The presence of these Christian insertions speaks to complex theological un-derstandings that have been renegotiated over time within a diasporic context. Given the centrality of ancestral veneration in Yoruba-Orisha religious cosmology, Trinidadian elders created ritual systems that accommodated a dual invocation of continental African ancestors and Trinidad-born, African-descended ancestors. They formulated what I call *ritual bilingualism,* which utilizes familiar Christian prayers to revere and summon Trinidadian ancestors and recites Yoruba prayers for those African ancestors who continue to navigate the spiritual landscape in their native tongue. This innovation represents a creative response to the situa-tion of the African diaspora. In ways that parallel transplanted people's ability to code switch appropriately between their native language and the prevalent language of the society they enter, Trinidadian Orisha practitioners have enlarged their ritual repertoire to include Trinidadian ancestors, who can guide them in the place they live, alongside African ancestors, who link them to their place of origin. To disregard this important theological innovation, reducing it to a matter of ritual syncretism or situational adaptation, underestimates the complex ways in which Trinidadian elders have engaged in ritual translation and reproduction.

Some Trinidadians, like Rawle Gibbons, are invested in maintaining and preserving the elders' ritual authority. He believes that the "main strength is the openness that [Trinidadians] have, the very integration that *they* are fighting against." In other words, the elders' defense of the specifically Trinidadian forms of ritual involves an acceptance of the tolerant pluralism of their society, as well as of their position in the diaspora, while those who seek to Africanize local religious practice are rejecting the opportunities for integration that the religion now enjoys, as well as the diasporic development of their spiritual tradition. For Gibbons, this "integration" becomes an asset when various representatives of Trinidad's non-Orisha communities come to the Orisha priesthood as "clients for spiritual work." In these instances, "when they cannot be dealt with in a Christian way, by the priest or the pastor, . . . or it can't be dealt with by the Imam or the Pundit, they come to Orisha. That means that the Orisha has to understand their systems." Gibbons ultimately concludes that "the business about authority has to do with a lack of self-confidence on the part of African people in the diaspora." Orisha spiritual leaders who rest their authority on the spiritual power of the tradition they sustain need apologize neither for their incorporation of non-African elements into ritual nor for their willingness to offer spiritual guidance to persons who come from other ethnocultural groups and other religious traditions.

Gibbons's comments provide important insights into how local religious authorities in the African diaspora struggle to sustain themselves in the face of broader Africanization and globalization pressures. For women like Iya Sangowunmi, narratives of Africa remain key to religious ritualization and to the identity of the Orisha tradition in Trinidad. According to Charles Long, a historian of religion, "Africa" functions as a metaphor of "self-determined legitimacy" for a black diasporic citizenry and allows it to assuage often ambiguous questions of origins and identity. Long argues that, in the New World context, even if there was "no conscious memory of Africa, the image of Africa" played an enormous part in the religion of black people. "The image of Africa, an image related to historical beginnings has been one of the primordial religious images of great significance. It constitutes the religious revalorization of the land, a place where the natural and ordinary gestures of the blacks could be authenticated."[25]

In the current struggle to define authentic religious boundaries in Trinidad, the perspectives of Iya Rodney and Iya Sangowunmi represent divergent views on wider questions regarding the complex relationship between black diaspora communities and what Paul Gilroy calls African "parental cultures." Gilroy rightly argues, specifically in the case of music, that the "black Atlantic"—the African diaspora communities that exist in the Americas—explode "the dualistic structure which puts Africa, authenticity, purity, and origin in crude opposition to the Americas, hybridity, creolisation, and rootlessness."[26] This proposition applies to religion as well. The debate between proponents of Africanization and defenders of Trinidadian forms of Orisha reveals that there is no single meaning of Africanness or even a dualistic model of religious authenticity. In this context, I argue that a more nuanced theoretical approach to "Africa" accommodates the Africanist perspective of Iya Sangowunmi and the views expressed by Iya Rodney and her supporters that local innovation has spiritual legitimacy.

Public Advocacy and Legal Reform Among Trinidad's Orisha Women

A priestly descendant of Iya Rodney and a political descendant of the 1970 Black Power movement, Pearl Eintou Springer has been actively working in the political arena of Trinidad to legitimize and legalize the Orisha religious tradition. Springer came to the Orisha tradition by weaving together threads of religion and nationalism. Her nationalist identity is rooted in her extensive political activism in Trinidad, as well as in her activities in Grenada under its late prime minister Maurice Bishop.

In the 1960s and 1970s, Springer's generation criticized the postcolonial government of Dr. Eric Williams for muting Africa's historical importance in Trinidadian society. According to Springer, "This was a Black government with no consciousness or sense of Black pride that could root us as young Africans into a sense of ourselves. They could give us no direction, no values."[27] As a result, thousands of young Trinidadian activists like Springer, inspired by their revolutionary expatriate Stokely Carmichael, marched in the streets, adorned themselves in dashikis, politically mobilized themselves, draped and painted the saints in the Catholic Church in black, and ushered in Trinidad's Black Power movement. Springer remembers the religious dimension of this movement in a poem:

In Time
We smashed
Those statues
Or painted them
Black
Black like we
In vengeance wreaked
On a God
With seeming bias
Against our colour . . .[28]

Raised as a Catholic, Springer recalls the "point of catalyst" that severed her from the Catholic Church was her "exposure to the knowledge of the complicity of the Church in enslavement and in racism." This repudiation of Catholicism as part of the racist colonial order helped to reinforce her early nationalist consciousness.

From the early 1970s on, the Black Power movement sought to dismantle the social, political, and religious vestiges of colonial Europe that remained in Trinidad. As their black North American counterparts had done a decade earlier, these activists regarded religion as a powerful domain for contest and turned it into a site of nationalist transformation. Deploying rigid dichotomies, nationalists condemned Catholic and Protestant allegiances as "colonial" and hailed as "African" nationalist religious leanings toward Islam and Orisha. During this period of religious bifurcation, the Orisha tradition experienced a major resurgence among younger devotees, including Springer. "Out of the movement also came a new respect and attention to the scorned practices of traditional African religion. The Afrocentric religions in the country were associated with poverty and illiteracy. Everything African had been tarred and feathered by the negative philosophy that would make enslavement palatable to Christian Europe . . . The Orisa and Rada wallowed in this scorn, except when . . . every kind of person would come, at dead of night, seeking answers and solutions to their problems. All levels, all classes would come to find the reviled obeah man and woman."[29]

Black nationalism became an important beacon drawing young Trinidadians toward African religious identities, just as in North America black nationalism led African Americans toward Muslim affiliations and interest in African forms of spiritual practice. According to Springer, "Many of us came to the traditional African religion as an act of political and ideological self-expression."[30] Ultimately, the Black Power movement became the occasion where many young Trinidadian nationalists abandoned their Catholic upbringings in order to em-

brace the tradition of Orisha they had been taught to despise. Recalling the clandestine ceremonies in Trinidad's wooded areas, Springer stated, "I remember hearing the drums in the night but for us it was an association with things negative, things not quite clean, not quite pure, things very mysterious."[31] Shedding the colonialists' suspicions of African-derived religions and positively revaluing as authentic what had been socially maligned as "heathen" was part of the cultural transformation wrought by Black Power.

Now, nearly three decades after the Black Power movement, Springer is the director of the National Heritage Library, a priestess of the Orisha tradition, and poet laureate of Trinidad. Alongside other activist practitioners in the Orisha tradition, Springer has dedicated her public political life to getting all "anti-African legislation expunged from the statute books." In contrast to Iya Rodney and Iya Sangowunmi, Springer's leadership is not lodged in the traditional Orisha institution of the *palais* or shrine. Springer's religious activism has taken place in the public arena. She sees herself as having a dual role in the Orisha tradition. First, she aims "to champion and articulate the cause of Orisha [and] . . . to challenge this society . . . in public debates" on the question of "blood offerings" and other misunderstood aspects of the tradition.[32] Second, through television and radio debates, Springer seeks to instill pride in the tradition among Orisha practitioners and to equip them with a vocabulary to correct widespread negative stereotypes about the tradition. She attempts to "take the suppressed barely articulated hopes and dreams of our people and give it voice and tongue . . . when I talk, I give them the confidence to go out and deal with [it] . . . I give them the fuel and the ammunition . . . When I talk in public, I'm not really talking to the person who is asking me the question, I'm empowering African people out there. I'm giving them the knowledge . . . You don't have to be embarrassed. You don't have to be ashamed.[33]

Springer seeks to counter the social atmosphere of shame and disapproval that often stigmatizes Orisha. According to Trinidad's prime minister Patrick Manning, Springer's public advocacy as a "member of the Orisha faith" has meant that the "Orisha faith was recognized."[34] In the aftermath of the Black Power movement, Springer has sought to "articulate recognition and visibility for the [Orisha] belief system" and "to make the Orisha worldview more accessible to the general public so that people know what we believe and what we're about." In the final analysis, she contends that "the recognition of African religion is the ultimate step in the reclamation of self for the diaspora African."[35]

For Springer, as well as for many Afro-Trinidadian Orisha women, the "diaspora African" possesses a unique transatlantic identity which, while always recognizing its primordial ties to Africa, simultaneously negotiates its history of en-slavement and privileges its local religious and cultural innovations. Because Africa, as well as its diaspora world, experiences "the instability and mutability of identities which are always unfinished, always being remade,"[36] Springer understands the relationship of Trinidad Orisha to Africa as one of reciprocity, not hierarchy. Thus, she concludes, "The religion in Nigeria has to be and is being nourished by the Diaspora." In this respect, Springer espouses a view similar to that articulated by Iyalorisha Molly Ahye: Trinidad's Orisha tradition has developed differently from that in Nigeria, but its specifically diasporan features are valid forms of religious practice. Springer and Ahye seek to instill pride in local Orisha traditions and to raise the standing of Orisha.

In Trinidad, women's power and influence have been important in securing legislative victories that legitimized the Orisha tradition. Through the organizing strategies of Springer and Rodney, as well as Ahye and Sangowunmi, parliamentary legislation became an important vehicle for decriminalizing Orisha ritual practices, minimizing social repression, and obtaining religious autonomy. Over the past two decades, collective mobilization among Orisha practitioners has resulted in the elimination of lingering repressive and discriminatory nineteenth-century statutes and the enactment of new legislation conferring legal recognition of the tradition. During the 1980s and 1990s, three monumental laws were passed by Trinidad's Parliament: the Act for the Incorporation of the Orisha Movement of Trinidad and Tobago, Egbe Ile Wa (1981); the Opa Orisa Shango Movement Act (1991); and the Orisa Marriage Act (1999).

Trinidad's 1981 Act for the Incorporation of the Orisha Movement was the first legal enactment to legitimize the status of African derived religions in the diaspora world. It was the first time that these religions were granted formal recognition and their devotees designated the status of other conventional religious groups. Under the auspices of the Ministry of Culture, the aim of this preliminary act was to develop archival materials (written and audio) documenting the history and practice of the religion, to develop an educational component that taught African Yoruba language, and to invite African traditional practitioners from Nigeria to discuss methods of ritual and healing. As a result of this act, Iya Rodney's Orisha shrine *Egbe Orisa Ile Wa* received official organizational incorporation.

A decade later, the 1991 Opa Orisa Shango Movement Act incorporated the Orisha organization *Opa Orisha*. Iya Molly Ahye currently serves as its chief administrative minister. Iya Ahye holds a doctorate from New York University's School of Education and has written extensively on the Afro-Trinidadian dance tradition, as well as conducted fieldwork in Haiti, Grenada, and Brazil. Over the past three decades, Iya Ahye has been instrumental in bringing international exposure to the Trinidad Orisha tradition in her public lectures and representations of the religion throughout North America, South America, the Caribbean, and Africa. In 1979, when Orisha practitioners from across the globe gathered for the first time in New York City under the auspices of the Caribbean Cultural Center (then headed by Dr. Marta Vega), Iya Ahye was among the original delegates, along with other women, including Pearl Eintou Springer, officially representing Trinidad.

Born in the Belmont section of Trinidad, Iya Ahye attended Orisha feasts as a child and remembers how "they had to hide from the police." According to Ahye, "There was always persecution against the drum beating. You always had this religious division because the orthodox Church had this [fight] against the 'devil worship' but they couldn't stamp it out. [The police] used to go in and for spite break up the people's equipment and run them. This was in the forties. It was a British law against the drum beating . . . so people used to go in the woods . . . and clear bushes and have their thing . . . and they used to always have people look out for police coming. That is part of the history." Again, this history of civil repression forced many Orisha practitioners to seek veiled protection under the guise of observing the country's dominant Catholic faith. Ahye recounts the duplicity and pretence that many Orisha practitioners had to employ as they publicly assumed a Catholic religious identity and secretly practiced Orisha. "There was a kind of, not persecution, but victimization if you had to confirm in the Catholic Church . . . [because] you couldn't let them know that you . . . were Orisha or any such thing like that."[37]

Over the past decade, Iya Ahye's organizational labors have been devoted to promoting religious autonomy, securing legal protection, and advancing the status of the Orisha tradition. She helped to incorporate the World Congress of Orisha in New York State with Dr. Marta Vega and assisted in the incorporation of *Opa Orisha* in Trinidad. She also worked with Orisha leaders in Trinidad to draft the initial Marriage Act petition, which was submitted and rejected in the early 1990s. She was an original signatory on a deed for five acres of government land designated for Orisha activities and gatherings.

Ahye has spent considerable time and effort concentrating on the physical and religious needs of women. For twenty-one years, she ran a fitness and wellness center that served several thousand Trinidadian women. She became a key founder and organizer of the public ritual ceremony in honor of Oshun, the female deity whose spiritual power oversees women's fertility and childbirth. Although she chose not to become the head of a local shrine, Ahye received much empowerment from her dual roles as a public activist and Orisha practitioner. She understood her contribution to Orisha women as one of "organizing, opening doors, carrying them forward, showing them the future, elevating them, . . . changing the way of clothing, . . . and when you look at them you see the beauty in black women."

Ahye and Springer, along with other Orisha women, spearheaded the effort to change the legal status of the religion in Trinidad. This effort took Ahye and Springer directly into the political arena and culminated in the passage of the Orisa Marriage Act in 1999. According to Ahye, "I was just organizing. I was looking for structure, looking for [Orisha] to have a voice and the only way we could have a voice [was] for us to go to Parliament." While awaiting the parliament's decision on the act, which granted legal recognition to marriages performed by the Orisha priesthood, Springer remarked to the press: "We have been waiting for years. In order for there to be an erosion of the fears, distrust and negativities of the Orisa faith, the state must begin to give validation. Since 1979 when the first World Congress was held in New York, I was trying but our own people did not believe in us. It is basically fear and the perception of what Orisa is."[38]

Changing the legal position of Orisha practitioners in Trinidad not only transformed public perceptions of Orisha but also changed the position of Orisha spiritual practices in the Afro-Caribbean diaspora. Later in 1999, during deliberations in the House of Representatives, the then–prime minister expressed his support for the Orisa Marriage Bill, calling its passage a victory not only for the Orisha community but for Trinidad as a nation. According to the House minutes, Prime Minister Basdeo Panday remarked, "When this Bill is passed . . . I am reminded that it will be the only Act of its kind in the entire world. There is no such Act even in Brazil, where I believe there are some 10 million people of the Orisa faith." He concluded, "Not only is Government committed to delivering on its promise to give the Orisas their own Marriage Act, but we are committed to putting them on an equal footing with other citizens."[39]

The successful legislative achievements of the past twenty years have revolutionized the status of the Orisha priesthood in Trinidad, creating an environment of recognition and acceptance that even activist Orisha women like Ahye, Rodney, Sangowunmi, and Springer could scarcely have envisioned. In reflecting on their long and arduous engagement with Trinidad's political system, many women reveal that these public labors were marked by conflict, tension, and competition with men. Yet their collective efforts show that women in Trinidad have consistently worked to shift the axis of religious legitimacy from Africa to their own domestic diaspora context. Their energies as women were channeled less into seeking religious validation from their Nigerian, or even male, counterparts than into achieving social and legal standing for the Orisha tradition in their native Trinidad. Ultimately, these women illustrate the broader ways in which diaspora identities reclaim authority, voice, and ownership.

"All is mines. All is mines."

Pearl Eintou Springer recalls a wonderful story about her grandfather of Congolese origin, Daniel Artley, who was known as "Pa Jimpy." Living to a vintage age of around 108, Pa Jimpy, a renowned herbalist, would gather his grandchildren around him and bless them with the verbal affirmation, "All is mines. All is mines."[40] This is an apt metaphor for Trinidad Orisha in all of its diversity and divergence, continuity and innovation. With the increasing globalization of Yoruba-based religions, local Orisha religiosity has undergone major transformations as it has tried to maintain its efficacy and legitimacy. Trinidadian women such as Iyas Rodney, Ahye, Sangowunmi, and Springer represent important elements in the legitimation of Orisha's social standing within the wider spectrum of Orisha power and pluralism. As women, they have wrestled with the challenges of male authority in Trinidad's government and civil society and the larger Orisha priesthood. Despite these obstacles, they have proven themselves to be forerunners in religious survival, institution building, and legal advocacy. Although situated differently in terms of education, economic position, international exposure, national prominence, and religious foci, these women have all worked out of the strength of their sundry paths for the solidification and elevation of the Orisha tradition in Trinidad. Within their larger narratives, the women speak to their fortuitous roads to the Orisha and of having never imagined themselves as serving in the capacities of Iyas or spiritual mothers, healers, legal advocates, and public servants. Yet they have done so with great success, and in the process they have sustained and broadened the spiritual tradition. Their unique contributions echo Iya Molly Ahye's reflection about her work on behalf of the Orisha tradition: "I took care of things; I took care of people; I smoothed the way; I opened doors."

CHAPTER THREE

Joining the African Diaspora

Migration and Diasporic Religious Culture among the Garífuna in Honduras and New York

PAUL CHRISTOPHER JOHNSON

How does the consciousness of belonging to the African diaspora figure in the discourse and practice of religious communities? This essay takes identification with the African diaspora not as given but rather as acquired and negotiated in dynamic processes of group self-definition and social exchange. The inquiry is anchored in a case study of the Garífuna, or "Black Caribs," a group of mixed African and Amerindian descent living on the Central American coast of the Caribbean Sea. During the last generation, as a result of growing transnational migration and cultural connections, its religious leaders have begun to view and present their religion as being in and of the African diaspora.

The Garífuna are joining the African diaspora through mass migration to U.S. urban centers, especially New York City, which locates them in new religious networks. The homeland religion takes on new meanings as it becomes situated in the foreign metropole, and the acquisition of a new religious repertoire—ritual enactments, objects, words, and ideas—from other migrant Afro-Caribbean communities changes the very contents and emphases of "traditional Garífuna religion" from the valuation of local and Carib markers and identifications to the valuation of pan-African ones. The process of religious transformation parallels shifts in ethnic and racial identifications undergone by transmigrants between the United States and the Caribbean. Garífuna move from being situated within the complex racial logic of Central America and the Caribbean—comprised of manifold factors including ethnicity and cultural affiliation, physical features of color and hair, and socio-economic class—to the bipolar racial logic of the United States, in which Garífuna or Carib identifications disappear as migrants are regarded as simply "black." The processes of becoming racially "black" and religiously "African" are distinct but cross-referenced conversions that reinforce one another. Moreover, these two parallel processes occur both in New York City and in Honduran villages. Religious innovations in the United States are remitted to the homeland, leading to agonic exchanges among migrants returning for visits and those who remained at home.[1] Women are key agents in these shifts, yet this chapter does not describe the specific roles of women as much as chapters 1 and 2. Rather, it yields center stage to the shifting meanings of the African diaspora and diasporic religious culture. By giving provisional analytical precision to these key terms, we can better understand the transformative roles of women in religious change discussed in subsequent chapters.

To engage the question that animates this inquiry, consider the phrase "joining the African diaspora." The term *diaspora* commonly refers to an involuntary dispersion from a homeland and expresses a longing for redemption and return. How can a people *join* a diaspora? If the verb rings dissonant, it is because it is common, though specious, to think of diaspora affiliations as given by virtue of biological descent. I begin by explaining how this essay (along with others in this volume) parts ways with such a view.

Diaspora as Sentiment and Subjectivity

Let us start by distinguishing the use of *diaspora* as an empirical observation of the territorial dislocation, within a given temporal frame,[2] of a group of more or less shared ancestral, linguistic, or territorial derivation, from the use of diaspora as culture, the semiotic repertoire of discourses and practices activating and reproducing affinity and perceived likeness in agents' subjectivities.[3] Our concern here is with the second sense of the term. This definition, which centers on consciousness, sidesteps the bipolar debate over observable "retention" versus "invention" in comparisons across communities of multiply sited ethnic groups. It considers instead how diasporas are made and maintained as individually carried and partially shared sentiments of continuity and connection between one locale and another, putatively more original one. Diaspora, in this sense, is a structure of feeling made of human discourses and enactments.[4] Such relatively shared sentiments may emerge and solidify at specific historical junctures and dissolve at others,[5] depending on "the ways in which the politics of the present encourage certain processes of selective emphasis, invention, or suppression of histories of dispersal and transnational connection."[6]

Culturally speaking, *diasporas* do not exist without their repeated invocation and collective commemoration, although they may exist in an archeological sense, as a trail of bones or arrowheads.[7] Diaspora discourses, enactments, and sensibilities do not simply express existing relations between spatially distant groups; they create those connections. Through them, the lines marking insider from outsider are redrawn; through them, religious practice is transformed among both cosmopolitan migrants and those remaining in homelands. Since the specific character of the diaspora banner under which spatially disjoined communities rally is always in flux, diaspora identifications are as much a source of religious friction and change as they are an attempt to establish likeness, unity, and stability.

The dissonances generated by diasporic connections are as audible as the harmonies. Does being "in the diaspora" depend on perceived likenesses in language, music and dance rhythms, religious practice, skin color, sartorial style, the memory of enslavement and oppression, or a subtly negotiated combination of all of these? By what authority are such attributes ranked so as to certify, reject, or qualify groups for diaspora membership? The attempt to answer such questions remains quixotic. Any concord implied by the notion of diaspora is never self-evident but precarious and contingent on relations of power.

The Garífuna have been defined—and have defined themselves—as other than African during significant phases of their history. At the end of the eighteenth century, they were despised by other groups of African descent living on the British-controlled Caribbean island of St. Vincent. Africans enslaved by the British, as well as white colonists, disparaged the "Black Caribs" as "flatheads" for allegedly applying boards to elongate their children's foreheads, a practice they adopted from Carib Indians to distinguish them from African slaves.[8] Several Black Caribs, most notoriously the leader Chatoyer's brother, Du Vallée, even owned African slaves, pressing them into the production of export crops such as tobacco. In the Carib Wars leading to the Black Caribs' deportation in 1796 and 1797, "British" African slaves and Black Caribs fought against each other rather than in alliance against their colonial masters. Although we might imagine these rival groups as cells of a single diaspora organism because of their shared biological descent from Africa, they clearly did not conceive of themselves as kin or conduct themselves as groups with common concerns. No shared diaspora culture existed among distinct groups of African descent on St. Vincent.

"Diaspora-ization," to take Stuart Hall's awkward neologism, entails a shift in consciousness and a conversion of identifying practices.[9] Under what conditions do such conversions occur? How does a "local" religion change when it engages the broader nexus of diaspora? What specific cultural transmissions bring about shifts in sentiment, such that we could begin to speak not only of theories but also of ethnographies of diaspora-ization?[10] And why does diaspora-ization guarantee so little consensus once the shared moniker is adopted? We need to ask how "the African diaspora" signifies variously in different contexts and for different ethnic groups and how pressures called forth by the attempt to discern deep sources of affinity may catalyze social rifts rather than coalitions.

The Garífuna have joined the African diaspora through their recent mass migration from the Central American coast to urban centers in the United States. They were forged as a distinct ethnic group on the island of St. Vincent out of the transculturation between Amerindian and African settlements. As one third of their society has migrated from Honduras to New York City, the Garífuna are becoming less hybrid in their own identifying practices. This occurs in parallel processes of dual conversions: religiously joining the African diaspora,[11] and undergoing a racialization of ethnicity to become "black."[12]

Three major factors shape the process. First, joining the religious African diaspora implies a specific directionality toward prescribed ethnic niches in the new religious field. If the representation of deep Africa by African Americans once favored Ethiopia and Egypt as synecdochic tropes, it now relies on the Yoruba of southwest Nigeria. To join the African diaspora today follows a predictable pattern: *Yorubize it!* Second, religious and racial shifts among the Garífuna are related not only to entering an already circumscribed religious field but also to meeting new needs generated in the move from rural Honduras to the dense concrete battlements and iron crenellations of the Bronx. Urban Garífuna seek protection against the threat of intrusion and harm, physical and spiritual,[13] and assemble spirit "warriors" to secure and guard entryways of apartments and bodies. Garífuna migrants in the Bronx find and adapt these spiritual protectors from Cuban redactions of "Yoruba" and "Kongo" religions, Santería and Palo Monte.[14] Third, as the Garífuna entered a foreign religious field that presented new social, practical, and religious needs, they encountered a new set of definitions of ethnic identity. Joining the African diaspora is related to Garífuna adaptation to an identity marketplace where cultural alliances and their discursive articulation in the public sphere are fundamental to securing resources in the city: meeting places, offices, sponsorship for performance arts, seed money for social service organizations, détente with police forces, and so on. "Being Garífuna," religiously as well as ethnically, becomes a matter of conscious, practical action, rather than a state of being that can be taken for granted, as it is in homeland villages. This new North American "market" is far from free, and only a limited range of identifications are open to Garífuna social actors. The imperative to articulate identity generates a drive to discourse, an impulse to secure authenticity through speaking and writing rather than ritual practice alone. Hence the "theologization" of Garífuna religion, which I have called "protestantization" in the case of Brazilian Candomblé: the push toward verbal articulations of meaning in a religion once expressed and transmitted primarily through ritual.[15]

This chapter traces how diaspora identifications are adopted, explores the dynamics through which the transformations undergone in diaspora elicit friction between rival versions of "tradition" and rival authorities seeking to affix authenticity, and elucidates the relationship between religious and racial identifications as they shift through transnational circulation. It first examines Garífuna religion as constituted in the Caribbean world and in its contemporary Bronx vernacular to trace the process of becoming an African diaspora religion. It then describes attempts to remit such innovations to the homeland and the fissures produced by contests between versions of orthopraxy. Homeland religious leaders posit the authority of territory against diaspora religious leaders' cosmopolitan expertise. The next section highlights the active roles of Garífuna women in homeland and diaspora religious practice. The concluding section rethinks the concept of diaspora as a set of discourses and enactments of desire that bring social affinities into being rather than merely expressing them.

The development of the Garífuna in Honduras and in New York City illuminates the processes through which the religion of a group derived from African, Amerindian, and European ethnic sources is being remade as a more clearly signified "African diaspora religion"—a set of practices consciously related to a specific religious family that includes Santería, Palo Monte, Vodou, Candomblé, and Spiritism.

The Religion of the Garífuna in the Homeland and Diaspora

The Garífuna were from the outset a hybrid group whose origins as a distinct society with a specific set of religious practices confused European interlocutors. The Garífuna were called Black Caribs[16] in English nomenclature, possibly by their own choice.[17] This name was reinforced in the histories about them and in their own oral tradition until the relatively recent shift to "Garífuna" as a standard ethnic title.[18] The Garífuna are descendants of Africans and of Carib and Arawak Amerindians who lived on the Caribbean island of St. Vincent from the second half of the seventeenth century. The African presence on St. Vincent derived from three sources: survivors of slaver shipwrecks near the island around midcentury, slaves taken from Puerto Rico by Carib raiders, and *maroons* (runaway slaves, from the Spanish *cimarróne*, "wild" or "unruly") fleeing neighboring Barbados and other island colonies.[19] The British deported between four and five thousand Black Caribs from St. Vincent in 1796 and 1797. Following a horrific six-month internment on the neighboring small isle of Baliceaux, during which many succumbed to epidemic disease, half the original number was finally deposited on the island of Roatan, just off the Honduran coast.

Among the first modern ethnographers of the Garífuna writing in the early 1950s, Douglas Taylor stressed their Amerindian cultural features, while Ruy Coelho emphasized their African derivation.[20] Perhaps the foremost recent ethnohistorian of the Garífuna, Nancie Gonzalez, argued that the Garífuna downplayed references to their Africanness through the 1950s but became more comfortable with such a view as Africanness became tolerated and even fashionably "modern" in some venues.[21] Virginia Kerns's fieldwork from the 1970s documents that the Garífuna of Belize referred to themselves as Carib as often as Garífuna, depending on with whom they were speaking.[22] Crisanto Meléndez, the foremost Honduran Garífuna activist from the 1970s until the present, reports that throughout his education during the 1950s and 1960s, Africanness was never mentioned and that he came to this knowledge later through attending international conferences.[23] Garífuna over forty years of age who now live in the Bronx report similar experiences, as documented in my own and other scholars' contemporary observations.[24]

The historical record does not permit us to know to what degree the Garífuna maintained a sense of their distinctive religious practices as African. Even before their deportation, most Garífuna described themselves as Catholic when speaking to Europeans.[25] It is possible to hazard a morphology of their traditional religion as comprised of aspects typically associated with given cultures: the "African" use of drums to induce trance and possession by ancestral spirits, the "Carib" shaman (*buyei*) who blows smoke on an afflicted patient's body to extract malevolent penetrations, and "Catholic" baptism and images of saints. But all this is speculation; the ability to sift out geographically and temporally distinct religious elements from this syncretic mélange is long forfeit, and current moves to plot that religious history as Carib versus African, or even more specifically as Yoruba or Kongo, must be viewed as in large part a contemporary discursive effort to create a religious genealogy from its absence.[26]

A century ago, the Garífuna were settled in around sixty beachfront villages dotting the Caribbean coast of Belize, Guatemala, Nicaragua, and especially Honduras. The Caribbean fruit industry had begun to boom, and the Standard and United Fruit companies provided steady jobs in many of the largest settlements of the so-called banana republic for four generations. Many Garífuna nostalgically recall this neocolonial period as a time of plenty. Today, most Honduran Garífuna households depend on monthly contributions from relatives working in New York or on the ships of international cruise lines. Many Garífuna migrate yearly to jobs in textile sweat shops outside such large cities as San Pedro Sula or Tegucigalpa. Even those who stay home dwell increasingly in a global imaginary of media broadcasts from Miami, Mexico City, and Rio de Janeiro. With the arrival of electricity and television in most villages around 1980, a global imaginary took hold in previously more insulated locales. *Telenovelas* (daily soap operas) from Mexico and Brazil provide the narrative frame for everyday chat among village women, as soccer games do for men.

This global imaginary takes on flesh with the periodic return of migrants from U.S. urban centers, especially the Bronx.[27] Loaded with goods like VCRs, NBA jerseys, and Nikes, they also come bearing new signifying codes. The new codes have to do not only with consumption patterns but also with discourses of race and ethnic identification. Migrants in U.S. cities are subjected to an unfamiliar racial system, in which Garífuna is subsumed by the categories of black or black Hispanic, and they return with a different classifying consciousness from those at home.[28] The new, racialized consciousness is expressed—and disputed—in discourses of self-representation. The terms *black* and *black Hispanic* were strongly resisted until recently and remain contested because they confound Garífuna identity with that of other Afro-Caribbean communities. The territorial disjunctions of migration and the subjection to U.S. classifiers come home to roost in the ethnic reclassification from Carib and Amerindian to Garífuna, black, and African.[29]

This changed consciousness is also manifested aesthetically, and its values are contested in that domain as well. Movement toward global black modernity occurs along two vectors. The first move comes through the mimesis of U.S. urban style: hip-hop music, "black" movies and videos, "African"-patterned clothing purchased in New York City, heavy jewelry, oversized clothing, and playing basketball instead of soccer. The second move follows the route of burgeoning Protestant neo-Pentecostal affiliations that, through hi-tech sound systems, formal dress codes, and "black" preaching styles, emulate and are often funded by denominational patrons in the United States. Other Garífuna discourses and practices congeal around a quite different form of cultural invention: the idea of deep, authentic religious roots nourished by the elaboration and acceleration of traditional ritual events increasingly understood, presented, and performed as specifically African. These two directions, cultural innovation directed toward modernity and cultural innovation directed toward tradition, are not socially bifurcated but rather work in tandem, although their signs signify over and against each other.

Both developments proffer membership in global networks rather than local, village-based communities. Tradition as a matter of consciousness is forged in the culturally plural context of New York City and relies on the most modern technologies of semiotic reproduction. The Garífuna quest for authenticity, like that of other groups, is a deeply modern search for the lost aura of what was[30] and the deliberate filling in of the historical erasures of slavery. Local tradition must be given global range—be witnessed to, recorded, publicized, discursively defended, and disseminated—in order to acquire exchange value in the new identity market.[31] The Garífuna have recently sought and received coverage from *National Geographic*, the *New York Times*, UNESCO, and other publicizing organs in a mirroring process out of which tradition is dialectically built. Traditional religion is as much part and parcel of globalization as neo-Pentecostalism, hip-hop style, or other forms of black modernity activated within Garífuna communities.

The key question remains, however, of how and where such religious and ethnic shifts—especially the traditionalist movement—occur. Three sites for interpretation are visible to empirical documentation: shamans' declared spirit geographies, the identities and locations of the ancestral spirit guides who are the source of their power; shamans' altars, the symbols through which religious power is constituted, located, and directed on behalf of their clients; and shamans' religious autobiographies. Shamans are central to this investigation because they act as local brokers of meaning, determining through overt discourse or ritual leadership what should be remembered, preserved, discarded, or revised as authentically Garífuna. In Honduran villages, such culture brokers are few: typically one or two shamans per village, who are regarded as local intellectuals and authorized historical speakers.

Shamans' Spirit Geographies in the Homeland and the Bronx

In the homeland, shamans (*buyei*) are responsible for leading periodic large-scale rituals (*chugu* and *dügü*), but their primary daily occupation consists of consulting with individual clients who seek physical cures, interventions in matters of luck, love, and finances, or divination of the future. Shamans' power to accomplish such tasks derives from their selection by spirits of ancestors (*hiuruha*) and undergoing initiation and apprenticeship with an established shaman in order to learn to communicate with these spirits and intercede with them on behalf of clients. As keepers of the ancestral spirits, shamans are, practically if implicitly, keepers of memory and history, as mediated by the geographies and biographies of their spirits.

Never in my extensive work with five shamans in three Honduran communities (Corozal, San Juan, and Triunfo de la Cruz) has Africa appeared without my first introducing the term into the discussion. Tutelary spirits who aid shamans in their healing enterprise were never located as African. For example, the three spirits of the senior shaman of the village of San Juan—Dongal, Domingo, and Delores—are described as "little people" from Yurumein, the Garífuna name for the isle of St. Vincent. The spirits of the primary shaman of the village of Corozal are reported to be Dabwi, Baba, Da, and Mama. One is from Corozal; another is from neighboring Sambu (Sambo Creek); and the others are from Garífuna villages in Belize. Though the spirit Dabwi is described as "universal" and is said to speak "French, *orisha*, all languages!" his spiritual geography is local.

All nine of the Bronx-based shamans I interviewed have at least one key tutelary spirit identified as African. A shaman I will call Maria works with three spirits. Matuco is an indigenous Indian of Honduras. Cresencia is from Maria's own familial ancestors, a great-grandmother who acted, in her time, as midwife. Hermanito, also called el negro, was the "chief of an African tribe." Maria's three spirits represent three sources of her contemporary Garífuna identity: familial, indigenous Caribbean, and African. Another shaman, who I will call Mayha, used to have many spirits but now wields two of primary influence: Lulu, from Belize, and Oyendi, a male African "from Kongo." Mayha has undergone initiation into Cuban Palo Monte, a religious complex explicitly invoking Kongo origins. Indeed, the majority of shamans in the Bronx report having either *nkisi* (Kongo) or *orisha* (Yoruba) spirits. Although Cuban Palo and Santería refer respectively to Kongo and Yoruba origins, in practice they are often cross-referenced and ritually worked in tandem.[32]

Several Bronx shamans wear plastic-bead necklaces (*elekes* or *collares*) marking their *orisha* affiliation. Belgium wears five such necklaces. Edwin, a male shaman from Belize, wears a wrist bracelet linking him to Ifa, the patron of Yoruba divination. Others report considering initiation into Santería (the Yoruba-derived religion of Cuba) or Palo (Cuba's Kongo-derived religion), having been told by Cuban neighbors that they need to undergo them. In the homes of most Bronx-based Garífuna shamans, altars to Eleggua or his *palero* [adjectival form of Palo Monte] counterpart, Lucero, guard corners and doorways. These warrior or guardian spirits, whom Mayha called "my gang" in a brilliant double entendre relating the spirit world to the street, are foreign to the repertoire of homeland Garí-funa practices.

Altar Symbols

Homeland shamans' altars, which mediate their interactions with ancestral spirits, are void of overtly African symbols. They are assembled from a repertoire of traditional Garífuna implements: maracas (*sisiri*), pipes, candles, bottles of *aguardiente* (sugarcane rum), beach sand, wands (*murewa*) used to call ancestor spirits and temper spirit possession, miniature hammocks or boats, images of the Virgin, and icons of Jesus of the Sacred Heart. While this collection is itself a collage, as an ensemble the altar objects present a fairly coherent symbolic representation of a "Garífuna-ness" that has a certain temporal depth, dating at least to the nineteenth century and probably earlier.[33]

Bronx-based shamans' representations of their spirit helpers and their physical altars are replete with objects familiar to students of West African–influenced religions in the Americas. These include the trickster, messenger, and keeper of doorways and crossroads, Eshu-Eleggua, or his *palero* counterpart, Lucero; the goddess of oceans, Yemaya, or her Palo Monte analogues, Madre de Aguas and Tiembla Tierra; the forest hunter, Oshossi, or his Cuban and Brazilian representation as an Amerindian *caboclo;* the god of iron and war, Ogun, and his *palero* counterpart, Zarabanda; and Shango, god of fire and lightning, or his palero counterpart, Siete Rayos. The use of dolls and pins suggests popularized influences from a new religious field that also includes Vodou derived from West and Central Africa (especially Dahomey and Kongo). In addition, the altars of Bronx Garífuna shamans have incorporated the iron *calderons* (also called *prenda,* or *nganga*) from Cuban Palo, the black fortune-teller called "La Madama" from Puerto Rican popular practice, and the entire *orisha* complex from what has become the semiotically hegemonic pan-African religious system of representations, a condensed and standardized canon of the Yoruba-Benin pantheon.

Garífuna shamans in the Bronx have incorporated new rituals to secure and protect apartments and communal religious sites, treating entrances and crossroads and making sacrifices and offerings to pay, feed, and replenish the warrior "gang." This practice resonates of Cuban-redacted Kongo and Yoruba ritual, with its focus on mediators and protectors who defend against unwanted intrusions. These ritualizations indicate that Garífuna have entered a new religious field with social needs that no traditional entities are seen as equipped or trained to serve.

Religious Autobiographies

Looking closely at the religious autobiographies of the nine Bronx-based shamans with whom I have worked makes these innovations seem less surprising. Most shamans report taking little interest in religion during their childhood in the homeland and undergoing conversion to traditional Garífuna practice only after their arrival in the United States. Their heightened consciousness as Garífuna was mediated through the pan-African religious network of New York City. How had they embarked on their occupations as Garífuna traditional religious specialists?

One shaman began his spiritual search by phoning a Yoruba priestess on a radio call-in program in New York. He followed her recommendation to study at Oyotunji, a reconstructed Yoruba community in South Carolina that seeks a desyncretized African purity, where he discovered his need to pursue his own ancestral lineage. Finally, he found like-minded seekers in New York. Another Bronx-based Garífuna shaman was a professional dancer who studied Yoruba *orisha* dance moves before she undertook initiation in her own tradition. Based on these experiences and her reading about Yoruba *orishas,* she had already equated the African and Garífuna traditions before initiating her specifically Garífuna practice. A third Garífuna shaman in the Bronx was saved from a psychic crisis by her building superintendent, a Cuban *santera,* who found her on the floor staring fixedly at an overhead light bulb. Regarding her helper as "spiritually more advanced," the Garífuna woman underwent preliminary initiation in Cuban Santería before being possessed by spirits speaking in Garífuna. Only then did she pursue her own religious tradition. Another shaman, a young man living in the Bronx who also leads rituals during yearly returns to the Honduran village of his birth, has been advised by his Garífuna ancestors that he needs to "seat" (be initiated to) Santería deities and is actively seeking the required funds. Finally, the preeminent Bronx Garífuna religious leader, an older woman, frequently visits Palo and Santería ceremonies and has attended at least one Vodou ritual. She has invited leaders of these other Afro-Caribbean religions to visit Garífuna villages with her and has shown to and discussed with them videotapes of homeland rituals.

All these Bronx shamans consume popular books about the Yoruba pantheon. Along avenues in the Bronx, Brooklyn, and Harlem, they shop for ritual herbs and implements at the Cuban or Dominican shops (*botanica*), which commingle Spiritist and Afro-Latin products among their wares. From such shopkeepers,

Garífuna leaders acquire advice on the herbs' and implements' correct usage— "correct," that is, from the purview of Santería's and Spiritism's visions of orthopraxy.

Garífuna religious leaders in New York City are articulating their notions of ancestry and orthodoxy within a dramatically different religious field from that of the homeland. In entering this new religious field and taking advantage of its established economic and social niches—its *botanica* stores, popular literature, meeting places, and clientele—Bronx Garífuna religious leaders now view their traditional religion as part of the African diaspora, which is defined by groups long established in major U.S. cities.[34] Reflecting a sentiment widely reported by Bronx-based Garífuna, one shaman declared: "We didn't know exactly who we were or where our roots were. To survive here [in New York], Garífuna made themselves pass for blacks of other nationalities"—Cubans, Haitians, Dominicans, Puerto Ricans, and Jamaicans. The available black and pan-African identity was predominantly Yoruba and to a lesser degree Kongo and Spiritist, as mediated by "blacks of other nationalities." The Garífuna, relative newcomers to the religious marketplace of New York City, take their place in an urban territory already parsed and marked by others.

These patterns suggest a process of indigenous transculturation—not the ballyhooed syncretism of African diaspora religions with the Catholic saints, but the transculturation of Garífuna religion with Cuban Santería and West African Yoruba symbols. It justifies a view of the Garífuna as a dramatically innovative and "additive" religion.[35] Through this urban transfusion, Garífuna religion is also changed. Its leaders become purveyors of a new religious system that is ethnically narrowed and semantically expanded. Its signs and symbols are clearly defined as African, but, in the quest for authenticity and depth and for a clear distinction from U.S.-style blackness, the term becomes Yoruba-focused. This move is semantically expansive as well. Garífuna ritual practice not only signifies the reverence of family ancestors but also extends broadly toward Africa, Africanness, and the multiple neighboring religions that represent and construct their meanings.

Africa Remitted to the Homeland

How are these transformations in the Bronx diaspora transmitted to the homeland? There are at least two primary avenues of religious communication: the periodic return of Bronx Garífuna shamans to lead rituals at home, and literature produced by homeland Garífuna with international experience for consumption by those in Honduras, Guatemala, and Belize. Stability or change in homeland religious practice does not depend wholly on transnational networks, but the culture brokers motivated to assign discursive "meaning" to homeland practices are those who have negotiated the religiously plural contexts abroad and articulated defenses of what is distinctively "Garífuna" in contexts where such definitions and boundaries matter.[36] These spokespersons are "modern traditionals" because they write, grant interviews to newspapers and magazines, and consolidate the locations of histories and origins through the drive to discourse. Such articulations do not go uncontested. As the Garífuna remake their religious identity in the diaspora, the prospect of a reform of religious practice in the homeland is also engaged, and a turf war is fought between those claiming the authority of place, the enduring occupation of the homeland, and those claiming the cosmopolitan authority of the globalized metropole and the African diaspora.

African diaspora religious identity arrives in the homeland with the periodic return of Bronx-based religious leaders to Honduras to visit relatives and to guide ritual events. Bronx families are key instigators and patrons of homeland rituals. Garífuna residing in New York City are motivated to accelerate homeland ritual performance by their nostalgia for "home" and are disproportionately able to fund and influence such expensive ventures because of their wage-earning capacity in the United States.[37] Since the shamans they know best are located in the Bronx, and since these are the shamans whose divination has determined the need for such rituals, Bronx-based shamans are central actors in homeland rites.

In the summer of 2001, I accompanied a group of Bronx shamans to the homeland and documented tensions between Honduran villagers and New York residents, as reported by both. Homeland shamans perceived the New York visitors as threatening because they arrived as an ideological block, with a consensus on the meanings of Garífuna religion formed by locating the tradition in the comparative framework of the African diaspora; and they presented an institutional anomaly by acting as officiants in rituals not necessarily related to their family lineage. They take part as professionals who are there to sharpen their skills and hone their craft. They serve in the mundane ritual capacities like the constant "cleansing" of the temple with aguardiente and smoke, and taking part in the chorus of maracas played by shamans to call the spirits. They do not mediate the family spirits, however, and are viewed by local family members with a certain mistrust; as such, they occupy a middle space between the foreign ethnographer and the homeland ritualizer.

There were more basic concerns as well. Those arriving from New York were perceived to have better clothes and the disposable wealth such clothes imply.

Complained one homeland shaman, "They arrive with suitcases full of clothing changes instead of food" for ritual offerings, criticizing the materialism of those in the diaspora as well as their ignorance of ritual protocol. Such criticisms were put into practice by excluding Bronx shamans from gossip networks and practical tasks demanding overt instruction. The need for instruction was one hinge of the problem. Homeland shamans disparaged those from the Bronx by declaring that they lacked the practical knowledge acquired through years of routine ritual work and that they did not treat the ritual with the respectful secrecy it mandates, regarding it as knowledge learned "like in school."

Bronx-based shamans countered with comments criticizing their homeland counterparts: "They know what to do, but they don't *why* they do what they do." The homeland ritual specialists "don't know any better; they've been doing the same thing forever." Bronx-based shamans' romantic notions of a pilgrimage toward the simplicity, beauty, and purity of the village was tempered after several weeks by a gnawing sense that they were dwelling among country cousins. Their "city knowledge" of other religions of the African diaspora was not welcome but rather regarded as problematic.

The new knowledge claimed by Bronx-based shamans, which they sought to instill in Honduran villages, was a comparative perspective based on and valued in relation to deep Africanness. They interpreted their tradition in terms of its similarities to other religions of the African diaspora, adopting that phrase as key to their practical lexicon. Locating Garífuna religion in a network of Africanness elevated ethnic and racial designations that previously were ambiguous, unspoken, or irrelevant to a central position. Traditional Garífuna religion's similarity or dissimilarity to "African religious practice" (that is, Yoruba or Kongo mediated through Cuban Santería and Palo) was tendered as vital to orthopraxy. In Honduran villages, such accretions were viewed as aggressive foreign incursions on what is regarded as simply "our tradition." The Bronx returnees' presence was welcome but perturbing to the village.

The quest for authentic religious Africanness arrived in tandem with the clothing, music, technology, and tastes of the metropole and the tropes of U.S.-style blackness brought by Bronx-based Garífuna. Diaspora religious sensibilities and spirit geographies located in a primordial Africa comport awkwardly with such modern black signs and symbols, but they do so more plausibly in New York City than in Honduran villages. Shamans based in the homeland derided their U.S. counterparts as "materialistic," "lacking in generosity," "lost," and "know-it-alls." Central American Garífuna perceived Bronx shamans' children as disturbingly "like American blacks." Their style, music, movies, culinary preferences, jewelry, and "lack of respect for elders" disrupted village life, especially because the city cousins became "the talk of the town." Bearing gifts and currency made them pivotal social players in ways beyond the means of those who remained in the village.

This corrosive gossip represented an ongoing debate between two kinds of authority: that of remaining "on the land," with its implied habitus of corporeal and largely unspoken practical knowledge; and that of the cosmopolis, with the interreligious perspective and discursive skills called forth in that site. The Bronx-based Garífuna religious leaders have thoroughly joined the African diaspora, but such an identification remains uncertain in the homeland. A pan-African consciousness appears to be under construction, but this development has also met with opposition.

Garífuna Women Joining the Religious African Diaspora

Since the Herskovitses' account of Trinidad and Ruth Landes's book on Brazilian Candomblé, both published in 1947, it has been a commonplace that women play vital, sustaining roles in religions of the African diaspora. Landes called Brazilian Candomblé a "city of women," although the assertion has since been disputed.[38] Rachel Harding in chapter 1 and Tracy Hucks in chapter 2 bring those early accounts of women in Brazil and Trinidad into the present in fascinating new ways, demonstrating the import of the basic insight and the need for that insight to be given greater complexity.

Ruy Coelho's account of Honduran villages, first published in 1955, declared that eighty percent of the members of Catholic organizations were women and that these organizations were the main source of the human resources required for traditional ancestor rituals.[39] Douglas Taylor's 1951 report of the primary Garífuna ritual event, the *dügü*, estimated a ratio of four women to each man among participants.[40] My own field notes, as well as other accounts, suggest an even higher proportion of women in contemporary ritual performances.[41]

In the past, men and women were more equally balanced among participants in Garífuna rituals. Thomas Young's mid-nineteenth-century description of the *dügü* mentioned the "great numbers" of women participating but did not remark any striking disparity in the proportion of women and men.[42] The existence of an elaborate corpus of "men's songs" (*arumahani*), considered an important part of an ideal Garífuna ritual, suggests relative parity, at least in the formal terms of ritual construction, in the gender of participants. So, why did this balance shift over time? Men traditionally traveled for work more frequently than women did. Labor migration accelerated around 1950, with the relative decline of the fruit industry whose jobs had sustained many communities. Migrants also ventured further, with the gradual pioneering of legal and illegal migration channels to the north. Today, Kerns's account of Belizean communities in the 1970s and my own observations from contemporary Honduras indicate the difficulty of finding a group of men who are willing and able to sing "men's songs." In their absence, that task goes by default to women, who periodically playact as men during rituals, singing the men's songs while hiking up their skirts and sometimes even holding a stick in place as a mock phallus, an act accompanied by enormous mirth.

Although women make up the great majority of participants at rituals to honor the ancestors, men play specific roles as drummers, as sacrificers of animals, as "traditional fishermen" whose arrival initiates the *dügü* ancestor rites, and as shamans (*buyei*). In fact, women and men are relatively evenly represented in the role of *buyei*, directing and orchestrating large-scale rituals. The gender balance in leadership positions, compared with the overwhelming predominance of women in supporting roles, may result from *buyei* being a "profession" rewarded with financial compensation and conforming to social norms that give males authority in the public domain. The position of shaman attracts men in ways that simple ritual participation does not.

In the Bronx diaspora, it appears that the majority of shamans are female. Six of the nine shamans I interviewed were women. Many of the religious shifts documented in this essay have been accomplished in New York and remitted to the homeland by women. Why do Garífuna women hold positions of religious leadership more often in the Bronx than in Central America?

Women are now nearly as likely to migrate as men.[43] This shift is related to the availability of gender-specific niches in the U.S. labor market at specific junctures. The demand for domestics during the 1970s enabled more women to immigrate legally, since they fit the profile.[44] Currently, demand is highest for home-care workers, live-in caregivers for the sick or disabled whose services are subsidized by the state; women seem to be able to obtain these positions more easily than men.

Yet, women's increasing propensity to migrate reflects more than the availability of job opportunities in New York City. Women may also accrue more social benefits through migration than do men. When men working away from home leave their wives and children behind in homeland villages, they enjoy radical independence from domestic ties. As Garífuna women constantly complain, such men frequently engender multiple family households in different places.

Women traditionally tend the home, children, and gardens, but subsistence-producing activities are increasingly untenable in the face of decreasing yields from gardens and fishing. Nancie Gonzalez explained that many Garífuna migrants will remain in the United States, making only periodic visits to the homeland, and that "the women are often more insistent on remaining than are the men, possibly because they find the housework in the village onerous and the amenities primitive."[45] Many Garífuna women living in the United States enjoy financial independence by engaging in paid employment, a relatively rare phenomenon in Central American villages, though they also pay a high price for these new freedoms, often remaining away from their own families much of the week as "live-in" home-care workers.

It is possible that the increased proportion of female traditional religious leaders in New York correlates with women's greater independence in the city. Many of the Bronx-based shamans are single women supporting children, and the network of women shamans and devotees provides valuable personal support. Through this network, women maintain and rehearse their traditions even as they expand them in terms of a religious idiom—"African diaspora religions"—that matches their growing cultural capital and transnational experiences. The identification with African diaspora religions leads these women not only to a shared intellectual journey among themselves but also into new trans-Caribbean social networks and even outward into the public domain: to museums, workshops, lectures, and an ever-expanding literature.

Diaspora as Discourse and Enactment of Desire

The Garífuna are in the process of joining the African diaspora because key culture brokers have undergone conversion to diaspora consciousness through their proximity to more established African-descended religions, especially Cuban Santería and the Yoruba-centricity it reproduces.[46] This shift can be seen as an adaptive response of Bronx-based Garífuna shamans to taking their place in an urban religious landscape—already marked by earlier migrant groups—which generates new social needs. This religious expansion is accompanied by an ethnoracial narrowing of Garífuna identity. As Garífuna religion becomes one spoke in the wheel of the African diaspora, Bronx-based Garífuna begin to view themselves as more definitively African and black than they did a generation ago in the homeland, where a unique Carib identity was equally prominent and discursively locating identity was not at issue. These related processes of religious expansion and ethnoracial narrowing originate in the Bronx but are carried to Honduras when shamans return to homeland villages as emissaries of reform.

The Garífuna present a persuasive example of how the African diaspora does not simply exist as a stable form, but rather is enjoined and shaped through specific cultural transmissions and at specific historical junctures. This perspective raises new questions and suggests a new agenda for research on religions in diaspora. These concluding pages consider what the Garífuna case suggests for the study of the African diaspora, religious diasporas, and diasporas in general.

Multiple Diasporic Horizons

Ethnic groups like the Garífuna who dwell in several locations live within multiple *diasporic horizons,* each with distinct functions and features. Honduran homeland villages provide one diasporic horizon, a site to which migrants aspire to return, the place where the extended family retains its hub, and the locus for over two hundred years of Garífuna history. The island of St. Vincent provides a second diasporic horizon, as the birthplace of Garífuna culture and the location of an idealized independence prior to European domination. This second diasporic horizon remains an imagined homeland. There are no Garífuna settlements there now, and almost no Garífuna will ever visit the island. Nevertheless, it serves as an imagined place that links Garífuna of diverse Central American nations in a transnational community through a shared historical trajectory.

Africa is now emerging as a third diasporic horizon, a place of mythic historical origins. This remote horizon remains wholly opaque for almost all Garífuna, apart from the simple knowledge of being descendants *of that place.* As such, Africa constitutes an open semiotic site for rethinking identity in relation to contemporary concerns, especially migration. The Garífuna increasingly view their cycles of migration to the United States through the prism of an imagined Africa that serves to articulate and focus critical perspectives on their experience of exile in the United States. Joining the African diaspora through religion becomes a way of thinking and acting critically in relation to race, as racialism and racism are constituted and confronted differently in Honduras and in the United States. This third diasporic horizon presents an array of new political and social opportunities for Garífuna in New York City and elsewhere. Other transnational structures could serve an analogous purpose for the Garífuna, such as "indigenousness" or "Latin American-ness," and the Garífuna engage these when it is advantageous to do so.[47] But Africanness becomes primary. The Garífuna are perceived by whites, African Americans, and other Afro-Caribbean migrants in the host land as black, so the African diaspora network provides the most readily accessible social and institutional niches.

Diaspora as Habitus, Subjectivity, and Ideology

From the inception of this project, I have followed in the wake of such key contemporary theorists of the African diaspora as Stuart Hall and Paul Gilroy. Yet I follow them reluctantly. The source of my hesitation is that even these scholars who cut the notion of the African diaspora free from its essentialist, race-based stakes have held fast to the idea of real continuity, transferred now from race to a shared cultural "grammar" or set of tendencies in styles of movement and musicality[48] and experiences derived from subjection and resistance to institutionalized terror.[49] The Garífuna provide good evidence for such an argument, since in the Bronx they have readily adopted elements from Afro-Caribbean religious systems that were not their own. This affinity suggests mutual recognition between disparate religions, perhaps based in perceptions of a family resemblance among such key features as connecting with ancestors through possession and trance, altars as sites of material exchange with spirit powers, and the central role of drumming and dance.

Still, there is reason to tread carefully. As Sidney Mintz has pointed out, the consensus on transhistorical features out of which the African diaspora is supposed to be composed, while drawing on cultural rather than genetic categories, may distort or level differences between cases worth keeping distinct.[50] The second reason, on which I focus here, is that in studying religious diasporas we are dealing with not one but three distinct social phenomena: (1) diaspora in the form of seemingly (to an outside observer) shared cultural dispositions across multiple sites which may or may not exist as an internalized consciousness among religious actors; (2) diaspora as an internalized conversion of consciousness, the subjective self-understanding as belonging to a diaspora, whether or not a multi-sited cultural resemblance empirically exists; and (3) diaspora as ideology, a discursive artifact articulated in speech and the public sphere in order to achieve unity between previously disjoined groups for political or other desired effects.

The three forms of diaspora are inter-calibrated in complex ways, which is why it may be worthwhile to keep them analytically distinct. Until the 1950s, the Garífuna belonged to the African diaspora in the first but not in the second or third senses of the term. When they joined the diaspora as a matter of self-conscious ideology, the first sense was shifted; the underlying set of shared cultural dispositions was tilted toward the Yoruba version of Africanness. The discourse of diaspora is distinct from senses one and two. One group's claims of durable continuity with another, more or less distant one may actually increase in the face of evidence calling such continuity into question. Diaspora discourse may be articulated more frequently and stridently in consequence of the perceived weakening, or even absence, of bonds based on common enactments or sentiments. The discourse of diaspora and the empirically observable relationship between disjoined communities must be seen as separate though overlapping social phenomena. The following cases illustrate why it is useful to differentiate analytically between these three senses of *diaspora*.

The first example, the inclusion of the Caribbean, Brazil, and the U.S. South within a single network, shows the disjunction between diaspora in sense one, a shared set of cultural dispositions, and sense two, the sentiment of being in diaspora. To speak simply of an African diaspora religious repertoire that links the Caribbean and Brazil with the U.S. South hides as much as it reveals. Cuba and Brazil accelerated the importation of "raw" African slaves (*bossales*) through the first half of the nineteenth century as sugar markets expanded, "Africanizing" slave culture with constant new arrivals. The United States curtailed slave imports after 1808, so its slave culture underwent a process of American creolization in the absence of new African arrivals and the cultural tools they carried with them.[51] This historical contingency goes a long way toward explaining why overtly African religions were maintained in Brazil and the Caribbean, while indigenous African religious practices were largely absorbed into the black Christian churches in the United States.

Such dramatically different trajectories suggest that it is one thing to speak of a cultural diaspora, including religion, as a relatively delimited repertoire of symbolic resources that might have been available at some point in time to different communities in exile. It is quite another to assume that the repertoire is equally or simultaneously available, considered desirable, or activated in divergent locations. A style of musicality and possession by ancestral spirits may have been present as cultural options to varying degrees among distinct slave cultures in the Americas. But that they were not historically exercised in a consistent way makes their designation as characteristic of the whole African diaspora suspect. Their invocation as a shared repertoire that defines the African diaspora is a constructive effort, a composite aimed as much at contemporary political practice as at establishing historical or analytical purchase. It is not a description of what already exists in any specific case but rather a selection of features from among various cultural repertoires at hand. The goal of the discourse of diaspora is to create sentiments of proximity to a distant group and place at a time when such sentiments are politically expedient.

The second example, the Brazilian religion called Candomblé, demonstrates that some of those who deploy the diaspora concept in its second and third senses are not of African descent yet identify themselves as adherents of African diaspora religions. Here we witness not the complexity of drawing boundaries circumscribing the African diaspora but rather the problem of knowing what the identification means once it is discursively affirmed.

Prominent Candomblé houses view themselves as constituents of a broader entity called "African diaspora religion." If this notion is used as the rationale for "re-Africanizing" religious practice, this claim brings these groups into conflict with other houses of Candomblé, whose members understand themselves as distinctly and markedly Brazilian and remain uninterested in purging their practice of Catholic and Spiritist elements, which many regard as part and parcel of authentic Candomblé. In this case, a transnational ethnic location of the religion as purely African competes with a national and ethnic location, mirroring a century of scholarly debates on the relative African versus creole Brazilian character of religions like Candomblé. In chapter 1, Harding eloquently points to the embodied and performative continuities of ritual that link Afro-Brazilians and Africans across space and time. Hucks, in chapter 2, indicates the tensions evoked within Trinidadian communities by the discursive reifications and amplifications of those embodied continuities, and provides hints too of the attempts to build religious authority through more and less persuasive representations of "authentic Africa."

As the discourse of diaspora seeks to simplify the problem of origins, it complicates other matters of identity. Candomblé claimants to African diaspora identity cannot help but note that half the practitioners of the religion are not biologically descended from Africans at all, especially in the southern states of Brazil around Rio de Janeiro and São Paulo.[52] Does belonging to the African religious diaspora involve merely acknowledging African liturgical and theological origins or something more? Alternatively, does it include all the religions performed by persons of African descent, even Episcopalians or Zen Buddhists, or only those displaying "traditional" African features? This question needs to be clarified to define the "diasporic field" under study.

These comparisons suggest that the concept of diaspora is inherently unstable and contingent, in terms not only of when and how it comes into being but also what it implies once established. While Brazilian Candomblé has been nationalized and become transracial through its wide dissemination in the public sphere, Garífuna ancestor religion has narrowed these boundaries, purging possible Amerindian genealogy to become more purely African. Joining the African diaspora through religion in Candomblé implies a liturgical investment in practicing a religion derived from Africa, regardless of the racial identities of practitioners, but in the Garífuna case, it involves a serious ethnoracial investment in becoming ancestrally and exclusively African.

Considering *diaspora* not merely as an expression of social relations or cultural predispositions that already exist but also as an acquired subjectivity and an identity discourse devoted to creating desired relations opens new questions about religions in transit and the boundary work in which collective sentiments of affinity coalesce and divide across space. The very polyvalence of the term *diaspora* allows us to link and think through a series of otherwise disjoined theoretical fields: ethnic identifications, social movements, collective memory, religious stability and change, globalization and transmigration, the meanings of space and place, the problem of authenticity, and more. Just as the invocation of *diaspora* as a term of practice can build new bridges between formerly dislocated religious communities, its invocation as an analytical term can build bridges of thought between artificially partitioned fields of scholarship. This is much to the good. Let us, then, ask questions promiscuously. How and why do diasporic desires emerge? How do they develop divergently in different locales, even if from what is defined as the same culture? How is the consciousness of being in or belonging to diaspora created, implemented, and maintained through specific objects, enactments, and narratives? How are those desires contested by rival ones, so that the boundaries of diaspora remain porous and always under construction?

Finally, how does gender play into each of these questions? How and to what extent do men and women differ in the ways they carry and transmit African diaspora religious consciousness? Garífuna women are both the key culture bearers of ancestral religion in the homeland and the central agents of change in neotraditional movements seeded in the U.S. diaspora. Other contributions to this volume suggest that this is a common rather than anomalous case and begin to offer explanations for the increasingly prominent roles of women in African diaspora religions.

CHAPTER FOUR

Women of the African Diaspora Within

The Masowe Apostles, an African Initiated Church

ISABEL MUKONYORA

The suggestion that Masowe Apostles, an African Initiated Church whose members are scattered across sub-Saharan Africa and gather to worship in the literal and metaphorical wilderness rather than in central places, belong to "the African diaspora within" poses a challenge to prevailing conceptions of *diaspora*. Masowe Apostles are displaced Shona-speaking people who interpret their marginality and dispersion as exile, which they associate with journeying from place to place, seeking out the periphery for worship, and practicing rituals focused on longing for redemption. My use of the word *redemption* is not with specific reference to the death and resurrection of Christ, although the Apostles think of themselves as followers of Christ, but is meant more broadly to describe social and religious processes through which adherents become uplifted materially and spiritually. Redemption is a quest in which individuals hope to rise above trauma, oppression, and misfortune.[1] Perceived in terms of its religious dimension, the phrase "African diaspora within" involves spiritual as well as physical meanings.

Africa is ordinarily conceived as the place of origin of many diasporan peoples; it is not normally thought of as a location of diasporan peoples. And, despite the Judeo-Christian referents of the term, recent reconceptualizations of the African diaspora have not paid much attention to religion.[2] I take up the religious dimension of the term *disapora* in order to create a platform for dialogue between the women of Africa who have been displaced by the legacy of colonialism and those daughters of Africa who were dispersed throughout the world by their ancestors' enslavement.

Let us look, then, at the multiple meanings of *diaspora*. In the history of Western civilization, there are two main groups of people whose dispersions have been central to the hegemonic understanding of this term. The Jewish people, whose long history of oppression takes us back to ancient slavery, give meaning to the Greek word. English-language dictionaries cite the exile of the Jews after the destruction of the first and second temples in Jerusalem, their captivity in Babylon during the period just before the Common Era, and the repeated expulsions of Jews from European states over many centuries. The suffering that the Jews experienced in their dispersion and the hope for redemption they expressed in their sense of themselves as "the chosen people" created a powerful conjunction. This condition and trajectory laid the basis for an entire religious tradition by which the distressing situation of *dia-spora* (being scattered)—not just exiled but also fragmented—nurtured aspirations for redemption, for the restoration of peace and harmony on earth and, with it, a return to the promised land. The term *diaspora* thus draws attention not only to movements from place to place but also, and more importantly, to the expression of aspirations for emancipation that are profoundly religious.

The second group of people whose dispersion has been described by many historians of Western civilization as diasporic is comprised of African slaves and their descendants in the Americas and beyond. People of African origins have been scattered abroad since Europeans enslaved Africans to advance capitalism in their American colonies between the fourteenth and nineteenth centuries.[3] Studies of recent migrations of Africans to Europe and North America complicate this notion, for these new members of the African diaspora bring new identities with them. Significantly, these diasporic Africans are predominantly Christian, with their own understandings of the meanings of exile and redemption. The anthropologists Gerrie ter Haar and Elias Bangomba argue that we must redefine the African diaspora in light of encounters between new migrants from Africa and persons of African descent in Europe and America.[4] Deidre H. Crumbley makes a similar suggestion in her study of an African Initiated Church that has reached out from its origins in Nigeria through missionary efforts to other parts of Africa and followed Nigerian immigrants to the Americas. (See chapter 5.) What happens if we further enlarge the term *African diaspora* to include recent instances of Africans migrating *within* the continent to escape violence and hunger?

Focusing on the religious interpretation of experiences of displacement in colonial and postcolonial Africa expands the term *diaspora* to encompass a quest for redemption through journeying and enacting rituals in peripheral places. Masowe Apostles confront us with ways of thinking and acting in religious communities where diaspora means more than being scattered abroad; it suggests a human condition marked by fragmentation, displacement, marginality, and oppression. The term *diaspora* is thus translated into an African spiritual quest or discourse of redemption.

Who are Masowe Apostles, why do they imagine themselves in diaspora, and what difference does it make when we examine their spiritual vision through women's eyes? Although this religious group has a significant presence in contemporary sub-Saharan Africa, it is relatively little known. African Initiated Churches are not generally understood outside Africa except by religious studies scholars, and within Africa the Masowe Apostles intentionally locate themselves in the less visible parts of the physical as well as institutional landscape. Introducing the women who are central participants in this religious group to an English-language audience involves a double act of translation: articulating the group's sense of identity and its prophetic spiritual vision, and, at the same time, placing it in social-historical context and in relation to religious movements now emerging on the African continent.

In this essay, women of the African diaspora within exist as agents of knowledge whose powerful presence, deeply informed understandings of cultural traditions, and transformative spirituality would be easy to miss if the approach to Masowe Apostles remained centered on what men say in their capacity as official leaders. The centrality of women to this case study rests on underlying principles and key questions that also shape the other chapters, albeit in very different ways given the vast differences in their spatial, temporal, and cultural settings. The Masowe Apostles, like many of the African-derived and African American diasporic religions examined in these essays, are comprised overwhelmingly of women, although the group's founder and its most visible leaders were men. The social relations that give rise to this contradictory situation and the tensions that arise from it and are expressed within spiritual practice reveal much about the dynamics that shape this religious movement.

What do women devotees bring to and seek in the experience of prayer on the margins? What experiences of suffering and longings for redemption draw so many women to the sacred wilderness again and again? How do Apostles' prayer gatherings express women's marginality and heal their pain? Looking at Masowe Apostles' rituals from the point of view of female adherents and in relation to the symbolic meanings of gender illuminates how this movement is rooted in social-historical conditions of patriarchy and gender conflict, as well as conditions of colonial and postcolonial displacement shared by Shona-speaking women and men, and it highlights the spiritual elements within the tradition in which women worshippers find strength despite its more visible patriarchal characteristics. Women draw healing power from a deep well of gendered symbols that remain available within Masowe Apostles' ritual repertoire and connect this African Initiated Church to indigenous beliefs and practices that it has only partially superceded and suppressed. The subversive meanings that women find in Masowe Apostles' gendered symbols and acts of communal prayer are the source of their redemption. Placing women at the center of our analysis offers an alternative perspective on this religious movement, enlarging and even transforming the understandings that would be available if we studied the Apostles from the outside, from the point of view of men and the patriarchal order they seem to uphold. In doing so, we attend to not only the voices, experiences, and viewpoints of women but also the powerfully gendered dynamics of exile and redemption that animate this emergent religious movement and underlie its wide appeal across the African continent and beyond.

Keeping in mind these ideas about women and gender as the key to whatever goes on in the places where women of the Masowe Apostles gather to enact prayer rituals that they fervently believe bring benefit to them, let me return to the cultural matrix of Africa. I suggest that Masowe Apostles practice a spirituality that accommodates those who suffer from oppression and marginality, journey from place to place within Africa, and translate their experiences into a religious quest for a redemption they dramatize as part of prayer.

The Historical Origins of Masowe Apostles

The name Masowe Apostles is used by Shona-speaking[5] members of a popular African Initiated Church (AIC) that thrives in sub-Saharan Africa. Altogether, there are approximately three million Masowe Apostles scattered among the wide spectrum of Bantu people in southern, central, and east Africa (see Fig. 1). The leaders and members of this AIC speak Shona as they express their religious ideas and participate in rituals. Generally associated with eight or nine groups of Bantu people colonized by the British in what is now known as Zimbabwe, Shona is the most widely spoken indigenous language in the country. Nowadays, many Ndebele people who live alongside the Shona speak the language, as do migrant workers from Malawi, Mozambique, and Zambia. Some non-Shona people join the Masowe Apostles; the group has a powerful presence among popular religious movements.

The dynamic relationship between language, peoplehood, and culture in precolonial, colonial, and postcolonial Africa is a matter of considerable scholarly debate. The historian David Beach asserts that central and east Africa is a region filled with groups of Bantu, and that Shona are nothing but groups of Bantu peo-

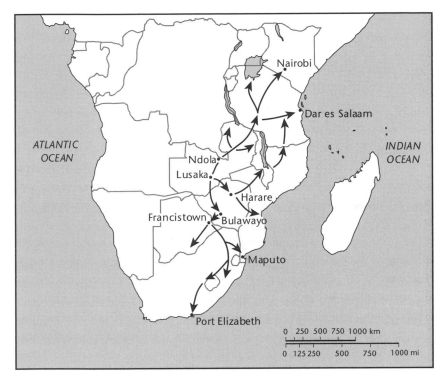

Fig. 4.1. The Journey of Masowe Apostles, 1930s–2005.

ple who were conquered alongside the Ndebele by the British at the end of the nineteenth century. The various dialects of Bantu spoken by the Shona can be understood by many other groups of Bantu people in southern and central Africa.[6] The social histories of these millions of people in the region put them in roughly the same cultural matrix in the precolonial, colonial, and postcolonial periods, a remarkable degree of cultural continuity given the multiple displacements that colonialism entailed and that have followed the achievement of national independence. The setting for my study is contemporary Zimbabwe. This society is in decline under the leadership of an indigenous government and patriarchy that is widely recognized as corrupt and authoritarian, as well as oppressive to women.[7]

The phrase "the African diaspora within" comes from the fact that colonialism brought about an African modernity known for the harshness of its material and political conditions. In postindependence central and southern Africa, the scars of these disruptive and incomplete historical transitions show in the sharp divisions between rich and poor, political conflicts that sometimes erupt in civil war, and the corruption of indigenous governmental leaders in failed states.[8] The African diaspora within refers to a condition of displacement within the continent, as people leave their homelands to find work or temporary shelter in other societies. The common talk about refugees that we hear in the news about sub-Saharan Africa makes explicit that these are forced migrations. The African continent keeps within it many people who are lost to their homelands and who suffer from their condition of exile.

This expanded definition of the African diaspora shares much with the third definition of diaspora offered by Paul C. Johnson in chapter 3. He develops the idea of the African disapora by drawing attention to it as a state of mind, a sense of shared identity that emerges through intricate cycles of dispersion and reconnection. In the case he studies, repeated migrations, feelings of displacement, and related ways of thinking about the spiritual dimension of cultural transformations give meaning to the term *African diaspora*. I am also struck by Rachel Harding's discussion of the Afro-Brazilian religion of Candomblé (chapter 1). Harding's analysis, like my own, examines ritual practices in order to illuminate consciousness. Candomblé rituals are a means of transmitting knowledge about the experiential aspects of suffering in the history of oppression in this Brazilian setting. Harding's work powerfully echoes the central thesis of Rosalind Shaw's recent book on religious rituals in contemporary Africa, *Memories of the Slave Trade*.[9] Doing fieldwork in contemporary Sierra Leone, Shaw found people using ritual to dramatize enslavement as if it happened yesterday. Harding, like Shaw, helped me realize just how much knowledge can be retained and transmitted through ritual behavior. These scholars also confirm the idea I explore here of a discourse of redemption that begins with the acknowledgement of forms of suffering entailed in a history of oppression and displacement.

This essay uses this enlarged concept of diaspora to explore and explain the ritual practices of Masowe Apostles. The fieldwork on which this study draws was conducted among groups of Shona-speaking people I met in and around the city of Harare, Zimbabwe, during the last decade of the twentieth century. Masowe Apostles are easy to spot when they are in motion. They dress in white robes and walk to the fringes of the landscape to pray. Prayers are sometimes held at odd hours around sunset. Weekends are a popular time for meetings that can last as long as eight hours or all night. The sites for prayer, from which I learnt about the spiritual practices of the Masowe Apostles, are called *masowe* (sacred wilderness).

The history of Masowe Apostles begins with groups of Shona people from

Zimbabwe who responded to the social upheavals caused by colonialism by creating religious rituals dramatizing their displacement. Terence Ranger, Clive Dillon-Malone, Bennetta Jules-Rosette, and Richard Werbner all discuss Masowe Apostles migrating into other African societies, expressing their hope for a better world in the religious and political terms of a promised land.[10] Today, among the estimated 3 million members of Masowe Apostles scattered across sub-Saharan Africa, the majority are either Shona-speaking or understand it well enough at prayer meetings to become followers. The migratory behavior of Masowe Apostles throughout southern, central, and east Africa (see Fig. 1) is suggestive of a diasporan mentality. Groups of Shona people who worship in this wilderness church ritualize their displacement, enacting their marginalization and expressing their aspirations for redemption.

In an African church that welcomes victims of oppression and draws large numbers of women, it makes sense to examine this concept of the African diaspora within from women's perspective. Studying women among Masowe Apostles deepens our understanding of this religious movement, which has hitherto been portrayed as an exodus led by men. Women form the overwhelming majority of Masowe Apostles despite the norm of choosing only men as official leaders.[11] Women's sense of social marginality, their gendered experience of rejection by and ejection from home, and their hope for healing from wounds that arise from physical, psychic, and social ailments are central to the rituals that the group conducts in the wilderness the Apostles find at the edge of the communities where they live in exile. Women feature in this multidimensional quest as active participants in ritual practice and signifiers of meaning whose longing for emancipation from the patriarchal oppression of Shona society is part and parcel of the desire for transcendence. Women who participate in these rituals articulate their sense of social marginality at the same time that they enact their centrality to the redeemed world they envision.

Johane Masowe and His Apostles

The Masowe Apostles, like many religious movements in which women play central roles, was founded by a man whose spiritual vision and prophetic message did not seem particularly addressed to women. Understanding what women have found in and made of this movement requires us to trace its development, especially its theology and ritual practices, from its origin in the early twentieth century. The acknowledged founder of what Richard Werbner calls the Wilderness Church[12] was known by the religious title of Johane Masowe. Although the exact year of his birth is uncertain, he was born in 1914 or 1915, about the time the Great War broke out.[13] According to Ranger, Johane Masowe grew up under the family name Shoniwa Masedza, Tandi Moyo.[14] When he began preaching in the 1930s, he went by the nickname "Sixpence" to draw attention to the low wages earned by African workers recruited by British settlers.[15]

The economic depression in Europe affected colonial societies such as Rhodesia. Ranger suggests that youths had begun running away from their home villages in search of a livelihood well before the 1930s. The depression made them even more restless, especially those from the lower ranks of society. Johane Masowe was born poor in Gandanzara village in Makoni District. The name *Gandanzara* means "a land of hunger"; the soil was barren, water was scarce, and it was next to impossible to grow crops during droughts.[16] Throughout the 1920s, when white settlers took over large tracts of land for farming, mining, and the building of towns, Africans were pushed to marginal lands like Gandanzara.[17] According to the Anglican missionary Arthur Shirley Cripps, these were deliberate acts of injustice on the part of "greedy" settlers who found Africans easy to push around.[18] Angela Carter, however, points out that these actions met with resistance.[19]

Johane Masowe started preaching during the drought and economic depression of the 1930s. People traveled far and wide to find employment in white-owned commercial farms, mines, and industries in southern Rhodesia and the diamond mines of the Transvaal.[20] Johane was among many youths who migrated to the cities in the hope of finding work. In those days, Africans were not allowed in urban areas unless they were labor recruits. Colonial authorities used "passes," or registration certificates, to control workers. The unemployed were restricted to rural areas.

In 1932, Johane Masowe drew the attention of the police in Mashonaland for the first time.[21] He was reported to be turning up at places of work in towns, at mines, and on commercial farms around the capital city of Harare, then known as Salisbury, without a registration certificate. In the eyes of colonial administrators, he made matters worse by gathering people for prayer in open-air places that became popularly known as *masowe*. He called the sites of prayer close to water *Jorodani:* there he could baptize those who repented their sins. By preaching at the fringes of the landscape in places that colonial administrators considered too poor to exploit and therefore left unoccupied, and by describing his activities in familiar religious language of resistance to oppression, Johane Masowe aroused so much suspicion among the white rulers that he became a target of police investigations.[22]

The religious name Johane Masowe means John of the Wilderness and is derived from John the Baptist. Like the biblical prophet, Johane Masowe articulated sociopolitical problems as well as promoted religious beliefs. The founder of the Masowe Apostles demonstrated that those in power had displaced African people, taking over their lands and pushing them to the periphery. Johane Masowe did not breach the norms imposed by colonial rule by demanding black people's right to mix with whites in areas they wished to keep to themselves.[23] Rather, the sacred wilderness that Johane constructed in the minds of his followers became a landscape in which the gospel was proclaimed for the victims of colonial oppression.

Johane was arrested at least five times during the 1930s for walking around preaching a gospel of repentance from sin and baptism through the power of the Holy Spirit. As far as the European masters were concerned, Johane Masowe disturbed the peace by calling people out to pray in places that colonial administrators wished to keep empty. The nuisance of waking up to apparitions of white-robed Christians and loud choruses of men and women praising God around the fire at all-night prayer meetings called *pungwe* aside, colonial administrators dreaded groups of Africans meeting without white supervision or control. Johane Masowe's use of the Bible to dramatize colonial oppression was easy to comprehend as a language of resistance in political terms and of hopes for redemption in spiritual terms.

The Exodus Within Africa

Nengomasha, one of Johane Masowe's immediate followers, explained the repression that prompted the migrations of Masowe Apostles within Rhodesia (which finally became independent as Zimbabwe in 1960) and then to other countries: "When the word of God was being spread [among Africans] the government of Rhodesia was not happy . . . People were arrested and thrown in prison . . . so the church decided to find another place they could spread the gospel unmolested."[24] Clive Dillon-Malone traced the migration of Johane Masowe and some of his followers from Zimbabwe to Botswana and Zambia. By the time Johane Masowe died of cardiovascular disease in 1973, he had crossed the borders of Zambia to Malawi and made his way to Tanzania. To this day, some Masowe Apostles live in Nairobi, Kenya; apparently they can be found in London as well.[25]

Werbner conceptualizes the movements of Masowe Apostles to peripheral sites for prayer by using the term *Exodus*. In his view, the ritual behavior enacted

by Johane Masowe paralleled the history of Shona people driven away from ancestral homelands into the wilderness. Werbner focuses on the marginality of
Africans as victims of colonialism during Johane Masowe's lifetime. Highlighting the power of imagination behind the construction of *masowe* as a reconcep-
tualization of space, Werbner describes the sacred wilderness phenomenon as a
"disharmonic image" for people "migrating towards the Promised Land" after experiencing displacement.[26]

Werbner's thesis accords with much of what I observed among women of the
Masowe Apostles and is central to my extended conceptualization of the term
African diaspora. Throughout Masowe's ministry, the people of Rhodesia were
deeply involved in armed conflict over the control of land. Ian Smith's racist
regime declared war on African nationalists and often attacked civilians for walking around after six o'clock in the evening. Curfews were put in place in many
rural areas by the Rhodesian army.[27] In towns and other venues for work, the
colonial regime prohibited Africans from gathering for religious meetings without European supervision. The sacred wilderness emerged in a context of oppression that made ideas about the possession and control of land by white colonialists central and the Exodus a powerful religious symbol that black people
could use to express their marginality and quest for freedom.

The Masowe Apostles are not the only Wilderness Church Richard Werbner
studied; another group was led by Johane Maranke. Both men promoted *masowe*
beliefs, making believers wear white robes and worship *mumatongo* (in the wilderness or forest). Both leaders chose the name Johane to give legitimacy to their
activities as African prophets in a society fast becoming acquainted with European missionary appeals to the Bible. The choice of name, like the other religious
symbols surfacing at prayer meetings, was a way of communicating a profound
spiritual message.[28]

The African Apostolic Exodus that Werbner observed thus began with two
Shona men called John the Baptist. When their paths crossed, these groups developed ways of creating distinctions between them. For example, in Mount
Pleasant, Harare, where I did field research during the 1990s, Maranke Apostles
completely shaved their heads and one or two male elders used walking sticks as
symbols of authority, while the majority of Masowe Apostles kept short hair and
did not make a point of their leaders looking like Moses in the desert. Given my
interest in how these believers understood themselves in relation to the places
where they chose to pray, I was fascinated to find these nonverbal signs: a man
dressed in a white robe with a walking stick symbolized a message of redemp-

tion. By going to the margins of the city, the African Apostles demonstrate their conceptualization of the site of prayer in classic biblical imagery associated with wandering through the wilderness. I call this formulation of a theological concept in action *communicative praxis*.

This exodus within Africa was enacted not only in periodic prayer at the edges of settlements but also through long journeys to faraway places in southern and central Africa. Bennetta Jules-Rosette traced Johane Maranke Apostles in Zambia and Kongo. I remember my grandmother describing the Kongo Basin as the original sacred wilderness for Shona-speaking people: she said it was "from somewhere in the wild wetlands of the Kongo that we came." Maranke Apostles reached Kongo in the 1970s and established themselves in the sacred wilderness there and throughout central Africa.[29] Masowe Apostolic communities continued to grow in faraway places.

Several scholars, including Richard Werbner, have speculated that precolonial African people were nomadic, believed in a creator god, and treated their ancestors as mediators between God and humanity. The consonance between this cosmological view and that articulated in biblical texts makes it easy to understand Africans' attraction to ancient Hebrew stories about patriarchs to whom God sent messages as his children wandered through the wilderness in search of "the land of milk and honey."[30] Masowe Apostles construct an African Exodus led by Moses, whom the male leaders often invoke to legitimate their authority in Masowe communities. When I asked the first evangelist I met during my fieldwork about the meaning of the name Johane Masowe, he said: "Johane Masowe is a name for the way we pray. Moses, Abraham, John the Baptist, and Johane Masowe are names of messengers of God from times gone by. They stood for truths about God's love that we experience as followers of the same faith."[31]

Observing Women's Ritual Practices

In order to explore women's experiences among Masowe Apostles, I joined a group of clandestine members who agreed to serve as my informants and let me wander with them, observing and participating in the rituals they conducted. We traveled around to different groups to learn various ways of handling the sacred wilderness. Masowe Apostles welcome strangers, provided they follow the basic rule requiring those not yet baptized to dress simply and observe the customary discipline during prayer meetings. Departing from the tendency of theologians to base their inquiries on texts rather than on practices, I conducted fieldwork in order to observe and talk with women in the places where they bring into the open the religious aspirations that are their own and outside the control of patriarchy. Original fieldwork was necessary to document and analyze the meaning of the communicative praxis of women, who comprise the overwhelming majority of Masowe Apostles, on their own terms.

Women's religious responses to the distinctive challenges they face in patriarchal society make their conception of the diaspora within different from the male leadership's conception of the African diaspora. In her analysis of the changing predicament of Shona women during the colonial period, Elizabeth Schmidt states that women became beholden to "two patriarchies."[32] Under the first patriarchy, women were victims of oppression in precolonial culture, cultivating the land and bearing children for male-dominated patrilineages. The second patriarchy, imported and enforced by European colonialists, did not reduce the patriarchal attitudes of Shona men but rather reinforced their sense of superiority. Colonial patriarchy made harsher the lives of women who worked the land and pushed them to the margins of the new social hierarchy. Under colonial rule, Shona men were exploited as cheap labor controlled by whites, while women suffered on the fringes of the landscape to which they were relegated by the European takeover of African lands.[33] In terms of the religious practices and beliefs found among Masowe Apostles today, the experiences of Shona women in independent Zimbabwe have inspired a set of religious responses that make women agents of knowledge about the diaspora within.

The initial impetus for this project came from seeing groups of mothers and children accompanied by one or two men wander into the sacred wilderness every other day. My main informant in Harare, Susan, prayed with her circle of friends every Tuesday and Thursday evening for about two hours. She would say that she needed God's blessings. Susan was one of thousands of women whose participation in Masowe prayer meetings outsiders could not always see or comprehend. Between 1996 and 2000, I followed groups of five, twenty, thirty, fifty, eighty, and sometimes a hundred or more white-robed Masowe Apostles as they moved toward the shade of trees located near main roads, behind factories, on golf courses, in small forests, beside lakes, and in other fringe places. Women always outnumbered men by a large margin, comprising between 80 percent and 90 percent of these groups.[34] In these circumstances, the agency of women is apparent. Masowe Apostles articulate a distinctly African concept of being in disapora within the mother continent, and women Apostles express religious conceptions of marginalization and emancipation that give voice to their distinctively gendered experiences and viewpoints.

Finding God in the Margins

Well-known ideas about precolonial Shona religion and culture shed light on the central roles women hold in religious practice despite the power of patriarchy. In *Guns and Rain: Guerillas and Spirit Mediums,* David Lan observed that beliefs in male ancestors as guardian spirits were all-important among Shona people in Dande, as among other groups of Shona in Zimbabwe. These ancestors were invoked in family politics involving the ownership and inheritance of land. When men gathered to venerate their ancestors, women were pushed to the margins, Lan maintains. Except for the odd woman serving the lineage as a spirit medium or an aunt honored to assist the family at marriage ceremonies, women were not wanted at these important meetings. If they did not pass their time singing and cooking for the men conducting the ritual, women made "ventures into the bush."[35] Michael Bourdillon, the author of one of the standard textbooks on the beliefs and practices of Shona people, confirms this point and discusses the repercussions of the ancestors' patriarchal claim for the status of Shona women. According to Bourdillon, "the Shona kinship system is basically patrilineal, which means that kinship through males is stressed over kinship through females . . . When a Shona man or woman wishes to show respect, he or she uses traditional clan names inherited from that person's father (rather similar to English names)."[36]

The patriarchal focus of customary ancestral rituals and the marginality of women to worship help explain women's readiness to seek God by walking away from the center of things once Johane Masowe appeared. Not only were women accustomed to working outdoors, but they sometimes wandered into the bush because men had excluded them from parts of their ritual activities. In Masowe spirituality, women can be said to find marginal places that are transformed into "schools of deliverance" and attractive havens of peace.

Women forge a close relationship to nature by working the land to produce food crops, their bodies are likened to Mother Earth, and they are expected to prove their fertility through childbearing.[37] This linkage between women, the earth, and fertility generates a woman-oriented religious language. The Shona high god/dess *Mwari* is male with a female dimension. According to Martinus Daneel, praise-names such as *Mbuya,* the Great-grandmother, and *Dzivaguru,* the Great Pool (she who nurtures life like a womb nurtures the life of a fetus), which refer to fertility, are very popular among *Mwari* worshippers.[38] The worship of *Mwari* takes people away from the homestead dominated by men's veneration of the ancestors. People worship *Mwari* in the forest or in such out-of-the-way places as the cave at Matonjeni located among the Matopo Hills.[39] Women, or persons occupying a role defined as feminine, are central to this ritual.

The title *Mbonga* designates a virgin or a postmenopausal woman or an elderly and ascetic woman or man, all of whom are called "wives" of God in the *Mwari* cult.[40] It is the *Mbonga*'s duty to proclaim the "voice" of *Mwari* at Matonjeni. Speaking in the ancient Rozvi dialect of Shona, *Mbonga* shares words of wisdom, warns people of dangers in times of war and drought, and addresses patriarchy. Even when male priests assume this role, the messages to the people are considered divine and feminine, coming out of the depth of groves and rock formations with caves containing water, all symbols of fertility. Serving this god/dess goes hand in hand with interests in the fertility of Mother Earth and the women who bear her image and bear children to fill the earth. In traditional logic, "the 'Mother of the nation' who represents *Mwari* becomes *Mwari*," writes Martinus Daneel.[41]

The woman-centered practice of *Mwari* worship provided a foundation upon which the Masowe Apostles built. Dillon-Malone observed that Johane Masowe called himself *Mbonga* and accommodated women as special agents of knowledge about God. Dillon-Malone collected a whole list of titles used by Masowe Apostles to draw attention to the significance of women in the diaspora within when he was following Masowe Apostles during the 1970s.[42] In *Korsten Basketmakers*, his famous book about them, Dillon-Malone listed words echoing the Bible that were used to interpret symbolic power of female priesthood in worshipping *Mwari*. Masowe Apostles referred to female "guardians of the ark of salvation," "sisters who are the temple," and spiritual wives of Johane, all taken straight from the precolonial religion, along with the popular expression that the *Izwi* (voice) of God speaks to all believers to advise, counsel, and nurture life.[43]

Masowe Apostles coined the compound term *Mwari-Baba* for the concept of God followed by the great patriarchs of the Bible, adapting the Shona belief in *Mwari* as the supreme being to emphasize the fatherhood of God. Although the feminine dimension of God as represented by the Earth still makes sense, the feminine side of the divine is no longer explicitly articulated. The Masowe seem to have suppressed the talk about *Mwari* as mother for the sake of patriarchy. Daneel observes that "Mwari (the male/female Being) was not lost sight of, but in the composite picture of traditional religion, Mwari sometimes became the Personal Being whom the ancestor venerators addressed in the masculine through the mediation of senior lineage figures" (e.g., kings and chiefs).[44]

Great Mother as Healing Spirit

One of the few opportunities I had to learn something about how the male leaders of groups of Masowe Apostles understood women and femininity took place near Rusape, the village of Johane Masowe's birth in Manicaland.[45] An evangelist known as Philemon made explicit reference to ideas about women that echoed the female dimension of the divine. Philemon explained that he was standing for prayer on typical *Gandanzara* soil, sandy and barren with withered plants dying in the hot sun.[46] "Although our suffering in the world causes us to withdraw onto this barren land, praying for healing all day is like drinking from Our Great Mother, the *tsime* (well) and giver of life."[47] When I asked him if this metaphor was his way of making a reference to God as mother, he denied it, arguing that for a Christian who could read the Bible, I seemed ignorant of the fact that *Mwari-Baba* is God the father.[48]

Philemon acknowledged the presence of the life-giving spirit of God on Earth, "Our Great Mother," only to turn around and denounce the suggestion of a feminine dimension of God. What was unusual here was not Philemon's assertion of the masculine character of the divinity but his invocation of a popular Shona tradition of feminine God language. For Philemon, as for other male preachers, God had become that masculine personal being above the hierarchies of African and biblical ancestors.[49] But his imagery evoked the feminine aspects of *Mwari* that also remain visible in the sites chosen for worship and in the ritual acts performed there.

Like Philemon, the women I met during my research would not use titles such as Great Mother Earth in any explicit fashion. Nor did they openly articulate the connection between their symbolic use of water to invoke the promise of life and well-being and the other popular praise-name for *Mwari, Dzivaguru* (the Great Pool).[50] They replaced this terminology with the word Holy Spirit (*Mweya Mutsvene*) as a way of translating the biblical idea of the divine presence in *Ecclesia* (the church) spoken of in the Acts of the Apostles in the New Testament. The use of symbols of femininity silently to show the immanence of God demonstrated the agency of women as healers with a view of themselves as guardians of knowledge about the Great Mother.

Releasing tension from the body, a pervasive feature of African rituals, is allowed by some (though not all) groups of Masowe Apostles, provided it is done at the allotted time in the proceedings. Meditating quietly by oneself and talking at length about personal problems with other women is standard procedure. At healing ceremonies, I witnessed lengthy and carefully organized ways of turning into practice the belief in God as the source of life that forms the core of Masowe spirituality. "Great Mother Earth," from whose well Apostles drink, nurtures life, and protects and heals through prayer. I watched women speak in tongues and lay hands on each other. The poor, the sick, and the depressed seemed to understand each other's hopes for redemption. In these dramatizations of the agony of living, many women were singing and dancing, while others raised their hands in the air, shook themselves about, fell to the ground, or wept quietly. Against the background of songs repeating God's promise of "deliverance from evil," it seemed especially meaningful to watch women weep. The drama included men as well. Men often held earthenware bowls "made from the soil of our birth and shaped like the mother womb," Susan explained. The bowls were usually filled with water, creating meaning in an oral Christian tradition constructed in a society where symbols of Shona womanhood came with the worship of *Mwari* as the source of life.

Healing among Masowe Apostles is not restricted to miracles.[51] In the six years I spent frequenting Masowe gatherings, sick people would come and go, but belonging to these communities was not always based on testifying to miraculous healing. Masowe practice felt more like a school open to the prayerful expression of all the emotions that arise from participants' anguished condition. Worshippers left on a higher plane and at peace. When Daneel says that healing is the main attraction of Masowe Apostles, he draws attention to a particular function of the sacred space created in the wilderness.[52] Dillon-Malone calls this "holistic" healing, since these practices are sensitive to social, psychological, and physical ailments in a unified system of therapy. This holistic approach to healing is one of the key features of the African diaspora within, a way of affirming hopes for redemption in the midst of suffering and dispersion.

Women Accused of Witchcraft

The social implications of the feminine elements of God language and of the symbols invoked in ritual were intensified by the presence of so many women in prayer gatherings. The position of women was a subject of some tension, even controversy, among Masowe Apostles. Prophet Nzira, leader of one of the groups that prayed on lands that mark the border of the city of Harare in Chitungwiza, went so far as to banish women healers.[53] "You prostitutes and witches—be quiet," he shouted. He directed one of his assistants to pass him an earthenware pot from which he took holy water to sprinkle on the crowds, demanding also that someone pass him some milk and honey to use in prayers for the healing of infertile women. Prophet Nzira tried to silence women in order to assert his own authority. Nzira's hostility toward women is unrepresentative of other groups of Masowe Apostles, and his views on gender and women healers landed him in trouble. Shortly thereafter, much to the dismay of his followers, he was found guilty of rape and put in prison.[54]

Nzira's condemnation of women healers as witches deserves investigation for two reasons. First, it highlights a major concern that most male leaders of Masowe Apostles are sexist. This aspect of Masowe ritual behavior is not discussed in detail here because I aim to examine women's own ways of experiencing reality. Second, Nzira's abusive language raises awareness about the acute marginality of women in the wider society as a key reason why they actively participate in the open-air prayer meetings. In other words, Nzira points to a human condition in which women's cries for redemption make sense in Shona society. Nzira was confronted by a situation in which the active interest of women in healing ceremonies gave scope for them to challenge his authority in the name of the silent yet fully represented Great Mother and healing spirit.

Accusations of witchcraft (*kuroya*) are central to the dynamic that generates the practices of this Wilderness Church. Among the Shona, accusations of *kuroya* often came up in family disputes. Sometimes this talk was used to provoke people in situations where they calmed down quickly. But, once made formally before the male elders of the family, such charges carried the threat of public humiliation and exile. After all, witchcraft was an antisocial activity by which people could be maimed and die, so the punishment was commensurately severe. Women suspected of witchcraft could be chased away from their homes into the wild. The drawings based on stories about witches in Michael Gelfand's book about Shona peoples illustrate why places to hide became essential for women on the run. One image shows a young girl stabbed in the back of the head and another woman being drowned following accusations of witchcraft. The picture of a woman running from a village into a forest with the whole community and its dogs giving chase shows the vital importance of finding hiding places. Seeking refuge in the *sasa* (forest with places to hide) was a way those accused of witchcraft could escape a violent death.[55]

Although men were understood to be capable of witchcraft, accused women suffered more than accused men. The majority of myths about witches feature women. Women's myriad responsibilities to fathers-in-law, husbands, and children, as well as their obligations to work in the fields and to provide the household with fresh water from a well that could be a half-mile or a mile away, made women vulnerable to Shona patriarchy. Accusations of witchcraft continue to haunt society today, despite the influence of modernity upon many people.[56]

Women participants in the Masowe movement commonly refer to themselves as suffering on account of having been accused of witchcraft. Prominent among them are many women who were sent away from their husbands' homes because of alleged faults such as barrenness, failure to guarantee the continuity of the lineage by giving birth to sons, or conflicts with their husbands' parents. The keyword *masowe* has another significance that makes the African diaspora within profoundly meaningful to women. It symbolizes the experience of marginality but also creates a safe place where women can express their anxiety through shaking and tears. Accusations of witchcraft usually leave women tormented by feelings of being rejected by their families. Many make use of this sacred space to heal social wounds.

The places that used to be found deep in the forest known as *Gandavaroyi* deserve special consideration. In contrast to *Gandanzara*, the "land of hunger" of Johane Masowe's birth, this term designates a wilderness. *Gandavaroyi* connotes a place of exile where the female victims of patriarchy accused of witchcraft whom the community did not kill could live.[57] *Gandavaroyi* may be the opposite of *masowe*, defined as a place of healing and animated by the *tsime* (well) of life rather than death. In appropriating the richly fertile lands of the Shona people, white settlers allocated to those they displaced the sterile, wild lands that family heads had shunned in the past as dumping grounds for witches. This historical and gendered dimension of displacement doubles the anguish dramatized by women during Masowe Apostles prayer meetings.

Beliefs regarding *kuroya* do not focus on frightening stories about witches marauding gravesites for human flesh, riding on hyenas without wearing clothes, shadows appearing in the dark, and so on.[58] Witchcraft accusations are the commonplace results of unusual events and untoward circumstances. Anything that might befall people—infertility and miscarriage, extreme beauty or ugliness, unexpected misfortunes—could be used as incriminating evidence by those accustomed to finding scapegoats when the peace and harmony of the family home were disrupted.[59] In Shona culture, men are allowed to use violence to discipline their wives and children, in addition to exploiting their labor. Such behavior is not regarded as antisocial or immoral in a society organized around the interests of men. More women than men would take refuge in *sasa* (forest hiding places) because women are victims of oppression.

I recall a conversation with two male leaders of a Masowe Apostles group near Harare. The men complained that the drought conditions and the bareness of the soil that characterized the sacred wilderness around us resulted from the work of Satan. One commented: "It is a bit like my wife's womb, destroyed by Satan. She is too 'dry' to bear children, like this sand or the rock up there."[60] In Shona culture, infertile soil and infertile women are unwanted. A barren woman can be verbally abused and beaten: hence the common expression, *mukadzi ruware* (a woman is barren like a rock).[61] Infertile women are at risk of being sent away, usually into no-man's-land, if others are unwilling to intervene.

The construction of the concept of an African diaspora within defined in terms of fringe spaces too barren and too wild to be habitable can readily be related to the male domination of this movement and to women's endeavors to heal the wounds of oppression. Infertile women are welcome at *masowe*. Healing ceremonies are the important signifiers of meaning women give to the diaspora within. Shona religious language focuses on fertility in ways that bind women to the image of Mother Earth. The Wilderness Apostles who pray on barren soils come from a culture that connects the barrenness of the land with the infertility of women, an association that makes it easy to shift from honoring a woman to denigrating and abusing her. The site of suffering epitomized by women in the *Gandavaroyi* of the old world is a fearful symbol of the marginality that brings women to the sacred wilderness for prayer, fellowship, and healing.

In sum, the land and women are treated together as welcome possessions of men when they are fertile and as undesirable or dangerous when dry, unproductive, or difficult to control. In order to understand what happens in the sacred wilderness of Masowe Apostles today, we must comprehend the fundamental association of womanhood with a concept of nature as an object for men to dominate and exploit. At the same time, men yield ritual power to women. This phenomenon is very common in African and African-derived religions, as the studies in the first part of this collection attest. Women enjoy ritual power because of the meaningful ways in which women's experiences correspond with the human quest for redemption, aspirations for a world of peace and harmony that can be idealized as a world without oppression. The Masowe Apostles have created a new religious heritage easy to relate to the marginality of women and nature in a male-dominated society. Yet, for women adherents, this religious practice also offers the support of sisterly solidarity and holds a promise of redemption.

Colonial Modernity

To complete our consideration of the woman-oriented elements of the diaspora within, we turn to women who chose to leave their rural families and households, often because of conflicts with their husbands' parents or other relatives, and migrate to towns whose gates were initially shut to women. Johane Masowe addressed those at the margins of colonial society from the fringes of its landscape. By the 1930s, it was rare to find a piece of usable land that was not claimed by someone. Huge tracts of grasslands were fenced off as game reserves after white farmers, miners, and city-dwellers had all the land they desired. In Harare, some of the places that Masowe Apostles thought lay empty were developed into golf courses for whites to occupy during their leisure time. Johane Masowe was arrested many times for spoiling the landscape with his preaching.

According to Diana Jeater and Theresa Barnes, who studied this region of Zimbabwe, women who ran away from rural areas into towns were taking real risks. Since women were legally prohibited from living in towns, they could not obtain formal employment. In mining and manufacturing towns filled with male migrant laborers, women provided sexual favors to men as a means to get food and accommodation, an arrangement called *kuchaya mapto,* or cohabitation. Such women were despised as prostitutes or adulteresses who were lowering the standards of morality in the city.[62] Colonial administrators, who were accustomed to women being restricted to the margins of the public domain in Europe, did not welcome the way these "deserters of culture" (their term for those who had defected from the countryside) sneaked in through the cracks in the city walls and created a space for themselves. Women from rural areas, without formal education and unfamiliar with Europeans, were seen as backward and immoral.[63]

Marja Hinfelaar has countered that Jeater, Barnes, and other scholars who presume that cities were closed to women exaggerate Shona women's predicament. Hinfelaar shows that some places in this domesticated space were designated for women. If a woman had been schooled by missionaries, was married, and attended the women's groups organized by the churches, she was welcomed in town.[64] Although recent scholarship has become more attentive to social realities, it still erroneously presumes that colonial modernity was orderly. I see the colonial city as an urban wilderness frequented by women trying to eke out a living, away from places that were visible to colonial administrators but in secret places of the kind that Johane Masowe frequented.

For example, women brewed and sold *kachasu* (an alcoholic drink that resembles gin), even though colonial administrators forbade it. Sex and alcohol, like cohabitation, were considered bad influences because they distracted men from work. Some women, aware that male workers missed traditional cooking, would quietly stand behind factories with supplies of *sadza* served with delicacies, which women from rural areas brought to urban areas. Providing salt-dried foods such as peanuts, meat from small animals that women collected on their ventures into forests and fields, and wild fruit and roasted maize were important ways women endeared themselves to men in towns. The margins of the landscape served as the center of action for those at the bottom of the social hierarchy. So, during the colonial period, the sacred wilderness that is now the site of a multilayered diaspora on the fringe of the urban environment was used to brew beer, cook *sadza* to feed hundred of workers, and supply them with a homemade alcoholic drink.

Under contemporary social conditions marked by the prevalence of poverty and the AIDS pandemic, the popularity of Masowe Apostles comes as no surprise. Masowe Apostles are sophisticated enough to know that no treatment for AIDS is available in the parts of Africa where they travel. The healing ceremonies they conduct are open and holistic, offering places for people to learn to face death surrounded by the spiritual melodies of women healers. These spiritual guides remind those threatened by death to lay their hope in the promise of deliverance offered by the African diaspora within.

African Women's Diasporic Consciousness

Johane Masowe, the founder of the Masowe Apostles, spoke of *vanhu vatema*, literally meaning "black people migrating" on a journey "through the wilderness" to a promised land under African skies.[65] The African diaspora within is given a deep religious meaning, arising from Shona people's experiences of oppression and displacement. *Vanhu vatema* do not have to leave Africa to join the diaspora. The wilderness, in Johane Masowe's mind and in the practice of Masowe Apostles today, is the massive continent where *vanhu vatema* are conquered and exploited by Europeans and black people journey to sacred places on the margins of settlements in their quest for deliverance.

Masowe Apostles wander off to pray as if venturing into the wild. Their ritual movements to the fringes of the landscape are significant as a practice through which they internalize the diaspora mentality. Some Apostles express their religious aspirations by turning up in other African societies claiming that they are seeking the promised land, while others enact their hopes for redemption by seeking transcendence in the movement in and out of *masowe*, the sacred wilderness which symbolizes their journeying. Masowe women are also often seen selling homemade crafts, vegetables, and other small goods they carry to open-air markets in different towns to earn a living. In this material way, as in more spiritual practices and in the symbolic meanings that resonate with gendered power, they give meaning to the concept of the African diaspora within. Women have adapted the Judeo-Christian religious tradition of exile and redemption to their struggle for peace, harmony, and the well-being of body, mind, and spirit. By employing symbols of their femininity to express a theology of liberation that breaks down the boundaries between men, women, and children, the women of the African diaspora within explain the popularity of Masowe Apostles as places where people gather for healing ceremonies.

I end by pointing to the questions addressed by Deidre Crumbley in the next chapter. Male leaders have multifarious reasons for excluding women from sacred spaces and silencing them at prayer meetings. As in the case of Nzira, this discrimination can be so blatant that, instead of relegating women to the margins, it stimulates their quest for redemption and deepens their determination to recenter sacred space around them. I wonder whether women in the Church of the Lord-Aladura from West Africa express the same sense of social marginality and prayers for healing and redemption as these women among the Masowe Apostles of Zimbabwe.

CHAPTER FIVE

"Power in the Blood"

Menstrual Taboos and Women's Power in an African Instituted Church

DEIDRE HELEN CRUMBLEY

Religion has been a source of power for women, or a source of subordination, or both.

—*Cheryl Johnson-Odim and Margaret Strobel, 1999*

Menstrual taboos are often associated with low social status and the exclusion of women from arenas of explicit formal power.[1] However, the gender practices of the Church of the Lord-Aladura (CLA), an African Instituted Church (AIC) based in Nigeria, complicate this relationship. In this church, menstrual taboos coexist with the ordination of women and a symmetrical structure of parallel male and female offices.[2] While all menstruating women are prohibited from sacred space and ritual acts, a woman may theoretically rise to the primacy, the highest executive church office. Postmenopausal female clerics have the same duties and responsibilities as their male counterparts.

This essay investigates this complex conjunction of gender equality and sex-based, age-related ritual exclusion as it affects women's access to and exercise of power within church structures. It focuses on nexuses of power, rituals of control, and protocols of subordination. Although Isabel Mukonyora (see chapter 4) and I both bring questions about gender and power to our studies of contemporary African Instituted (or, in Mukonyora's terms, Initiated) Churches, Mukonyora offers a woman-focused exploration of agency and creative resistance in the face of explicit and divinely sanctioned patriarchy. While Mukonyora listens carefully to the voices of women and observes the gendered resonances of the Masowe Apostles' ritual actions, I focus on the structural relations of power and how menstrual taboos delimit women's access to authoritative ritual roles.[3]

Menstruation is a dramatic gender marker that distinguishes the male from the female body, even when the body is as feminized as the male bodies of *hijra*, a "third sex" of spiritual practitioners in India.[4] Church of the Lord menstrual taboos are explicit reminders of this procreative physiological distinctness. The CLA constitution contains this proviso: "Women shall remain behind the tent during the period of their menstruation. They are not permitted to enter any holy place until after the expiration of seven days of their menstruation."[5] Although this is the only menstruation-related restriction that is explicitly stated in church documents, it has significant implications for women and gender relations that ramify throughout the organization. CLA menstrual taboos set up patterns of male-female interaction, which, like all power relations, are nuanced by the complexities of power exchange.[6]

A dramatic incident that took place while I was doing fieldwork on the CLA in Nigeria highlights the multivalent meanings of menstrual ritual practices. When a young CLA priest invited me to enter the church building to complete an interview, I explained that I was menstruating. His response was: "Thank you, sister. You know, that could have harmed me." It would seem, then, that within this belief system, while being menstruous puts constraints on the physical movements of a woman, it also empowers her to cause harm or protect as she chooses. The cost of this empowerment is that she is excluded from sacred spaces, objects, and discourses.

African Instituted Churches tend to provide greater opportunity for female leadership than older mission churches. Oyeronke Olajubu explains this difference in women's power and position between European-derived and distinctly African forms of Christianity in contemporary Nigeria as a consequence of Yoruba culture and tradition.[7] She argues that, paradoxically, the same factor plays a strong role in limiting women's participation in certain ritual activities, providing insight into the coexistence of female ordination and menstrual taboos in CLA. In her study of women in new Nigerian religious movements, Rosalind Hackett notes that, although women play crucial roles in church life and development, they are often limited to church activities focused on children and women. Furthermore, even when a woman founds an AIC, her successor is often male.[8] While this has been the general pattern for Nigerian AICs, CLA is an exception. Its constitution specifically provides that women clergy serve as heads of their own congregations and direct regional and provincial units of the church organization as well.

The most germane interpretation of gender dynamics in AICs is the "ceremonial" versus "political" typology of authority suggested by Bennetta Jules-Rosette.

She finds that women in AICs are often assigned ceremonial leadership roles but are denied direct and explicit political authority.[9] Again, CLA departs from this pattern in complicated ways. As ordained clergy, CLA women participate in both types of power but not unconditionally, for they are excluded from selected rituals and sacraments until they are postmenopausal and are forbidden to exercise final authority in doctrinal arbitration throughout their lives.

How can we analyze such ambivalent situations and ambiguous meanings theoretically? Anthropological interpretations of menstrual taboos tend to fall into one of two camps: those that emphasize universal transcultural patterns, such as the classic viewpoint of Mary Douglas, and those that emphasize cultural particularities, as articulated more recently by Alma Buckley and Thomas Gottlieb.[10] Douglas argues convincingly that menstrual taboos reassert a simplified cultural consensus of male dominance in the face of contradicting cultural realities. Thus, in a society where men are "held to be in charge," as in patrilineal Yoruba society, but where women predominate in certain arenas of power, such as the marketplace, menstrual taboos may serve as symbolic reminders of gender norms that privilege males. These ritual reminders, Douglas suggests, carry a heavy "symbolic load" that reaffirms binary gender categories. What better medium for affirming binary male/female categories than menstruation? As the penis-incising bloodletting rituals of New Guinea Wogeo males demonstrate, only women menstruate naturally.[11]

In this light, CLA menstrual taboos can be interpreted as an affirmation of normative male authority in the face of contradicting female leadership, in the larger society and within the church's gender-symmetrical structures. However, this theory does not explain why CLA menstrual taboos coexist with female ordination. The beauty of Douglas's interpretation lies in its elegant lucidity and in the organizing clarity it lends when ethnographic minutiae threaten to obscure insight. However, to explain unique constellations of ritual and power within and between groups, it is necessary, as Buckley and Gottlieb argue, also to pursue multicausal and multivalent explanations germane to the particularities of a given case study.[12]

Interpretations of Menstrual Taboos from Within

The word *taboo*, connoting interdiction, relates to notions of the sacred as distinct from the profane, which were expressed in classical social theory by Durkheim.[13] Moreover, as Douglas pointed out, notions of the sacred, pollution, and taboo intersect in complex ways.[14] African scholars from cultural backgrounds, in which menstrual taboos are normative, have much to offer to the investigation of these complexities. Dr. Olabiyi Yai, a Yorubaist scholar and Republic of Benin's representative to UNESCO, has explained that Yoruba menstrual taboos have less to do with "dirtiness" than with wonder at the miracle of life associated with menstrual blood and the unpredictability of its interaction with other powerful things.[15]

At the Third International Interdisciplinary Conference of the African Christian Diaspora in Europe (CACDE), an interview with Dr. Abraham Akrong of the University of Ghana in Legon provided further insight into this topic. His research on Ghanaian religions and cultures has produced heuristic perspectives that highlight the multivalent meaning of the term *taboo*. Because of unhelpful negative associations with the term, he suggests that we substitute a transculturally applicable alternative, "menstrual ritual practices." Akrong notes that in certain indigenous Ghanaian cultures female paramount rulers and mediums, when menstruating, must not perform ritual duties that are usually associated with their offices. This restriction is not based on notions of "dirt" but is intended to avoid "interfering powers." The reasoning is that the gods might feel they are being attacked by the power emanating from the menstrual blood, and in order to defend themselves they might strike out and harm the menstruating woman.[16]

Akrong also cites cases of male rulers and traditional priests exercising caution when meeting women, lest they be menstruating and the power of that blood neutralize the power of the "charms" these men might be wearing for protection and power. In the same vein, he notes that, traditionally, menstruating wives of a king leave the palace at this time of the month in order not to neutralize his royal powers. Yet, under certain circumstances, Akrong has known menstrual blood to be sought out rather than avoided; for example, a man might intentionally have sexual intercourse with a menstruating woman for the purpose of gaining spiritual power. The use of menstrual blood in love potions is a well-known and seemingly transcultural phenomenon, reported by Dr. Akrong from his ethnographic data and by scholars in other spiritual traditions.[17]

In these cultural contexts, menstrual ritual practices are part of a constellation of beliefs in which menstrual blood and female fertility are highly valued. Still, at the end of the day, we are left with the task of making sense of power relations on the ground, that is, how valued traditions and nuanced interpretation of symbols translate into access to and control over resources. This is not the first study of menstrual ritual practices to struggle with reconciling the significance of cultural legacies with critically assessed power relations; this tension has been addressed in the interpretation of Jewish notions of *nidah* (menstrual and postpartum impurity) and the practice of *mikveh* (ritual bathing after menstruation).[18] The problem with interpreting menstrual ritual practices only as symbolic expressions of cosmological awe is that it tends to neutralize and draw attention away from the acts of exclusion and segregation that follow from these rituals in everyday organizational life. At the same time, the cost of ignoring the cultural significance of these practices is that this forfeits their value as indices of overarching meanings and values that defy reductionism.

This study acknowledges the elements of awe and respect for the procreative capacities of female bodies implied in the Yoruba cultural legacy that shapes CLA menstrual ritual practices. At the same time, it explores how this cultural legacy constrains female access to and exercise of power within CLA institutional structures. In sum, CLA menstrual ritual practices are viewed as multivalent expressions of transcultural gender patterns of conflict and competition, as well as windows on particular cultural cosmologies of shared values and unifying beliefs.

The Genesis of the Church of the Lord-Aladura

The Church of the Lord-Aladura is an African Instituted (or Initiated) Church. AICs are African manifestations of the "next Christendom," a global decentering of Christianity away from the Atlantic North to the developing South.[19] Allan Anderson argues that the significance of AICs rivals that of the Protestant Reformation; Dr. Rev. Ositelu describes them as examples of "mission in reverse" which are revitalizing Western Christianity by an infusion of African liturgies and spirituality.[20] The CLA is one of many AICs to emerge among the Yoruba people of southwestern Nigeria in the 1920s, as part of the Aladura (*ala* owners of, *duura* prayer) movement, which selectively combines features of Yoruba and Christian religious traditions.

The CLA is self-described as biblical in pattern, evangelical in ministry, ecumenical in outlook, and Pentecostal in power.[21] It has survived the death of its founder (in 1966), a critical time in the institutional history of a new religious movement. The church was not destined to remain a Yoruba or even an African phenomenon, for it has spread throughout West Africa and into the United Kingdom, Europe, and the United States. Today the Church of the Lord (Aladura) Worldwide is globally accessible through its Internet website at www.aladura/de/, which lists its American Provincial Head office as being in the Bronx in New York.

Between 1992 and 2002, half a million African immigrants were admitted into the United States. The largest group of these was Nigerian; 75,814 new arrivals joined the many Nigerians who had immigrated twenty years earlier during the civil war.[22] Some of these immigrants brought Aladura beliefs, practices, and gender practices with them into what can be conceived as a second-wave African diaspora in the New World. This is a study, then, not only of an African church but also of a church in the African diaspora, thereby expanding the concept of the African diaspora to accommodate its evolving formation over historical time and geographic and social space.

The Church of the Lord-Aladura, like other Aladura denominations, weds selected Christian and Yoruba religious traditions. These include belief in the redeeming power of Jesus Christ, the Trinity, religious dance, the use of holy water, prophesying, intervening evocable divinity, constrained but potent witchcraft, spiritual healing, and the centrality of fervent prayers to effect the healing of body, mind, and circumstances. The symbolic complexity and ritual richness of Aladura Christianity cannot be reduced to the social-historical conditions that marked the period of its emergence, yet it is impossible to ignore the especially exiguous circumstances within which the Aladura movement arose: the 1918 worldwide influenza epidemic, the bubonic plague of 1924 to 1926, the 1932 famine in Nigeria, and the worldwide economic depression of the 1930s.[23]

It was during these troubled times that Josiah Olunowo Ositelu, a Yoruba man from the town of Ogere and an Anglican catechist-in-training at Eruke, awoke at 2 a.m. on May 17, 1925, to the vision of a resplendent eye. This vision was the start of his new life as an Aladura prophet, healer, and preacher. On July 27, 1930, Ositelu inaugurated the Church of the Lord-Aladura in Ogere.[24] Early in his career, the founder received a vision that he would "teach . . . those that are beyond the sea"; the Church of the Lord-Aladura would be a church for all people of the world.[25] Thus, for believers, the encounter between Emmanuel Owoade Adeleke Adejobi, the founder's right-hand aide and eventual successor as CLA primate, and the British scholar-cleric Harold Turner was not simply (as Turner described it) "a casual encounter on Lumley Beach, Freetown, in 1957."[26]

Primate Adejobi, in his historical account *Authentic Traditions, Customs, and Early Practices of the Church of the Lord (Aladura)*, writes of the far-reaching ecumenical consequences of this meeting with Dr. Rev. Turner.[27] Turner went on to write a seminal two-volume work on the history and doctrine of the CLA. Through Turner, Adejobi met Andrew Walls, then of King's College, Aberdeen, Scotland, who directed him to the Bible Training Institute in Glasgow, where he completed two years of formal training before succeeding Ositelu as CLA primate. Dr. Turner was also instrumental in Adejobi's meeting the Anglican Archbishop of Canterbury and the head of the World Council of Churches (WCC) in Geneva.[28] The CLA became a member of the World Council of Churches in 1975, and in

1979 Primate Adejobi spearheaded the formation of the Nigerian Association of Aladura Churches.[29] In 1971, the CLA established the Aladura Theological Seminary and Prophets and Prophetesses Training Institute in Lagos and became a member of the West African Association of Theological Institutes.

Although the CLA founding disciples were all male, women began entering the ministry as early as the 1930s.[30] Women enrolled along with men in the seminary, where a female president shared the leadership of the student body. Women helped to expand the church throughout Nigeria, West Africa, and abroad. At a WCC meeting, Primate Adejobi chastised the Roman Catholic and other older Western Christian churches for relegating women to the role of servants, in contrast to his rather young African church, which ordained women and had a parallel structure of male and female church offices.

Yoruba and Western Cultural Sources of Menstrual Ritual Practices

Yoruba women were not a *tabula rasa* on which colonial British officers and foreign missionaries simply imposed European Christian gender norms and practices. Yoruba people brought to this cross-cultural contact situation their own culture's extensive latitude regarding gender roles. In Yoruba society, as in other West African societies in which women and men negotiate a dual-sex gender system, domestic and public lives overlap, and women's roles of mother, entrepreneur, and wife are inextricably intertwined.[31] Yoruba women have been *oba*, traditional rulers, of major Yoruba kingdoms and have taken chieftaincy titles.[32] Traditionally, Yoruba women did not lose jural rights when they married, and if they chose to divorce, they were free to repay the bride wealth and marry again.[33] In the arena of ritual and symbol, while the identity of Olodumare, the supreme being, lies beyond gender categories, the *orisa,* or divinities, are represented as male or female beings. In the precolonial period, Yoruba women predominated as *orisa* priests; and some became *babalawo,* a position usually held by men, serving as herbalist-priest-diviners of the most powerful Yoruba oracle, Ifa. Equally important, *orisa* possession is transgender: a male *orisa* may possess a female devotee, who then takes on masculinized mannerisms and vice versa.[34]

Despite the breadth and flexibility of Yoruba women's roles within local cultural and religious traditions, there are certain constraints to their leadership.[35] The female *orisa* Osun is venerated as mother of the many children, the wealthy market woman, the pampered lady, protector of warriors, empowerer of kings, and head of all *aje,* a term that is often mistranslated as "witch."[36] According to

Yoruba lore, Osun was given the opportunity to learn Ifa, the paramount oracle of Yoruba divination, but to gain this knowledge she was required to sacrifice her beautiful gowns.[37] When she refused to do so, the male Orunmila became the *orisa* of this deep knowledge. The female *orisa* Osun has more limited power because she chose the superficial and material over the profound and spiritual.

Ambivalence surrounds the notion of *aje* in Yoruba tradition. Unlike the uniformly malevolent witches in European Christian traditions, *aje* merely manipulate power. Since power is traditionally conceived as neutral and is rendered evil or good by the will of the practitioner, an *aje* may be a good or bad *aje*, wielding this power for good or evil. Indeed, the term *aje* is sometimes used affectionately, though with an element of awe, to refer to older women. For example, Ann Neil, a missionary, nurse, and teacher for twenty-seven years in Nigeria, reported the mixed sentiments expressed by a young Christian male: "These witches are our mothers; we love and fear them greatly."[38] If an *aje* were deemed evil, her behavior would come under the jurisdiction of all-male secret societies, such as Gelede, Oro, Egungun, and Ogboni. While a male might conceivably be an *aje*, the general pattern was that the accusers and enactors of this judgment were male, and the accused were female, most often barren, postmenopausal, or wealthy women who had been indiscreet about their economic success.[39] In sum, the roles of women in Yoruba society and religious traditions were flexible and broadly defined. Although women were not explicitly prohibited from achieving high-status positions, their ability to access and maintain power could be compromised by ideologically subtle messages about female leadership and by the threat of witchcraft accusation.

The indigenous Yoruba menstrual practices that were reported to me during my fieldwork in Nigeria took the form of avoidance and separation. During this time of the month, a woman might sleep on a separate mat from her husband and use a different aperture than other members of the household for departing and entering a dwelling. If her husband were a *babalawo,* she must strictly avoid his ritual objects. Nor would she cook her husband's meals; in a polygamous family arrangement, this task would be performed by a cowife.[40]

The European patterns of gender relations and Christian beliefs and practices that were introduced to Yoruba people by the British colonial government, colonial business enterprises, and the Anglican Church in Nigeria were fundamentally different from those that prevailed among the Yoruba in the precolonial period. Yet there were some points of cultural and spiritual overlap as well as points of contradiction in the ways that gender figured in this cross-cultural interaction. The colonial state, capitalist businesses, and Christian missions were all white,

male-dominated institutions. The schools and informal modes of education prop-
agated by these institutions offered sharply sex-differentiated curricula that prepared girls for lives of domestic labor, not for participation in the market economy.[41] Colonial mission Christianity introduced a faith with a unitary male
supreme being, the "Father-God," his "Savior Son," twelve male disciples, and
polygamous patriarchs.

Furthermore, the holy text of this new religion contained menstrual rituals associated with notions of separation, impurity, and atonement for sin.[42] In the English Revised Standard Version, the biblical text reads:

> When a woman has a discharge of blood, which is her regular discharge from her
> body, she shall be in her impurity for seven days, and whoever touches her shall be
> unclean until the evening . . . If a woman has a discharge of blood of many days, not
> at the time of her impurity, or if she has discharge beyond the time of her impurity,
> all the days of the discharge, she shall continue in uncleanness . . . But if she is
> cleansed of her discharge, she shall count for herself seven days and after that, she
> shall be clean. And on the eighth day, she shall take two turtle doves or two young
> pigeons and bring them to the priest, to the door of the tent of the meeting. And the
> priest shall offer one for a sin offering . . . (Leviticus 15:19, 25, 28–29, RSV)

The "unclean" status of new mothers, like that of menstruating women, required
purification, atonement, and a sin offering:

> If a woman conceives, and bears a male child, then she shall be unclean seven days;
> as in menstruation, she shall be unclean . . . Then she shall continue for thirty-three
> days in the blood of her purifying . . . But if she bears a female child, then she shall
> be unclean two weeks, as in her menstruation, and she shall continue in the blood
> of her purifying for sixty-six days . . . And when the days of her purifying are com-
> pleted, whether for a son or for a daughter, she shall bring to the priest at the door
> of the tent of meeting a lamb a year old for a burnt offering, and a young pigeon or
> a turtle dove for a sin offering . . . (Leviticus 12:1–7, RSV)

These passages from the Hebrew Bible reached Yoruba people in Nigeria through
the Christian redactions and interpretations that were brought by Western mission churches, such as the Anglican Church, which predominated in the Yorubaland region of southwestern Nigeria. The Catholic presence was strongest in Lagos among repatriated ex-slaves from Brazil, many of whom were also Yoruba in
origin. In Catholic and Anglican traditions, Levitical purification rites have been
expressed in the liturgical rite known as "churching of mothers."

The place of this ritual in the life of the colonial mission church is documented in the Church Missionary Society (CMS) Journal Extracts for the quarter ending March 25, 1865, which were entered by the Sierra Leonean priest and missionary James White from the town of Ota. "To match the heathen practice after childbirth of women going to their idol house, to give thanks and make an offering, Mrs. White comes to church while JW reads the service for the Churching of Women. She makes an offering of 5 heads of cowries for a 'country cloth' to give to a poor destitute old woman found in the street and brought to our house."[43] The Churching of Women liturgy continues to be performed today in Anglican parishes around the world, though the contemporary discourse surrounding the rite emphasizes thanksgiving. But the more ancient resonances of the ritual have not been entirely lost. Indeed, the newsletter of St. Michael's Church in Great Torrington in England connects the "Thanksgiving of Women after Childbirth" commonly called "Churching" with Mary taking Jesus to the temple to "do what the law prescribed after childbirth." Although the language refers to blessings, thanksgiving, joy, and protection, the heading of this section of the newsletter is "Purification."[44]

According to some Nigerian scholars, the theme of purification is more explicit in some of the older mission churches in Nigeria today. For example, Rosemary Edet, writing in 1995, pleaded with church leaders to rid the churching of mothers "of its purificatory aspect." She also reported that rural Ibibio and Qua women of Cross River State, Nigeria, avoid church-related events during their menstrual period and after childbirth.[45] Olajubu, writing in 2003, notes under the heading "Women in Mission Churches" that women in some mission churches choose to attend worship regardless of their menstrual state, while others apparently avoid the sanctuary while menstruating.[46]

Early Yoruba female converts to Christianity, who regarded female religious leadership as normative because women were spiritual leaders in *orisa* worship, found themselves barred from the Christian pulpit. European mission churches allowed—indeed, depended upon—women to spread the gospel by "speaking," but they prohibited women from "preaching" the gospel.[47] We can only imagine what radical behavioral and cognitive shifts conversion to Christianity must have entailed for these women. However, they were not entirely silenced by sacralized exclusion; instead, they exploited institutional spaces within mission church structures to serve as teachers and missionaries. Importing a doctrine of corporate existence from traditional Yoruba society into their new Christian experience, these women not only helped to establish the mission church but also became bulwarks of its expansion.[48]

Despite normative male domination of engendered church hierarchies, the holy text and religious ideals of this new faith held a source of critique and contestation. The biblical texts that African Christian women found to support their participation and validate their spiritual authority were familiar to Christian women in other places as well, and the interpretation and gender implications of these texts have long been contested within Christian churches in the Western tradition. Did not Jehovah deliver the enemy of Israel "into the hand of a woman," the warrior-prophetess judge Deborah (Judges 4:9)? Did not Paul, writing from Rome, commend to the saints "Phoebe our sister, who is a servant of the church which is at Cenchrea" (Romans 16:1)? Was not the entirety of 2 John addressed to the "elect lady" whose "children" could be found "walking in truth?" Does not Galatians 3:28 (King James Version) state that "there is neither Jew nor Greek, there is neither bond nor free, there is neither male nor female, for ye are all one in Christ?"

Exemplary practice as well as theological statements might serve as precedents for women's spiritual and ritual equality. Jesus, on whom the Christian faith is founded, ate with publicans and interacted with women—including women of ill repute, like the Samaritan women by the well, and the ritually unclean woman with the issue of blood (Mark 5:25–34, Luke 8:43–48, RSV). Jesus entered the world through gestation inside a woman's body. The crucial role of the female body in human salvation has perennially been used to criticize the church's prohibition of female ordination. As the African American church founder Bishop Ida Robinson asked pointedly, "If Mary the Mother of Jesus could carry the Word of God in her womb, why can't holy women carry the word of God in their mouth?"[49]

Christian praxis has sacralized the exclusion of women from high office, yet its egalitarian ideals afford grounds for an ethical critique of male privilege within church structures.[50] Contradictions in gender relations as constituted by religious beliefs and practices have also existed within indigenous Yoruba traditions. Yoruba women's social roles are characterized by breadth and flexibility, yet in spiritual matters men have tended to hold the highest offices, and all-male secret organizations could execute judgment on witches who were usually women. In sum, Yoruba and Christian traditions both have empowered and disempowered women, resulting in a culturally mixed reservoir of gender practices that might reinforce or neutralize each other. But why, in the admittedly exceptional case of the Church of the Lord-Aladura, did these elements combine in ways that promoted explicit political female leadership rather than form an "unholy alliance" to prohibit female ordination?[51] To address this question, it is necessary to explore particularities of CLA history, leadership, and doctrine.

Gender Policies and Practices in the CLA

Consider these two passages:

The doctrine of the equalness of man and women gave birth to prostitution. The popular doctrine is that if a man is [able] to be a clerk, a woman is also fit to be one . . . forgetting the purpose for which woman is created . . . a helper to man in the home . . .[52]

In the days of your special prayer, consecrate yourself highly and avoid women entirely . . . Menstruation and fornication are deadly enemies to the Angels, who fly away at the slightest smell of them.[53]

The first of these two quotations, entitled "Prostitution in Disguise," is excerpted from an article by a layman in a 1946 church magazine. The second, from a lecture by Bishop Orebanjo recovered from his correspondence in 1956, is entitled "Woman the Woe." If these attitudes are representative of that era in Nigerian social history, then the CLA's 1959 ordination of women is outstanding for going against prevailing opinions at the time.

The Church of the Lord-Aladura was characterized by a remarkable openness toward female spiritual leadership from its founding and at the highest levels. As early as 1930, when the church was formally established, Primate Ositelu, recorded in his journal that a prophetess arrived in Ogere and preached to the town. From the church's inception, then, there was a place for women preachers. The founder assigned his mother to the post of "lady president of the whole organization"—a female-designated position of authority within the church, not a subordinate position with authority only over the women.[54]

Primate Adejobi documents the place of women as an integral part of the narrative in his historical work *The Early Diary of the Church of the Lord,* noting women's presence in major church developments rather than placing women's affairs under a separate subheading.[55] He records the initiation into the ministry in 1938 of Julie Ositelu, the youngest wife of the founder, and the appointment of Beatrice Talabi of Iperu as the "first Lady Evangelist" in the CLA in 1939. During the first decade of the church's history, women preached, prophesied, and received training for church duties, although women's ministerial roles were not fully articulated until the 1954 constitution. While an earlier constitution had made little reference to women, the 1954 church constitution delineated their offices and gave women the right to carry the ceremonial "iron rod" of ministers. Still, women were not allowed to "speak" in church unless the male minister or male lay leader was unavailable. Women were also prohibited from the sacred space of the altar.[56] In his undated work, *The Authentic Traditions, Customs, and Early Practices of the Church of the Lord-Aladura,* Primate Adejobi laments:

> In the past, women were disallowed (if even they were ministers) to enter into, and minister to their churches from the altars. They had to stand outside the Chancel to perform their church assignments . . . In those bygone years, female ministers were not allowed to pronounce grace and benediction at the end of the service though they may have been the conductor of the service from the start to the end, the reason being that they are simply females (women), the weaker vessel.
>
> Thanks be unto God for changes have come, whereby men and women ministers alike pronounce grace and say benediction. This is derivable through the redeeming blood of our Lord Jesus Christ into a new society (the Church) wherein St. Paul the apostle said there is no class distinction, no segregation, no racial discrimination, nor male or female, but in Christ Jesus they are one and the same.[57]

Primate Adejobe hailed the decision to ordain female clergy as a change that aligned CLA practice with principles revealed in the Bible.

In 1959, the founder, Primate Josiah Ositelu, who led the church until his death in 1966, proclaimed that "the establishment of Women Ministry in the Church of the Lord is a divine injunction, and as long as the church exists it shall not cease." Women were already functioning as spiritual leaders within the CLA, so the extension of formal ordination was followed by the rapid recognition of women's ministry rather than requiring a long, gradual process of training and development. Indeed, a 1961 ruling determined that if a husband and wife are presiding ministers, the one who has been in the ministry longer is the one to say the benediction, "whether male or female."[58] An essentially parallel hierarchical structure of male and female offices is delineated in the CLA constitution, and the use of "he/she" pronouns makes it clear that the men and women who hold these posts have the same responsibilities.[59] By-law 30 prohibits deacons and deaconesses alike from conducting services from within the alter area; instead "he/she is to place his/her table in front of the altar where he/she shall perform his/her divine activity."[60] Regarding the bishop/reverend mother, the constitution says:

> In addition to the work of a Bishop/Reverend Mother as administrative Overseer in a Diocese within a Province, he/she shall have the right to perform the following duties.
>
> (i)   To promote the gospel of Christ and to establish new branches . . .
>
> (ii) To perform Baptism to those qualified to be members

(iii)   To administer the Holy Communion

(iv)   To solemnize Holy Matrimony

(v)   To perform other duties that may be assigned to him/her by the primate.[61]

At the lower end of the hierarchy, probationary ministers "shall perform Pastoral duties under the observation and guidance of a senior Minister, but shall not perform Baptism, Holy Communion, Holy Wedlock and funerals."[62]

Up to this point, the CLA constitution extends privileges and powers equally to women and men who occupy parallel positions in the church hierarchy. However, this article of the constitution ends with an explicit, sex-linked prohibition:

No female Minster can perform the following duties:

(i)   Holy Communion

(ii)   Holy Wedlock

(iii) Baptism by Immersion

(iv)   Burial

Except she has reached the age of 60 years and has also reached the state of menopause.[63]

Thus, while the bishop and reverend mother have the same duties, a woman must be postmenopausal before she is qualified to perform the sacraments associated with this post. Until she is postmenopausal, she—like a probationary priest— cannot perform the four sacraments. The CLA seems to have embraced its Yoruba legacy of beliefs about menstrual blood as a competing powerful substance not to be mixed with other powerful substances in the sacraments. This belief also assigns women roles that put them on a timeline different from that of males, who may assume all the duties of high office without waiting for a change in their physiology.

In the CLA, the highest office is unitary, and to date the position of primate has always been filled by a male. Still, as the late Primate Adejobi pointed out, there is no explicit constitutional prohibition against a woman moving up the ranks to become primate. He added, however, that a female primate would be as unusual as Judge Deborah in ancient Israel—an exception rather than the rule. Primate Adejobi explained that women were totally excluded from only one arena of church life: determining doctrine. The rationale for this was two-pronged. First, he explained, Jesus and his disciples, who established the doctrinal foundation of Christianity, were all male. The second explanation entails a unique interpretation of 1 Timothy 2:11–14. Primate Adejobi wrote: "We firmly believe in the doctrine of the priesthood of all believers (males and females alike) . . . And we opine that when St. Paul said 'I do not permit a woman to teach' . . . this is not an absolute denial of a women's chance to preach, but it forbids a woman to be the ultimate arbiter of doctrine."[64]

In the final analysis, the CLA ordains women to the ministry, but only when they are postmenopausal may they perform all the sacraments of the church, and they are prohibited from doctrinal arbitration throughout their lifetimes. Menstrual ritual practices do not exclude CLA women from seminary preparation or ordination. Female clergy administer their own local parishes and climb up church hierarchies, and the CLA does not prohibit them from aspiring to the primacy. The availability of clerical training, ordination, local congregational autonomy, and upward professional mobility for women distinguishes the Church of the Lord not only from other major Aladura churches but also from many "born again," charismatic, and Pentecostal churches, not to mention older mission churches in Nigeria today.

Ecumenical Internationalism and the Position of Women

The CLA entered the World Council of Churches (WCC) at a time when the ordination of women in Christendom was being hotly debated and the movement to ordain women was gaining momentum. In the Anglican Church, with which CLA had established a strong historical connection, Rev. Li Tim Oi of Hong Kong had resigned her priesthood in the 1940s to protect the bishop who had ordained her from censure by his superiors. In the United States, Phyllis Edward entered the Episcopal deaconate in 1965. In 1974 eleven Episcopal women were ordained "illegally" at the historically African American Episcopal Church of the Advocate, located in Philadelphia.

The following year, when the Church of the Lord joined the WCC, four more American women were irregularly ordained, and in 1981, a worldwide grassroots consultation on the issue was held in Sheffield, England. In 1984 the African Anglican provinces of Uganda, Burundi, Rwanda, and Zaire began unofficially ordaining women. Four years later, Barbara Harris, an African American, became the first female bishop in the worldwide Anglican Communion.[65] Joining the worldwide ecumenical Christian community at this time, the Church of the Lord-Aladura, with its policy of female ordination, was allied with an international movement identified with justice and progress. This affiliation enhanced the image of the CLA as an international pacesetter and a global leader among equals on the issue of female ordination.

Spiritual Powers and Female Bodies

The gender practices of the Church of the Lord-Aladura confound the "ceremonial" versus "political" dualism proposed by feminist theories of religion; women are not allowed full access to ritual roles while being excluded from positions of organizational authority but have parallel positions in both domains. The case of the CLA also effectively challenges the notion that menstrual taboos are always correlated with low female status; women are ordained to the ministry despite the observance of ritual restrictions associated with menstruation. Menstrual ritual practices do not preclude explicit ritual responsibilities and political leadership by CLA women, but the full ritual and political inclusion of women occurs only when they become postmenopausal. It is only when their bodies lose the physiological feature that most sharply distinguishes them from men—the ability to menstruate—that women may perform the four sacraments. Furthermore, whether postmenopausal or not, women are excluded from doctrinal arbitration because persons with female bodies are seen as disqualified from exercising ultimate doctrinal authority.

Female leadership in CLA derives, in part, from the latitude in gender roles that was normative in precolonial Yoruba society; and this flexibility and gender symmetry has been selectively reinforced by Christian egalitarian ideals and bolstered by ecumenical acclaim. The mutual reinforcement of these foreign and local elements is fostered by the agency of CLA church leaders, male and female. From the founder to its current head, Dr. Rev. Rufus Ositelu, CLA's male primates have championed female ordination as a divine ordinance that may have been recognized only in 1959 but should be upheld forever as foundational to the church. CLA women have risen to the occasion, assuming leadership at home and abroad. For example, Senior Prophetess Gloria Cline-Smythe, a university-educated former local government official and a Krio of Yoruba descent from Freetown, Sierra Leone, became head of the Eastern Province of the CLA in the United States.[66]

In the conversational exchange about my remaining outside the sanctuary when I was menstruating, the CLA priest and I acted out a social drama, which, in Mary Douglas's terms, reasserted the norm of "male-in-chargeness." Although the priest expressed sincere appreciation that I did not harm him, as a woman, I was, nevertheless, reporting to a man. While the belief system lent me power, which I could choose to exercise to harm or protect him, the very fact that I had to make such a choice—between excluding myself from sacred space or risking harm to him and perhaps myself by provoking a spiritual conflict between the powers of the divine and the powers of female fertility—was a consequence of a social role assigned to me because I was born female, a bodily condition over which I have no control.

Truly, there is power in menstrual blood, but cosmological appreciation does not automatically translate into political equity. Gender equity requires more than the cosmological privileging of women's procreative capacity. It requires taking concrete steps to put in place the necessary attitudes, rules, and regulations that foster equal access to and exercise of authority, regardless of the body with which a person is born. The Church of the Lord, more than any other major Aladura church, has boldly pursued female inclusion in leadership roles, bravely ordaining women in 1959 and championing women's inclusion in ecumenical circles when it joined the World Council of Churches in 1975. The question facing CLA in the twenty-first century is what steps this AIC pacesetter will take to reconcile its menstrual ritual practices with its principled and progressive record of proactive gender inclusion.

PART II

POWER, AUTHORITY, AND SUBVERSION

CHAPTER SIX

"The Spirit of the Holy Ghost is a Male Spirit"

African American Preaching Women and the Paradoxes of Gender

WALLACE BEST

African American women played crucial roles in the development of black urban religion in the Unites States during the Great Migration. That diasporic component of black women faithful who, in the words of Richard Wright, left the land "for the streets of the city"[1] served as church builders and spiritual leaders. In a striking departure from prevalent patterns in the rural South, black women assumed visible leadership in the many storefront churches and even in the larger independent institutions that emerged during the migration. For most of the twentieth century in U.S. urban centers, women have constituted the majority membership in all denominations, from mainline black Baptist and Methodist to Pentecostal. African American women, as the womanist scholar Jacquelyn Grant has asserted, have been the "backbone" of black churches, wielding enormous influence in setting the theological and cultural tone. Yet, many Americans still consider churches to be the domain of men; women are routinely cut off from access to power and ministerial authority in mainstream churches and some Pentecostal denominations. In Chicago during the early 1940s, an African American minister who allowed the women of his small congregation to preach was brought before his district council and rebuked. Explaining the incident, St. Clair Drake and Horace Cayton, two chroniclers of black life during the migration era, revealed the paradox. "The preachers jealously guard the pulpit against female infiltration, but they must depend upon women for the bulk of their regular attendance, financial support, and general church work." Speaking generally about women as the majority participants in American religion, Ann Braude has observed this paradox in more contemporary contexts, noting that churches "have relied for their existence on the very group they have disenfranchised."[2]

The notion that churches are the domain of men while in fact the overwhelming majority of members are women is perhaps the central paradox in African American religion. This gender imbalance is especially significant given many denominations' resistance to women in positions of clerical authority. Historically, fewer than 5 percent of clergy among the mainstream African American Baptist, Methodist, Presbyterian, and Congregational churches have been women. Although many of these churches have recently altered their policies, and indeed some black churches have found it difficult to exclude women entirely from clerical leadership because of women's overwhelming numbers within their congregations, a culture of resistance to black women in the pulpit has prevailed across denominations.

What is at the core of this resistance? What are the issues that have proved so troubling with regard to a black woman in the pulpit? Or, what is threatened by a black woman in a position of church leadership? This chapter analyzes the historic culture of resistance to black women preachers, noting particularly what the folklorist Eileen J. Lawless has called "layers of religious, historical, and cultural beliefs and perceptions about women which have uniformly served to deny them access to religious power and authority."[3] Drawing on this and other scholarship, I argue that the resistance to black women in positions of ministerial power has stemmed primarily from culturally reinforced notions about black women's bodies and paradoxically configured gender expectations. In making this argument about deeply rooted perceptions of black women's bodies as a primary factor in the culture of resistance to black preaching women, I do not wish to reinscribe patriarchal notions and merely refocus an objectifying gaze. Rather, I mean carefully to scrutinize how cultural beliefs about the black female body shaped perceptions of women who led churches and created complex conditions within which they had to maneuver in order to legitimate their ministerial authority.

Throughout the migration era in the urban north, ideas about black women's bodies, sex, gender, and conventional gender expectations played a paradoxical role in the religious identities of black women preachers. The perceived biblical injunctions against women in ministry ("women keep silent in the churches," 1 Cor. 14:34) received strong support from cultural perceptions about women, their bodies, and sexuality. The two case studies presented here show that migration-era black preaching women developed inventive strategies to subvert and manipulate conventional gender expectations and to deflect attention away from their bodies, sex, and sexuality. They rendered themselves sexually ambiguous or entirely ensconced in a female sacred world beyond the reach of male perspectives or male power.

Analysis of the resistance to black preaching women and black women's inventive responses to that resistance must foreground a discussion of the body for a number of reasons. First, Kathleen Canning's relatively recent assertion is correct: despite the burgeoning of scholarship on the body in recent years, the "body remains a largely unexplicated and under theorized historical concept."[4] Scholars within the interdisciplinary fields of women's, gender and sexuality, and slavery studies have attempted to grapple with the implications of the "body" as a signifier, metaphor, and allegorical emblem, a site of intervention or inscription, but many of these studies undervalue the body as a historical entity in favor of discursive constructions and symbolizing abstractions. The body for our purposes is not understood as an abstract concept. It is a historically inscribed site of physical experience. We are concerned with real bodies that endure a range of experiences with profound consequences for daily life and self-understanding. African American history reveals that women's bodies have long been contested terrain. Power relations between slave owners and the enslaved were often enacted, resisted, and subverted in physical, sexualized form. Stephanie Camp, for instance, has shown that despite slaveholders' attempts to control black people's movements and bodily experiences, slaves maintained a "rival geography" characterized by mobility and used their bodies for their own pleasure and purposes. In this "rival geography," slaves assumed periodic "ownership" of their bodies in order to control their physical existence.[5]

The definitions of black women's bodies that emerged during that struggle still hold cultural power and not simply because after emancipation black women remained vulnerable to sexual violation by white men and actively defended their bodily integrity. Even when women are free from coercion and live within a predominantly black community, they navigate a terrain that remains shaped by black people's collective efforts to define themselves under circumstances in which the body is a highly charged site of freedom and identity. Indeed, recent scholarship on women in black churches has placed women's efforts to demonstrate and defend their sexual respectability as central to their religious activities.

Second, scholars of African American religion, in particular, have been lax in taking seriously the relationship between black religion and bodily experience. One of the few works that directly addresses African American religion and the body is Anthony Pinn's "Black Theology, Black Bodies, and Pedagogy." Less directly, but perhaps more effectively, E. Patrick Johnson explores this relationship in "Feeling the Spirit in the Dark: Expanding Notions of the Sacred in African American Gay Communities." Inspired by cultural theorist Michel de Certeau's formulation of "place" and "space," Johnson argues that black gay men transverse the sacred place of the black church to the secular space of the nightclub, where "feeling the Spirit in the dark" celebrates "the black gay body as well as a communion with the Holy Spirit."[6] These few contemporary analyses demonstrate the rich potential of examining embodied experience in African American religion so as to bridge the cultural divide between the sacred and the sexual.

The third reason for scrutinizing the body and embodied experience cuts closer to my purposes in this essay. Historically, when the subject of black women in positions of ministerial leadership comes up, the discussion leads directly to a dialogue about women's bodies, sex, and sexuality. They are inextricably tied together. The following story illustrates this phenomenon.

In October of 1939, Works Progress Administration (WPA) worker, Alvin N. Canon walked into a storefront church on East 45th Street in Chicago. It was an independent Pentecostal church, "The Royal Prayer Band," headed by a woman identified only as "Mrs. Williams." (Whether that was her choice or the choice of her interviewers is not known.) Her husband, whom she did not identify, had died the year before leaving her the sole pastor of the small congregation. After noting a "few crude paintings of Christ and the Crucifixion hanging on the walls," Canon made his way to the "living quarters" at the back of the church. Canon found that area to be "likewise untidy." When "Mrs. Williams" appeared, a southern migrant widow of "about sixty years old" with a "kindly motherly face," Canon started the interview. "What is the thing which distinguishes your church from the Pentecostal and the Church of God?" Canon asked. Mrs. Williams gave a most remarkable answer.

> Well, the Church of God in Christ says that only men can preach—women can only do missionary work. Well in a sense they are right because according to the Bible, the spirit of the Holy Ghost is a male spirit. But when a woman receives that spirit she is no longer a woman—then she has the right to perform the duties of a man, like preaching. Until then she should only do missionary work and teaching work. The word of God is a "he" and women are the flesh of the world . . . Now I believe that some people are born with a unity to God. These people are devoted to the work of the Lord—they don't have time to think about sex and the things of the world.[7]

This remarkable declaration was recorded by one of the many unemployed Americans who found work documenting various aspects of life during the Depression under the auspices of the WPA-sponsored Federal Writers' Project (FWP). It gives voice to highly charged, paradoxical notions of sex, gender, and spirituality which are brought together in dynamic tension. Some elements of Mrs. Williams's statement reflect a long tradition in Christian history, and others pertain to the specific situation of a Chicago storefront church whose spiritual spokesperson was a woman. The views she articulates do not entirely correspond to orthodox Christian tradition but rather constitute one interpretation of that tradition; these questions have been the subject of longstanding theological debates. Women's bodies, the gender of the Holy Spirit, and the gendered relationship between God and the preacher all figure centrally in these discussions of women in ministry. Even a woman determined to assert her legitimate role as a spiritual leader has to justify it in terms that arise within that debate, and the entire encounter demonstrates powerful connections between the matter of women in the ministry and historically based cultural perceptions about women, their bodies, and sex. So the statement and story merit deeper explication.

Mrs. Williams's statement first makes a dichotomy between flesh and spirit, that is, between the realms of the flesh (human) and the spirit (divine), and then attributes a male gender to the Holy Spirit. Attempts to attribute a specific gender or gender characteristics to the first and second persons of the Trinity have varied throughout Christian history. Gendered characteristics attributed to Jesus, for example, have included the "Jesus-as-Mother" images intrinsic to some forms of High Middle Ages spirituality. Evelyn Brooks Higginbotham discovered a "double gender consciousness" among black Baptist women of the late nineteenth and early twentieth centuries which espoused "the dialogic imagery of Christ as simultaneously feminine and masculine." The "manly" Jesus of "muscular Christianity," an idea forged during the same period, responded to what some held to be the "feminization of Christianity," which they feared made religious men effeminate or simply drove them away from the church.[8] There is, however, no theological tradition in the American Christian church for a gendering of the Holy Spirit. Throughout Christian history there have been discussions that work toward a gendering of the Holy Spirit, but at best the gender of the Holy Spirit has been rendered ambiguous. Certainly, the Bible makes no clear statement on this point, contrary to Mrs. Williams's assertion.

Mrs. Williams's gendering of the Holy Spirit has far-reaching implications. She assigns a spiritual superiority to maleness, pitting that superiority to an inherent carnality of women. To say "women are the flesh of the world" is to suggest an inherent, essential connection between the three terms. The phrasing resonates with biblical imagery and maxims that depict the world and the flesh in unequivocally pejorative terms: "Walk in the Spirit and you will not fulfill the lusts of the flesh" (Gal. 5:16); "Those who are in the flesh cannot please God" (Rom. 8:8); and "Do not love the world, for all that is in the world, the lust of the flesh, the lust of the eyes and the pride of life is not of the Father, but is of the world"

(1 John 2:15–16). As a preacher with some knowledge of scripture, Mrs. Williams would have been aware of these verses, as well as the implications of drawing such a direct connection between women, the flesh, and the world. Indeed, carrying the connection to its logical extension would seem to mark women's bodies as particularly and inherently unspiritual in contrast to men's. In stating that "women are the flesh of the world," she is implying that men are not; the sexes are in contrast on this plane. This corollary flows directly from the theological notion that the Holy Spirit is male, but its most profound spiritual consequences are human: women's embodiment is signified as defining their spiritual status, while men's bodily existence does not impinge negatively on their spirituality. This contrast between the sexes is the final implication of the dichotomy she makes between flesh (humanity) and spirit (divinity). As "the flesh of the world," women could only represent that which is human or carnal. Men (maleness) embody that realm which is fitted to represent the divine.

Mrs. Williams stands in a long line of religious women who have wrestled with the implications of this aspect of Christian theology. Notions that women's bodies render them originally prone to sin have a long history in the church. Since the Middle Ages, female theological thinkers have adopted the fundamental contrast of men/spirit with women/flesh but interpreted it in ways that opened up spiritual possibilities for women rather than using it to exclude and subordinate them, as many male theologians did. Indeed, Mrs. Williams's statement is reminiscent of a theological construct developed by Hildegard of Bingen, who declared, "woman is to man as flesh is to spirit." Bingen, an early female theologian in the Christian tradition, asserted that whereas men represented Christ's "divinity," women represented his "humanity." As Caroline Walker Bynum explains, "women theologians in the later Middle Ages saw woman as the symbol of humanity, where humanity was understood as physicality."[9] Bynum's interpretation of Bingen does not suggest that physicality was pejorative. As representatives of Christ's humanity, women reflected the part of God that was closer to humankind in identification and sympathy. However, the logical extension of Bingen's theological construct and Mrs. Williams's statement, given the way they associate women with the flesh, implicates women's bodies as a deterrent to spirituality and assigns women to a second-class spiritual status vis-à-vis men. Thus, in order to do the work of the ministry, Mrs. Williams had to deny herself, her gender, and "the flesh of woman," and embrace the Holy Spirit and the superior spirituality of maleness. She had to incorporate the power and authority that comes with "maleness" into her female body.

What is remarkable about this contention is that it contradicts and confirms certain historical depictions of Christian religion and "women's nature" extant in the United States for the past two centuries. Or, more precisely, it confirms the historically contradictory depictions of "women's nature" with regard to black and white women. Since the nineteenth century, the ideology of "separate spheres" has represented women as spiritual by nature, the pious embodiment of religious and moral virtue. This depiction was often used to exclude women from the public sphere, with the rationale that their delicate nature unfitted them for active participation in politics, the capitalist economy, and the formal leadership in the institutions of civil society—a domain that was represented not only as masculine but also as competitive, combative, and even violent, morally corrupt and potentially corrupting. Yet women found ways to subvert these implications in order to assert themselves in public life, arguing that because of their piety they should have a greater role in society, bringing to politics, civic organizations, and especially the church the domestic virtues that they embodied. White women preachers deftly employed this argument, asserting that their right to preach stemmed not only from a divine call but also from their duty as women. Religious sects such as the Society of Friends (Quakers) and the United Society of Believers (Shakers) had long shown greater tolerance of women preachers than did Protestants. During the nineteenth century, some Baptist and Methodist denominations also began to allow women to preach not in spite of their gender but rather because of it. This shift related to profound economic and cultural changes in Jacksonian America.[10] As market relations spread and the ideology of domesticity was elaborated, the private world of home life emerged as the exclusive domain of women. Amid anxieties about the potential of the new capitalist order for conflict and corruption, the home became a refuge of familial and moral values. White women became the safeguards of the home and exemplars of Christian virtue.[11]

Only white women, however, were represented as virtuous and pious by nature. The dominant American culture did not recognize black women as embodying moral virtue or pure spirituality; indeed, in the ideology that had developed under slavery, black women did not qualify to the exalted status of natural womanhood. Black women who chose to act in a public way had difficulty invoking feminine virtue as a defense of their right to speak out or preach in a climate in which they were regarded as inherently lascivious. By the late nineteenth and early twentieth centuries, the stereotype of the lascivious, promiscuous, and morally corrupt black woman had congealed in the white mind. For example, a self-described "Southern white woman" proclaimed in a progressive newspaper in 1904, "I can not imagine such a creation as a virtuous black woman." White male religious and civic leaders such as A. H. Shannon, William Picket, and William Smith wrote numerous tracts disparaging the lack of "personal chastity" among black women and suggesting that their "depravity" accounted for black people's lack of progress.[12] The specter of sex and sexual impropriety lingered as a barrier to black women's preaching.

The stigma of sexual immorality that was attached to black women because of white men's long history of claiming access to their bodies intensified the objections, even antagonism, that black women who dared to operate in a public manner encountered. The rage that the African American preaching woman, Zilpha Elaw, saw in the eyes of a man who taunted and circled her as she preached was shot through with sexual aggression.[13] To counter charges of natural lasciviousness, some black preaching women attempted to demonstrate that they were feminine and virtuous. Indeed, the degree to which black women were regarded as unwomanly sometimes called into question even their biological sex, especially when they crossed gender boundaries to engage in public religious or political activity. For example, in an 1858 incident that was notorious at the time and is now famous in American women's history, Sojourner Truth, a preaching woman whose spiritual calling and abolitionist feminism were inextricably intertwined, bared her breasts to demonstrate her "womanhood" when it had been called into question by a white man who conjoined femininity with physical weakness. Jarena Lee, the freeborn African Methodist Episcopal (AME) preacher, had to address claims that she was actually "a man dressed in female clothes." In her autobiography, *The Life and Religious Experiences of Mrs. Jarena Lee, A Coloured Lady* (1836), she declared repeatedly that she was a "true woman." Even though she donned a simple bonnet and wore a shawl that covered her entire body throughout her preaching career, charges that she was a Jezebel persisted.[14]

Because they could not justify their ministerial calls with claims of feminine virtue, black women, more so than white women, based their right to preach on dramatic experiences of divine inspiration. They often layered descriptions of their call with religious rhetoric and biblical imagery. Maria Stewart, an AME preacher, declared herself an "instrument of God" divinely appointed to improve the moral character and social position of the African American race. A passionate plea she made in 1833 before white Baptists in Boston was replete with biblical imagery. She justified her preaching by invoking exemplary women of the Bible. "What if I am a woman? Is not the God of ancient times the God of these modern days? Did he not raise up Deborah, to be a mother and a judge in Israel? Did not Queen Esther save the lives of the Jews? And Mary Magdalene first declare the resurrection of Christ from the dead?"[15] Many African American women preachers of the nineteenth century tried to convince their detractors that they were compelled to preach, countering charges that they were inappropriately putting themselves forward by saying they were merely obeying God's commands. Zilpha Elaw maintained that "no ambition of mine, but the special appointment of God, [has] put me into the ministry, and therefore I had no option in the matter."[16] Jarena Lee, who was given to dreams and visions, declared that she had "distinctly heard" God tell her to "Go Preach the Gospel!" She, too, insisted that biblical examples supported a woman's right to preach, situating herself and other black women in a long line of female prophets and disregarding any difference that whites saw as arising from her race. "Did not Mary, a woman, preach the Gospel?" she asked.[17]

Despite their claims of feminine virtue and divine inspiration, nineteenth-century black preaching women could not escape speculation about their bodies, sex, and perceived innate carnality. Black women preachers during the migration era faced the same negative stereotypes, directed at them with perhaps even greater intensity. As a southern migrant, Mrs. Williams would have been particularly attuned to this stigma because, as Hazel Carby put it, black women migrants were routinely "characterized as sexually degenerate and, therefore, socially dangerous." By the 1920s the notion of the sexually immoral black woman, which was crafted during the nineteenth century by the white male imagination, was being embraced by some African Americans. Northern blacks, who had struggled to attain reputations for respectability and acceptance by whites, worried that black southerners in particular brought habits that marked them as different, rural, immoral, and lower class, and therefore jeopardized northern blacks' own standing. The literature of the Harlem Renaissance is rife with images of "hypersexualized" black women, particularly women from the South. Claude McKay, for example, in his novel *Home to Harlem* describes a scene witnessed by Jake, the protagonist, in a night club where girls from the South have presumably come to seduce men. "A jungle atmosphere pervaded the room, and, like shameless wild animals hungry for raw meat, the females savagely searched the eyes of the males . . . [Jake] had concluded that a woman could always go farther than a man in coarseness, depravity and sheer cupidity."[18]

An awareness of this image of black women is perhaps evidenced by the last part of Mrs. Williams's statement, which was not merely an offhand comment about sex. Perhaps her statement that people who are devoted to the work of God "don't have time to think about sex and the things of the world" was meant to refer to what would now be called gender, meaning that women who served as spiritual leaders were exempt from ordinary women's concerns—the burdens of earning a living, bearing and raising children, sustaining families, and wrestling with worldly cares. But Mrs. Williams's remark seems to refer more pointedly to sexual activity, given the prevalent stereotypical depictions of black women as sexually immoral and the connections she herself drew between women, the flesh, and the world. The conjunction of these concerns culminated for her in a perception that womanhood was incompatible with formal spiritual leadership, and perhaps—given the historical and cultural association between black womanhood and the sexualized body—black womanhood in particular was unfitted for such a position. That is perhaps the ultimate underpinning of Mrs. Williams's statement "women are the flesh of the world." In this one comment given in the back of a storefront church on Chicago's South Side, all the connections were made: the Holy Spirit, the body, women's leadership, and sex. As the accounts of Sojourner Truth and Jarena Lee show, these connections and the contradictions they create have confronted African American preaching women since their emergence within black Christianity.[19]

They have found expression in African American literature as well. James Baldwin's play and Great Migration narrative, "The Amen Corner," turns on the incompatibility of Christian ministry with a notion of black "womanhood" as implicitly connected to the body and sex. Margaret Alexander, the pastor of a small Harlem storefront church, is ousted by her congregation when her husband appears on the scene. They had thought she had been "born holy" and was without "much nature." Her husband, Luke, is undeniable evidence of her sexuality, and the real possibility of sexual desire in Margaret unfits her for spiritual leadership. As one of her congregants declares, she "ain't nothing but flesh and blood."[20]

So, we return to the general question and ask how it might apply particularly to the lives of African American preaching women in the migration-era urban north. What has been the problem with, or the threat posed by, a black woman in the pulpit? The answer is: perceptions about the black woman's body and its implicit connection to sex and sexuality. As Mrs. Williams's comment shows, the discrimination against women in ministerial leadership has first to do with a theological ordering: the divinely endorsed superiority of males which, expressed in Christian terms, means a male Father, a male Son, and a male Holy Ghost. Among African Americans, as among European American Christians, this theological ordering has given ready support to a male-dominated social order and a male monopoly on the ministry. As one AME minister who objected to the proposed pastorate of Sarah Ann Hughes in 1884 said, "God has circumscribed her [woman's] sphere and whenever she goes out of it, injury is done to society."[21] But more lurks here. Besides the obvious implication in this theological framework that women don't "look like" God is the ironic implication of the asexuality of God and of male ministers. A woman in the pulpit evokes the body and sexuality in a way that men do not. Social and theological constructs mask a male minister's sexuality, while a female minister's sexuality is written in her body. She cannot be understood outside sexual terms.

There is little question that neither female nor male ministers jettison their sexualities when they occupy sacred space in their sacerdotal roles. But the woman minister's body is sexually marked primarily because of her role as child bearer and all that entails and implies about her body. Debates have raged throughout Christian history (Jewish and Islamic history also, for that matter) about the participation of women in sacred space because of their capacity to menstruate and to give birth. In chapter 5, Deidre H. Crumbley shows that restrictions against women in sacred space have more to do with menstruation as a marker of gender difference than with ritual uncleanness. Indeed, only post-menopausal women are allowed to perform the same clerical duties as their male counterparts because that primary physiological difference has been removed. However, many churches throughout the world, including those in Africa, have made associations between menstruating women and "uncleanness" according to the Judeo-Christian tradition as depicted in Leviticus chapters 12 and 15. I would argue, however, that the spatial restrictions placed on women in the Judeo-Christian tradition had and still have as much to do with the woman's body as a site of sexual provocation in general as with particular issues of ritual uncleanness before and after childbirth. This would seem particularly the case in the current debate about women in the ministry since notions of a woman's impurity during menstruation, pregnancy, and childbirth no longer play any part in the discussion.[22] An example drawn from migration-era Chicago substantiates this point. Horace Clarence Boyer, the historian of black gospel music, recalls that in the early career of Mahalia Jackson—who was childless and, though not a preacher, occupied a public ministerial role—black ministers insisted that, when she sang in their churches, she don a clerical robe to render the movement of her body less obvious.[23] In her position as a spiritual leader, Jackson's body became something to be covered in the interest of modesty at the request of male ministers whose bodies, I assert, would not have been similarly subjected to this level of objectification.

The Catholic Church has for centuries predicated an all-male, celibate priesthood on the idea of asexual male ministers, or a male clergy beyond speculation about the body and sex. According to a Catholic tradition ratified by the Second Vatican Council, priests, as "princes" of the church, serve as representatives of

God, including God's male gender and asexuality. They serve *in persona Christi,* "in the person of Christ." Indeed, in everything, including their physicality and "maleness," priests are meant to represent *alter Christus*—"another Christ."[24] According to the medieval theological construct that the divine spirit is male and the flesh is female, only men are equipped to represent the divinity of God in their bodies. A male priest in his sacramental role is, therefore, considered beyond speculations about his body and sex. This claim remains the chief Catholic argument against women priests.

The erotic dynamics of black preaching and of black worship complicate any unequivocal conception of African American male clergy as asexual or beyond speculation about their bodies. But there are parallels to the Catholic model within black religious communities. The black female body has often been scrutinized and marked as sexually immoral when the "wayward" black male minister has not. In some cases when a male minister's tendency to succumb to sexual temptation has become known, he has generously been forgiven for his human fallibility rather than regarded as disqualified for spiritual leadership because of his carnality. Black male preachers' illicit sexual relationships, often with female congregants, are common knowledge. Scholars, writers, and ethnographers have long noted a close relationship between black preaching, worship, and sexuality. As Michael Eric Dyson has contended, "there is a relentless procession, circulation, and movement of black bodies in the black church." It is from this notion of the sensuality of black worship that we get depictions of the libidinous or wayward male preacher. He is just as much a part of African American church lore as the righteous male minister, having been celebrated in song, sermon, film, and literature.

The African American filmmaker Oscar Micheaux explored this theme in a number of his movies, most notably in *Body and Soul,* in which Paul Robeson, in his first film role, plays a duplicitous preacher in a southern town. In *Hallelujah,* the first all-black film produced by a major studio, the protagonist Zeke Johnson is drawn by his lust during a highly sexualized revival meeting to have sex with and then elope with Chick. Although the filmmaker, King W. Vidor, makes certain that the viewer understands that Zeke is motivated by his passions, he is equally keen on portraying the sexually loose Chick as Zeke's temptress and the one chiefly responsible for his fall. In her novel, *Quicksand,* which she wrote in part to counter migration-era images of the hypersexualized black woman, Nella Larsen nevertheless suggests that it is female sexual desire that needs controlling, not the wayward black minister. The Rev. Pleasant Green is a man of indisputably bad character, who is drawn to Helga for her aberrant sexuality. Although he is portrayed as a "hypocrite," it is still Helga who needs redemption. Green's lust for her becomes socially sanctioned through their marriage, while the marriage effectively redeems Helga and places her into a respectable social space. More than that, the marriage tames the "hardiness of [her] insistent desire."[25]

A similar dynamic takes place within African American sacred space. Although black male ministers are sexual and sexualized, the black female preacher evokes the body and sex in a way the black male preacher does not. Her body is objectified, her sexuality is at issue, and the nature of her desire is held suspect. Consider again the case of James Baldwin's Harlem storefront preacher Margaret Alexander. In his final confrontation with his ousted former pastor, Brother Boxer, one of the few men of the church, chides Margaret. "You ain't no better than the rest of them (women)," he declares. "You done sweated and cried in the nighttime, too, you'd like to be doing it again . . . You ain't as good."[26] Brother Boxer has become convinced that Margaret is just like other women, unable by nature to control her sexual passions.

Mrs. Williams's statement indicates that her approach to dealing with the perceived incompatibility of womanhood, and its implied connection to carnality, with ministerial leadership was to deny her body, herself, her femaleness. As she put it, when she came under the influence of the Holy Ghost "she . . . [was] no longer a woman." Then and only then did she have "the right to perform the duties of a man." By becoming a "man," Mrs. Williams did not so much assume the male gender or have her gender transformed; rather, she ironically desexed herself so that, in a sense, she transcended gender altogether. In order to exercise an authority to preach the Christian gospel, she had to embrace the spiritual superiority of maleness and by doing so place herself beyond speculation about her body and about sex.

Although few black preaching women have been known to articulate claims about the Holy Spirit, gender, and the body in the same terms as Mrs. Williams, the attempt to desexualize themselves was widespread among those who sought to defend their presence in the pulpit. It was part of a complex strategy employed by black preaching women who aimed to detract attention from their bodies and sexuality by rendering themselves sexually ambiguous or by complicating the very notion of "femaleness." They manipulated what Elaine Lawless terms a set of "confused gender expectations," which required that they be maternal (nurturing) and pragmatic (rational), occupying both gendered realms but fully ensconced in neither. Rejecting domesticity, these black preaching women indicated that they were mothers but not wives. They and their parishioners understood wifehood to carry a bodily or sexual connotation that motherhood, ironically, did

not. Through this strategy, they attempted to take control of their self-representation as women and as ministers. They sought to authenticate their religious
power and authority and to reframe the gendered discourse with regard to black
women in ministry. The Rev. Mary G. Evans and Elder Lucy Smith, two of Chicago's most prominent African American preaching women during the first half
of the twentieth century, were keen exemplars of this strategy.

A "Mannish" Woman as Businesslike and Motherly Minister

In interviews conducted in the late 1990s for a biographical sketch of Mary
Evans, longtime members of the Cosmopolitan Community Church recalled that
rumors that Evans was a lesbian had started not long after she came to Chicago
in 1932. According to church members' recollections, there was sufficient substance to lend the rumors credibility. Evans never married but maintained two
long-term relationships with other women. The first relationship was with Harriet Kelley, a schoolteacher and parishioner at St. Johns, the Indiana AME church
Evans had headed before coming to Chicago. Evans and Kelley worked on similar projects at the church and even shared a residence, which apparently "confused many." For reasons that are not entirely clear, Evans listed herself as head
of the household and listed Kelley as her sister on the 1930 census. If this kin
term was an effort to shield the nature of the relationship, the guise was not fool-
proof. It was clear the two women were not related. The same census record
showed that Evans's parents were born in Virginia, while Kelley's parents had
been born in Illinois and Kentucky.[27] One could argue that the women used the
term *sister* in the familial way with which many African Americans would be familiar and in a way some anthropologists would describe as "fictive kinship." It
is also possible that they meant it in spiritual terms, considering themselves as
"sisters in Christ." Evans and Kelley must have known that the terms *boarder* or
roomer were the categories census takers would more readily recognize, yet they
chose not to use them. Although eventually Evans developed a relationship with
Edna Cook that lasted until Evans's death in 1966, her relationship with Kelley
lasted in some form for many years after Evans had left Indiana.

Mary Evans never publicly spoke of the nature of her relationships with Kelley and Cook, so it is impossible to know for certain that Evans was lesbian. The
known aspects of the two relationships suggest the possibility that Evans was, if
not self-identified as lesbian, then at least "womanist," to use Alice Walker's term.
A *womanist*, according to Walker, is a woman who "loves other women, sexually
and/or nonsexually." She prefers women's culture, emotional flexibility, and

strength.[28] The long time during which Evans and Cook lived together and their apparent closeness indicate a relationship that was emotionally and possibly physically intimate. It must have been obvious to the congregation and to the wider African American community that the two women understood themselves to be in a primary relationship. Despite the unconventionality that lay in both partners being female, perhaps theirs mirrored the type of relationship that feminist theorists term *heteronormativity*; perhaps they acted toward one another as husbands and wives do, sharing a household and a sexual connection. Or, perhaps it was a relationship similar to what historians of women call *romantic friendships*; during the nineteenth century, some women were, in the words of John D'Emilio and Estelle Freedman, "passionately attached to each other and committed to a lifetime together."[29]

Evans's personal demeanor fueled the gay rumors. She dressed in an austere manner, wearing the same "shiny black suit" for years and refusing to buy new clothes until the church had made progress in raising money for one of its building projects. She was known to wear a "severe hairstyle" and "no makeup."[30] That 1930s WPA workers found her to be businesslike and the church to reflect business efficiency was due, in part, to Evans's strict style of leadership. Her career in Chicago was dominated by ambitious building projects as well as active involvement in civic culture and politics, arenas deemed to be the province of the city's male clerical leadership. In addition to reducing the church's debt, Evans was the only Chicago minister, male or female, to design and build a community house and a retirement home on church property. The AME minister John Harvey claimed that Evans's facility at fundraising and church administration was the primary reason he invited her to assume the leadership of Cosmopolitan. She exceeded his expectations in endeavors that black Chicagoans hardly expected from a single woman pastor. Though she never spoke of social issues from her pulpit, Evans demonstrated a keen interest in racial betterment. Under her leadership, Cosmopolitan outdistanced all other Chicago churches in membership drives for the NAACP.

In time, people throughout the congregation and wider community commented on Evans's "mannish" ways and her leadership style, which a former congregant described as a propensity to "dot every *i* and cross every *t*."[31] Another member of Cosmopolitan Community Church recalled that she had not immediately taken to Evans upon joining the church in 1932 because she felt Evans was "too mannish." Others concurred.[32] The accusation of mannishness was often directed toward black preaching women and was a crucial aspect of the discourse centering on the woman minister's body and sexuality. A wide range of 1930s sources characterized black preaching women as "plain," "buxom," "plump and brown," and "homely." Many commented on their unusually "deep voices." A WPA worker who witnessed Rebecca Porter of All Nations Pentecostal Church preach in 1938 remarked, "She was a very emotional speaker with a strong husky male voice. Her movements were likewise very masculine." One of the African American informants in a 1940 study by Samuel Strong, a University of Chicago doctoral student of Robert Park, concluded that "women preachers are somewhat mannish, overweight, and hoarse." Another noted that they are "usually of a mannish type and imitate men preachers."[33] To be sure, these perceptions stemmed from the rise in masculinist conceptions of American evangelical Christianity. As an element of the movement some scholars have called "muscular Christianity," the surge in masculinist sentiment within mainline denominations sought to reverse the perceived feminization of American religion. It framed the discussion about women ministers not in terms of naturally predetermined gender spheres but more simply in terms of the gender definition of proper work roles.[34] Indeed, according to a story she later told, when young Mary Evans first mounted the pulpit of her Baptist church to deliver an extemporaneous sermon, her shocked parents reprimanded her, saying that preaching was "man's work."[35] Evans did not follow her parents' advice and became a minister at the age of twelve, assuming a personal and professional style that prompted speculation that she was lesbian throughout her long career. The case of Mary Evans shows that publicly transgressing gender boundaries and rumors of personal sexual deviance were linked. One, however, was not reducible to the other.

Whether Mary Evans was actually a lesbian is beside the point. She apparently never made a public proclamation of her sexual orientation and would have been disinclined to do so, given her position and her repeated claim to be a "private person."[36] Remarkably, the unsubstantiated rumors did not halt her career; they did not even deter support for her or her church. As remarkable was Clarence Cobbs, a contemporary of Evans's and pastor of the First Church of Deliverance "Spiritualist," who, despite being a known homosexual and living a flamboyant lifestyle, headed one of Chicago's most prominent churches with thousands of members. The support and acclaim he and Evans received, particularly during the 1930s and 1940s, seems to corroborate George Chauncey's argument that gays were more visible and liberal attitudes toward homosexuality perhaps more prevalent prior to the Cold War period.[37]

It was not likely that a woman living in a long-term relationship with another woman could escape speculation about her sexuality. But Evans had historical precedent for the strategy she adopted. When Rebecca Cox Jackson, an African

American Shaker, joined the celibate religious sect in 1836 and later engaged in a lifelong relationship with Rebeccah Perot, it was because she wanted to be rid of sex with her husband. She held to the view that sexual relations, even with a married partner, were incompatible with a spiritual life. Jackson also intimated that she left her husband in order to take control over the use of her body. Even so, the close relationship she maintained with Perot continues to generate assertions by some scholars that the women were lesbian.[38] While it is likely that Evans was lesbian and that, given her commitment to celibacy, Jackson was not, what is more important is how Evans carefully manipulated the images of motherliness and mannishness to create her own self-presentation, to navigate a "confused set of gender expectations" for black preaching women, and to deflect attention from her body as well as her sexuality.

African American preaching women in black urban churches were expected to "mother" their congregations. Indeed, their ability to mother the congregation was one of the ways black preaching women authenticated their calls to ministry. Mary Evans utilized the mother typology to great effect, asserting herself as the primary matriarchal figure in the church. She also took pragmatic steps to insure her mother status and occasionally addressed her congregation as "children." Former Cosmopolitan members recalled that Evans sent them birthday cards and they, in turn, "minded her just like we were children."[39] They also recalled that Evans, who had borne no children, had a particular fondness for them and considered one of the Cosmopolitan girls her "adopted daughter."[40] (That adopted daughter referred to Kelley as "Aunt Harriet.") Evans's fondness for children perhaps motivated the construction of the nearby Martha Carter Playground, equipped with "everything a young heart could wish for." Federal Writers' Project researchers found that Evans's sermons had a maternal quality; after waxing "sharp like a two-edged sword," she then would become "kind and entreative [*sic*]."[41]

But Evans's appropriation of the mother image had a larger aim and more important effect. Mothering her congregation effectively desexualized her, deflecting focus on her body or the nature of her personal relationships. Ironically, the mother image presented the best way for black preaching women to deemphasize the body, sex, and sexuality. The category of mother and "church mother"— an official title in some denominations—remains the most desexualized in the black church tradition. What little available literature exists on this all-important feature of black Protestantism does not draw direct connections between mothers of the church, the body, and sex. These descriptions do, however, suggest that mothers in the black church tradition are presumed to occupy a space beyond physical concerns and, notably, even beyond biological reproduction. Drawing on West African models of women elders, mothers in some interpretations of the black church tradition are sagacious leaders of the young, particularly young women, and serve as mediators between the sexes. This position of honor is not bestowed indiscriminately. As C. Eric Lincoln and Lawrence Mamiya have intimated, the role of church mother is not available to young women. It is given to older women, the "most respected" within the congregation, and those presumably past their sexual prime. Often women are not elevated to the position of "mother" until they are widows, the implication being that they are to be considered mothers but not wives.[42] The Catholic Church again serves as an example here. "Mother Mary" in Catholic iconography is a desexualized and de-eroticized figure, and when she has not been so characterized, there has been trouble.[43] In traditional Catholic Mariology, Mary's virginal conception and motherhood takes precedence over her wifehood. The doctrine of her "perpetual virginity" means to portray Mary as a mother who has never had "carnal knowledge" of her husband Joseph.

The nonsexual or sexless black mother image has roots in the secular arena as well. To counter the stereotype of the hypersexualized black woman, African American activists such as W. E. B. Du Bois and Alexander Crummell promoted a notion of idealized black womanhood. The ideal black woman, or "true black woman" as Claudia Tate has called her, drew from the dominant white culture's "cult of true womanhood" and reflected its values. The ideal black woman was a "moral mother" who also held the responsibility to "uplift" the race. However, encumbering the ideal black woman with a philosophy of moral motherhood, when combined with the aim of refuting notions of her hypersexuality, tended to construct a sexless and dour black mother. "Motherly" became equated with "sexless" in some African American contexts.[44] The nonsexual "moral mother" emerged as one of the key representations among the shifting and colliding images of black womanhood found in Nella Larsen's *Passing*. Larsen depicts Irene as a "true black woman" who has devoted herself to home, family, and racial uplift. When her husband looses interest in her sexually, however, Irene attributes it to having taking her role as a mother "rather seriously." As a consequence, her husband considers sex between them to be "a grand joke." To him, Irene has become "only the mother of his sons. That was all."[45] Mary Evans played upon this nonsexual maternal imagery to her advantage. By doing so, she perhaps hoped to mitigate speculation about her body and sexuality.

Similarly, it is likely that Evans' "mannishness" was a deliberate and self-conscious display that was misread by contemporary observers. Perhaps by some gender conventions her austere dress, autocratic style of leadership, and skill at debt reduction and administration were tangible proof enough of her mannishness in the minds of some. And to an extent that perception was unavoidable, given that she worked in a realm considered the sole province of men. Complicating all of this was the paradoxical expectation that black women preachers demonstrate the rational and pragmatic qualities attributed to male ministers in order to legitimate their roles as clerical leaders. Rather than aiming for a mannish display outright, it is likely that Evans was working toward a personal display or performance of gender ambiguity. Such display would tend to deemphasize the body and sex altogether.

Numerous photographs of Evans, most of which were taken later in her career, suggest that she was particularly interested in controlling her public image. Certainly, for historians the use of photographs raises some interesting epistemological questions, or as Nell Irvin Painter would say, questions regarding "ways of knowing and being known."[46] However, as Evans left relatively few written records—none of her sermons were published, and no documents pertaining to her personal life have been found—these photos are a valuable means by which to understand her. They serve as a "text" of her life in the same way as the abundance of institutional records that she left with the church. All the portraits were done in clerical garb and some were posed in profile, where the body and often not even the face were emphasized. The photos are evocative in that they do not explicitly suggest a particular gender. They contrast strikingly with verbal descriptions from earlier in her career. She was once declared "the Bobbed Haired Evangelist" whose voice was "mellowed with a touch of sweetness that makes it thoroughly feminine."[47] So, whether motherly or mannish, lesbian or not, she situated herself in that desexualized category of "minister," which pointedly disinvited speculation about the body, "femaleness," or sexuality. A statement Evans made to an interviewer in 1940 came closest to encapsulating this view. "I am a minister and a leader of my followers who need my advice and guidance," she asserted. "Women preachers are important . . . There is no doubt that we encounter a great deal of opposition, but our work is needed."[48]

A Physically Imposing Woman as Overseer and Motherly Minister

In a neighborhood only blocks from Cosmopolitan, Elder Lucy Smith, pastor and founder of the All Nations Pentecostal Church, faced the same challenges as Mary Evans. Smith developed different strategies to deal with confused gender expectations and to deflect attention from her body and sex, presenting herself as a deserted wife motivated by her maternal responsibilities as well as her spiritual calling to enter the ministry. Smith reported to her biographer that she had come to the city after being abandoned in Georgia by her husband, William. The biography, *From Farm to Pulpit*, told the story of her early life as a narrative of deprivation, loss, and struggle.[49] She arrived at the Illinois Central train station in May 1910. Surrounded by her nine children, she had nowhere to go, no idea of how to secure shelter for the night, and no contacts. Depicting herself as alone with the children in a large, unfamiliar, and potentially hostile city, Smith was absolutely clear on one point: there was no man in her life; her husband of fourteen years was not with her. "My husband left his family," she said, "and went to another city. I had to work to keep the children from starving and going naked."[50]

Although it made for compelling drama, the story of Lucy Smith's separation from her husband played out differently than the way she told it. William Smith actually joined her a short while after she arrived in Chicago and stayed with her until his death in 1938.[51] Whether he had planned to do so all along is not certain. Nor is it clear that he lived in the same residence with his wife during all of his years in Chicago. What is clear is that Smith reunited with his wife and the union produced two additional children. Indeed, he was instrumental in helping her build and maintain the first All Nations Pentecostal Church on Langley Avenue. The only surviving record that unequivocally identified him as her husband is his obituary. The "William Smith" and "brother Smith" that she referred to in her biography is not identified as her husband; rather, he is depicted as one of the few male workers at the church.[52]

Why did Lucy Smith veil her husband from public view? Why did she find it necessary or advantageous to present herself as a woman abandoned by her husband? The exact reasons could lie deeply embedded in the particulars of that relationship, which are beyond historical grasp. Perhaps she considered the biography her story, not his. Perhaps she considered this telling a way to exert some control over her life, or at least over how her life was remembered. Smith was among a long line of African American women who realized the significance of "I"—the self—and the act of telling her story as self-declaration.[53] That her husband was not a Christian may have played an important part in her refusal to acknowledge their relationship in her church and in her narrative of her ministry.[54] Perhaps she did not want to besmirch her testimony of doing the work of God with an account that featured an ungodly husband. All these are likely possibilities. It is just as likely, however, that this construction of her life narrative had just as much to do with deflecting attention from her body and sex as with drawing attention to her ministry. As in the case of Margaret Alexander in James Baldwin's play, the presence of a husband invited unwanted and troublesome speculation about her body and sexuality.

Unlike Evans, Smith was not subject to overt speculation about her sexuality, but she suffered from others' seemingly endless preoccupation with her physical stature. Standing six feet tall and weighing over three hundred pounds, Smith was compelled on a number of occasions to respond to inquiries about her body and size. Few sources fail to mention her imposing presence. In *Black Metropolis*, Drake and Cayton describe her as "elderly, corpulent, dark-skinned and maternal." After his initial visit to the church, Fenton Johnson, an African American poet working for the FWP during the mid-1930s, reported flatly that Elder Smith was "a large, gray haired, black woman."[55] White FWP workers, who also frequented All Nations during the late 1930s and early 1940s, wrote insensitive and degrading descriptions of Smith's body. Their portrayals reveal as much about their class biases—since Smith represented the black poor and working class—as they do any inhibitions the workers may have held about women in ministry. Alvin N. Canon (who also interviewed Mrs. Williams) articulated white people's typical responses to Smith's body in a report filled with vivid pejorative detail. "When the assembly had finished singing the opening hymn, Elder Smith squirmed her way out of the tightly fitting cushioned chair in which she was voluptuously ensconced, and wobbled over to the pulpit. As Elder Smith leaned on the lectern which was draped with blue cloth on which was inscribed the words: 'god is love,' she shifted some of the responsibility of carrying three hundred and fifty pounds from her large but weary looking feet."[56] Smith must have known that chroniclers of her life would fixate on the size of her body. But, by portraying herself as a woman preacher seemingly without a husband, she mitigated unwanted speculation about sex.

Similarly, Smith made use of her image as "mother to the drifting black masses," a phrase attributed to her by Drake and Cayton. Like Evans, Smith worked with the maternal expectations placed upon black preaching women of the era. One of the many ways people (in her church and in the wider black Chicago community) addressed her was as "Mother Smith." She, too, was known to "mother" her congregation, and the many descriptions of her in the WPA files and other sources recognized the maternal aspect of her work. Primarily, Smith suggested herself as the sole matriarchal figure in the church, having gathered her congregation from "the back streets of Chicago."[57]

Although Smith considered herself a mother, she did not consider herself a wife in any conventional sense. She was a mother to her children, her congregation, and "the drifting black masses" of the city, but she was not "Mrs. William Smith." In responding to one of the many inquiries about her weight, she unconsciously but revealingly asserted her rejection of womanly "domesticity." She told an interviewer in 1935 that she had once been "small," but since becoming a pastor God had taken her "out of the kitchen" and "fleshened her up."[58] Smith had not "cooked a meal in about 20 years," and all her domestic concerns were handled by a group of women who comprised the entirety of her private world. Smith's main contacts were her surviving daughters (several children preceded her in death); her personal secretary, Anna Johnson; her dressmaker, Mrs. Sutton; Rebecca Porter, a family friend from Alabama; and her granddaughter, "Little Lucy."[59] By 1930, most of these women lived with Smith in a household near the church on Langley Avenue. Smith had purchased the home some years earlier, signing the contract with a small "x." The census listed Lucy Smith as head of the household; the other occupants included Smith's youngest children, Henry and Ardella; Anna Johnson and her young two sons; and seven "lodgers," five of whom were women (including Rebecca Porter) and two of whom were single, young men. All the adults were migrants from the South, and their ages ranged from thirty-one to forty-seven. Only two of the women were listed as having ever been married.[60]

Just as Smith lived in a private world of women, her church constituted a female sacred world. And it was the construction of a female sacred world that comprised a significant part of her strategy to place herself beyond questions about her body and sex. Indeed, the female sacred world of All Nations placed Smith and the women of her congregation beyond the objective gaze, authority, and perspectives of men altogether. They provided the leadership in all major departments of the church. Clear lines of authority and succession were defining aspects of the institution. Smith functioned as sole pastor of the church and as "Overseer" of the All Nations Pentecostal Convention. The official title "Overseer," with all its historically masculine and racialized connotations, sharply contrasted with Smith's maternal image. White-garbed women "saints" served as her closest ministerial and administrative companions. These women sat in the place of honor in the front of the congregation and had the responsibility to assist Smith in her faith healing work. Men of the church were not regarded as "saints." Smith operated without an official assistant pastor until she appointed her daughter Ardella as her successor in the late 1940s. She elevated Rebecca Porter to "subleader" largely because of Porter's remarkable preaching skills. Porter delivered most of the sermons at All Nations, while Smith concentrated on the radio broadcast, *Glorious Church of the Air,* and the faith healing services.

Although some men at All Nations served as ushers, it is not clear if any male members served as ordained ministers with regular appointments during Smith's pastorate. Only upon her death, under the direction of her daughter Ardella, did men clearly assume regular clerical duties at All Nations. For many years, the most visible male at the church was Edgar G. Holly, a Haitian who had left Tuskeegee Institute for Chicago. ("I didn't want to study agriculture. I wanted to study art," he explained.) Smith's twelve-year-old granddaughter "Little Lucy" later replaced Holly as church pianist.

The female sacred world constructed by Smith did not so much render men powerless as silent and apparently marginal to the church's operations. The leadership of Evans's church was also predominantly female. Although All Nations and Cosmopolitan contained at least a few men among the congregations, the historical record bares little evidence of their actions and perspectives. Federal Writers' Project workers made repeated visits to All Nations over a three-year period in the late 1930s, but the only male voice recorded in those interviews is that of Brother Holly. The exhaustive studies of black churches, including All Nations, done in 1935 by Herbert Smith and in 1940 by Samuel Strong contain no voices of male members. Only in photographs taken for Richard Wright's *12 Million Black Voices* and for the Farm Security Administration do we get a sense of the male presence in the church. In those photographs, men exist literally on the margins of the congregation. Mary Evans's church had as members several prominent African American male professionals, including Dr. William Moses Jones who ran a free clinic out of the church's basement.[61] But neither his voice nor that of any other male member testifies to their role in the church. The "ritual and guidance" of All Nations in particular came from women, who elided the closed system of male clerical power.[62]

The predominance of women prompted Herbert Smith to characterize All Nations as "overwhelmingly feminine."[63] This characterization was apt and ironic. Women held all the leadership positions at the church and the congregation was about 90 percent female, which was remarkably high even for a Pentecostal congregation. "Quite a few" of these women were between the ages of fifty and sixty, reported another survey in the late 1930s. Most were married and employed in domestic service.[64] But the women of All Nations, like their pastor, occupied a space that subverted traditional gender expectations. The silence and invisibility of men at the church suggests that in their private lives they were "wives" and in the urban economy they were "domestics," but in the female sacred world Smith created they were simply "saints." Theirs was a self-contained black womanhood configured in relation to other women and defined without reference to men.

While Mary Evans was attempting to render herself sexually ambiguous, Smith was reconfiguring femaleness altogether. Her strategy of being "mother" and "Overseer," as well as rejecting domesticity, has some roots in Smith's Pentecostal faith. It was clear from the inception of the modern Pentecostal movement that it tended to confirm gender norms even as it subverted them. On the one hand, this modern-day revival supported the fundamental order of home and family, God, and man and woman. At the same time, however, the tradition decentralized the home, instilling a new order of priority: Jesus first, the institution of the church second, and family last. This order was especially applicable for Smith. She presented herself as a mother but not a wife and said that "since becoming a Pastor God has taken me out of the kitchen." The Pentecostal movement supported a broad-based egalitarianism with regard to gender and race. Paul's injunction in Galatians 3:28 became the mantra of the movement: "There is neither Jew nor Greek, slave nor free, male nor female, for you are all one in Christ Jesus." The racial equality that was fundamental to early Pentecostalism was a primary motivation for Smith's embracing the movement. She later recalled that when she saw black and white people worshipping together at the Stone Church, a predominately white Pentecostal church on Indiana Avenue with which she briefly affiliated in 1914, she realized that "there must be something to it." Smith insisted that interracialism motivated her to name the church All Nations, and it contained a larger racial mix, including whites and ethnic minorities, than any predominately black church in Chicago.

Ultimately, the influence of Pentecostalism on Smith's life was to reconfigure prevailing gender norms and restructure gender relations within the church. The Pentecostal tradition allowed her to subvert conventional notions of gender in practice while in theory working within them, to be an overseer who was also motherly. Lucy Smith's strategy, which aimed at desexualizing herself and undermining speculations about her body and sexuality, complicated the very notion of what it meant to be female. She was a church leader and a minister, but not a wife, heading a church that was overwhelmingly feminine, full of other women with veiled husbands. These were women, who as Mrs. Williams suggested, didn't "have time to think about sex and the things of the world."

Women Ministers as Problematically Embodied Souls

Prevailing perceptions about black women's bodies and their implied connection to sex and sexuality have been key components in a culture of resistance to black preaching women in American urban settings over the past century.

Rooted in mutually reinforcing historical, cultural, and theological understandings of "women's nature," this resistance has considered black women's bodies as inherently carnal and evocative of sex. As Mrs. Williams asserted, "Women are the flesh of the world." The logical extension of this perception is that womanhood as such, and black womanhood in particular, is incompatible with ministerial leadership. Mrs. Williams, Mary G. Evans, and Elder Lucy Smith developed and employed inventive strategies that effectively subverted dominant notions and conventions of gender, even as they represented themselves as asexual and maternal. These strategies deflected attention away from their bodies. Working paradoxically within and outside conventionally gendered understandings of womanhood, these women rejected domesticity and created female sacred worlds that reimagined femaleness. In doing so, each woman engaged in what French feminist theorists would call *écriture féminine*, writing the body. They put primacy on their subjective experiences as women rather than on the objective and objectifying gaze of men. They even reinterpreted the seemingly prohibitive sacred texts concerning women's place in sacred arenas.[65]

The modern city itself played a significant role in the development of these strategies. Amid and despite the shifting and colliding images of black womanhood during the era of the Great Migration, black preaching women found a more expansive place in public life. Like their male counterparts, African American preaching women were able to found and lead churches according to their own specifications, particularly outside of the mainstream denominations. Evans left the AME church to serve as pastor at the Cosmopolitan Community Church, while Smith founded an independent Pentecostal church. Some black women preachers not only worked outside accepted ecclesiastical boundaries but also operated outside the confines of a religiously marked physical space altogether. A woman who regularly preached at the corner of Thirty-first and State streets in 1917 incurred the wrath of a *Chicago Defender* reader who called her an "old woman mock preacher" and termed her preaching "a regular vaudeville show."[66] Others on the margins, "spiritualists" and "divine healers" such as Madam Cassyain Fletcher, Mother Naomi Bagby, and Rev. Sadie B. Owens, carved out substantial spaces for themselves in Chicago's African American religious scene. Bishop M. W. Hall maintained a church on South State Street and regularly advertised her ministry in the *Chicago Defender* and other African American newspapers. Other black women preachers included local evangelists, like Rev. Dorothy Sutton Branch and Rev. Evelyn Hooks, and traveling evangelists and pastors of smaller groups characterized as "cults." Rev. Pauline J. Coffee, a former actress, held numerous revival services in Chicago during the 1930s and 1940s. An evangelist and associate of Aimee Semple-McPherson, the Los Angeles–based founder of the International Church of the Four Square Gospel, Rev. Coffee preached to large crowds in churches of various denominations.[67] The ability of this eclectic assortment of women to exercise ecclesiastical power did not always represent or lead to changing attitudes with regard to women in ministry, but it did grow from the opportunities to work in the public realm that urban culture afforded.

This narrative of black women's inventive, collective strategies to evade and subvert prevailing gender norms and notions of female nature is nonetheless a cautionary tale. Despite some changes in church policies and the effective strategies adopted by black preaching women during the migration era, a persistent gaze upon black preaching women's bodies supports the continued cultural insistence that the ministry is the province of men. The example of Vashti McKenzie, the first female bishop in the 215-year history of the African Methodist Episcopal church, is a case in point. McKenzie's elevation was hailed as a pathbreaking development for women religious generally. According to McKenzie, "The stain[ed] glass ceiling has been pierced and broken." But the resistance to McKenzie's bishopric, as well as to her ministry, revealed a fixation upon her womanhood that led her to address it. In a book she wrote several years before her elevation, McKenzie declared as the first of "Ten Womanist Commandments for Clergy": "Thou Shalt Not Compromise Your Femininity for the Sake of the Ministry." The implication was clear. A woman's "femininity" is precisely what gets compromised when she dares to serve in a position of clerical leadership. An African American male preacher interviewed by C. Eric Lincoln and Lawrence Mamiya for their monumental 1990 study of leadership development for African American women in ministry corroborated this notion. He asserted that a woman shouldn't preach because "she loses her femininity" and "diminishes her womanhood."[68]

Scholars of African American religion and gender can be helpful in this discussion. The literature and the debates on these questions need an infusion of new thoughts about gender and its relationship to black women's clerical power. We must interrogate the layers of meaning that accrue to gender relations in ecclesiastical contexts. This analysis of Lucy Smith, Mary Evans, and other African American preaching women may tell us that their experience of religion was a transcendent liberty. Answering the call to spiritual leadership offered black women liberty from all kinds of restrictive norms, including domesticity and the notion of a singular gender category to which individual women had to conform. The idea that preaching is "man's work" simply has no application. In constructing a female sacred world, these women rewrote notions not only of women's place but also of men's place, and in the process undermined the prevailing hegemonic gender ideology. Perhaps they also unwittingly called into question the very existence of gender norms in the ecclesiastical realm. If this is so, the notion of separate spheres ideology has to be rethought. If there is a lesson to be learned, it might be that (as some African American scholars have begun to suggest) black church culture needs an open discussion about the relationship between sex, the body, and the church. If black preaching women's bodies are evocative of sex and sexuality, dare we recognize the crucial role the body plays in religious practice? Perhaps the embodiment that black women evoke necessarily projects our attention back to the incarnational aspect of the Christian faith, leading black churches and the wider black community to new understandings of the sanctity of sexuality and the paradoxes of gender.

CHAPTER SEVEN

"Make Us a Power"

African American Methodists Debate the "Woman Question," 1870–1900

MARTHA S. JONES

By the mid-1880s, black Methodists throughout the United States were debating the woman question. In the African Methodist Episcopal (AME) church, they asked whether women should be licensed to preach, ultimately affirming that while they were eligible for such licenses, women were disqualified from holding a pastoral charge. In the Colored Methodist Episcopal (CME) church, a proposal to create the office of stewardess, while initially met with laughter, was finally approved. In the African Methodist Episcopal Zion (AME Zion) church, a debate erupted when a woman was appointed to serve on a conference committee until the presiding officer ruled that church law permitted female officeholding. In the years following Emancipation, African American Methodists engaged these and other questions as part of a broad reconsideration of women's religious authority. Denominational activists forged new roles for women in the public life of the church through contests over biblical precepts, church law, and denominational culture. Their deliberations were closely connected with debates unfolding in other realms of African American life. The optimism of Reconstruction, the degradations of Jim Crow, and finally the new ambitions of U.S. imperialism all informed black Methodists' debates on the woman question.

Eliza Ann Gardner, an AME Zion activist, captured the tenor of these exchanges when she urged her denomination's leaders to "strengthen [women's] efforts and make us a power." While the debate over the "woman question" encompassed many post–Civil War issues, most notably those related to labor and familial relations, it took on a particular meaning for black Methodists. "What should be the standing of women in the formal sites of denominational governance?" they asked. What roles should black Methodist women play in church-based campaigns for civil, economic, and political justice? These questions were taken up by what one AME commentator termed a "woman movement" in the religious realm, a movement that sought female power in the highest echelons of black Methodism's institutional hierarchy.[1]

These changes did not take place uniformly across the three denominations; differences in their history, polity, and leadership gave them different vantage points on questions of women's religious authority. The AME and AME Zion churches had their origins in northern cities during the late eighteenth century. The CME church was born during the years after the Civil War, and its leaders came largely from the ranks of former slaves. During the last quarter of the nineteenth century, the AME church was dominated by men who had led the denomination during the years before the Civil War, while the AME Zion church was directed by a cadre of ministers who had come of age during the tumult of Reconstruction. Yet, these institutions had a great deal in common. All had been born out of conflict within the white Methodist denominations with which they had initially been affiliated. In the postwar era, all were singularly focused upon ministering to freed people; by the 1870s, formerly northern-based black Methodists had relocated the center of church life to the South, where the overwhelming majority of African Americans lived. The three denominations' laws and practices were uniquely Methodist. Each was governed by a similar code, *The Doctrines and Discipline,* which was legislated by a network of local, regional, and national decision-making conferences, and each had congregants who were ranked from lay members and local exhorters to ordained ministers and bishops. Their debates over the woman question were conducted within these structures, as conference delegates deliberated over changes in church law aimed at elevating women within the leadership hierarchy. These shared histories, objectives, and structures were reinforced through shared rituals and a sense of spiritual, liturgical, and institutional kinship. Each denomination included the leaders from the other two as guests during deliberative conferences. In these settings, black Methodist women struggled for the right to vote, hold office, control missionary societies, and, in some cases, be ordained to the ministry. Along the way, they and their male allies challenged the gendered premises that shaped their denominations and their relations to a broader public culture.

The relationship between black Methodists and broader publics is this chapter's central concern. While these religious activists were bound together as Methodists, their considerations of the woman question were also animated by ideas and innovations generated in the realm of politics. Thus, while there is evidence of what Wallace Best, in his examination of Pentecostal female preachers of the 1940s, has characterized as a "culture of resistance" to women's religious authority, we also find that deliberations in black Methodist circles turned on broader shifts in public culture, of which churches were but one part.[2] During Reconstruction, a time of optimism and openness to change when the national Methodist denominations were reorganizing themselves, revisions of law and practice made women visible members of formal decision-making bodies as conference delegates and officers, explicitly recognizing women's position in the churches and extending their power within them. However, the collapse of Reconstruction ushered in the degradations of the Jim Crow era, and efforts to extend women's religious authority took on controversial meanings. As male leaders struggled to maintain their public footing in the face of an increasingly aggressive political program of white supremacy, they moved within churches to oppose female control of missionary societies and access to ordination. As black Methodist missionary aspirations became linked to U.S. imperial endeavors in the 1890s, it was men who forged new ties with diasporic people of African descent throughout the world.

The debate over the woman question was not limited to churches; it touched all realms of black public culture in the decades following the Civil War. This public culture was comprised of the many communal institutions that were characteristic of the period: churches, political conventions, fraternal orders, lyceums, literary clubs, schools, and civil rights organizations.[3] In those spaces and institutions, black Americans came together to meet their material needs, extending educational and employment opportunities, creating burial societies and cemeteries, setting up widows' pensions and funds for the needy. These were bounded spaces, the parameters of which were defined by racism, on the one hand, and on the other by a strong desire for the authority and autonomy that independent institutions made possible. Most black Americans lived and died, worshipped and mourned, read and debated, strategized and sought assistance in African American institutions.

The term *public culture* is intended to convey more than the material sustenance and organizational capacities provided by institutions, however. Public culture also encompasses a realm of ideas, a community of interests, and a collective understanding of the issues of the day and the relationship of black Americans to them. African American religious life was an important site for sustained and far-reaching intellectual dialogue, political analysis, and civic discussion. Through exchanges within conventions and conferences, through the written word and in oral debates, African American activists built an intellectual community. In this realm of deliberation, they developed tactics and strategies that sustained community well-being and enhanced their standing in the broader society.[4] This aspect of public culture did not suffer from the same bounded quality that institutions did, and in the realm of ideas African American activists were as cosmopolitan as any.[5] Men and women were as likely to take up world cultures or national politics as the Sunday sermon or the upcoming ladies' bazaar. They read widely, attended public forums when people of color were welcome, and forged connections to the broader society, its issues and trends, challenges and triumphs.

As women and men traversed this complex and always evolving public culture, ideas about women moved between the various sites of black discussion and collective action. An increasingly robust print culture extended the debate, as newspapers and pamphlets allowed people in widely dispersed places to participate in a common dialogue. Lively and multifaceted deliberations were carried on across all these spaces and media. Questions arose about women's public authority and autonomy as some female activists sought parity with their male counterparts, aspiring to speak from the podium, vote in decision-making bodies, be licensed to preach, and thereby determine their community's future.[6] Eventually, these activist women forged a movement that was intimately bound up with allied reforms and constituencies; their movement was mindful of the contemporaneous movement for rights among white women and was shaped by civil rights struggles carried on by black men but was defined by neither. "What shall be the standing of women within African American public culture?" was the movement's central question. How would women exercise authority by taking part in collective decision-making, and to what extent could their decisions remain independent from male oversight? As black Americans took up the issues of the day and developed strategies by which they engaged in struggles for freedom, citizenship, and civil rights, they also grappled with the limits on and possibilities for women.

Reconstructing Churchwomen

What most clearly distinguishes the post–Civil War decades is the extent to which African American women capitalized on their long-standing contributions to community building to demand formal recognition in some of the most powerful black institutions. By the 1880s, the relationship of gender to power had been permanently altered as by-laws, constitutions, doctrines, and charters were rewritten. Women's access to sites of black publicity was formalized as fraternal orders, schools, political organizations, and churches recognized women's work as essential to overcoming the challenges posed by Reconstruction and its premature end. Organizations and positions designated specifically for women, such as the Masons' Order of the Eastern Star and the Methodist Office of the Stewardess, were created along with numerous other ladies' departments and female auxiliaries.[7] This was a complex process laden with multiple meanings. On the one hand, these innovations acknowledged that women were vital for maintaining a viable public culture; their organizing and fundraising had long sustained institutions in a community without a capital or philanthropic class. On the other hand, these innovations subjected women's public work to the scrutiny of male leaders, inviting a series of struggles over the limits of women's authority relative to that of their male counterparts. Despite these tensions, Reconstruction saw the emergence of a new base from which women engaged the public realm, and formal officeholding ensured that women were no longer wholly subject to the capriciousness of male leaders. The earliest of these debates erupted in the realm of politics.

The issue of the Fifteenth Amendment, more than any other, forced African American activists to consider their views about women's standing in the political realm. The proposed addition to the Constitution provided: "The rights of citizens of the United States to vote shall not be denied or abridged by the United States or by any State on account of race, color, or previous condition of servitude." These terms brought to the fore the issue of black women's public authority because the amendment would establish the voting rights of African American men but not those of women of any race. A bitter debate ensued, which many historians have interpreted as a splintering of what before the Civil War had been an enduring, if not untroubled, alliance between abolitionists and women's rights advocates.[8] This interpretation holds to the extent that many white women's rights advocates abandoned any commitment to interracial political alliances. Yet, for black people the Fifteenth Amendment debate was not as sharp a point of demarcation as some have suggested. African American activists did not turn their backs on women's rights. Indeed, in postwar African American public culture, the rights of women remained among the most important issues of the day.

The "colored convention movement" was among the long-standing sites of political culture. In the postwar period, black Americans came together to grapple with women's rights questions even after the terms of the Fifteenth Amendment had been finalized.[9] The debate reverberated through these conventions. For example, at the 1869 Colored Men's Labor Convention meeting in Washington, D.C., a women's suffrage committee successfully put forth a resolution that urged women be included in all African American efforts at labor organizing.[10] In that same year, at the meeting of the National Convention of the Colored Men of America, Helen Johnson of Philadelphia was seated as a delegate because, as one attendee put it, African Americans "had but one voice in the South, and that was to know no distinctions of color or sex. Unless they concentrated their power they would never attain to any political power."[11] Black activists also joined the ranks of the National Women's Suffrage Association and the American Women's Suffrage Association, campaigning for women's right to the vote.[12]

New outlets for the expression of African American political energies also took up the question of women's rights. Activists entered the realm of electoral politics during Reconstruction and were among those that placed women's suffrage on the agenda of constitutional conventions and state legislatures. For instance, William Whipper, a delegate to the South Carolina constitutional convention of 1868, called for that body to enfranchise black women as well as men.[13] Men like Whipper acted as allies to their female counterparts. The following year, his sister-in-law Louisa Rollin, a member of the American Women's Suffrage Association, addressed the South Carolina House of Representatives and urged that body to support universal suffrage.[14]

Beyond the formal institutions of state-level politics, African Americans operated in an "internal" realm with differing purposes and rules. In these spaces, women were enfranchised and participated in the parades, rallies, mass meetings, and conventions through which African Americans "enacted their understandings of democratic political" culture, as borne out in settings from Virginia and South Carolina, Arkansas and Louisiana to California.[15] In San Jose, when it was learned that women had voted for representatives to a black state convention, the results were declared null and void, prompting some to term the gathering the "free speech crushing meeting."[16] For some, women's rights were regarded as integral to fundamental democratic rights.

Ideas about women's public authority helped to shape African American political culture in the postwar years. Women sometimes participated without controversy as members of deliberative bodies, and other times the matter of their rights was the focus of deliberations. Yet, during Reconstruction it appeared that black female activists had for the moment ceded political leadership to their male counterparts. Rarely were they to be found among the formal leadership in political circles. Still, ideas about women's rights as democratic rights had a remarkable impact, not in the arena of politics but in the church.

Churches rivaled political organizations as the most important sites of African American public culture. In his 1903 study of black churches, W. E. B. Du Bois reported that 2.7 million of the nation's 12 million African Americans were active church members—that is, nearly one out of every four to five people. Of these, 95 percent lived in the South, a statistic that dramatically illustrates the transfor-

mation of the black church from a northern- to a southern-based institution during Reconstruction.[17] Black Methodists numbered 1.2 million in 1903. One out
of every ten African Americans was a member of a black Methodist denomination at the close of the century, which represented a tenfold increase since the end
of the Civil War.[18]

Focusing on numbers alone would elide the broader significance of these religious institutions. While they were important sites of spiritual refuge, churches
were also highly public venues that sponsored civil rights campaigns, lyceums,
and widows' funds. They financed educational institutions, ranging from elementary through secondary schools to theological seminaries and normal training institutes. Their sanctuaries, often the largest local gathering place, hosted
political conventions, fraternal order celebrations, temperance rallies, and schools.
Ministers were often political leaders. For example, of the nearly two thousand
black male officeholders in the Reconstruction era, 276, or nearly 14 percent, were
ministers. Several of these men came to exercise tremendous authority within
black Methodism. AME bishop Richard Cain served as congressman from South
Carolina for two years, and Bishop Theophilus Steward was a Republican Party
activist in Georgia. James Hood, an AME Zion bishop, served as president of
the North Carolina Colored Convention of 1865 and later as the state's assistant
superintendent of education.[19] Consequently, during church conferences, spiritual matters and church business shared the agenda with party politics, civil
rights, temperance, and education. These were vibrant and well-attended occasions for deliberation, and their influence was enhanced by church-sponsored
publications of the proceedings. For many church leaders, the realms of politics
and religion were compatible if not interdependent, and their movement back
and forth between conferences and conventions met with little resistance in either organizational forum.

The interrelatedness of religion and politics shaped church leaders' views
about the rights of women. Some saw an important connection between the
movement for women's right to vote and the influence of spiritual forces. Laud-
ing the 1875 election of Methodist Episcopal Church (North) bishop Gilbert
Haven as president of Boston's American Female Suffrage Association, Benjamin Tanner, the editor of the *Christian Recorder,* remarked that the "good" movement appeared to be on its way toward seeking "success on the basis of a religion
that honors God and Christ."[20] Tanner endorsed women's suffrage in the positive terms often bestowed upon antislavery and temperance campaigns and attributed the movement's likelihood of success to its reliance upon religious, particularly Methodist, leadership. The women's rights activism of Haven, a white

Methodist, exemplifies how political interests were not only compatible with but perhaps even enhanced by leaders' engagement with the church. Such ideas paved the way for the incorporation of political tenets into church-based deliberations, especially shaping views about the rights of churchwomen.

Many of the era's key challenges were manifested in the workings of black Methodist churches. Older institutions had to grow and transform themselves. The AME and AME Zion churches reached out actively to freed men and women in the South and shifted priorities as they encountered new social conditions and challenges. New institutions were born. The CME church was created when the Methodist Episcopal Church (South) decided to exclude those former slaves who still worshipped in its sanctuaries. These institutions struggled for legitimacy in relation to their white counterparts, asking whether black churches would best distinguish themselves through conformity or through innovation. The tensions associated with the coming together of formerly enslaved and already free people were evident in debates about the desirability of an educated ministry, the role of lay leaders, and styles of worship. Alongside these issues emerged questions about women's authority in the religious realm.

Changes implemented in the postwar era altered the gendered character of church policy and practice in lasting ways. Prior to the 1870s, while black Methodist churchwomen had consistently performed essential fundraising and benevolent work, they were not formally recognized in church law. During the postwar years, however, these practices gave way as women gained substantial formal authority. By the early 1880s, women had secured the right to vote and hold office in decision-making bodies, serving as officers to home and foreign missionary societies, overseeing local church governance as stewardesses, and spreading the gospel as duly licensed preachers. In the realm of ideas, these innovations arose from and promoted shifting views about women's rights in the church, and in practice they transformed women's relationships to the rituals, deliberations, and administration of religious bodies. Female authority and autonomy became visible dimensions of the religious realm.

The earliest of these innovations were changes in church law. Throughout the 1870s, the AME and the AME Zion churches amended their governing texts, *The Doctrines and Discipline,* granting women "the same rights and privileges as male members."[21] The issue first came before the AME general conference in 1872, when Rev. Thomas W. Henderson, a member of the Missouri conference, proposed that the law be amended such that the "the word 'male' wherever it occurs as a qualification of electors be struck from the Discipline."[22] A veteran of Republican Party politics in Kansas, Henderson was educated at Oberlin College during the Civil War years. There, in one of the nation's few coeducational and interracial colleges, he likely encountered debates about the rights of women generated by alumnae including Lucy Stone, the women's rights and antislavery activist, and Antoinette Brown, the first women to be ordained a minister in the United States.[23] Henderson's proposal was seconded in spirit by a subsequent motion that all church members over age twenty-one, regardless of sex, be permitted to vote for local trustees. Four years later, gender qualifications were struck from all provisions related to Sunday School personnel.[24] In the AME Zion church, similar revisions were taken up in 1876 when the general conference voted to "strike out the word male in the *Discipline*."[25] Apparently this directive was not fully complied with, and in 1880 a group of Boston churchwomen petitioned "to strike out the words 'man' and 'men' in the *Discipline*" and specified those sections of church law that had not been so amended.[26]

Churchwomen's gaining the right to vote through changes in the denominations' governing documents drew little attention at the time. There was no debate; indeed, there was no opposition. The nature of the innovation, particularly the striking of the words *male* and *man*, echo the Fifteenth Amendment debates during which women's rights advocates called for a gender-neutral amendment that would guarantee the voting rights of all citizens. The commentary on the 1880 AME Zion petition supports this view. The Boston-based petitioners had offered a rationale for their proposed amendments, "giving women the same rights in the church as men." This was an ambitious objective that extended well beyond the right to vote for trustees or serve as Sunday School superintendent, and the significance of these changes in religious and secular law would not have been lost on their contemporaries active in secular politics. For example, Mary Ann Shadd Cary, who was active in the National Women's Suffrage Association, was not permitted to graduate from the Howard University Law School because women were prohibited from admission to the bar by the District of Columbia. Cary charged sex discrimination but ultimately withdrew from her studies. A short time later, Cary's fellow suffragist, Charlotte E. Ray completed her law studies at Howard and was duly graduated and recommended to the bar as qualified. Ray benefited from an intervening change in the District of Columbia Code that struck the word *male* as a qualification for admission.[27] Changes in law had the potential to enhance women's autonomy and authority in public life.

For those who advocated that church law be rendered gender neutral and envisioned women rising to positions previously held only by men, the AME's creation of the office of stewardess must have engendered an ambivalent reaction at best. In 1872, during the same general conference meeting that granted women the right to vote for trustees, AME church leaders authorized local congregations to designate between three and nine women to sit as a board of stewardesses.[28] In 1876, the AME Zion church followed suit, although in that denomination the stewardesses were to be appointed by the quarterly, or regional conference.[29] In the CME church, when the office was first proposed in 1882, the suggestion "produced laughter throughout the General Conference" that was punctuated by the tabling of the matter.[30] Three general conferences deliberated the issue over the course of eight years before finally approving the office.[31]

Ambivalence about female religious authority was woven into the resolutions that authorized the appointment of stewardesses. While the title stewardess might suggest that this office was equivalent to the long-standing office of steward, the authority extended to women was hardly equal to that of the men. Stewards were, by church law, aids to local ministers, while stewardesses were assigned to work "in assisting the preacher's steward in providing the necessary comfort for the minister."[32] They were envisioned as assistants to the minister's assistants, or a sort of ladies auxiliary to the stewards.[33] In some cases, women were held accountable to the stewards, who were empowered to "confirm or reject the nomination of the Stewardesses; and hold them responsible for a faithful performance of their duty."[34] This innovation hardly led to women's full equality within the church. Still, the establishment of the office gave formal standing to work women had long performed in their local congregations. It enhanced their visibility, increased their authority, and for some raised questions about where the changes in women's roles might end.

Just a few years after the establishment of the office, the AME's *Christian Recorder* published a commentary asking if such offices would ultimately lead to a political end—woman suffrage—or, more likely, to women "taking hold" and "speaking" in religious gatherings.[35] For the time being, carefully crafted by-laws ensured that the stewardess had a subordinate status but some men feared the possible consequences of the new office. Others welcomed women's service. When attempting to appoint a board of stewardesses in a local congregation, the Rev. Henry McNeal Turner saw in practice the ambivalence expressed in the wording of the new law and in the commentary that surrounded it. The stewards in his congregation refused to approve his female nominees until he threatened them with removal. Stymied by the men, Turner had nothing but praise for the women. They were "worth more than all the male officers put together," he concluded.[36] This remark hinted at the potential of this innovation: although men might retain authority to approve the selection of stewardesses, after they were appointed women might prove to be effective, even superior, leaders.

The ambivalence reflected in defining the position of stewardess was also manifested through the terms under which female missionary societies were chartered. The AME church created the Women's Parent Mite Missionary Society in 1874.[37] The AME Zion church followed, founding the Ladies' Home and Foreign Missionary Society in 1880.[38] The CME church authorized its Women's Missionary Society in 1890.[39] Like stewardesses, female missionary society leaders remained subject to male oversight. In some cases this meant that members were to be elected from among those women perceived to be most loyal to the male leadership, the "wives and daughters of our bishops and elders, and other influential ladies of our churches." Sometimes women were deprived of a final say over missionary affairs. Governing boards comprised of male ministers oversaw women's work, or by-laws required the election of men to a society's executive board.[40]

The founding of women's missionary societies formally recognized work women had long performed but extended their control over fundraising and outreach work. This addition to the church's organizational structure was intended to be a tribute to women's church work, and it offered them an unprecedented opportunity to exercise leadership and independence in missionary endeavors. As with other changes in women's standing, female-headed missionary societies were tinged with political connotations, leading one AME commentator to term such societies the " 'woman movement' of our church."[41] The terms under which missionary societies were constituted reflected ambivalence about the claims women were making on church authority. It was true that women could exercise unprecedented leadership and visibility. For the first time they served as officers, spoke from the podium, and presided over the proceedings at church conferences. They conducted fundraising and relief work pursuant to a constitution and by-laws rather than at the discretion of male leaders. Yet, women's missionary societies were hardly unfettered spaces for the expression of women's ambitions and authority; the very constitutions and by-laws that guaranteed their authority also ensured that their work would be subject to male supervision.

Changes in law and structure do not inevitably lead to changes in practice. As was the case when Rev. Turner sought to appoint his first stewardess board, it was at those moments when churchwomen sought to inhabit their new positions of authority that the ambivalences hinted at in the by-laws came to the surface. When women began to test the possibilities for their public authority by voting, holding office, and taking part in deliberative bodies, they met with what had likely been long-standing if muted opposition. What had changed were the tools that women had at their disposal as they stood their ground. Changes in law recognized the *rights* of churchwomen, and while they did not yet possess "the same rights in the church as men," churchwomen used the new laws to insert them-selves into the deliberations of decision-making bodies and to withstand assaults on their authority.

By the beginning of the 1880s, women began to appear regularly as active members of church conferences at all levels. They were no longer merely thanked for serving a meal or raising funds, although these sorts of tributes to women's work continued. Instead, churchwomen were reported as conference delegates and even officeholders. For example, Amanda Beatty served as a secretary of the AME Zion West Tennessee and Mississippi conference in 1884.[42] Beatty's service in her local conference led to her election as a "fraternal delegate" to the regional meeting held in Memphis the following year. Although the conference minutes report that a male ally, Brother W. L. Carr, nominated Beatty to her new post, among those present during her election were Nannie Riddick, who had earlier in the year been elected conference clerk, and the officers of the Ladies' Home and Foreign Missionary Society.[43] Beatty's appointments went through without remark, as part of her conference's regular business.

Some appointments of women to conventions and administrative committees were marked by open controversy. During the July 1885 meeting of the AME Zion Church Baltimore District Conference, presiding elder William Howard Day in-cluded a woman, thirty-eight-year-old Selena Bungay, a resident of Washington, D.C., on the committee that would determine the presiding elder's salary. A con-test ensued as Bungay's opponents insisted that, as a Sabbath school delegate, she should be "rejected from being appointed on any business of the conference." Day defended his choice and Bungay's right to sit on the committee, reasoning that his action was fully in accordance with church law. His opponents main-tained their objections. When Day finally prevailed, it was by way of a somewhat awkward-sounding resolution that read, "We bow with humble submission to the decision of the Presiding Elder and beg him to appoint sister Selena Bungay."[44] This statement expressed a formal concession to the church hierarchy rather than an acceptance of the principle of women's participation in decision-making bod-ies. Earlier changes to church law ensured that duly appointed female officers could resist such challenges. The women's rights significance of a seemingly small victory was not lost on a man like Day, a veteran champion of women's rights struggles since his years as a student at Oberlin College.

Most women who served as conference officers did so in their capacities as missionary society leaders. As early as 1880, officers of the AME's Mite Mission-ary Society appeared as conference officers and delivered reports on their work.[45]

Women's societies were credited from the outset with providing indispensable support for missionary endeavors. At the same 1880 general conference, the Women's Parent Mite Missionary Society was praised for single-handedly supporting the AME's Haitian station.[46] But missionary society leaders soon found themselves returning to the very conferences that had authorized them to plead for ministerial support at the state and local levels. The women reported meeting with deeply held indifference, if not outright hostility, from ministers. Their assessment was affirmed by some male church leaders, such as AME Zion bishop Singleton Jones, who told his general conference that female missionary societies "were greatly hindered last year in consequence of a want of cooperation on the part of the brethren . . . that is, to come down to plain English, they did not encourage their sisters in their praiseworthy effort."[47] The power of women as conference officers was soon felt as they used their access to the podium to make a case for the value of their autonomous missionary work.

Some women adopted a deferential posture. Catherine Thompson, treasurer of the AME Zion Ladies Home and Foreign Missionary Society, beseeched the ministers: "Help us! Help us! dear brethren, by your cooperation, and we will try, under God, to do what we can to make the missionary work of our church a grand success."[48] Others, like AME Zion vice president Jane Hamer, offered reassurances to those who might misunderstand the women's assertion of autonomy as somehow disloyal to the church. "I am for Zion," she pledged.[49] Still others laid the blame for the limited success of missionary work at the feet of uncooperative male ministers. In the AME church, Mrs. S. C. Watson of the New Jersey conference offered her own pointed analysis of the situation: "I do not blame the ladies for this. The fault is with the ministers. They do not like to have the society organized in their charges . . . I hope brethren you will get out of the ladies' way and let them work."[50] To solve the problem, Watson asked the bishops to "make it binding on every minister to be compelled to see to it that this society is organized in this charge."[51] Still other women, like AME Zion's Eliza Gardner, were not satisfied to depend upon men's cooperation or noncooperation for the fate of their missionary societies.

Gardner was discouraged when she stepped to the podium at her church's 1884 general conference to champion women's missionary work. Earlier in the session, she had witnessed an unsuccessful but concerted effort to limit the impact of the church's gender-neutral law and constrain the rights of women. Two ministerial delegates, A. L. Scott and S. Deary, put forth a proposal that read: "Resolved, That females have all the rights and immunities of males, except the rights of orders and of the pastorate. They may be licensed as evangelists."[52] Gardner's response was neither deferential nor reassuring: "I do not think I felt quite so Christian-like as my dear sisters. I come from old Massachusetts, where we have declared that all, not only men, but women, too, are created free and equal, with certain inalienable rights which men are bound to respect." Gardner made explicit the political underpinnings of women's quest for religious authority. The rights of churchwomen were bound up with equality and freedom, as specified in the Revolutionary-era constitution of the Commonwealth of Massachusetts and as an extension of the "inalienable rights" provided for in the Declaration of Independence. In a twist on Justice Taney's notorious pronouncement in *Dred Scott v. Sanford,* she claimed for churchwomen rights that "men *were* bound to respect."[53]

Gardner situated the women's efforts in the context of church history, explaining that the struggle for women's rights had been born alongside "other good movements" dear to black Methodists, including "temperance reform and the anti-slavery cause." Like Benjamin Tanner, she cast churchwomen's contemporary struggles as part and parcel of the "good" cause of women's rights. She concluded by proposing a bargain that allied the debates unfolding in the religious realm with secular issues of gender and power. The church's standing in broader political circles, she explained, was at risk: "If I would go back to Boston and tell the people that some of the members of this conference were against the women, it might have a tendency to prejudice our interests in that city with those upon whom we can rely for assistance." Gardner suggested an exchange; women would continue to ensure the good standing of the church, but only if they received the support and respect of male leaders. "If you will try to do by us the best you can . . . you will strengthen our efforts and make us a power; but if you commence to talk about the superiority of men, if you persist in telling us that after the fall of man we were put under your feet and that we are intended to be subject to your will, we cannot help you in New England one bit."[54] By the mid-1880s, while churchwomen like Gardner continued to hold themselves out as doers of good works, they also understood their struggles to be part of black women's broader claims for public power and authority. The tenor of the woman question debate was shifting, with conciliation and ambivalence being replaced by confrontation and acrimony.

Gardner's threat was hardly idle. Black Methodist leaders knew well the case of the itinerant preacher Amanda Berry Smith, who had in the mid-1870s left the AME church to work with white Christians. Smith was criticized for depriving black Americans, "who need it most," of her skills and of her tremendous capacity to raise funds for AME missionary endeavors.[55] Gardner and other black women in New England were already beginning to organize in the secular realm, coming together in what by the mid-1890s emerged as the black women's club movement. Gardner would lead hundreds of female church activists into a secular organization as an officer to the inaugural meeting of the National Conference of Colored Women in 1895, offering opening and closing prayers as that group's chaplain.[56] Black churchwomen were beginning to imagine alternative sites for their public aspirations, and they were using the confidence and the collective sensibilities that came from their secular activities to elevate their standing as religious leaders.

Engendering Jim Crow

The increasing tensions within Methodist churches paralleled those emerging within African American public culture more generally. By the 1890s, American race relations had seriously deteriorated, reaching a state of affairs Rayford Logan retrospectively characterized as the "nadir."[57] The sense of political empowerment that black Americans had enjoyed during the 1870s and sustained through the 1880s had turned into disillusionment. In 1890 Mississippi adopted a disfranchisement plan that served as a model for the rest of the South. Literacy tests, poll taxes, and other state election laws, along with social and psychological oppression, economic sanctions, and actual and threatened violence pushed black Americans out of the nation's political life.

Black men lost the ballot and many other rights that the constitution and federal civil rights laws theoretically protected: the right to hold public office, to sit on juries, and to allocate tax dollars for schools and other social services. Southern states imposed discriminatory laws that routinized the separate and inferior status of African Americans. Violence and intimidation intensified, and between 1884 and 1900, more than 2,500 lynchings of African Americans were recorded. Segregation quickly circumscribed every part of life: employment, housing, places of amusement, public transportation, schools, hospitals, and cemeteries. In the face of these restrictions, black communities turned increasingly inward. African Americans could no longer even hope for the protection of the federal government. In 1883 the Supreme Court declared unconstitutional the federal Civil Rights Act of 1875, a law prohibiting racial discrimination in places of public accommodation, and in 1896 the court sanctioned the "separate but equal" doctrine in *Plessy v. Ferguson*. In this climate, independent African American churches endured as settings for discussion and debate, as promoters of education and economic cooperation, and as arenas for the development and assertion of leadership.[58]

Black churchwomen were among the first to articulate the relationship between women's activism and the problems generated by broader social forces. In an essay entitled "A Woman's View on Current Topics," AME Zion church member May M. Brown considered what she termed the "race problem" and queried, "what will the Negro of the United States do to gain just and merited recognition?" Brown's characterization of this challenge aptly characterized the conflicts at the heart of the problem. "Affairs are now reaching a climax. The whites are struggling to retain the supremacy. The Negroes are struggling for right and justice." Although Brown formulated the problem in terms of the poor state of race relations, she suggested that the solution would be found, in part, through women's activism. "The women cannot, must not, dare not be idle," she proclaimed. Brown delivered an ambitious charge to her "own women," her sisters in the church. They must be prepared to "read, to study, to keep . . . abreast with the thoughts of the day . . . take part in the social, religious, philanthropic and intellectual subjects which have never been found so exacting or so diffuse as now."[59] Writing in 1891, Brown still expressed optimism, seeing the sensibilities of what many termed the "New Woman" as a weapon in the battle against the "race problem." However, by the decade's end this kind of optimism was severely tried, and hopes for a successful defense of civil rights were tempered by a realistic assessment of the obstacles African Americans faced. As black communities looked to churches as arenas where some autonomy could be exercised, tensions between women and men over gendered relations of power were exacerbated. As the imposition of Jim Crow took its toll upon black men's standing within public culture, as their power and authority grew decidedly constrained, it became increasingly difficult for black women to imagine their lives as unfettered by gendered boundaries. Churchwomen, in particular, tested the limits of their expanding authority.

Women's roles as decision makers, delegates, and officers were familiar dimensions of post-Reconstruction black Methodist life, even though the expansion of women's authority was marked by controversy. By the late nineteenth century, women's missionary societies had become such an accepted feature of church governance that some of the most pointed controversies erupted between competing groups of women. In the AME church, women affiliated with the denomination's southern conferences organized an alternative society, the Ladies' Home and Foreign Missionary Society, in a challenge to the supremacy of the older, northern-dominated Women's Parent Mite Mission Society.[60]

The crucial issue of female ordination remained outstanding, and during the late 1880s and 1890s it surfaced as perhaps the most challenging woman question of the era. The question of women's ordination came to the floor of the AME general conference when the ordination of Sarah Ann Hughes of the North Carolina annual conference was revoked by the denomination's supreme body. Hughes began her career as a freelance evangelist in the early 1880s and was licensed to preach in 1882.[61] While she held a number of pastorships throughout the region, Hughes's aspirations to the ordained ministry were frustrated until 1885 when Bishop Henry McNeal Turner arrived to oversee the North Carolina conference.[62] Turner was an outspoken supporter of female preachers, and at the November 1885 session he ordained Hughes to the ministry as a deacon. Dissenting voices were raised almost immediately, and by the 1887 session an opponent of women's ordination, Bishop Jabez Campbell, replaced Turner. Campbell ruled Hughes's ordination contrary to church law. Her name was summarily stricken from the list of deacons.[63]

The bishops squared off over the issue in the pages of the quarterly *A.M.E. Church Review* in 1886.[64] Bishop Campbell argued that the Bible did not sanction the ordination of women. He grounded his case in the concept of separate spheres for men and women: "Man cannot do woman's work and fill her place under the divine economy, and women cannot do man's work and fill his place under the same divine economy . . . Women always have been and are now recognized as helpers . . . for that is the will of the Lord."[65] Bishop John Mifflin Brown, Turner's mentor, argued in support of women's ordination while also making a case for their right to vote, a discussion that underscored how religious and political ideas were related. Brown squarely placed the dispute in terms of the woman question and pressed the analogy between the issues confronting women and those confronting African Americans generally. "Two questions have disturbed the public mind for some time. These are 1. What shall be done with the Negro? 2. What shall be done with the women?" While never directly addressing Hughes's case, Brown pointed to women whom he deemed to be among the leading thinkers of the day. In addition to Lucy Stone Blackwell and Olympia Brown, he named several AME churchwomen, including Jarena Lee, Martha Low, and Emily Rodney Williams, all of whom he thought had been excellent "pastors." Brown argued that women needed a voice in politics and urged that their status in society be clearly defined so they could take part in public culture as voters, office holders, and ministers.[66]

Presiding at the following year's general conference was Bishop Daniel Payne who, over his long career as a leader of the AME church, had steadfastly held that women's roles should be confined generally to the domestic sphere.[67] The 1888 conference affirmed Bishop Campbell's action and formally prohibited women's ordination, amending *The Doctrines and Discipline* to expressly direct that bishops "shall not ordain any woman to the order of Deacon or Elder in the A.M.E. Church."[68]

Nearly a decade later, the matter of women's ordination arose in the AME Zion Church. Here, too, the arguments linked the debate within the church to the contemporary contest over the standing of women in public life. The controversy began in the spring of 1898, when Bishop Charles Pettey ordained Deacon Mary Small to the station of elder. Small now stood formally shoulder to shoulder with all of the church's male leaders, save the bishops. She was empowered to administer church ritual and oversee her own congregation, which would enable her to exercise authority over male leaders, including deacons, preachers, trustees, and stewards. Most church members learned of this development through an item in the church's weekly newspaper, the *Star of Zion*. The initial notice sounds almost naïve, given the furious debates it unleashed. "After a spirited discussion, Mrs. Mary J. Small, wife of Bishop J. B. Small, was, by a vote of 34 to 13, elected and ordained an elder . . . Mrs. Small has the same rights now as the ministers. The way is open now for her to pastor a church and be a presiding elder and bishop. She is the first woman to be ordained an elder. We have a few more female preachers who are deacons who will doubtless follow Mrs. Small."[69]

It is unlikely that Pettey anticipated the furor that would erupt when he ordained Small. Dissent had been expressed at the annual conference, but few efforts to expand women's authority had gone wholly unremarked. To his surprise, and to the surprise of many of Small's supporters, in 1898 polite disagreement would not suffice. During the next six months, the denomination was consumed with the question of women's ordination. Nearly 60 percent of the pages in the church's weekly newspaper were devoted to this issue, with bishops, ministers, and lay people, male and female, weighing in. A debate ensued over the shape of church policy, and long-standing questions about the relationship of women to the church and to public culture were revisited.

The changes of the preceding decades ensured that women were situated as influential members of AME Zion, and when the debate over women's ordination erupted, the denomination's female members were among the first to jump into the fray. Seemingly without hesitation or fear of reprisal, churchwomen took on their male counterparts, arguing in favor of Small's elevation to the ministry. While they continued to perform the full range of church-related work, including fundraising and missionary endeavors, churchwomen were vocal contributors to discussions of church policy and issues of general interest. They were redefining their relationship to the church and, in doing so, throwing over those ideas that had limited their place. Evalina Badham asked rhetorically: "Could I place [women] in one prescribed circle and say stay thou here, step not forward nor backward; swerve neither to the right nor left?" Her answer was, "No, I could not." In the pages of the *AME Zion Quarterly Review,* Badham asserted that a woman's role was any she took up under the influence of the "Holy Spirit." Her list was long; Badham claimed for women authority as class leaders, missionaries, Sabbath schoolteachers, fundraisers, trustees, stewardesses, deaconesses, and members of church societies.[70] Women also carved out expanded territory in the realm of ideas. Sarah Pettey, whose husband Charles had ordained Mary Small, through her "Woman's Column," made clear the extent to which she deemed her sphere to include business, higher education, medicine, and even international affairs, commenting on matters that included Cuban independence.[71] As churchwomen projected themselves as entitled to power and authority within AME Zion, they set the tone for their forceful contributions to the 1898 debate over women's ordination. Such ambitions paralleled those being articulated by women outside of religious circles. The 1890s were the "woman's era" for black women, poet and activist Frances Ellen Watkins Harper first declared in 1893; it was a period in which changing laws and attitudes were removing barriers to women's property rights, education, and the suffrage, with African American women working together on a national scale to gain unprecedented visibility, authority, independence, and influence within public culture generally.

The ordination debate aired competing views. Church members exchanged ideas about women's relationship to the church and to public culture generally, and they touched upon issues ranging from women's rights, the equality of the sexes, and the nature of women's sphere to the worth of fundraising work. Some revealed their enduring commitment to ideals of women's equality, and they were joined in this general sentiment by the newest generation of young women; others argued for curtailing women's roles within the church.

Women's ordination, argued the Rev. J. Harvey Anderson, was an action "based upon the 'equality of the sexes.'" Anderson, a Civil War veteran, argued that church law was grounded in a principle that imposed "no limit nor restriction . . . upon female membership . . . 'she' being entitled to the same immunities as the 'he,' from start to finish."[72] To the extent that this position was considered anomalous among Methodist sects generally, the Rev. J. J. Adams explained that it was nonetheless grounded in political precedents. Adams maintained that when the church law was made gender neutral, women had been given "equal rights in the 'political economy' of the church" because "taxation without representation was declared wrong from the foundation of our free American government and is nonetheless true in the church as well as state."[73]

Others argued that women's ordination was not only proper as an abstract principle but also followed from women's long-standing contributions to the church and to public culture generally. Women had "earned" the right to be ordained. Boston's Eliza Gardner lamented the tenor of the debate: "I have read with some pain some of the articles [against women's ordination] that have been sent to the *Star* vilifying woman." She pointed out the irony that at the very moment in which some church members would deny women the right of ordination, "a strong appeal was made to the women of the church to come to the rescue of some of its departments."[74] Women demanded the consideration of the church's male leadership. An anonymous woman wrote: "We form a majority of the membership; we furnish a large part of the spiritual life, and we collect most of the money of the church. We believe that this entitles us to share in the government of the Church; and whether the Church law provides for it or prohibits it, cuts no figure with us. We shall continue to claim our rights."[75]

Church members argued that, even in light of women's significant contributions, female ministers must be qualified on the merits; they must have served in the lower ranks and passed the requisite examinations, just the same as male aspirants to the ministry. Beyond this, women's ordination was linked to ideas about women's rights that had long undergirded changes in women's religious standing. In the difficult climate of the late 1890s, even the Rev. R. A. Morrisey, an outspoken advocate of women's ordination, felt the need to qualify his position. He explained that there would never be "wholesale and indiscriminate" ordination of women and that only those with "special qualification and fitness . . . should be admitted to the ministry."[76] Clara Betties argued that it was Mary Small's "genuine calling" that rendered her fit to serve as a minister.[77] B. F. Grant, a layman who had voted in favor of Small's ordination, explained her qualifications in terms of church law: "After we ordained her a deacon in York, and she passed a creditable examination the other week in Baltimore, she had a right to receive orders . . . She prepared herself . . . and of course she won her position by merit—no favor in it."[78]

The opposition was equally resourceful and at least as vocal, resurrecting arguments that supported a constrained standing for churchwomen which came close to relegating them to the position of silent helpmeets. The Rev. S. A. Chambers opposed women's ordination with a sweeping assertion that "woman is not man's equal, and the claim is simply ridiculous."[79] An editorial in the *Star of Zion* considered the concept of qualifications quite differently, arguing that a woman was "not physically able to pastor a church. She is too timid and fearful to get up at one or two o'clock in the night, unless some man is with her, and go across the city to see the sick or pray with some one ready to die . . . It would be too hot and dusty in the summer and too cold and slushy in the winter for her to walk ten, fifteen and twenty miles on a circuit in the country to try to preach the gospel."[80] Others, like Reverend Chambers, sounded the alarm and rallied opposition by claiming that "the next thing it will be women pastors, presiding elders and Bishops, then we shall be 'into it' up to our necks."[81] He and others feared that, once granted access to the ministry, religious women would upend the church's gendered order. In an editorial reprinted in the *Star of Zion*, C. H. J. Taylor, who was personally acquainted with Mary Small, argued that ordination took women beyond the limits of their place within the church and within society: "There is plenty of work for good women like Mrs. Small to do in this world, without unsexing them by making them elders . . . There are mannish women who, by this example, will come forward and do God's church any amount of damage. A woman in a river baptizing men; a woman in the army acting as chaplain; a woman celebrating marriage and a woman in the pulpit divesting herself of wig and teeth, when under religious excitement, are sights that even angels would be shocked to see, much less men."[82] Taylor's remarks anticipated concerns about the emergence of black female Pentecostal preachers of the 1940s, especially to anxieties expressed about black women's bodies.[83] Yet, Taylor's concern about the "unsexing" of women such as Mary Small, was likely shared by Small and numerous other black female activists of the period, although clearly they too had a different view of how female ministers might be read by their peers. Indeed, it was the circulation of ideas that denigrated black women's sexuality which had led women like Gardner to establish the 1890s black women's club movement and adopt "respectability" as a strategy by which to resist white supremacy.[84]

Taylor's remarks suggest the ongoing interrelatedness of the ideas circulating between the realms of religion and politics. Despite his familiarity with the issues and his clear engagement with the controversy unfolding within the AME Zion church, his reputation was not that of a religious activist. By the late 1890s Taylor, who had been born a slave in Alabama, was well known in African American public culture as a lawyer, journalist, and politician. In the wake of Reconstruction's collapse, Taylor generated controversy as he, in a scheme to establish African American political independence, broke ranks with Republicans and became a Democratic Party activist. He achieved some personal success, for example, being appointed in 1887 by Grover Cleveland as U.S. minister to Liberia. Yet, by 1898, Taylor's strategy had crumbled as white supremacy became the Democrat's defining tenet.[85] Thus, even men like Taylor turned to the church as a critical site of African American resistance to the degradations of Jim Crow and to an understanding of how gender might shape strategies of resistance. "If God had intended woman to do the work of a man along all lines, he would have made her a man and not a woman," Taylor remarked, a broad enough point of view that suggests how ideas reflecting a long-standing culture of resistance may have operated to oppose women's suffrage just as they did the ordination of women to the ministry.[86]

Although the AME Zion debate reflected long-standing permutations of the woman question, within and outside the church, one aspect of the ordination controversy was new, reflecting tensions among male church leaders that were generated by the collapse of Reconstruction and the rise of the Jim Crow order of the 1890s. The debate became the terrain upon which men on both sides of the question manifested their differences with one another. Through the deployment of metaphors of combat and violence, critiques of men's capacities as ministers, challenges to the church's hierarchical structure, and shows of intellectual prowess, AME Zion's male leaders vied for what little public authority had been left to them. What began as the woman question during the optimistic climate of Reconstruction became, with the degradations of Jim Crow, the man question.

The pervasive use of metaphors of combat and violence was the first hint that church men had more at stake in the debate than the standing of women. An early *Star of Zion* editorial recast the controversy in terms suggestive of a physical confrontation, speculating that "a great war is expected."[87] Bishop John Small, husband of the new elder, interjected the notion of a physical challenge: "A man who strikes a woman is a coward, and I think I will commit no sin if I strike a coward for striking my wife."[88] The Rev. S. A. Chambers, a vocal opponent of women's ordination, dramatically wrote that one of his opponents "laid off his coat, rolled up his sleeves, threw aside his silk beaver, thrust his fingers through his hair, foaming at the mouth and came dashing at us with his eyes flashing fire, breathing out epithets peculiar only to himself, shouting, as he advanced, 'Shoo! Shoo! Begone! Begone!' trying to scare us off the warpath, but we have not given back one inch, and never intend to as long as there is the least scent of powder smoke in the air." Chambers also took up the war metaphor. "We have waged war against ordaining women to Holy Orders in the absence of Biblical authority and shall cease firing only long enough to wipe out our gun and sink something or be sunk. The brother fired at us with a 2-inch gun and dodged around the corner and peeped to see what effect it would have, but he missed his mark and his target [that is, Chambers himself] stands as before."[89] In anticipation of a reply, Chambers wrote, "We pause for a heavier shot."[90]

The debate devolved quickly into an opportunity to vent criticism of male ministers. One *Star of Zion* editorial complained that there was already "too much useless ordained male timber lying around in all of our conferences," such that female ministers were unnecessary.[91] Clara Betties admonished the men to withdraw their objections because churchwomen like Mrs. Small were already more hardworking than male ministers: "She is doing what you won't do. I will be glad when the time comes that those men will find something to do and let Rev. Mrs. Small alone."[92] Mrs. Rev. W. L. Moore criticized the opponents of women's ordination, concluding that they did not see "through the eyes of faith, but look at Sister Small with eyes of jealousy." The move to ordain female ministers was due, in part, to inept male leadership: "My dear brother, do not worry any more about the sisters, but help see after Zion's property more than you do, then we will not have to ordain women."[93] Small's supporters were not spared ridicule, and the men who had endorsed the adoption of gender-neutral church law were chided: "kicking ministers, you made the law. Now take your own medicine."[94]

These debates offered an occasion for challenging the church hierarchy—in particular, the relationships between bishops, elders, and deacons—and the deference paid to highly placed leaders such as the bishops by lesser ministers and lay people. Some, like the Rev. J. Harvey Anderson, defended the ordination of Mrs. Small as a reasonable exercise of a bishop's authority: "In ordaining females, [they] have in no way transcended their authority nor antagonized the polity of the A.M.E. Zion Church." Critics of the bishopric would be ostracized and "vanish in queer glances at the General Conference," he warned.[95] Bishop Hood himself sought to silence his critics with words that revealed the profound extent to which he demanded deference: "I should like to know when the General Conference authorized any one to tell the Bishops how to discharge the duties of their office. The suggestion is not only presumptuous, but it also lacks wisdom . . . I think it likely that a bishop would follow his own judgment regardless of any advice from those who are not authorized to advise him."[96] Others took up this invitation to counter the bishops' expectations. Rev. J. H. McMullen claimed the right to oppose the bishops, insisting that "our ministers don't feel that they must act without consulting their own minds simply because they are discussing a question in which a bishop's wife [Mary Small] is involved."[97] In the majority, however, were ministers like Rev. F. M. Jacobs, who argued that "there is an amount of respect due a Bishop in advance of a clergyman in the lower sea . . . the ministry and many of the young men have either lost their respect or have never received proper training."[98] In Jacobs's view, young men were using the occasion of the women's ordination debate to test the limits of the bishops' authority.

This debate furnished an opportunity for AME Zion men to demonstrate their intellectual capacities for interpreting church law, as well as their comprehensive knowledge of Zion's history. B. F. Grant explained that, while he was generally opposed to women's ordination, his reading of church law had obligated him to support it. "As a lay delegate, I voted for her ordination, not so much for my belief in the ordination of women but because I did not see anything against it. She [Mrs. Small] only asked for what [the general conference, as the denomination's law-making body] said she could have if she was competent," he reasoned.[99] Rev. F. M. Jacobs also felt legally bound to support women's ordination, and he revealed his intimate knowledge of Zion's history: "I was opposed to the action at that time [in the 1870s when the law was made gender neutral], as I am opposed to it now, but since it is a woman's right to aspire to these high positions in the church under the law as it now exists . . . I take the ground and position as a defender of her rights only on account of the gap in the law."[100]

The issue of biblical interpretation became one of the bitterest aspects of the debate. Bishops, ministers, and laymen engaged in lengthy exchanges over the relevance and proper interpretation of numerous biblical passages. Demonstrating their thorough knowledge of the scriptures, those on both sides presented an exhaustive range of examples chosen to convey women's proper standing in religious life. They competed to see who could demonstrate superior intellect and education through facility with languages—English, Greek, and Latin—in the reading of biblical texts. These were far more than polite academic disagreements about women's standing in the church or the meanings of biblical texts: the very standing and authority of male church leaders was being contested through this debate.

By the close of 1898 the debate within the AME Zion church had subsided, after many factors conspired to quell it. Church activists were concerned that the debate had become so rancorous, bitter, and volatile that the church itself could not withstand the divisions. Zionites admonished one another to let the matter rest until the next general conference, scheduled for 1900, during which, they were assured, rationality would prevail. But the decisive factor in ending the debate was the united front presented by the bishopric. While they had not, as a body, ruled directly on the propriety of women's ordination, informal polls and their related pronouncements suggested that the bishops were of one mind in their support for the ordination of women.[101] In a seeming effort to keep their denomination committed to the exercise of women's authority, the bishops had closed ranks in a powerful demonstration of Methodism's hierarchical mode of governance.

Bishop Cicero Harris explicitly invoked what he held out as the principles of the prewar decades, calling upon church history and tradition as he defended the ordination of women. Women's rights were, at the close of the century, as they had been since the Civil War—on par with the principles of antislavery and civil rights. Harris urged, "For a hundred years we have been pleading for and demanding the equal rights of citizens, without regard to color. Is it any wonder that we recognize the fact that the same arguments which, as to the equality of rights [also] abolish the sex line; and that as a rule where a white man was an abolitionist he was per consequence an advocate of women suffrage? Fred Douglass was consistently an ardent advocate of both Negro and of woman suffrage. These lines are from his pen: Right is of no sex, Truth is of no color, God is our common Father, And all mankind are brothers. To me these words are not only epigrammatic, but immortal."[102]

Harris's rhetoric powerfully expressed one of the most salient dimensions of the debates among black Methodists about the woman question during the preceding two decades: the shared principle that ideas about women's rights in the political realm should also guide the definition of their standing in the religious sphere. For activist churchwomen, Harris aptly recast church history to bring it into alignment with their vision of women's rights to autonomy and authority that transcended institutional boundaries and encompassed all of African American public culture.

Manning Foreign Missions

Harris's rhetoric, which proclaimed these foundational principles as universally accepted among African American Methodists in particular and black Christians in general, failed to acknowledge the dissension that the ordination of a qualified woman evoked. Moreover, it elided what was emerging as an equally contentious issue within his denomination—churchwomen were seeking exclusive control over their missionary societies.

By the 1890s, the meaning of missionary work was being transformed. In the immediate postwar decades women had shouldered much of black Methodist missionary work, principally by raising funds and ministering to former slaves in the southern states while supporting a modest number of foreign missionaries in such places as Liberia and Haiti. However, the turn of the twentieth century was the age of U.S. imperialism, and black Methodist leaders seized upon this expanding field, aiming to extend their influence to the world's people of color. This was a profoundly masculine reenvisioning of the missionary project that sought to rescue African American manhood from the degradations of a domestic Jim Crow order. As the Civil War had been a proving ground for an earlier generation of men, U.S. imperialism furnished an opportunity for black religious leaders to reestablish themselves as men and as citizens.[103]

Churchwomen had an alternative vision in which they would take exclusive control over the missionary societies within which they had long labored. For them, missionary societies were sites for the expression of an idealized womanhood and represented the culmination of a four-decade-long struggle for the rights of women within the church. If their claims were now familiar to church leaders, the faces of the women at the fore of this struggle were new. Female activists of the immediate postwar generation shared the podium with their daughters who had come of age under the guidance of female voters, officers, delegates, and preachers.

First during AME Zion's centennial celebration in 1896 and again at the general conference of 1900, female church leaders took every advantage of their standing as officers to press for control of missionary societies. Mrs. Maggie Hood-Banks, daughter of Bishop James Hood, called attention to women's work: "The great missionary cause of our Church has been in the hands of the women ever since it has been a department of the Church. They have toiled early and late, sacrificing time and money, to build up the work."[104] Also at stake was the church's commitment to women's equality. Should women not "take an equal part in all things that have a common interest for both, whether, politically, socially or religiously?" asked Sarah Janifer, a thirty-eight-year-old Washington, D.C., schoolteacher. Woman "must organize, originate and mould sentiment, and in fact, take her place on the broadening platform of equality and justice," Janifer urged.[105]

Janifer's remarks hinted at two important themes. The places of women in the political, social, and religious realms were analogous, and principles of equality should best guide women in their public work. Rosina Nickson pointed to the work of the Women's Christian Temperance Union as one model of female autonomy to which black Methodists might look as they contemplated female control over missionary affairs. These connections were also understood by women active in secular organizations. The black women's club movement leader Mary Church Terrell addressed a meeting of the National Women's Suffrage Association in 1900. While arguing for women's political enfranchisement, Terrell made clear that her objective was to remedy the fact that "the most honorable and lucrative positions in Church and State have been reserved for men."[106] For all of these female leaders, church and state remained critical sites of power, and women's struggles within them were closely allied.

Janifer saw churchwomen's challenges as bound up with those faced by women in politics, and she saw their futures as connected with changes in the nature of missionary work itself. The "broadening platform of equality and justice" to which she referred increasingly included international settings through which African American Methodists hoped to extend their influence. The women's male allies also saw the particular significance of robust female missionary societies in the imperial age. Rev. J. N. Manly argued that the turn of the century, more so than any other moment in church history, required the harnessing of all that churchwomen had to offer to missionary endeavors: "To fail in giving women charge of the Missionary Department would be a great sacrifice to the spread of our Zion Methodism throughout the United States and the world."[107]

"The great object of our church is to disciple the world," Manly urged. The idea that black Methodists were charged with bringing their faith to people of color throughout the world, and especially to those fields of interest that U.S. imperialism appeared to be opening up, was key to the debate. The question that faced black Methodists was the extent to which women would control or take part in such encounters. Missionary work not only had the potential to make African American churches "great," it had the potential to restore to those men who found themselves suddenly and forcefully evicted from politics a type of greatness that most were unwilling to share with their female counterparts.

At the AME Zion general conference of 1900, the century's two final woman questions were put on the table. The first—may women be properly ordained to the ministry?—was answered in the affirmative. This victory secured the standing of a small number of women who sought out such duties in the early twentieth century. But the tenor of the times was better captured by the answer to the second question—should women be granted exclusive control over their missionary societies? The answer was an unequivocal no. Ideas about politics and religion would remain intertwined. In a world of Jim Crow limitations and imperial possibilities the woman question was being redrawn to ask about the possibilities for women's standing in the realm of international missionary endeavors. As African American women, religious and nonreligious activists alike, mobilized through women's clubs to challenge state-sanctioned Jim Crow, they too were confronting new questions about the possibilities and limits for women in public culture.[108] Developments in religion and politics would ensure that black Methodists would be debating the woman question for decades to come.

CHAPTER EIGHT

"Only a Woman Would Do"

Bible Reading and African American Women's Organizing Work

ANTHEA D. BUTLER

Sometimes, the best ideas for research come from others observing what you take for granted. One of my colleagues, a New Testament scholar, was summoned for jury duty in the large city where we both reside. When I inquired about the process of jury selection, he remarked: "You know, it makes for a boring day, but all of the African American women read their Bibles. At least they received something out of the long, boring day. Why do so many black women carry Bibles to read?" I gave a vague answer, but later I reconsidered the question. Why do African American women still read their Bibles, when so many popular magazines and self-help books target black women? What do they glean from the intense scrutiny of scripture? How did Bible reading become such a prevalent practice among African American women?

The answer lies not so much in the present as in a shared past. During the late nineteenth century, African American women established strong networks for education and empowerment. Black Baptist women, some of whom later joined the Church of God in Christ, participated in Bible Bands, which were bible reading and study groups started by Joanna P. Moore, a white American Baptist home missionary who worked in the South after Reconstruction.[1] These groups, sometimes led by "church mothers" with an eye to proper Bible exposition and home training, were started in 1884, according to Moore, in order to "commit to memory the word of God for our education and comfort, to teach it to others, and to supply the destitute with bibles."[2] Bible Bands not only encouraged group study but also lent themselves to entrepreneurial endeavors, as black women sold Bibles, collected dues, and raised funds for missions. These groups provided African American women with a sacred space of their own, giving them some autonomy for their personal and collective spiritual lives, despite their marginalized status within the black church. In addition, Bible Bands often became the main-stay of women's church organization, providing an education in domestic duties and social activism.[3] Most importantly, Bible Bands enabled women to pursue their spirituality in a realm primarily designed by and for women, even though men at times shared their study space.[4] Although they are not womanist by pre-vailing contemporary definitions, Bible Band groups enabled women to acquire and practice organizational skills that they also used to serve their communities. The networks established through the Bible Band movement led them to advo-cacy and activism on behalf of women's concerns within their wider church de-nominations and, in some cases, helped to establish other women's organiza-tions.[5]

Bible Band networks facilitated the expansion of autonomy, education, and en-trepreneurial opportunity for African American women in the South during the late nineteenth and early twentieth centuries. The movement allowed women to teach one another how to read, how to interpret scripture, and how to make a "Christian home." For black women like Lizzie Woods Robinson, the Bible Band "got her hands out of the washtub and on the Bible," enabling women like her to improve their educational and their social status.[6] Most importantly, Bible Bands provided a framework for African American women's religious organizing that assisted in the formation of the Women's Convention of the National Baptist Convention and the Women's Work of the Church of God in Christ (COGIC).[7] The biblical text became a lifeline, linking women in Bible Bands and eventually in women's convention groups to pursue shared goals of spirituality, personal uplift, and social improvement. Indeed, the zeal that Bible Band women brought to their organizing eventually caused controversy with men over the work of women's groups and their roles in the church.[8]

Bible Bands offer a valuable lens through which to trace the development of the practice of regular Bible study among African American women and to ex-amine the role of scripture in the promotion of reading literacy. Although many Protestant groups during this period introduced Sunday School literature and some sent missionaries to work among African Americans in the South after Re-construction, the Bible Band system provided autonomy outside of the mission-ary/missionized relationship, which was almost unavoidably asymmetrical. In contrast to missionary activities and schools run by white people, missionaries within black church groups and communities organized and conducted Bible Bands independently. They were assisted in this endeavor by the national maga-zine *Hope*. Created by Moore specifically to provide daily lessons for use in Bible Band meetings, *Hope* became an effective text and mode of communication among African American women in the rural South. The magazine articulated commonplace nineteenth-century tropes of domesticity, piety, and the primacy of scripture, but it played a more dynamic role as a point of connection for women and missionary workers. Letters from African American women were published in *Hope,* generating a dialogue and support network across the region. Used in tandem with the Bible, *Hope* was an important tool in the promotion of literacy and community among African American women.

Alternative educational opportunities like Bible Bands reached women in rural areas and in the lower socioeconomic classes who were unable to attend college, obtain secondary education, or even get access to enough formal schooling to become fluent readers and writers. Informal, community-based education was crucial to many black women living in regions where publicly funded educational facilities were absent or inferior and the black community's resources to support schooling were already stretched thin. Using a home study system with scripture married religion and literacy, allowing women to explore moral questions and social issues within their homes and with others from their own social location. Concerns about temperance, thrift, and racial uplift articulated by many middle-class African Americans were communicated to and upheld by those in more straitened circumstances. Impoverished women subscribed to the same ideals as their better-off and better-educated sisters and were able to achieve a measure of respectability.[9] Their notion of respectability, however, found its locus and meaning in their belief in scripture and in putting its lessons into practice in their daily lives, rather than in imitating the demeanor and styles of the black middle class or seeking recognition from white people.[10] By upholding moral values based on scripture, these women furthered the goals of racial pride and uplift.

The other unique aspect of African American Bible Bands was the interracial relationship that black women participants and activists forged with the white missionary Moore, which lasted from the late nineteenth century until her death in 1916. Virginia Broughton, a Holiness Baptist who was instrumental in the inception of the Women's Convention of the National Baptist Convention, and Lizzie Woods Robinson, a laundress who became the first overseer of women's work in the Church of God in Christ, played important roles in the dissemination of *Hope* magazine. The work of black women in the Bible Band movement and their friendship with Joanna Moore illuminate how black and white women in the South could find a common ground in Bible study. The Bible as a text helped people to navigate not only the minefield of race but also the differences that came with class and the complex contradictions of gender. The biblically based intersection of Moore's work with African American women in the South challenged the common conventions of Jim Crow and facilitated the building of an alternative structure for African American women's organizing work outside of the women's club movement. The Bible joined black women into a larger diasporan community linked to a sacred text that, like the talking book, held power and authority for the women who could wield it.

Joanna P. Moore, "Swamp Angel of the South"

The missionary work of the white missionary Joanna P. Moore in the late nineteenth-century South intriguingly combined a single-minded pursuit—the promotion of her ideal of the happy Christian home—with genuine service to women who were profoundly different from her. Moore, born into a poor family of thirteen children in Clarion County, Pennsylvania, was raised with family prayer and Bible reading. Like many who went to the mission field, Moore had suffered tragedy; three of her siblings had died during a three-week period. At the age of fourteen, she worked in an Episcopalian school to help pay part of her board, and the next year she began teaching in a private school in her neighborhood. With an Episcopalian father and Presbyterian mother, Moore was brought up as a liberal rather than an evangelical Protestant. However, after attending a revival meeting in 1852, she joined the Baptist church, much to the consternation of her father. Shortly thereafter she entered Rockford Female Seminary to become (in her words) a "first class teacher." In February 1863, a missionary who had been stationed on Island #10 in the Mississippi River came to the seminary to give a talk on his experience of ministering to "1100 colored women and children in distress." Deeply affected by hearing his stories of pathos and woe among the ex-slaves on the island, Moore resonated to the words of the speaker when he asked: "What can a man do to help such a suffering mass of humanity? Nothing. A woman is needed, nothing else will do." The message stirred Moore into action. In 1863, after settling her widowed mother into a smaller cottage, she left with four dollars collected from her Baptist Sabbath School and a commission from the American Baptist Home Mission Society (ABHMS).[11] Like many white women who worked as teachers in the South during and after the Civil War, Moore was a northerner activated by religious motives. Unlike many of her peers, however, she remained in the South and devoted her life to missionary work with African Americans.

The first missionary appointed to go South by the ABHMS, Moore arrived at Island #10 in the middle of the Mississippi River near Memphis, Tennessee, to begin her work with black women and children who had fled to the Union Army camp there.[12] Moore worked there for a time and then traveled throughout the South, doing substantial work in Louisiana, Arkansas, and Tennessee. Settling in New Orleans in 1879, she established a "faith home" for former slaves and used the city as a base for her work throughout Louisiana. Moore clearly described the need for a charitably supported home to provide care for some of the freed women: "The most pitiful objects that I found in New Orleans were the old Freed women worn out with years of slavery. They were, usually, rag pickers and had a little hut where they lodged at night, and ate old scraps that they had begged during the day . . . The colored people had tried several times to collect money for a home, but something always happened to the treasurer before they got enough to open a home."[13]

Moore's initial attitude toward African Americans was typical of many northern missionaries who went south. She had a great desire to help with the temporal as well as spiritual needs of ex-slaves, but her own fears and prejudices about African Americans held her captive for a time. Her aside about the treasurer in the passage quoted above hints at her initial perceptions of the black community, which seemed to her unstable and prone to entrusting its financial resources to feckless men. More blatant comments in her memoirs indicate that the deplorable ignorance she found among the "colored people" challenged her Christian principles and middle-class sensibilities. "I've told you how repulsive most of those old people were to me. God showed me that I only pitied them, but did not love them, as Christ loved me when I was all covered with sin and was in rebellion against him. I did not love even to shake their hands, and yet I would have shared my last piece of bread with them. I knew this feeling was wrong and spent many hours in prayer for a baptism of love."[14] Moore recognized that her racism stood in contradiction to the Gospel and struggled with her repulsion through prayer.

Moore's attitude toward African Americans shifted over time, as she overcame her initial repugnance and condescension and adopted a more comfortable and generous stance toward her black coworkers. By living with African American families in their meager homes in the bayou country during her missionary excursions, she gained an appreciation of the costs of slavery and the struggles facing freed people. After establishing the faith home for the elderly in New Orleans, Moore traveled throughout southern Louisiana, conducting Bible study in small churches and homes.

Her chief concern was the lack of educational opportunities for African Americans. Realizing that the pervasive illiteracy of former slaves resulted from whites' prohibitions on instruction and that the white supremacist governments of the "redeemed" South did not offer integrated public schools, she wrote in her memoirs, titled *In Christ's Stead*, "The black man didn't choose to have separate schools or churches, but he now chooses to take them rather than to have his manhood insulted. As I said before, there is no problem before me. I know what to do. First, be loving, helpful and cheerful myself. Then help my fallen brother."[15]

Moore's relationships with African Americans in the South during this period were shaped by the ideals that many missionary workers and northern white Protestants held during the late nineteenth century. She felt that Bible reading would bring "civilization" to African Americans who had remained uncivilized under slavery. Like many women who espoused racial uplift for African Americans, Moore worked first and foremost to promote Christianity; in her mind, religious faith would serve as a foundation for self-improvement, material success, and social elevation. As time went on, however, she came to advocate self-determination for African Americans and to see religion as an arena in which they could organize themselves. For Moore, it was a sin that whites had made it impossible for African Americans to advance. She recognized that (as she put it) the black man "seldom received the courtesy and respect that was given to white men as ignorant as he was."[16]

Moore was even more emphatic that black women deserved to be treated as equals. Her memoirs include a ringing statement proclaiming the equality and sisterhood of women across lines of race, asserting black women's entitlement to the same privileges that white men were supposed to extend to white women.

> I do beseech you to be kind to my black sister and treat her with the same courtesy and respect that you do other women who come to your church, or whom you meet on the street or in a public conveyance. If she has a basket of clothes or a baby in her arms, help her on and off the cars in a kind, manly way. I do not ask these favors for her because she is a Negro. No, no, but because she is a woman, with all the high and holy feelings that live in the hearts of other women. Her purity and good name are dear to her. She is not naturally any better nor any worse than women of other races, except I think she has a little more motherly, loving kindness.[17]

In a society where people of color were being relegated to second-class status by the imposition of Jim Crow on the streets and public accommodations and where most white Protestant churches excluded people of African descent, such a principled and religiously motivated call to defy segregation was startling indeed. Even more important was Moore's statement that a black woman is entitled to courtesy and respect not "because she is a Negro" but "because she is a woman." The entire history of American slavery excluded women of African descent from the category of womanhood, whose "high and holy feelings" and "purity" earned her a "good name." Enslaved women and their free descendants were represented as animals whose physical strength was to be exploited in co-erced or low-paid labor and as Jezebels whose innate licentiousness served as an excuse for their sexual violation by white men. Moore's careful choice of words echoed the slogan of abolitionist feminists before the Civil War, which was often visually presented as spoken by an African American woman in chains kneeling and lifting her hands in prayer: "Am I not a Woman and a Sister?" In the post-Reconstruction era, the repetition of such a refrain had deep significance, calling white men and women to uphold their Christian ideals rather than succumb to popular stereotypes.

Moore's declaration that African American women deserved to be treated with the same respect as white women in the South differed profoundly from the atti-tudes and actions of most white people who lived in the areas where she con-ducted her missionary work. Moore's championship of equality for African Americans came from her experiences of living in their homes and from her Christian beliefs about equality which served as a template for her missionary ser-vice. These ideals of education and empowerment for black people provoked open hostility to her work in Louisiana. That she lived among black people controverted the social mores that defined white womanhood and, for the average white south-erner, made her as licentious as African American women and as unworthy of the privileges of southern womanhood.

Social conventions forbidding racial intermingling on terms of equality and prohibiting white people from offering educational opportunities to black peo-ple came into play in what Moore called "one of the greatest trials" in her life. Moore had established a Wives' and Mothers' Training School in Baton Rouge, Louisiana, in 1886 for the benefit of African American women. The school, which was intended to train women in domestic duties, was met with resentment by lo-cal white people, who, Moore explained, were motivated by "jealousy because of the improvement the Negro was making." Perhaps the interracial nature of the school angered whites as well. The White League, a Louisiana precursor to the Ku Klux Klan, threatened Moore by posting a skull and crossbones at the school's gate and leaving a signed note ordering her to "close the school and leave the place." The group severely beat one of the pastors who was working there, and the women enrolled in the school left immediately out of fear.[18]

Moore had originally hoped that the school would be permanent, but these events forced it to close. Nevertheless, she did not abandon her aspirations to teach black women in the rural South and Bible study remained her most compelling connection to them. She resumed her work as an itinerant missionary, and decentralized Bible Bands became her primary tool for reaching African Americans in Louisiana and other points across the South. Bible Bands began with brief teachings written on note cards, which Moore took with her as she held mothers' training schools around Louisiana. Moore was dismayed at the lack of reading skills among pastors and church members, and the cards were a way to leave behind scripture teachings in the homes she visited. The cards would encourage the participants to learn to read and then to study scripture. Although the cards were useful, Bibles, though coveted by many African Americans, were expensive and oftentimes unavailable. Moore saw access to a Bible as crucial in order to instill reading literacy and biblical literacy. Reading scripture and leaving study cards wherever she visited, she established a communal method of Bible study, so that people who did not own a Bible could pair up to study scripture with someone who did. Moore drew up a formal constitution for the Bible Band outlining its purpose and goals. "The object of the organization is: First, to study and commit to memory the word of God for our own edification and comfort. Second, to teach it to others. Third, to supply the destitute with Bibles, and if possible to get every man, woman and child who can read to own a Bible." These three principles guided Moore and the black women who worked with her in establishing Bible Bands throughout the South.

What Moore could not have envisioned was that structures and cultural practices already in place among African Americans enabled the Bible Bands to become successful. Because so little written material was available, memorization of scripture had already begun through listening carefully to sermons. Moore repeatedly complained in her memoirs that black preachers were untrained and did not quote scripture well. Yet this very orality laid the basis for the Bible Band. The organized study and memorization of scripture assisted in the creation of a shared story and memory that called women into accountability to their Bible Bands.[19] By studying scripture in groups, men and especially women could use the cards to bring together their understandings of scripture.

It is not clear precisely where in Louisiana the first Bible Band meeting was held, but Moore began to implement the teaching method during her missionary tours in southern Louisiana beginning in 1874. Her lessons did not quote the entire scripture but rather referred to it by book, chapter, and verse. This method required the reader to look up the text. Most Sunday School quarterlies printed the text and then the accompanying commentary, which made allowances for those who lacked a Bible but also meant that they had only the verses they were given.[20] Moore's manner of study made it more important to own a Bible. Moore adopted this method because she was determined to make sure that every woman could read the Bible for herself. If the woman was enterprising, she could also sell Bibles.

While serving as an agent for the American Bible Society in New Orleans, Moore encouraged the Bible Band women to go out into the community and sell Bibles. The demand for Bibles to aid the study of scripture provided an obvious entrepreneurial opportunity. In order to keep track of the number of Bibles sold and distributed, Moore created a simple system of tallying; each month, the treasurer of the Bible Band would record how many members read their Bible regularly, how many were without a Bible, and how many had been supplied with a Bible. These statistics are very useful in ascertaining the spread of the movement and the numbers of women involved in the Bible Band endeavor.

Planting Bible Bands alone would not ensure the spread of the movement. These small groups were located in relatively isolated rural areas and had no readily available means of communication. One traveling missionary could not possibly serve them all, even if she left behind study cards and Bibles. The tool that helped birth the movement outside of Louisiana was *Hope*. Before she started publishing the magazine in 1885, Moore had created cards that outlined a lesson a day for a six-month period. Moore then began writing a leaflet that had Bible lessons for a month and sending it out to subscribers, so that Bible Band members and others could have lessons to accompany their reading of scripture. Moore's ultimate purpose in publishing *Hope* grew out of her experiences with women in the Louisiana community with which she had been intimately involved:

> I had been studying the condition of the colored people for twenty-two years, and all that time had been at work among them, and I asked myself, what do they need most of all? After careful thought and prayer I came to the conclusion that what they needed most was Hopefulness, encouragement,—someone to tell them that they had as much natural ability as any race, and all that they needed was patient, persevering effort to cultivate the talents that God had given them. During the days of slavery they were discouraged and hopeless. There was nothing to live for, and this old feeling still clings to me, I wanted to encourage them, I wanted to inspire them with *Hope* and cheer them on.[21]

Moore's intimate knowledge of the difficulties faced by African Americans, from poverty to racism and persecution, led her to name her magazine *Hope*. The title expresses the aspiration, that she and African Americans shared, to attain the freedom to prosper spiritually and materially in everyday life. She understood the obstacles that too often made "patient, persevering effort" seem useless, even to those who realized that "they had as much natural ability as any race" and should "cultivate the talents that God had given them." Over the years between 1863 and 1885, Moore's work with African Americans had profoundly changed her outlook, and she chose to offer hope rather than succumb to the forces of white supremacy that had hampered and threatened to end her mission work.

Moore's mission was not just about making Christians but also about making citizens. Even mailing the magazine to subscribers was a daring act. Moore knew that in the South it was dangerous (in her words) "for colored people to get papers through the mail" because whites feared that "some political scheme or something inside would tend to upset the established plans of society."[22] Despite her doubts, she was deliberately cheerful, filling *Hope* with Bible teachings, instructions, and admonitions intended to create a "Happy and Bright home life." *Hope* provided daily Bible lessons for group and individual study. The frontispiece of the magazine featured two guiding phrases: "Love one another" and "Have Faith in God." At first, Moore wrote most of the Bible studies, promoting basic and biblical literacy.[23]

Hope began in 1885 with a run of five hundred copies printed in Plaquemine, Louisiana. The first few issues featured short sermonettes, a Bible study plan, and letters that members had written to Moore. Using *Hope* as a guide, Bible Band participants were forced to read their Bibles, but those who could not read were still able to participate.

Tigerville, LA.

June 25, 1886

Dear Miss Moore:

I write to send you a report of our Bible Band. We have 60 who read the Bible every day and 21 who hear it read. They cannot read it themselves, but some one *reads it to them every day.* We are glad to get your plan of Bible Study. The parables these months have taught us many wonderful lessons. We close with Much Love and Blessing on you sister.

I am your Brother, Silas Teems, pres.

Men as well as women availed themselves of Bible Bands, and some of the men who participated were pastors. Women comprised the majority of the membership, however, and many local groups were conducted entirely by women. Teems's letter illustrates how Bible Bands promoted literacy by having some members read aloud to others in the group. The principles and practices of an oral culture, coupled with group Bible study, helped to inculcate a shared goal of members being able to study scripture for themselves. Reading fluency was not necessarily accompanied by skill in writing, which perhaps explains why "Brother" Teems wrote on behalf of the group. By publishing letters like this one, *Hope* promoted writing literacy as well. The magazine extended the culture of Bible study from face-to-face groups who met to read and talk about scripture toward written communication linking these study groups across the South.

A letter from a "sister" in an early Bible Band in Louisiana attests to the close connections between Bible study, learning to read and write, and selling Bibles that were generated by the Bible Band project.

> St. Martinsville, La.
>
> August 15, 1886
>
> Dear Sister Moore:
>
> I was so glad to get *Hope* and also your kind letter. Our Bible Band numbers 28, of these, 5 daily read the Bible and learn the verses. I have at last gotten 20 subscribers for *Hope*, at 30 c each. Will send you $2 for missions. I have sent the $6 for the paper . . .
>
> Your sister in the Lord, Palmy Hughs

Hughs's letter suggests that the majority of participants in her group could not read or had no access to a Bible. In Bible Band meetings, listeners could ask questions, see the scripture passage, and begin to pick up words and phrases. Participants showed varying degrees of skill at reading and writing, but all were invested in increasing their literacy along with their spiritual knowledge. Susan Mixon of Millers Ferry, Alabama, wrote to Moore: "I cannot write so well, but I thank the Lord for what I have learned. I did not know anything before I went to the mission school. I have been taking *Hope* for seven years. I don't want to be without it, because it has taught me so much about the gospel."[24]

Moore may have edited the letters she published in *Hope* in order to put them in what she regarded as proper form, but this letter makes clear that reading and writing skills did not necessarily go together. Reading was but one step toward complete literacy. Writing to *Hope* encouraged women to express themselves to Moore and each other and promoted the next step in the learning process. The profusion of letters and reports about meetings that were published in *Hope* indicate that networks of Bible Band workers in southern Louisiana and other states were established rapidly.

Some of the most interesting letters that Moore published in the early issues of *Hope* are from children. For the most part, their race is not mentioned. These letters give tantalizing details about how new Bible Bands were organized.

Memphis, Tenn.

January 26, 1886

Dear Miss Moore:

I was at your meeting Thursday Morning and Thursday evening. The meeting was very nice and it made me read the Bible more than ever, and this is what makes me feel so bad, that my grandma and my two sisters are God's children but I am not. But I am going to be one of God's children. I am eleven years old.

Your little Lizzie Owens[25]

It is impossible to discern how much redaction was done with this letter; since it is as well written as the published letters signed by adults.[26] It is important to note, however, that given the lack of access to education in the South before Emancipation and the rapid spread of schools during Reconstruction, some children likely learned to read before their parents or grandparents did. Children were welcome at the meetings, which were held daily around the Memphis area. Perhaps children read the Bible to their parents at home, facilitating the family study of scripture that Moore sought to promote. But the Bible Bands were not only an effective tool for reading; they were also a powerful force toward conversion. Their evangelical function was clear to participants. Even the eleven-year-old Lizzie felt the pressure of not being "one of God's children" when the other women in her family were.

The Bible Bands promoted moral reform along with scripture study; in these groups, as in church services, lessons were learned in order to be applied to daily life. Many of the readers who wrote to *Hope* testified that the Bible Bands "convicted them of sin, stopped them from drinking and snuff dipping, and made them read their bibles."[27]

Hope became an indispensable resource for the burgeoning movement. By 1888, there were ninety Bible Bands with 1,683 members in the Louisiana area, and by 1889 there were 115 Bible Bands in Louisiana and other places in the South, including North Carolina and Virginia.[28] In addition to promoting literacy, Bible Bands promoted entrepreneurial activities through sales of Bibles and *Hope*. Moore encouraged women to write to the magazine and report on the progress of their Bible Bands, how much money was raised, and how many Bibles had been sold. The letter writing began to link women from varying social strata and educational backgrounds who had the Bible in common.

Letters poured into *Hope* describing women's successes in selling Bibles and magazines door to door in their communities.

Homa, La.

Aug. 6th

Dear Sister Moore:

Enclosed is 50c for *Hope*. I have engaged several other subscribers who will send money soon. I am studying my Bible daily and memorizing verses. On Sunday I will organize a Bible Band. I have read *Hope* to the sisters and it has aroused them greatly. You have encouraged me greatly to read my Bible, and live a better Christian life.

I am your sister, Sallie Brown.[29]

Bible Band women were canvassing for sales and souls. Moore advised *Hope* subscribers how to do "house to house visitation." "You visit in order to get help for yourself and your work. You go to your neighbor and tell her what you need and what you are doing and that sets her to thinking how she can help. You say to her . . . I have a little meeting with the children once a week. I am teaching them how to sew, but I can't read and they ought to have lessons from the Bible and be taught rules of politeness, etc. The children do need help so much. You say all this and more in such a kind, pleading way, because you are yourself in such deep earnestness."[30] Moore's shrewd instructions about home visitation yielded evangelistic and entrepreneurial success. Women who became invested in helping with an established group would feel needed and become committed to the success of the Bible Band and its teaching endeavors, regardless of the limitations of their skills.

Moore elaborates on how even nonliterate women making home visits on behalf of the Bible Band could exemplify its values. The goal of reaching women in need of the education that Bible Bands offered was served by having members from all educational backgrounds make person-to-person contacts with their neighbors. "Who to do it . . . It must be a person who has good common sense, good judgment, one who knows something that will help others. It matters not how she learned it, whether from books or observation. She may not know how to read, and yet be a far better visitor than one who has a good education."[31] Moore's insightful advice provided women like Sallie Brown, who were without the benefit of formal education, with an avenue to do missionary work within their communities. In her view, women who were oriented toward serving others were best suited to recruit others to join the Bible Bands.

These African American women, whose rural location and class position placed them outside the fortunate "talented tenth" that Du Bois called to serve as teachers of their race, worked in the Bible Band movement to provide an alternative, informal education that cultivated spirituality and self-esteem close to home. The education that *Hope* offered was not solely concerned with homemaking and child rearing but aimed more broadly to provide a religious education that gave identity and purpose to lives otherwise spent toiling in the fields and doing manual labor for white people. In this sense, *Hope* helped to accomplish goals that leaders like Booker T. Washington and W. E .B. Du Bois placed high on the agenda for African Americans; it inculcated respectability and self-respect. The inspiration for that goal, religious faith, was not the primary source from which these two men believed the impetus would come, but it was effective, nonetheless.

These letters from African Americans and their interactions with Moore show how the Bible Band movement provided leadership opportunities for African American women beyond the limited roles open to them within the patriarchal structure of the Baptist church. Although there were many fraternal orders and organizations that women could join, Bible Bands were a low-cost alternative that focused on everyday life and child rearing, all with a spiritual connection that pushed the reader toward "holy living." In addition, *Hope* promoted biblical and everyday literacy among African Americans in rural and urban areas across the South. The popularity of the groups also facilitated more formal organizing activities by and among African American women. Scripture reading in groups provided a space for literate and nonliterate neighbors to meet outside of the environs of the church and to open the scriptures for themselves. For women who moved beyond this level of participation and became "Bible Band entrepreneurs," the possibilities for organizational leadership expanded. Such was the case with two African American Bible Band women, Virginia Broughton and Lizzie Woods Robinson.

Virginia Broughton, Black Missionary

Virginia Broughton's autobiography, *Twenty Years' Experience of a Missionary*, chronicles the mission work she embarked upon after joining a Bible Band in Memphis, Tennessee. What is amazing about Broughton's story is that, unlike most of the women who populated Bible Bands, she was college educated, holding the distinction of being the first female graduate of Fisk University in Nashville, Tennessee, in the class of 1875. After graduation, she moved to Memphis, married, and began teaching in the city's public schools. She worked as a teacher for twelve years, rising to the position of principal of a school for African Americans. Invited to a missionary meeting by Joanna P. Moore, Broughton joined a Bible Band group formed at that meeting. Broughton recounted her first encounter with Moore in her autobiography, in which speaks of herself in the third person as "Virginia":

> While teaching in the last position mentioned, a stranger introduced as Miss J. P. Moore, accompanied by Miss E. B. King, called to see Virginia, and invited her to attend a missionary meeting appointed for women only. As this was an entirely new thing under the sun twenty years ago, curiosity prompted Virginia to go and ascertain what such a meeting would be. Miss J. P. Moore, the good woman who called the meeting, stated the object and opened the service with an appropriate devotional exercise. She at once enlisted the sympathy and promised cooperation of the women in attendance. We organized what was then called a Bible Band. The principal object of the organization was the daily study of the bible.

In Broughton, Moore found a willing and educated coworker to assist in establishing Bible Bands throughout the South and within the Baptist Church. According to Broughton, "Soon, Bible Bands were organized throughout the city of Memphis and the women of our churches took on new life. Every Monday afternoon women could be seen in all sections of the city with Bibles in their hands, going to their Bible Band meetings."[32]

In the mid-1880s, as in the present, the sight of black women walking around carrying their Bibles must have been strange but intriguing for those who did not understand the persuasiveness of Bible study. Broughton's account of organizing Bible Bands in Memphis alludes to the uplift that women received from being recognized as capable expositors of scripture as well as eager workers. The local groups soon attracted the interest of some of the Baptist district association meetings held in Memphis. As a result, pastors were introduced to Bible Band work and began to ask for women to help in the establishment of these groups through Baptist churches.[33]

Broughton was pleased but had no designs to do outreach work herself until two major events changed her plans and priorities. The first occurrence was the failure of a Christian school intended to serve the Bible Band movement. The philanthropist who had earmarked funds for the Bible and Normal Institute was murdered, leaving the school incomplete and in debt. Broughton's spiritually defining experience, however, was illness. Her health deteriorated after her mother's death, so much that she started to put her affairs in order in preparation for her own death. Then she had a visionary moment that renewed her faith and health. She testified in her autobiography: "By and by the Lord Manifestly came, but not as she expected, to bear her ransomed spirit home, but she was overshadowed with the veritable presence of God, and made to understand thoroughly and clearly in language spoken to the soul, that God was not ready for her then, but He had a work for her to do. That marvelous experience was accompanied with renewed strength of body that continued to increase from that moment until she was able to leave her bed."[34] In this context, the third-person narrative stance she adopted seems to have been an expression of humility; she was called not to self but to service.

For Broughton, as for many religious workers during this period, her healing was the beginning of a "calling" narrative that led her into Christian service. After being appointed as a missionary with the ABHMS, Broughton set up Bible Bands in rural areas, setting aside her own trepidation along the way. "Upon invitation of a certain pastor, Virginia started on her first missionary journey up the Mississippi river. She was naturally afraid to travel on water, and needed special encouragement as well as preparation for that first trip. Accordingly, after much hesitation on her part amidst doubts and fears, she was assured that God was on the water as well as on the land."[35] Traveling along the Mississippi establishing Bible Bands might not seem like the proper occupation for a schoolteacher with a college degree. Yet organizing religious women into a strong regional network helped Broughton to help pave the way for the formation of the National Baptist Women's Convention in 1900.

Initially Broughton supported women in existing Bible Bands, in part by dealing with men who had grown suspicious of the movement. In the Woodlawn District Association, one of ten district meetings, Broughton struggled with pastors who were intimidated by the Bible Bands and what she termed "women's work." "Virginia was tried to the uttermost, and persecuted with cruel hatred for no other cause than her contention for holiness of heart and uprightness of daily deportment. A general awakening in the study of the Bible followed these great meetings . . . a general reform was evidently going on toward the development of women and the betterment of the home and church life of the people. Women were giving up the vile habits of beer drinking and snuff-dipping, and using their little mites thus saved in getting our Christian literature and contributing to our missionary and educational work."[36]

Bible Band women were interested in spiritual life and social issues. This phenomenon perplexed and infuriated pastors who were preaching similar messages with little success. Even more galling to ministers was that the women criticized practices that some pastors engaged in, like dipping snuff and drinking alcohol. The tensions between the inefficacy of pastors' messages, their own behavior, and a general feeling that women like Broughton had usurped men's positions began to take hold, and the support for Bible Bands dwindled in some churches. As women became more literate, not just in reading but also in interpreting scripture, these tensions between men and women increased. Broughton observed:

> The work (Bible Band) had taken root too deeply in the hearts of our women ever to be uprooted, and for a season the work seemed to stand still. The separate associational meeting was broken up, many local Bible bands disbanded . . . Bretheren would come to our meetings to catch every word spoken if thereby they might have some just cause to condemn our teaching, as being false doctrine. One minister was so desirous to destroy the work like Saul of Tarsus, he desired letters of authority that he might follow in the wake of our missionaries and destroy whatever good they might have accomplished.[37]

Baptist preachers indeed had much to fear from the women whose organizing work had begun with the lowly Bible Bands. The coordination of groups through *Hope* magazine enabled women to form collective opinions about the proper interpretation of scripture and to articulate their concerns about home, hearth, and holy living through their study groups. Men's opposition did not stop either the proliferation of Bible Bands or the growth of other organizations that spun off from this movement, but it did cause much hardship and consternation for the Bible Band women.

With women like Broughton promoting Bible Bands, networks of women organized around the study of biblical texts began to spread across the South. Groups that ministered to women began to overlap. Conferences for mothers and parents held in local Baptist assemblies in Arkansas and nearby states also had their origins in *Hope*. Moore traveled to as many courses as she could, giving Bible lessons. Men and women attended, but joint meetings illuminated the need for separate women's work. Early issues of *Hope* addressed the Bible Band as the "Praying, Planning, Working Band." Some groups continued under that name in Baptist associational meetings alongside Bible Band groups. Separately formed mothers' groups existed alongside Bible Bands in other places.

The success of *Hope* spurred Moore to create other groups to support and extend the work of Bible Bands. First came Fireside Schools, an offshoot of the Praying, Planning, Working Band, which facilitated home-based training in domestic skills and the Bible by women who were already participants in Bible Bands. These schools also promoted literacy; one of their objects was to "put appropriate books in our homes and see that parent and child read them together as far as possible."[38] Fireside Schools were designed so that parents, especially mothers, would read *Hope* to their children in a three-year plan of study, improving upon the religious training that they received at church. Moore felt that Sunday or Sabbath schools separated parents from an important component of their children's religious lives. Fireside Schools, in tandem with *Hope*, were popular among the women who participated in Bible Bands. Black women eagerly wrote to Moore about their successes and sent pictures of their families. These family portraits demonstrate that African Americans sought to exemplify not so much mainstream values as Christian values.

For a time, Virginia Broughton worked at the Fireside School home base, located in Nashville, Tennessee. Her duties there consisted of serving as assistant editor for *Hope*, as well as supervisor of the school. Women with whom Broughton worked in the Fireside Schools came to board there to learn about scripture as well as receive training in domestic duties. These schools, much like the school that Nannie Helen Burroughs later established in Washington, D.C., followed a trade-school concept that taught women domestic duties and religious work. The success of the Fireside Schools could be measured by the substantial exhibit in the Negro building of the Tennessee Centennial held in Nashville in 1898. Over three hundred pledges from Fireside School participants to follow the rules of temperance, study the Bible, and read lined the walls of the exhibit, which was designed as a mock home with Bible and hearth. Mary Sweet, one of Moore's Fireside School workers and a missionary evangelist, was in charge of the booth and held daily devotional meetings for visitors.[39]

Out of these ancillary organizations, networks of women began to form into groups within state Baptist conventions, seeking the type of contact and fellowship that they received in Bible Bands. In her memoirs Broughton chronicled the steps to the formation of the National Baptist Women's Convention, connecting it firmly with her work with Bible Bands: "In the last National Baptist Conventions that Dr. Wm. J. Simmons attended in Louisville, Ky, Virginia spoke on the subject 'The ideal Woman' Prov. 31: 10–13. With other Bible women she contended for a woman's separate and distinctive organization in 1890. Dr. Simmons, however, did not approve that idea because he thought the men and women working together would do more effectual work."[40] Despite Simmons's rebuff, they continued to press for a separate women's auxiliary convention.[41] Through mothers' meetings paired with the state Baptist conventions, women found ways to connect and organize under the auspices of men who did not want them to act collectively as women. They continued to press for an organization at national meetings in Atlanta, Savannah, Washington, D.C., and Montgomery. The formal women's convention was finally founded at the National Baptist Convention in 1900, with the help of several Baptist men, including Rev. L. G. Jordan, secretary of foreign missions.[42] The organizational scope, connections, and fund-raising abilities of Bible Band women though the auspices of *Hope* magazine had helped the women to organize more cohesively to rally for their own organization within the national denomination. Without the group, it would have perhaps taken longer for the auxiliary organization to be formed. The two endeavors consolidated some functions after the women's convention was formed; in 1900, the publication of *Hope* was moved to the National Baptist Publishing Board, spearheaded by R. H. Boyd.[43]

Women's theological savvy also increased through participating in Bible Bands and reading *Hope*. One of the most important theological themes to shape the movement was sanctification. First articulated as the doctrine of "Christian Perfectionism" by John Wesley, sanctification was a second work of grace that allowed a Christian to pursue a life free from sin.[44] Those who experienced sanctification began to call their shared experiences the Holiness movement, a synonym for Christian Perfection which spread in evangelical circles during the nineteenth century.[45] The emergence of the Holiness movement during this period divided the Bible Bands along theological lines and intensified gender conflict.[46] Acting as a renewal movement within the black Baptists, pursuit of sanctification led to splits within the black Baptist churches and deepened the male/female divide.

The impetus to be "pure" as individuals and as a group became increasingly important to participants in the Bible Bands and Fireside Schools.[47] Moore wrote about her own experience of sanctification in *Hope*, in which she often referred to the work of the Holy Spirit.[48] Broughton, who also had an experience of sanctification, spoke about the conflicts that arose as the movement spread.

> About ten years after the beginning of Virginia's career as a missionary the doctrine of sanctification began to agitate the Christian church greatly, and our missionary encouraged the agitation as her own experience, and her conception of the Bible teaching of that truth led her to see the grave need of greater consecration and loyalty to Christ's cause on the part of both ministers and laity. A fresh anointing or filling of the Holy Spirit was given Virginia to give her the needed courage, wisdom and strength to contend for this truth and endure the persecutions that were sure to follow so aggressive a movement.[49]

The emphasis in Holiness theology on the work of the Holy Spirit to empower persons for service authorized them to move beyond customary nineteenth-century gender roles. Women like Broughton who embraced Holiness teachings held camp meetings, preached in tents and churches, and conducted revival meetings. Sanctification also emboldened them to take their places in ministry, without succumbing to the usual need for approval from a male hierarchy. By claiming divine authority through sanctification, women like Broughton could legitimize their leadership roles as missionaries and Bible Band women.

Donald Dayton, a historian of the Holiness movement, suggests a series of theological arguments that are useful in understanding the ministry of women in Holiness and Pentecostal traditions.

1. An emphasis on experience, and non-traditional forms of endorsement by the clerical hierarchy and education.
2. Radical or Low church movements emphasizing "sacramental" rather than priestly concerns.
3. A liberal standpoint that claims women have the "right" to preach (this falls in line with nineteenth-century liberation movements such as abolitionism and suffrage).[50]

These factors converged in the Holiness movement of the late nineteenth century, providing a way to pierce the formidable barriers against women preaching and teaching. Many of these same premises come into play for Bible Band women as well, enabling them to pursue sanctification as a means by which to empower their work within the Bible Band system and their service in their churches. The push to lead experienced by Virginia Broughton and others arose from their "sanctified lives" and study of scripture. The power of sanctification within the Bible Band movements affected many women within and beyond the Baptist denomination. Lizzie Woods Robinson, who began her religious activism in a Baptist Bible Band and eventually became overseer for women's work in the Church of God in Christ, exemplifies this process.

Lizzie Woods Robinson, Sanctified Bible Band Organizer

Sanctification teachings stressed not only a spiritual cleansing but also power for service. These messages resonated with many women. Lizzie Woods (later Robinson) testified that she became sanctified through her prayerful reading of *Hope*. Woods, who first joined a Bible Band in her hometown of Dermott, Arkansas, relates how she became sanctified in a brief memoir about her entry into women's work. "I moved from Helena (Arkansas) to Pine Bluff in 1892, but, I didn't get in touch with Sister Moore until 1901. I was then a member of the Baptist church. I received my first *Hope* Paper in the Bible Band of that church . . . I studied this paper until the Lord Sanctified me."[51] Woods's correspondence with Moore between 1901 and 1909 shows the transforming effects of Bible Band participation. Sanctification became not simply a theological construct to be embraced but an identity-defining practice that gave women like Lizzie the fortitude and perseverance to engage in missions and organizational activity, all in service of biblical principles.

Woods's first letter published in *Hope* gives an insight into how important the magazine could be to women who received it. "Sister Lizzie Woods of Pine Bluff, wrote: '*Hope* is my help in trouble, in sickness and in health. I will never forget the lessons in *Hope* about charity. Sister Moore, the Holy Ghost keeps me daily from my sins. Since reading *Hope,* I do not mind Satan, and I am happy in the Lord. Praise the Lord for this witness.'"[52] Woods relied on *Hope* to get her through the trials of mortal life. The phrase "in sickness and in health" speaks to the fact that for Woods—as for Broughton, Moore, and many other adherents—sanctification and healing went hand in hand.[53] Her letter reveals how women thought about the sanctified life; sanctification meant that one could call on the Holy Spirit to keep one free from the desire to sin. *Hope* gave Lizzie guidance by presenting scriptures related to the theme of sanctification and the tools for living a sanctified life. Sanctification was expected to change one's habits and tastes as well as one's spiritual life, enabling one to turn from suffering and sin to charity and service.

Sanctification had immediate and far-reaching consequences in Lizzie's life, beginning with her employment. In a 1908 *Hope* article, Moore reminisced about her first meeting with Woods. "Lizzie Woods did not have a good chance for an education and she has passed through many trials. One day several years ago I visited her home in Pine Bluff; she was earning her living by washing; I knelt with her by the washtub and asked God to take her hands out of that tub and fill them with Bibles and send her from house to house to feed hungry souls with the Bread of Life. God has answered my prayer. Glory to his Name!"[54] Soon after this visit, Woods began earnestly selling Bibles, a form of work that yielded material and spiritual sustenance, and starting Bible Band groups. In Moore's biblical metaphor, *Hope* and the Bible Band lifted Lizzie Woods from lowly labor and enabled her to emulate the women of the New Testament who offer others spiritual bounty. Traveling door to door, selling Bibles and subscriptions to *Hope* and starting groups to study scripture, Woods developed her missionary and organizational skills.

Woods's letters to Moore soon appeared regularly in *Hope*. A 1902 letter describes her beginning forays. "Sister Lizzie Woods, of Pine Bluff, has been doing some good work while visiting her sister in Brinkley. She sends us a club of ten subscribers. We are very glad this dear sister wants to see the work spread. She writes: 'I never saw *Hope* until Sister Bailey showed it to me and encouraged me to subscribe for it. Now I would not be without it. It has stirred me up to my sense of duty to God.'" Subsequent letters show the extent of her organizing activities on behalf of the Bible Bands. The August 1903 issue mentions that Woods had secured twenty-three subscribers for *Hope*. By 1906, she was engaging in extensive missionary work. "A Good Sister, Lizzie Woods, is scattering light in Lexa, Poplar Grove, and surrounding country in Ark. She has sold a large number of Bibles and secured subscribers to *Hope*. She says 'Once I loved only to read novels and foolish trash, but now the Bible is to me the best of all books.'"[55]

In addition to selling subscriptions and distributing Bibles, Woods was organizing Bible Bands and teaching women to read the scriptures. "Sister Lizzie Woods of Pine Bluff, Ark, is a very successful worker. She has supplied about thirty persons with Bibles during the last few months, and taught to read this book with the help of *Hope*, staying all night in homes and showing them how to have family worship and how to get time to read other good books with the children. She has the endorsement of the good people wherever she goes." By her accounts, Woods worked alongside ministers and enjoyed their support. She even held prayer meetings, a form of worship that women were permitted to lead. "I have good news to tell. Have sold in this district 66 Bibles. Thirty-five Bible Bands reported. About 100 persons bought their Bibles and *Hope*. The pastors were with us and greatly pleased with this great Bible work. I made 900 visits in homes in the district and had 500 prayer meetings."[56] In the communities where she traveled, Woods was accepted as a female evangelist.

Reading and distributing *Hope* played an important role in Woods's new sense of self, especially the sense of duty to God that led her to undertake missionary work with other poor, rural black women. Women like Woods, who could not afford to attend the National Baptist Conventions, could meet with other Baptist women, and their local networks enabled them to work together in an environment conducive to the reconstruction of their individual and group identities. Woods's zeal was exceptional, but women's enthusiasm in studying and distributing Bibles and holding their own prayer meetings could be attributed in part to the emphasis on sanctification.

The local church and Woods's work at home had been her main focus, so working and being recognized as a Bible Band worker and part-time missionary intensified her spiritual life and expanded her social connections. Her unstinting work so impressed Moore that she arranged for her to become matron of a Baptist academy in Dermott, Arkansas. The organizational skills Woods gained from participation in the Bible Bands translated into a position of some authority. Working as a matron was far from the educational and convention secretary posts that Virginia Broughton held with the National Baptists, but for a former washerwoman like Lizzie it was a profound career change. Woods held the post of matron, working as a teacher, housekeeper, and cleaner at the Baptist secondary school from 1909 to 1911. She was abruptly discharged after going on to embrace the next level of sanctification: the Pentecostal belief and practice of speaking in tongues. Subsequently, Woods went on to become the first overseer for women's work in the Church of God In Christ, which was lead by another Baptist convert to Pentecostalism, Charles Harrison Mason.

The Legacy of the Bible Band Movement

The Bible Band system provided African American women with a systematized method that enabled them to develop literacy, agency, leadership, and spiritual uplift. Expanding the meaning of literacy beyond being able to read for oneself and to write, the group study experience of Bible Bands allowed women with varying degrees of literacy to engage in activities that increased their knowledge of scripture and of reading and writing, enabling them to interpret and express the meaning of the Bible. The Bible Bands also provided entrepreneurial and organizational activities for women to engage in through the sale of Bibles and *Hope* magazine. This system allowed them to take ownership of their own groups within a loose organizational system. Study of scripture in these groups enabled women of different social classes to interact, allowing for a more egalitarian path toward leadership which did not solely rely on class-based structures, as the nascent black women's club movement did. Finally, the empowerment of women like Broughton and Woods through their Bible Band work enabled them to controvert some of the gender norms of the period, authorizing them to serve in leadership capacities that remained closed to them within the patriarchal structure of black Baptist churches. The Bible Bands created an alternative path to leadership positions that allowed women to participate in the exposition of scripture and offer spiritual guidance to their sisters beyond the limits imposed by their formal denominations.

Finally, the relationship of these black women to the white missionary Joanna P. Moore remains one of the most intriguing aspects of the Bible Band work.

Moore maintained her commitment to African American families throughout her lifetime, despite the segregation of civic life in the South. After her death in 1916, over seven thousand mourners attended her funeral at the Ryman Auditorium in Nashville, Tennessee. Eulogized by R. H. Boyd, former publisher of *Hope*, as well as by Virginia Broughton and the dean of Fisk University, Moore's funeral merited front-page coverage in the *Nashville Globe*. Resolutions of condolence were sent by many Baptist organizations, and the service culminated in her burial, at her request, in Nashville's Greenwood cemetery, the cemetery reserved for African Americans.

For African American women who read their Bible ubiquitously today, the legacy of the work of women like Broughton, Moore, and Woods points to the importance of connectivity to a sacred text that provides, much like Bible Bands did, a template for negotiating the tribulations that continue to press upon women of color. The popularity of many television Bible expositors, such as Juanita Bynum, Marilyn Hickey, and Joyce Meyer, with African American women speaks to the power of Bible study as a unique organizing tool for women of all classes. Like their predecessors, they look to the sacred book to provide them with the most important element of life: Hope.

CHAPTER NINE

Exploring the Religious Connection

Black Women Community Workers, Religious Agency, and the Force of Faith

CHERYL TOWNSEND GILKES

force n. 1 a: strength or energy brought to bear: cause of motion or change: active power. b: moral or mental strength. c (1): capacity to persuade or convince . . . 2 d: an individual or group having the power of effective action . . .

—*Webster's Collegiate Dictionary, 1965*

Now faith is the substance of things hoped for, the evidence of things not seen.

—*The Holy Bible,* Hebrews 11:1

Tell the women to stand together for God will never forsake us.

—*Harriet Tubman, 1913*

A month before she died in 1913, Harriet Tubman told club and race woman, Mary Talbert, that she was "at peace with God and all mankind." Tubman sent a message to the women with whom she had stood in 1896 when they formed the National Association of Colored Women, encouraging them "to stand together for God will never forsake us." We think of Harriet Tubman as "Moses," as the courageous abductor and conductor on the Underground Railroad who traveled back and forth between the slave South and the North, crossing and recrossing the border between the United States and Canada. Her last words to the club women remind us of the tremendous faith that undergirded her heroic exploits. Catherine Clinton describes her style of worship in the AME Zion Church of

Rochester as full of shouting and expressive singing, and as very much directed by the Holy Spirit.[1] Tubman's connection to the earliest national movement of African American women aimed at social change and community uplift highlights the need to appreciate the tremendous force of faith that has supported and guided the African American women who have worked hard and long for social justice and community transformation. Descriptions and explanations of African American women's community work often miss the religious connection.

According to Alice Walker, "They were women . . . / Husky of voice—Stout of / Step." In "In Search of Our Mothers' Gardens," Walker described the women of her mother's generation whose strength and organization, like Tubman's, confronted difficulties of war-zone proportions "to discover books / Desks / A place for us." Walker called these women "Headragged Generals," praising their strength, collectivism, and heroic forceful effort. These women achieved more expansive opportunities and inclusive futures for black children by breaking through the barriers that the powerful violently defended.[2] Walker recognized that the progress of black people was tied to the activism of black women who, despite derogatory stereotypes and exclusionary cultural icons, exhibited unusual fortitude in the face of opposition, particularly where the lives and futures of their children were concerned. In the autobiographies of black leaders, stories abound pointing to the vision and persistence of mothers and other women. These women insisted upon securing education for their children and thereby advancing the progress of the race.

African American women developed and built a myriad of organizations and institutions to attain their goals. Because the leaders of secular organizations such as the National Association for the Advancement of Colored People (NAACP) and the Urban League have been men and because some of the most visible leaders in the recent civil rights movement have been black clergymen, our understanding of women's activism has been limited to women's organizations and has tended to ignore their religious connections. In the case of the civil rights movement, because the women were not ministers, their roles have been seen as "lesser than" those of men, although the clergymen themselves admit that nothing would have happened without the women. They are described as grassroots organizers whose efforts were crucial to local community mobilization but not as leaders whose political vision and determined action was informed by their foundation in faith and in the church. While historians, sociologists, and political scientists have traditionally pointed to the role of the black church as a social center that generated social movements, communal cohesion, and indispensable leadership, they have not integrated their study of the roles of women with their studies of religious agency in the process of social change. In these accounts, nearly all of the religious leaders have been men and all of the religious women have been followers. There has been relatively little integration of black women's religious agency with the tremendous history of social change generated by women's activism.

I have been guilty of just such separation of perspective. In the late 1970s, I conducted a study of twenty-five black women who had achieved reputations as "women who had worked hard for a long time for change in the black community." That study was later augmented with interviews for the Radcliffe College Black Women's Oral History Project. For my own study, I developed a sample from a large list of women whom people in the community identified as their heroines and whose achievements were documented in black newspapers. I also sought nominations from clergymen. One politically active clergyman took the time to write a detailed letter explaining how one woman had been particularly helpful in connecting him with the larger religious community and with women activists when he first accepted his pastorate. He went on to say that he could have done nothing without her help and that she was the best person from whom to seek nominations.

When I interviewed this woman, she provided an extensive list of possible participants in the study. As we talked about the clergy and their activism, she provided me with my first characterization of the difference between male "preachers" and female "evangelists." I heard, internalized, and then ignored that discussion because I was conducting a study of politically active women, not church workers. The contested roles of women as ministers and evangelists served to mask the religious connections even more.

My study took place at a time when political assaults and funding cutbacks had reduced the Great Society programs of the 1960s until none but the truly committed remained in community work. At that time many black communities were beginning to confront the urban problems associated with economic restructuring and deindustrialization. Many community workers were particularly active in education, welfare reform, and health care. As a sociologist with a peculiarly secular bent, I did not make issues of faith and religious connection central to my study or place them high on the list of questions I asked. I was more interested in the provocations that had shaped these women's careers in volunteer and paid positions and had led to their becoming visible among the most admired black people in their communities.

Black women community workers were a force to be reckoned with. My own interest had been sparked by my father's insistence that the survival and progress of the black community was tied up in the activities of women who had raised scholarship money and opened doors for younger people like himself. He saw them as the prime movers in organizations in which he worked, such as the NAACP. These women knew how to make a difference *within* the community; at the same time they were effective in changing things *outside* of their communities. My father's story of growing up in Baltimore turned on the scholarship support that women managed to garner for college and graduate school educations. (For instance, they forced the state of Maryland to pay to send black students out of the state to programs that Maryland did not provide outside its white institutions.) Both my dad and Thurgood Marshall benefited from these programs, which exploited the contradictions of Jim Crow to enlarge educational opportunities. To this day, my father's description of Mrs. Juanita Jackson's activism enables him to recognize the importance of women's activism and grounds his enthusiastically positive evaluation of their work in the black community.

Over the course of my interviewing, I discovered that the importance of faith and religious experience ran so deep and was so taken for granted that my participants assumed that I, as a black woman, already knew all about it. When I asked about faith and religious connections, the women responded, "Of course!" or "That goes without saying." Combined with my sociological secularism, their taking the salience of faith for granted tended to relegate any discussion of spiritual motivations to a secondary place during the interviews. Often, indeed, it seemed an afterthought.

Only later did the importance of placing black women community workers' religious connections, faith, and spirituality in the foreground become clear. My subsequent research on religion, taken together with my interactions with women I'd interviewed, highlighted the centrality of women in shaping the religious centers of black communities. These women's religious connections and faith, a much ignored aspect of the process of social change within and beyond the black community, played an integral role in the organizational integrity of the black community and in the construction of a public culture (a meaning Martha Jones carefully defines in chapter 7) that not only assumed the importance of spirituality but also utilized "faith-based practices" as cultural strategies in political settings.[3]

Women's religious connections and practices are part of the forces that constitute and sustain African American political culture and at the same time strengthen, brace, and prepare women for a wide variety of struggles. The Latin root of the word *force* implies fortitude or the "strength of mind that enables a person to encounter danger or to bear pain or adversity with courage."[4] Black women's faith as a cultural force points us toward a more general understanding of the inextricable connection between African American women and the process of social change. Sexism and the exclusion of black women from a variety of leadership roles are not unimportant. However, we know more about the subordinate roles of black women in church and community than we know about the actual contributions they have made to the culture. Historically and currently, the centrality and force of black women's faith can be observed in spite of their marginalization.

Black Women's Leadership

During slavery, black women participated in all of the activities that fostered survival and generated resistance. Much has been said about the importance of religion and family as enduring institutions in the slave community.[5] Deborah Gray White demonstrates, however, that the black women's network was another key institution.[6] Women slaves organized themselves for survival, resistance, and leadership, and their autonomous, concerted action redounded to the benefit of the entire community. Women worked to make sure that their sisters, their brothers, and their families were properly cared for in sickness and death. In addition to working cooperatively to foster health and care for children, the women shared a collective spiritual life. Among themselves, away from white masters and mistresses and even their menfolk, black women worshipped and prayed together.[7]

Slave women's religious life included powerful women prophets who were respected leaders, listened to not only by women but by the entire community. In a manner similar to Nat Turner, these women interpreted the world apocalyptically.[8] They saw signs of God's judgment against slavery in nature and the weather. Their visions were recorded in quilts, such as those by Harriet Powers.[9] White describes a slave woman named Sinda who predicted the end of the world with such forcefulness that her fellow slaves refused to return to work until the designated day was past. Male slaves described their early religious socialization as beginning with hearing their mothers and aunts, both consanguine and fictive, praying for freedom. Multiple sources point to the importance of women's religious activity throughout the life of the community.

All of this was in addition to women's participation in the visible and invisible church as spiritual leaders, including their roles as preachers and exhorters in the slave community and the free northern churches.[10] Women agitated for ordination in the AME Church before the end of slavery, and they conducted revivals at camp meetings in the slave South.[11] Free black women participated in antislav-

ery and mutual aid organizations.[12] Women exhibited profound faith and religious activism. Sojourner Truth gained fame not only as an antislavery lecturer
but also as an Adventist preacher, although her spiritual inspiration and religious
leadership has often been forgotten.[13] Harriet Tubman was active in the AME
Zion church and openly utilized her faith and sacred music to carry out her role
as an abductor on the Underground Railroad.[14]

Immediately after freedom, as Tara Hunter points out, black women played vital roles in developing urban black churches.[15] They represented at least half of
the urban working class in the Reconstruction and post-Reconstruction South.
Women's money and labor built and supported churches. Churchwomen were
members of a variety of fraternal organizations, and the rules of these organizations often required that members also belong to churches. Prominent women
who served as "race leaders" during the late nineteenth century—women like
Maggie Lena Walker, Ida B. Wells, and Anna Julia Cooper—were invariably active churchwomen. Discrimination and cultural conventions guaranteed that
these women would not become acknowledged members of the clergy. However,
their activities required that they share the same social world with clergymen in
order to counter effectively the forces of violent repression and Jim Crow. They
spoke to religious gatherings that included men and participated in the deliberative bodies of their churches and denominations. (In chapter 7, Jones documents
this pattern among various Methodist groups.)

By the end of the nineteenth century, legal segregation was firmly in place and
black women had organized an extensive network of clubs and organizations to
resist discrimination, seek suffrage, end lynching, educate their children, and
uplift the race. In 1896, the National Association of Colored Women (NACW)
brought together over four hundred women's clubs and then launched an effort
to organize more. While scholars have focused on the prominence of middle-class
women in the club movement and criticized these women's elitism, what Evelyn
Brooks Higginbotham describes as "the politics of respectability" transcended
economic position.[16] Christian women of all social classes sought to live in accordance with their faith. In their eyes (as Butler points out in chapter 8), leading
an exemplary life was more important than economic position in defining a
woman's worth. By the end of the nineteenth century, the Holiness and Pentecostal movements inspired a large corps of women to fulfill their sense of Christian vocation by becoming missionaries and evangelists. The same women belonged to women's clubs and Bible Bands. They strove to meet the biblical
standards associated with women's dress and behavior at the same time they
served as educators and activists within and beyond their communities. This

shared Christian culture enabled the values we associate with the middle class to have a dominance and prominence in the club movement which masked the actual diversity among women.

I have argued elsewhere that the club movement represented a move by black churchwomen to become prominent public leaders in secular political settings. Blocked from full participation as leaders in their churches—that is, as ordained preachers—they sought to develop alternative spaces for their voices, energies, and leadership in the work for uplift and change. A few clergywomen, such as Florence Spearing Randolph, an ordained African Methodist Episcopal Zion (AME Zion) pastor, also led the club movement. While pastoring full time, Randolph served as national chaplain of the NACW and the president of the New Jersey state federation.[17] Some women found religious autonomy and greater access to sacred space in the Sanctified church, an outgrowth of the Holiness and Pentecostal movements (as Butler explains in some detail). Others raised their voices in gospel music, performing within their churches and in secular locations (see chapter 11). Substantial numbers of churchwomen found political autonomy and secular voice through their clubs and organizational efforts such as sororities and occupational associations. Since individual women tended to join multiple organizations, there was and still is tremendous organizational overlap.[18]

W. E. B. Du Bois, in a long-ignored and under-appreciated volume, *The Gift of Black Folk,* pointed out that black women's most significant contributions lay in the connections they established through their clubs and their missionary societies, which bridged secular and sacred settings.[19] Du Bois's observation invites a focus on the ways women established and maintained the organizational integrity of the black community. He also cited women's roles in sustaining the economic stability of black churches. His view implies that women provided a counterbalance for what he complained was the fractiousness of male preachers; while clergymen competed for congregants and prestige, jealously sowing the seeds of faction, laywomen cooperated across the lines of organizational division to further the cause of community. Women's activities were a vital form of leadership that helped advance and uplift all black people.

The organizational energy of black churchwomen was reorganized and more extensively galvanized when Mary McLeod Bethune organized the National Council of Negro Women (NCNW) in 1935. A protégé of Mary Church Terrell, Bethune developed extensive contacts with black women's religious and secular organizations across the country and served as president of the NACW in 1928. She used her experience and networks to leverage her friendship with Eleanor Roosevelt and bring pressure to bear upon the architects of the New Deal for more federal response to issues of civil rights, an effort that proved quite effective and had lasting political consequences. This Methodist, Presbyterian-educated woman studied at the Moody Bible Institute; as a student she worked as a street preacher and conducted a prison ministry. After being refused a position in the mission fields of Africa, she found an alternative as an educator and the founder of what became Bethune Cookman College. Her writings and activities placed Bethune squarely in the world of the religiously motivated. Her last will and testament is a brief exhortation rooted in Christian ethics and demonstrates the force of faith in her activism and philosophy of life.[20]

The civil rights movement, while eliminating Jim Crow, probably increased the level of misogyny that black women public leaders faced. For a variety of reasons, the movement pushed men—mostly clergy—to the forefront of acknowledged leadership. Although gender clearly shaped a number of key moments in the movement, particularly the Montgomery bus boycott, black women's leadership came to be viewed as "behind the scenes," "grassroots," "local," "bridge,"— a whole assortment of labels that marked womens' role as secondary to that of the men, who were regarded as leading the "real action." As a result, the centrality of women was ignored even when the evidence of their spiritual inspiration and organizational skills was everywhere, as in the lives and work of Ella Baker and Fannie Lou Hamer. As Belinda Robnett has observed, the complaints of white women participants in the civil rights movement received more prominence than the continued presence and power of black women in mobilizing their communities, and defined the lenses through which all women's roles were viewed.[21] The prophetic activities of black preachers of the period redefined images of ministry and leadership for black men, while black women activists were rarely viewed in terms of their prophetic leadership.[22]

Black Women's Prophetic Leadership

The force of faith, although much ignored, is clearly evident when black women activists tell their own stories. Religious connections were woven through the lives of the community workers I interviewed. Their spirituality was rooted in the African American tradition and encompassed innovative, idiosyncratic modes of religious expression. They evinced a deep faith that could be inferred from their religious affiliations and activities.

Some women actually held positions of leadership within their congregations at the same time that they exercised more publicly visible leadership in secular settings. Other women visited a variety of churches to construct a religious experience that matched their public activism. Even for those women who were not then members of churches, the church had operated as an early training ground for their political activities and shaped their effective leadership styles. When describing their various role models, they sometimes included their male pastors. Their first experiences of leadership—running meetings, managing treasuries, keeping minutes, electing officers—occurred in church youth groups.

Their religious experiences shaped a worldview comparable to that of a missionary, someone who possessed such a deep sense of vocation, experienced such a heightened sense of destiny, and perceived such deep levels of social injustice that she was moved to work to change the world for the better and to change the people within that world. Although all of these women spoke the language of the African American religious tradition, they described a variety of religious experiences. Some were more publicly embedded in religious traditions and institutions than others. None of the women wore her religion on her sleeve. Sometimes the true depths of their religious experiences were revealed only in their pastors' eulogies at their funerals or when I encountered them in religious settings. I discovered the dimensions of one woman's spirituality when giving her an account of my research on the Sanctified Church. All of these women had positive relationships with local pastors through their community work; although they might differ with these men over matters of theology or political strategy, not one woman spoke negatively of ministers in the local community.

Several women serve as important illustrations of how black women's faith operated as a creative and constitutive cultural and political force. They worked within and beyond black communities with the same prophetic styles and as much effectiveness as activist male preachers. These women were extremely persuasive public speakers and articulate advocates of the causes they espoused. Occasionally, their secular affiliations gained them access to places where their male counterparts' visible religious identification was a liability. Importantly, these women were part of highly effective public networks that linked them into cooperative working relationships with black preachers beyond the walls of the local congregation.

Personal Strength and Public Challenge

Mrs. Ellison (all of the names are pseudonyms) provided an especially instructive case study. In learning about her life as an activist, I attended meetings with her, served briefly as her chauffeur, and became, over the course of the research, a close friend. When I asked her about her role models, she actually pointed to Jesus, translating his status as Jewish and poor into contemporary terms that inspired her; because Jesus was able to keep his commitments and make sacrifices, she was able to keep hers. She had grown up in an older, established black church in the city. Early in her life, Mrs. Ellison taught Sunday School and managed a nursery in an affluent suburban church. The grown children from that nursery sometimes served as important resources for her diverse community activities. She maintained a membership in her childhood church but rarely attended, primarily because she was so busy with her community activism and her human service agency job, which periodically required her to visit a variety of local churches.

Mrs. Ellison had a personal relationship with nearly every black clergyman and many of the white clergy in her community. She organized Black History Month events with public funds, but that did not stop her from recruiting a variety of pastors to open and close her programs with prayer and to contribute remarks. Regardless of the topic of the program, she incorporated music and made sure that spirituals and gospel music as well as secular selections were represented. In spite of her very public municipal job, no one ever complained about Mrs. Ellison's inclusion of clergy and religious music in her public activities, since she always argued that such elements were "central to our culture."

These activities were not only cultural strategies but also personal fortifications. Any church choir that Mrs. Ellison recruited for her programs was expected to have in its repertoire certain songs, which she often requested ahead of time. These songs were personally meaningful to her. One of her favorites was "Going Up Yonder," popularized in the 1970s by the gospel singers Walter and Tramaine Hawkins. When Mrs. Ellison passed away, her funeral could not be held in her home church because it was simply too small; several local pastors competed for the privilege of hosting her funeral. This very efficient organizer and activist had left detailed instructions for her funeral, including the specific musical selections. Her relatives and the soloist she requested were able to carry out her wishes except for one song, "See My Savior Face to Face." When I arrived at the house, the soloist and the relatives were still discussing the music. They had poured over every accessible hymnbook and songbook they knew, but they could not find the song. They asked me if I had any idea what song she wanted. Because of our discussions about why she loved that song, I was able to tell them that Mrs. Ellison had actually misnamed her favorite gospel song, recalling it by the line that defined her religious hope rather than its actual title. The song she wanted was "Going Up Yonder." The presence and prominence of clergy at her funeral underscored her religious connections and motivation. Her religious connections enabled people to visualize the extent, complexity, and interconnectedness of community.

During her interview and in many of her public statements, Mrs. Ellison evinced a prophetic approach to her work. Her life centered on her concerns for and solidarity with the poor of all ethnic groups. This woman, who pointed to Jesus as her role model, lived by choice in a housing project in order to be an effective advocate for people in public housing. When she experienced upward mobility in her employment, she paid higher rents in order to remain in public housing. In spite of the considerable professional experience she amassed, she refused to be seen as enriching herself at the expense of the community.

The community workers were like the eighth-century prophets of the Hebrew Bible, thundering away in public places like the city council, the board of education, and the zoning commission. As was true of many community workers I interviewed, Mrs. Ellison's effective public voice could be loud, disruptive, even fearsome. She confronted the public housing agency, the city's elected officials, and the school committee, and she also waged an effective campaign for change in the local police department. She gathered a large group of undergraduate and graduate students and put them to work conducting an in-depth study of police policies and practices. Both the complaining community and organizations representing the police praised the results of her work.

Moral Authority and Faith in the Pulpit

Community workers' combination of faith and activism, along with their effectiveness as public prophets, provided them with access to pulpits as Women's Day speakers. Often local churches would invite prominent women who were secular leaders rather than women who were clergy or explicitly religious leaders, such as missionaries or evangelists. However, speaking in the Sunday morning service usually meant that the pastor and other church decision makers viewed the women's faith and spirituality to be exemplary.

One woman community worker, Mrs. James, became famous for her sermonic challenges to the black middle class. She passionately believed in the responsibility of the "talented tenth" to serve the people, and she was impatient with what she perceived as the complacency and political apathy of the more privileged members of her community. She was not alone. Most of these women did double duty as activists, working to change the unjust structures and at the same time challenging and exhorting people within their local communities to do more for their own uplift. When Mrs. James preached at the most affluent black congregation in her city, she made headlines in the black weekly newspaper for challenging middle-class people who were too exclusive in their social lives and too complacent in their politics. Her sermon echoed the complaints of E. Franklin Frazier in his book *Black Bourgeoisie*, without Frazier's pejorative approach toward black middle-class social organizations. She herself had grown up somewhat privileged, however, she developed a political style and a concentration on issues that bonded her with the poor and working classes. This sense of solidarity often extended to where community workers lived. Not all lived in public housing as Mrs. Ellison did, but many continued to reside in urban black neighborhoods by choice even when their and their husbands' combined incomes gave them access to more affluent and predominantly white suburban neighborhoods.

Activist women sometimes were catalysts for congregations' rethinking their attitudes toward women in the ministry. Mrs. Carroll, one of the senior members of the corps of community workers I interviewed, was the one with the most moral authority in the city. She was also the first woman ever to preach from the pulpit at what was arguably the leading Baptist church with the most visibly activist pastor. One pastor had held elective office while serving there full time. Mrs. Carroll had effectively mobilized the organizations affiliated with the National Association of Colored Women's Clubs to secure the election of the first woman president of the local NAACP chapter. She had been among that generation of black women who, despite their college or postsecondary education, had been unable to find work except as household domestics, and this experience had shaped her activist agenda. Mrs. Carroll became one of the prime movers behind legislation that provided access to Social Security benefits to private household employees. She ran workshops to teach household domestics effective strategies for challenging the most demeaning and exploitative aspects of their work. One of her organizations sent observers to bus stations during the 1930s, 1940s, and 1950s to look for newly arrived domestic workers from the South in order to offer them contacts in the local black community and the option of living away from their employers' households. Another one of her clubs purchased and administered a residence so that household domestics could become day workers rather than living in with their employers. She spoke of the experiences of poor people and their survival strategies as knowledge that could help many other people in need. In another one of her organizations, she and her club members organized cultural events, such as dances, teas, lectures, and musicals, that provided safe and less worldly social outlets for her fellow domestics. Her life exemplified an approach based on linking people across class lines, an inclusionary aspect of "racial uplift" that too often gets lost in criticisms of how middle-class women's concerns shaped the movements they led.

Community workers often approached the issue of their own mortality with the same assertiveness and realism with which they approached the problems of social injustice and the challenges of community transformation. Like Mrs. Ellison, Mrs. Carroll was "ready." When ministers learned of her impending death, they flocked to visit her. One talked openly about her attitude toward her approaching death. According to his account, as he attempted to rally her spirits, urging her to stay longer, she responded, "Boy! I can't stay here forever!" She sounded just as feisty in the face of death as she had been throughout her career as a community worker.

Preachers from her extensive network of political activist colleagues attended Mrs. Carroll's funeral in droves, along with two senators, the mayor, several congressmen, and governors past and present. In her interview with me she had spoken about the importance of her Christian faith, and the several ministers who eulogized her elaborated on its centrality to her life work. One minister in attendance was the pastor of the church where she had been the first woman ever to deliver a sermon. By the time of Mrs. Carroll's death, his Baptist congregation was known as a haven for women in the ministry and several had been ordained there.

Although Mrs. Carroll looked like the quintessential gentle great-grandmother, she could, like Mrs. Ellison, be a formidable public force. Once during a major sit-in that occupied a public building, the police threatened demonstrators with arrest. One of the coordinators phoned Mrs. Carroll, and she took a taxi to the sit-in and sat down with the demonstrators. Although the city had brought in the paddy wagons and a large force to arrest the protestors, her arrival prompted an order from police headquarters not to arrest the demonstrators. On another occasion young black militants publicly criticized her, saying that she had done "nothing for the revolution." Her forceful response, reported in the newspapers, was to remind them, "I was out raising scholarship money to send you to school so you can come back here and give me sass!"

Mrs. Tinsley, another senior member of the group of community activists I interviewed and a friend of Mrs. Carroll, also possessed moral authority and a powerful public presence. Mrs. Tinsley told me that her public career was shaped by the advice she received from her father before migrating from the South; he admonished her to join the church and the NAACP. Several other women were instructed by their parents to maintain church memberships regardless of their levels of faith. Like Mrs. Tinsley, they were told that they would not be able to do anything useful in their communities without the church connection. Mrs. Tinsley belonged to a large number of organizations but was known primarily for her devotion and long years of service to the NAACP. The local board created a permanent seat just for her.

After Mrs. Tinsley's death, I discovered that until shortly before she died in her early nineties, she faithfully attended Bible study at her church. She had told me how proud she was that she walked to church on Wednesday nights and Sunday. She confessed that she had kept her age (eighty-six at the time of our interview) a secret from the pastor and the church so that she could maintain her independence and mobility. By the time of her death, her church, a large and prominent older congregation, had, like Mrs. Carroll's church, become a haven for women in ministry.

Ministers, Religious Professionals, and Pastoral Helping Styles

Two women in my study were religious professionals. One was a pastor, and the other was the executive director of a religiously based organization. Rev. Talley, the pastor of a large Pentecostal congregation, talked extensively about her commitment to working on issues of educational quality and school desegregation. Before there was a "safe havens" program in the city, she made her church a place for students to come and talk about the violent conflicts they experienced in their newly desegregated schools. She did not say much about how she became a minister and talked entirely in a secular, activist mode, even though the interview took place in her church. That day, I never asked the right questions. Later, in another setting, I heard her speak about the process by which she became a minister. Like many black clergywomen, she had begun her spiritual journey in the Baptist church and struggled against discrimination there until she moved to a Pentecostal denomination that believed in the ordination of women. Her deep faith was evident in her story. The same faith that had carried her into the ministry was the source of the strength, fortitude, and calm with which she confronted public issues outside the walls of her church.

Dr. Burns, the director of an organization funded by a white mainline Protestant denomination, talked extensively about the various religious settings that had shaped her vocation. Not only had the Episcopal congregation of her youth helped to develop her, but she had spent time visiting with the Nation of Islam. Although she never became a Muslim, she acquired a deep sense of nationhood and community beyond her specific class and ethnic location as a child of Caribbean immigrants who saw themselves as better than black people born in the United States. Dr. Burns's faith motivated her to utilize her business experience and skills to push white religious organizations to confront racism. Like other women in the study, she was a prominent Women's Day speaker and a prophetic voice in political settings. From Dr. Burns's perspective, an important aspect of her public role was to confront white racism and to shake up the white Protestant mainline.

The women I interviewed who directed human services agencies resembled the pastors of large churches, managing and administering agencies that helped people. They had attained these positions of responsibility through various combinations of professional training and professionalized activism, obtaining the credentials and earning the credibility that the work required. Their approaches to helping people demonstrated a deep capacity for empathy. Often their relationships with so-called clients violated the presumptions of dominance and social distance that govern the helping professions. Since they often saw the people who received their services as "brothers and sisters," not as clients, their professional language sounded more congregational than clinical.[23] Furthermore, these women had experienced some of the same problems as those they were assisting. Mrs. Bullard was conscious of "what happens when the former receiver of services becomes the deliverer of services." These community workers built empathy into their philosophies of service. Further, they structured their programs in ways that provided opportunities for those they served to move from being in need of assistance to being able to assist others, a process that empowered people and contributed to making social change as well as ensuring that people's dignity was respected.

Mrs. Manning provided an extreme example of this empathetic approach. A woman whose faith story I almost missed, she was the director of a mental health program, which she had successfully moved from hospital grounds into the community. She was a stately, quiet woman who spoke in very low, slow, and elegant tones. It was clear that she was a native of the South. At the time I interviewed her, she was working with welfare mothers who had exhibited psychiatric symptoms. Her approach was to confront all of the problems related to their situation. While attempting to gather as many services for the women as she could, she also conducted training programs to help them manage their meager resources and reduce the stress they experienced from their poverty, motherhood, and diverse personal troubles. Her rationale in moving the program away from the hospital was her perception that these mothers would be stigmatized by having to receive their counseling and training at a mental hospital. Stigma only added to their stress, she explained. Her approach to providing services was consistent with her view that healing was an important community work activity.

When we got to the part of the interview where I asked the obligatory question about religious background, I learned that she was a member of a very traditional Baptist church and had been a missionary "in the Sanctified Church." She had left the Church of God in Christ because of a conflict with a bishop. What I did not realize at the time I interviewed her was that Mrs. Manning's role as a missionary meant that she was a gifted and charismatic evangelist. She was an experienced preacher, although such activity was called "speaking" or "teaching" when carried out by women.[24] Later, as I came to understand the force of her faith, I was able to comprehend what this history meant. As a missionary, she had probably worked under the authority of a bishop who sent her to various churches in his district to address problems and to teach doctrine within the denomination. Her conflict with him would have been very public and potentially divisive. Her leaving the church was probably an act of Christian professionalism, the kind of behavior expected when staff members of a church have conflicts with the pastor.[25] As Mrs. Manning listed her activities, she stated "I'm a member of the police commission." It was hard to imagine this elegant, graceful, soft-spoken woman hobnobbing with a bunch of rough and tumble, cigar-smoking white men, so I asked, somewhat incredulously, "How did you become a member of the police commission?" She leaned back in her chair and stated loudly and forcefully, "One night I turned Station A out!" Station A was considered one of the worst police substations in the black community, located in a rough neighborhood and legendary for the levels of violence prisoners experienced there. She proceeded to tell me the story.

One night the Station A police had raided a house where drugs were being sold. One of the people arrested was the mother of an infant. The police simply left the infant alone in the house. Of course, the baby eventually began crying. Because the neighbors were so afraid of this drug house, they called Mrs. Manning to report the crying infant. Undaunted, Mrs. Manning went to the house, found the baby, and placed the child with friends. She then proceeded to go to Station A where she loudly, forcefully, and prophetically informed the police of what they had done wrong. She raised so much turmoil in the station house that she was eventually appointed to serve on the police commission, and officers were required to secure care for infants and children when arresting their mothers. Mrs. Manning had taken all of the forcefulness and charisma of a Pentecostal evangelist and turned it loose on one of the most feared settings in the black community—a hostile police station. Her spirituality was a source of courage and public conviction.

Symbiosis, Cooperation, and Community

Several of the women maintained symbiotic relationships with activist ministers in the community. Women such as Mrs. Pimental often represented the black community on boards of directors. Sometimes the demands of board membership could mute their prophetic voices. At times like these, they would exploit their relationships with activist male pastors, informing them of the problems with an organization and its policies and encouraging these clergy to organize public confrontations and demonstrations. Mrs. Pimental told me of her cooperative but covert relationship with one minister. She had coordinated a demonstration to occur while she was sitting quietly in the board meeting; the minister conducted a picket line and sit-in that effectively shut the board into the building. The board was unaware that Mrs. Pimental had not only recruited this activist pastor but also had rented the busses he needed to transport the demonstrators to the downtown meeting site. When the board members attempted to ignore the demonstrators, Mrs. Pimental suggested that they should inquire about the demonstrators' grievances.

Mrs. Pimental's actions suggest the need to explore how gendered role expectations facilitate symbiosis and cooperation between preachers who control sacred space and community workers who control diverse secular settings. Such strategic symbiosis enabled the women's prophetic voices to be heard inside places where more visible activists, such as the publicly vocal ministers, would not be heard. Symbiotic relationships provided conduits of access to resources outside of deprived black communities when powerful white agencies were reluctant to deal with religious leaders. Conversely, sometimes the ministers were able to open doors to religious agencies when women community workers in secular settings could not. The ministers were also able to be present in spaces from which patriarchal norms and presumptions excluded women. These stories show that in some cases women and men understood their distinct activist roles as complementary, enabling them to bridge the secular and sacred, as well as the gender divide, and bring concerted pressure for change. This pattern of cooperation deserves further investigation.

These examples illustrate how religious connections and religiously informed patterns of behavior intertwine with political and social activism. These women's faith fortified them for effective service, affecting the community and their churches as well. The more dramatic examples among the community workers suggest that we explore the religious importance of women leaders in their own right and that we interrogate and foreground the meaning and consequences of their religious affiliations. These community workers make a difference in people's lives, in the neighborhoods where they live and work, and in the churches that provide them with a broad and deep base of support, key male ministerial allies, and a forum, if not a pulpit, from which to articulate an agenda for change. Their faith is a resource that sharpens their prophetic voice, calling the powerful to account for their actions and demanding change in unjust and oppressive institutions. Their spirituality, sense of vocation, and religiously based recognition of others as deserving of equal respect also shapes how they deliver services, healing and empowering individuals and enabling them to cope in an oppressive and hostile environment.

In 1924, W. E. B. Du Bois observed that African American women played a special role in connecting the black community.[26] He also noted that their work was done simultaneously in their missionary societies and in their clubs—in sacred and secular settings. Understanding the force of black women's faith requires that we understand how their spirituality empowers them to maintain multiple memberships in secular organizations, churches, and other religious organizations—their sense that they can do "all things" and "keep so busy." These black women community workers demonstrate that the prophetic role is not limited to the black preacher. They exercise leadership in a misogynistic world that is sometimes more comfortable with male preachers than female community workers. However, the ability of like-minded prophetic men and women to change structures and to transform and empower individuals may be a function of a shared faith—a faith that runs so deep and is so taken for granted that no one ever interrogates it.

Despite the discrimination women experience within their churches, people full of faith, especially black Christians, believe deeply that they are able to make a better world. That faith is typified by B. Alma Androzzo's song, "If I Can Help Somebody." Understanding the persistence of black people in seeking to change the world for the better means examining the faith of black women activists. In a world that seeks to make us believe that Dr. Martin Luther King said nothing after "I have a dream," why does it take a woman who formerly belonged to the Black Panther Party, Elaine Brown, to remind us that Dr. Martin Luther King insisted to this nation, "America, you must be born again"?[27] Such an admonition demonstrates the force of faith and the consequences of that faith for African American women, their communities, and this nation.

PART III

PERFORMING RELIGION

CHAPTER TEN

The Arts of Loving

LISA GAIL COLLINS

Empowered amorous objects are essential to the blues. In "Louisiana Hoodoo Blues," Gertrude "Ma" Rainey declares possessively:

Going to Louisiana bottom to get me a hoodoo hand
Going to Louisiana bottom to get me a hoodoo hand
Gotta stop these women from taking my man

Down in Algiers where the hoodoos live in their den
Down in Algiers where the hoodoos live in their den
Their chief occupation is separating women from men

The hoodoo told me to get me a black cat bone
The hoodoo told me to get me a black cat bone
And shake it over their heads, they'll leave your man alone.[1]

Central to the blueswoman's ballad is a black diasporic premise that expertly pre-scribed and properly charged objects—charms, roots, potions, gris-gris, jujus, to-bies, goofer dust, and, in this case, a hoodoo hand and a black cat bone—can harness an object of desire and abet hunger for emotional control.

Male swaggerers also assert the potency of empowered amorous objects within the blues. Muddy Waters in his heterosexual boast "(I'm Your) Hoochie Coochie Man" brashly touts the seductive powers of objects:

I got a black cat bone. I got a mojo too.
I got a John the Conqueror Root. I got to mess with you.
I'm gonner make you girls, lead me by my hand.
Then the world will know, I'm the Hoochie Coochie Man.[2]

Like Rainey in her blues ballad, Muddy Waters in his oral strut confidently claims that securing a charged charm—in this case, a black cat bone, a mojo, and a John the Conqueror root—will entice and seduce desired mates.

Like their musical peers, African American visual artists delve into the arts of enchantment for creative inspiration and spirited conversation. In so doing, they, too, encounter black Atlantic practices and beliefs that engage conjure and the amorous arts: the arts of finding and keeping a lover. Unlike musicians, visual artists approach the charged objects of conjure materially. Conjure, the practice of summoning spirits and forces, is an integral part of African American cultural history, and tales of love and the possibility of its manipulation through conjuring permeate black life. *Love Potion #9*, a 1988 multimedia installation by Alison Saar (1956–), visually converses with this dynamic black diasporic history as it serves as a visual meditation on conjure, particularly the links between empowered objects, faith, and the divine arts of seduction (Fig. 10.1). Borrowing its title from the Clovers' 1959 pop song, the broad subject of Saar's artistic environment of carved sculptures and mixed media assemblages is love and loving.[3] Like the blues, the gallery installation broods on the seamy sides of affairs of the heart, namely, emotional torment, mental chaos, and bodily lust.

Fig. 10.1. Alison Saar (1956–), *Love Potion #9*, 1988. Mixed media installation. Courtesy of the artist.

First situating us within the creolized complexity of New Orleans, the multi-media installation then guides us through nine separate works, or "stations," that engage conjure and the seductive arts. Each of the stations, Saar informs us, is devoted to "a specific amorous aspiration."[4] As each station refers to a specific yearning—to lure a mate, sate lust, connect deeply, avoid torment, alleviate anguish, and punish the competition—we walk through the created environment contemplating various love ailments and elixirs while deeply immersed in the cultural history of African America. Subtly echoing the ritual practice of making the fourteen Stations of the Cross in the Catholic Church, the nine "stations of the heart" that make up the installation serve as vibrant sites for imaginative contemplation. Mindful walking through the stations of the heart allows us to closely engage objects, intimately contemplate materials, and thoughtfully reflect on the practices and beliefs central to conjure in a secular setting. Playful in tone, the work simultaneously exposes cultural elements that can be traced to an African past and to communities of enslaved and free people in the New World and unearths the spiritual underpinnings of the seductive arts.

Upon approaching Saar's charmed stations, we pass through two cast paper gates reminiscent of the ornamental ironwork of the urban South. Serving as entryway and establishing shot, the black decorative gates suggest locale and set the context for the black diasporic beliefs, practices, and objects central to the room. The distinctive presence of the gates evokes the histories, movements, cultures, and creations of the people most associated with conjure and the seductive arts, for people of African descent have been central to the art and trade of blacksmithing in the United States since the eighteenth century.[5] Prior to the Civil War, southern metal work was heavily reliant on the skilled labor of enslaved black men. African American men produced much of the needed ironwork on both rural farms and in urban centers. During the eighteenth and nineteenth centuries, many blacksmiths of African descent worked to create the famed decorative wrought ironwork in southern cities such as Charleston, Savannah, Mobile, and New Orleans. Enslaved and free metalworkers forged ornamental gates, fences, balconies, and window grills for these historic cities. These skilled workers usually based their wrought-iron designs on European—typically French or Spanish—models. The material culture scholar John Michael Vlach argues that the port city of New Orleans offered the most room for cross-cultural artistic experimentation and improvisation with forged metal.[6] In Saar's installation, the blackened gates broadly evoke the tragic and resilient trajectory of people forced from Africa, transported across the Atlantic Ocean, and pressed into hard labor in the New World. More specifically, the latticed gates recall the complex history of the creolized hub at the base of the Mississippi River.

While the gates themselves suggest New Orleans' French Quarter, their design suggests two of that historic neighborhood's most famous residents, for woven into the intricacy of the gates is an abstracted heart. The heart was inspired by the artist's pilgrimage through the iron gates of St. Louis Cemetery #2 to the burial site for Marie Laveau, the legendary priestess commonly known as the Voodoo Queen of New Orleans. Marie Laveau (1783–1881) and her protégé daughter (1827–?), who went by the same title, were highly sought after Vodou-inspired diviners, herbalists, and healers.[7] Mother and daughter counseled numerous anxious clients on a wide range of issues, including domestic problems relating to passion and desire, and their prescriptions often included the faithful use of empowered objects. The subject of much twentieth-century legend and lore, these influential female spiritual counselors continue to animate the popular imagination. Contemporary devotees and admirers frequently visit the Laveau gravesite to leave material offerings, and they sometimes signal their journey by marking the tomb with symbols, most often with Xs or chalked hearts.

After witnessing these symbolic sojourns and markings and reflecting on their meanings, Alison Saar recreated their presence in her installation by painting the gallery walls the same mossy green as the aging above-ground tombs of the swampy burial grounds in New Orleans. She also marked the green painted walls with Xs and other referential insignia.[8] Concerning her interest in evoking a particular time, place, and cultural legacy in *Love Potion #9*, the artist explains: "This is an environment reminiscent of old New Orleans. Cool green moss-colored walls with two centuries worth of texture come alive with the shadows of magnolia trees and the spirits that dwell within."[9]

Both the heart on the gates and the hearts sometimes chalked onto the Laveau tomb echo the *vèvè* symbols used in Haitian Vodou to elicit Ezili Freda, the feminine spirit, or *lwa*, of love. The heart is a symbol for Ezili Freda, also known as Erzulie, the goddess of passion and ardor. Typically associated with sensuous luxury items such as fine clothes, jewelry, perfume, and lace, this deity of love and lovers most likely traveled with its adherents from the kingdom of Dahomey (located in what is now the southern part of Benin) and was transformed with its contact with Yoruba and BaKongo peoples as well as with Roman Catholicism in the New World. In leaving chalked hearts and other insignia on the Laveau tombstone, visitors quietly tap the cultural transformations based on the spatial and spiritual movements of the two priestesses' ancestors, as mother and daughter were the daughter and granddaughter of Haitian migrants.[10]

During Madame Laveau's childhood, Haitian migrants, a group that included French planters and free and enslaved people of African descent, arrived en masse in what is now the state of Louisiana. During the Haitian Revolution of 1791–1803, more than fifteen thousand *émigrés* fled the French sugar colony and settled around the banks of the Mississippi River; a considerable portion settled in New Orleans.[11] African-descended migrants continued to arrive in great numbers in the years directly following Haitian independence in 1804. These Haitians brought to the region many of the beliefs and practices of Vodou. Migrants also brought the essential practice of drawing *vèvè* symbols to invoke the presence of a spirit or deity. Often drawn on the ground, these symbols work, like conjure, to summon metaphysical forces.

Haitian migrants most likely introduced Vodou to a North American cultural landscape that already housed a less structured and even more diffuse set of beliefs and practices commonly referred to as voodoo, hoodoo, or conjure. Like Vodou, this set of West and Central African–influenced beliefs and practices developed when enslaved African people adapted their respective religious and philosophical traditions to the constraints of New World slavery and the doctrines of Christianity. Underlying many of the thoughts and actions of conjure is the conviction that events of the material world are shaped by a largely invisible world inhabited by powerful spirits. Also implicit is the assumption that these formidable forces can be influenced positively and negatively. Within this worldview, conjurers, root doctors, or other intermediaries are thought to carry the knowledge of how to guide the influential spirits and, in this way, to mediate successfully between the physical and spiritual worlds.

Within the blues, conjurers are frequently consulted for assistance with affairs of the heart. Deep desires to procure and secure love through conjuring are central to the world of the blues. Alison Saar's nine "stations of the heart" creatively participate in this rooted cultural history. Composed of a small iron heart bound with tin and attached to a metal ball and chain, station one, called *Love Potion #1, An Iron Clad Hex for Marriage,* is a petite but weighty assemblage that serves as a third-party curse on an unwanted proposal (Fig. 10.2). Positioned on a bright red (a frequent color of capture) square of cloth on the floor, this malevolent juju works assertively to undermine an undesired coupling. Displayed like a devotional altar, the second station, *Love Potion #2, To Tether a Ramblin' Man,* consists of a carved wooden heart covered with black shoe soles and strips of old tires (Fig. 10.3). Firmly nailed to the heart, the rubber soles and tires work by symbolically binding an incessant wanderer to his jealous and less mobile lover. The purpose of this charged prescription is to aid frustrated lovers in curtailing their desired

Fig. 10.2. Love Potion #1, An Iron Clad Hex for Marriage. Wood, tin, and iron. Courtesy of the artist.

mates' dreaded errant sojourns. As these first two "love potions" make clear, a desire to control the actions of others in the name of love underlies these assertive "cures."

The largest work in the installation, *Love Potion #3, Conkerin' John,* is a freestanding sculpture more than six feet high made of tin-covered wood (Fig. 10.4). A sculpture of a mythical man whose legs turn to a tangle of roots, the carved figure is a benevolent gris-gris for "a deeply rooted love."[12] This majestic love potion gives visual representation to oral expression, for in the living lore of African America the High John the Conqueror root is the ingredient most associated with romance. This is the potent root that Muddy Waters in his blues boast so brashly touts for its powers of entrapment and seduction. Famed for bringing luck in love as well as in gambling, this root enables risk taking. *Conkerin' John* gives visual life to this charged charm; it is a figurative representation of the legendary root. Half human and half tree, the figure is suggestively rooted in nature and grounded to the earth. In this way the figure, like his nonfigurative namesake, links the material world above the ground with the even more spiritual world beneath it. Fittingly, the figure is a blend of natural and manmade materials: his body is made of carved wood, while found pieces of rusty tin serve as skin, applied paint defines his face, and a discarded license plate covers his triangular chest.

Fig. 10.3. Love Potion #2, To Tether a Ramblin' Man. Wood, tin, nails, and mixed media. Courtesy of the artist.

The sculpture ingeniously unites verbal and visual creativity. Within African American folklore, charged roots with names such as High John, Big John, High John de Conquer, John de Conker, and High John the Conqueror are repeatedly sought out for their ability to tempt a mate, beguile him or her, secure the lover's emotional loyalty, and enhance sexual pleasure. These roots are ardently sought out for gallant and more sinister purposes. This tension befits the root itself, as it is often described in oral legends and lore as being particularly gnarled and knotty and thus potent enough to influence particularly gnarled and knotty love

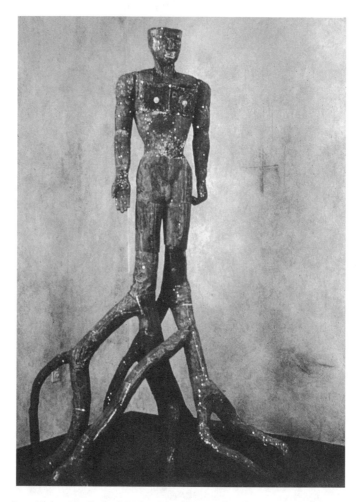

Fig. 10.4. Love Potion #3, Conkerin' John. Wood, tin, and nails. Courtesy of the artist.

affairs. The legendary root's contradictory purposes are made evident in the sculpted figure's gestures, for one of his hands is open, signaling his genuinely peaceful and noble intentions, while his other hand is partially closed, perhaps signaling more clandestine desires.

In giving figurative life to a nonfigurative root, Alison Saar's sculpture visually echoes one of Zora Neale Hurston's creative claims concerning African American folklore. In "High John de Conquer," a 1943 essay for *American Mercury,* Hurston contends that in the oral legends and lore of African America the slave trickster John—who figures in the popular John and "Old Massa" cycle of folktales—typically flies back to Africa after Emancipation.[13] She goes on to remark that heroic John's physical departure from the New World as well as his symbolic departure from oral lore after Emancipation is often rationally explained by lore enthusiasts in the following manner: when slavery was finally over, newly freed people no longer had an immediate psychological need for this favorite wish-fulfillment character. Creatively countering these premature claims of psychological and spiritual fulfillment by her colleagues, Hurston insists that the slave trickster John never entirely left American soil and that stories of him continue to abound. Other folklorists often overlook his presence, she suggests, because after Emancipation the trickster John was transformed from a human persona to an animate root. Hurston claims that though John did fly back to Africa after slavery ended, his spirit had separated from his body before departure and sunk into the southern soil where it had been transformed into the lucky life-enhancing root known as High John the Conquer. "High John de Conquer went back to Africa, but he left his power here, and placed his American dwelling in the root of a certain plant. Possess that root, and he can be summoned at any time."[14] As long as folks faithfully unearth the root, Hurston assures us, trickster John's powers remain ready.

Alison Saar's wooden root sculpture not only blends verbal and visual creativity but also affirms African American vernacular art, for there is a strong tradition of working with wood and roots among black folk artists. Saar has an intimate familiarity with the work of African American vernacular artists. As an undergraduate at Scripps College, she double majored in studio art and art history. There she studied with the artist and art historian Samella Lewis, whose work explores the African diaspora, and concentrated on the arts and religions of Africa and the Afro-Atlantic world. While an undergraduate and with the help of her mentor, the young artist was awarded a travel grant to study the works of southern folk artists.[15] This travel grant led to her senior thesis on four African American artists: William Edmondson, Minnie Evans, Clementine Hunter, and Sister Gertrude Morgan. Saar's close study of these visionary creators and their work, frequently left out of discussions of "mainstream" American and African American art, led to her development of a clear and democratic working definition of a successful artist. "What makes a great artist is having a vision and having something to say," she insists.[16]

Alison Saar has been visually and materially influenced by the work of African American folk artists. Her work shares the look of much vernacular art; it shows its seams and reveals the human hand of the artist. With its roughly carved wood and patched tin body, *Conkerin' John* frankly exposes the physical presence of its creator. The sculpture also shares a material affinity with much folk art, as it is made of found materials. Saar scoured urban streets, empty lots, abandoned buildings, and demolition sites for the vital stuff of her art: floor beams, ceiling tin, and old nails. By salvaging discarded materials, she upholds and extends a tradition of recycling and reuse central to many folk artists. This frugal practice also enables her to avoid dependence on expensive art store supplies and to think more deeply about the history behind her foraged materials. In working closely with previously used materials, Saar's nascent interest in the history of the aged objects grew. "I became very intrigued with the history of objects and that those objects had memory and spirit and a sense of that history. So I think that's why I use found materials. The wood I use is floor beams that came out of places built in the 1800s. The ceiling tin used in this exhibit was looking down and seeing lives come and go. These materials are older than me and maybe more wise than me, that's why I'm not attracted to new materials. I believe that the newer materials are stupid. They knew the factory and that's it."[17]

Alison Saar's visual and material link to folk art and artists is particularly apparent when we compare her work to the work of Bessie Harvey (1929–1994), an artist she especially admires. At the same time Saar was creating *Conkerin' John*, the late visionary artist was creating *Tribal Spirits*, a found wood and mixed media sculpture (Fig. 10.5). These two sculptures echo each other in terms of materials and technique. Created from pieces of discarded wood, Harvey's work consists of a motley mix of iconic human heads spread around a sturdy tree trunk. Decorated with small objects and paint, the masklike faces with inlaid eyes and teeth are gathered around and atop the two-foot-wide trunk base. Soaring at the top of the nearly four-foot sculptural group is a long lean stick painted to resemble the sinuous neck and sharp beak of a graceful bird. In describing this piece, Harvey explained that each human head was created to represent a different group of people.[18] The sculpture was to serve a moral purpose. Implicit in the exemplary sculpture, she stated, is the idea and ideal that—through faith—groups of people with competing interests can rise above conflict and find harmony with one another.[19] The bird of peace whose long beak points toward the heavens symbolizes the artist's lofty vision. Through her found wood and mixed media sculpture, Bessie Harvey sought to link the restorative power of nature, represented by the recycled tree parts, to the faith of a people she believed to be in need of guidance and restoration.

Tribal Spirits resonates materially and spiritually with *Conkerin' John*. Both privilege found objects and foraged materials. Until she passed away in 1994, Harvey frequently gathered wood (stumps, branches, and roots) from the hills near her Tennessee home. She believed that because found wood came from living

Fig. 10.5. Bessie Harvey (1929–1994), *Tribal Spirits,* 1988. Wood and mixed media. Dallas Museum of Art, Metropolitan Life Foundation Purchase Grant.

trees it contained spiritual forces. The elderly artist was especially keen on working with wood that outwardly displayed the visible traces of everyday life. For example, she delighted in working with wood that showed the natural effects of hungry insects, inclement weather, and aging.[20] Concerning her choice of materials and her creative process, Harvey explained, "You can go to the wood pile and all at once you see a face, in any piece of wood and it looks like it's just askin' for help, help to come out, ya know. There's something in there, we just know God creates the roots and stumps and shapes them by the insects, a lot of them, designing my pieces. Take Horace. Well, when I first found him he was a big limb but I know he was a beautiful man, I knew that when I pulled him out . . . I saw him and I just couldn't wait to get him home to get started bringing him out; what I saw was beautiful."[21] Like many visionary artists, Harvey saw herself and her work as conduits for a higher spiritual power. A devoutly Christian woman, she downplayed individual agency in her creative process; instead, she saw her work as a three-way collaboration between God, Nature, and herself. In this way, she also sensed that the subjects of her work, the human and animal figures, were already present in her materials—they were embedded in the wood—and that she simply released and adorned them.

While Saar more readily voices primary authorship than Harvey did, she, too, acknowledges intangible sources for her work. These sources, she tells us, are some of the links she sees between her work and the work of folk artists like Harvey. In reflecting on her art, Saar offers the following insight: "I see the work as being—well, I don't want to say spiritual because that sounds as if it's some organized belief out there—but the work deals with personal and spiritual elements. I think that is what I have in common with a lot of self-taught artists and a lot of visionary artists."[22] Raised in a creatively active and spiritually open home, Saar credits her 1960s upbringing for her keen interest in exploring aspects of religion, spirituality, and power in her art. "We were raised as Unitarians. The whole idea was there's always some sort of spirit power out there. It didn't matter what form it took—there was always this open door to see it however you wanted to. So I think that an awareness that there are powers beyond, not just the here and now, was heavily instilled by both my parents."[23] Like Harvey, Saar finds inspiration for her spiritually engaged work in her found and foraged materials. "Sometimes you pick up a piece of tin and it says something to you or a piece of wood looks like it might become something."[24]

Saar's and Harvey's works echo each other somewhat in terms of technique. Both artists work additively to adorn their found wood with other natural and manmade materials. Harvey embellished her tree trunk base with pieces of recycled wood, paint, glitter, beads, hair, and other found objects, while Saar covered her carved wooden figure with ceiling tin, paint, nails, and a discarded license plate. In essence, both artists draw from the hidden history and palpable presence of found objects and unearth their meaning. Although their work resonates in terms of material and technique, their subject matter is quite divergent. Passionate sex and ripe sexuality are not topics Harvey directly addressed in her work, while these topics are quite bawdily confronted in *Love Potion #9*. In this respect, Saar's environmental assemblage is much more in tune with blues singers who boldly voice the travails of the body, heart, and mind and offer potent recipes for their cure.

The installation's fourth station, *Love Potion #4, To Bring 'Em Knocking at Your Door*, is a recipe for enticement (Fig. 10.6). This temptation juju consists of an old door suspended from the ceiling with a thick wooden doormat positioned in front of it. The rustic door, the artist explains, "has been covered and encrusted with layers of libations."[25] An elongated heart framing a woman's torso and outstretched arms beckoning her desired lover is visible at the top of the empowered door. Reminiscent of the chalk marks often used to draw *vèvè* symbols and invoke the desired deity in Vodou, the wood plank doormat is inscribed with an eye-

Fig. 10.6. *Love Potion #4, To Bring 'Em Knocking at Your Door.* Wood, cement, iron, and dry pigments. Courtesy of the artist.

Fig. 10.7. *Love Potion #5, Fall For You Like a Sinkin' Stone*. Stone, water, and washtub.
Courtesy of the artist.

catching cobalt blue circle made of dry pigment and magnetic filings "to bring 'em beggin' at your doorstep."[26]

A simple metal bucket partially filled with water is the vehicle for *Love Potion #5, Fall For You Like a Sinkin' Stone* (Fig. 10.7). A carved stone in the shape of a human heart rests at the bottom of the galvanized washtub. The centrally placed and entirely submerged red heart works to assure complete emotional and bodily fidelity.

Displayed like an altar, *Love Potion #6, Motel 6 for One Night Stands*, is a provocative station where fiery passions are enshrined (Fig. 10.8). Central to the wall altar is a small framed painting of the backside flesh of a light-skinned woman in red in the throes of undressing for a darker man whose black top hat cockily rests just below her buxom bottom. A pair of bright red flickering electric candles flanks this sensual scene, accenting its warm hues and dramatizing its illicit connotations. On the altar's ledge, a long forgotten room key has served its literal purpose of opening the motel door and now serves as an offering to enable two ravenous lovers to enjoy a night of hotly desired passion.

The final two nonfigurative charms that make up the installation include *Love Potion #7, Wallflowers*, a "carved heart split open in the center" from the force of the flora growing within it (Fig. 10.9). This fertile and flayed heart is strapped to

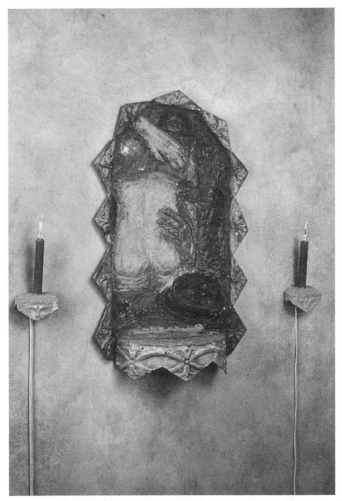

Fig. 10.8. *Love Potion #6, Motel 6 for One Night Stands*. Fresco and mixed media. Courtesy of the artist.

the gallery wall by strips of flowered tin. The intended work of this bright red enticement spell is to "draw love to wallflowers."[27] Another vehicle for attraction, *Love Potion #8, Evocation of a Storybook Romance*, is a charmed vessel for procuring an idyllic relationship (Fig. 10.10). It consists of a colorful decorated vase laden with plastic flowers. Painted with bright primary colors to attract and including figurative forms to instruct, the gorgeous vase rests ready for use atop a sinuous iron pedestal.

The final station is another carved and embellished figurative sculpture. Like

Fig. 10.9. Love Potion #7, Wallflowers. Wood, tin, plastic flowers, and encaustic. Courtesy of the artist.

Conkerin' John, Love Potion #9, Love Zombie looms within the vernacularly inspired and Eros-identified installation environment (Fig. 10.11). This figurative sculpture depicts a life-size, busty, lipstick-wearing woman in a tight blood-red dress. An embodiment of a femme fatale, the woman stands for "a dangerous infatuation, that robs its victims of all sense."[28] The woman's body is made of carved wood and is covered with oxidized copper, making her taut skin appear green. Her sleeveless dress and short black hair are made of painted patterned ceiling tin. With her full breasts, thin waist, rounded hips, short red dress, decorated lips, and heat-conducting flesh, the woman exudes sex and sexuality. Similarly, her strength is made evident through her sculpted arms, firm legs, and stoic gaze. Yet the female figure's vivacious sexuality and visible strength stand in stark contrast to the vulnerability displayed by her partly open chest, for a door to the figure's left breast swings open to reveal a telling assemblage: a wooden heart punctured by a snarl of rusty old nails.

Like the tangled root legs on *Conkerin' John,* which link him to the material world above ground and with the even more spiritual world beneath it, the tangled nails in *Love Zombie* suggest a straddling of seemingly opposing elements. While the carved figure connotes strength, the mixed media assemblage lodged in its chest conveys pain and fragility. This blend of figurative sculpture and mixed

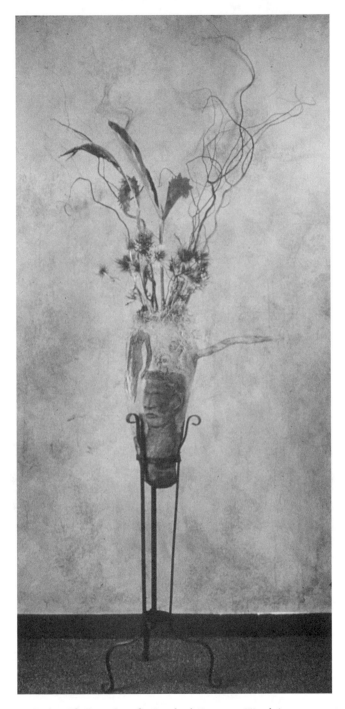

Fig. 10.10. Love Potion #8, Evocation of a Storybook Romance. Wood, iron, cement, and dry pigments. Courtesy of the artist.

Fig. 10.11. Love Potion #9, Love Zombie. Wood, tin, copper, and nails. Courtesy of the artist.

media materials captures the mortal complexity of the woman's robust exterior and her wounded interior. It also gives visual life to one of the artist's preoccupations. "Sometimes what is immediately apparent and what's inside of all that, the spirit, are alike; sometimes they are direct opposites. I'm interested in depicting what can't be seen—the forces within life," Saar asserts.[29] Because of the figure's intricacy, we as viewers are uncertain if the woman has been the source or the victim of the "dangerous infatuation" she purportedly represents. The title of the sculpture, however, implies that she has been held captive by anguish. Drawing from the concept of a *zonbi*, which in Haitian Vodou refers to a spirit that has been separated from its body and forced to work, the figure, echoing its namesake, is a hostage and clearly in need of a well-rooted cure to heal her aching and belabored heart. Concerning the female figure's infatuated entrapment, Saar explains,

> She's a zombie because she's at this state when you're so infatuated with someone that you can't see, so she doesn't have pupils in her eyes, and you can't hear. So you can't see him cheating on you, and you can't hear your friends saying what a dog the person is; you have this kind of bronze skin so you can't feel anything and you're sort of impervious to anything outside of your infatuation for this person. The breasts lift open. This is more about the heart than the breast per se; a kind of charred sort of heart that's been bound and there's a heavy whammy on this heart that has this power over her. Her heart has totally cut her off from everything else.[30]

The wood and nail assemblage embedded in the female figure's chest evokes a set of traditional West Central African beliefs and practices that have crossed the Atlantic Ocean with their adherents. Specifically, the materials and their placement in the body suggest *minkisi,* the potent medicines and charms long prepared in Kongo territory (part of present-day Democratic Republic of Congo and Angola).[31] Typically containing such things as leaves, earth, ashes, seeds, stones, herbs, and sticks, these sacred cures are made for benevolent and malevolent purposes, including for the varied purposes of love. Practitioners believe that when combined with faith, *minkisi* take on life and can effect a wide range of changes, from resisting colonization and bringing someone back to health to securing emotional fidelity. Although these empowered objects can also take nonfigurative forms, figurative *minkisi* often contain open cavities embedded with properly charged ingredients.

With its open chest laden with potent materials and its allusions to harm and healing, *Love Zombie* recalls and resembles figurative Kongo *minkisi.* The cavity's contents—the weathered nails and wood—suggest a particularly powerful oath-taking object, the traditional *nkisi nkondi* figure, a subset of the larger category of *minkisi* (Fig. 10.12). Typically the *nkisi nkondi* figure is an iconic wood figure pierced with nails, blades, pins, and other pointed objects. The sharp punctures in the wood visualize and symbolize the nailings of various arguments, vows, punishments, and other grave dealings. With its scores of weathered nails riddled in its wooden heart, *Love Zombie* visually suggests this mightily charged ritual object.[32] And with its references to the empowered medicines and potent charms known as Kongo *minkisi,* the sculpture also visually hints at the influence of BaKongo spiritual and material traditions on Haitian Vodou and the related set

Fig. 10.12. Kongo (Yombe) people, *Nkisi Nkondi,* 19th century. Wood, iron, glass, mirror, resin, and pigment. Brooklyn Museum of Art.

of beliefs and practices commonly known as voodoo or conjure in the United States.[33]

Love Zombie not only engages elements of African American vernacular culture that can be traced to an African past and to communities of enslaved and free people in the New World but also it, like *Conkerin' John,* engages the work of African American folk artists. This link is particularly apparent when we compare *Love Zombie* to the sculpture of William Edmondson (1874–1951). Edmondson, a central subject of Saar's undergraduate thesis, started work as a sculptor when he began carving tombstones for the middle Tennessee gravesites of African Americans in 1931.[34] For the next two decades, the former railroad worker and hospital orderly made tombstones, garden ornaments, and other carved stone sculptures for Nashville's African American community and for the mainstream art world.[35] Edmondson's typical subjects included biblical figures, real people, human types, mythical characters, folk motifs, and numerous animals, particularly birds and rabbits.

Measuring nearly two feet in height, *Miss Louisa* is based on either a real or an imagined person (Fig. 10.13). Cut out of a piece of limestone, the sculpture depicts a prim woman in a long-sleeved shirt and an ankle-skimming dress. She tightly clasps a man's bowler hat at her cinched waist. This sculpture resonates materially with Saar's sculpture, as both were created from recycled architectural remains. A half-century before Saar began rummaging buildings and lots for floor beams, ceiling tin, and old nails, Edmondson sought out the vital materials for his art—discarded rectangular limestone blocks—from demolished buildings and construction sites.[36] Unlike Saar, who was attracted to these materials for their history and presence, the master stonecarver claimed sills, lintels, steps, building foundations, and street curbs because they were available for free or at low cost.

Edmondson's body of work resonates visually with Saar's work as well. In terms of their carving, both work reductively to create elemental sculptures based on iconic figures. Both privilege an economy of form. Edmondson's carved figure retains some of its original blocky shape, while Saar's carved female figure is roughly hewn. Similarly, *Miss Louisa* and *Love Zombie* lack expressive detail; their faces are pared down to uncommunicative essentials. Thus, the two sculptures are more suggestive than delineated. Yet while both artists show restraint in altering their materials, they also share a concern with surfaces. Edmondson's figure reveals various textures: the woman's shirt has been chiseled to suggest vertical stripes, and her hair has been modeled to suggest its lively texture. Echoing Edmondson's creative surface modifications, Saar's wooden figure is decoratively garbed in textured ceiling tin.

The two carvers also echo each other technically. Both practice the dusty work of carving directly into their respective materials. The stonecarver worked largely with three simple tools: homemade flat chisels of varying sizes, a hammer, and a file.[37] His process involved first cutting out a form from a limestone block with his chisels and then refining it with a file. Saar's technique is also straightforward

Fig. 10.13. William Edmondson (1874–1951), *Miss Louisa*, ca. 1930s–1940s. Limestone. Philadelphia Museum of Art. Gift of Paul W. McCloskey in memory of Maris Madeira McCloskey.

and physically taxing. The woodcarver has slightly adapted Edmondson's process, however; she starts with a chainsaw to rough out the form and then relies on a chisel to give it shape and detail. Concerning her creative process, Saar explains, "I take an orderly piece of wood and wreak havoc on it with a chainsaw. It's very aggressive, hit-and-miss, frenzied and out of control."[38]

Edmondson's *Miss Louisa* may have been a vital source for the subject matter of *Love Potion #9*. While his work typically features biblical figures and animals, the bowler hat–carrying female figure may actually be a visual representation of verbal lore. Within African American folklore, men's hats and women's hearts are frequently linked. Wise women can clearly pronounce their desire to marry a wanted mate by picking up his idle hat and returning it.[39] Perhaps Edmondson's seemingly prim Louisa is quite assertively using the hat she holds at her waist like a charm, as an empowered object to secure love. Perhaps, using the worn hat like all the potions and roots, the gris-gris, mojos, and jujus, the woman is seeking to enter the world of the seductive arts.

Much like his fellow Tennessee resident Bessie Harvey, Edmondson understood his work as the Lord's work. A devoutly Christian man who frequented Nashville's Mount Sinai Primitive Baptist Church, Edmondson saw himself as a disciple and his work as God's creation.[40] He explained, "This here stone and all those out there in the yard come from God. It's the work in Jesus speaking His mind in my mind. I must be one of His disciples. These here is miracles I can do . . . Well, I know I'm going to carve. Jesus has planted the seed of carving in me."[41] In contrast to Edmondson's understanding of his art making as a conduit for a higher spiritual power, Saar explains that, while her artwork is spiritually attentive, her process is anything but divinely guided. "For me, it's often more of a fight with materials than a collaboration with materials—I have all of these scars on my hands."[42] It seems fitting that, just as seductive arts attempt to order the chaos of our most passionate emotions, Saar enters the world of conjure by attempting to control the initially resistant found materials of her art.

With her belief in the power of found objects and their ability to express spiritual energy, as well as her commitment to create heartfelt communicative work that reveals the palpable presence of its creator, Alison Saar is closely aligned with visionary vernacular artists like Bessie Harvey and William Edmondson. Yet in her belief that the travails of the body, heart, and mind must be mined for all their seamy human complexity, Saar's work is attuned with the blues. Deeply enmeshed in the creativity, spirituality, and sensuality of the black diaspora, Alison Saar in *Love Potion #9* joins the provocative dialogue regarding the evocative arts of seduction.

CHAPTER ELEVEN

"Truths that Liberate the Soul"

Eva Jessye and the Politics of Religious Performance

JUDITH WEISENFELD

In writing about her birth on a Sunday morning in Coffeyville, Kansas, Eva Jessye (1895–1992) highlighted a convergence that seemed to portend her life-long commitment to interpreting and performing spirituals and other religious music. At the very moment she was born in her parents' house, "the 'Amen Corner' in the Macedonia Baptist Church across the street was at the boiling point. 'Hallelujahs,' 'Praises to God' and the frenzied 'stomp' of sisters in the throes of religious ecstasy resounded in the air."[1] Her parents, children of former slaves, were not religious, Jessye wrote. Nevertheless, she felt keenly the influence of black Baptists and Methodists and the affectionately competitive relationship between the two groups that dominated Coffeyville's religious landscape, where Baptists far outnumbered Methodists. The presence of these two denominations also shaped the broader culture of African American life in the small city. Jessye mused that the coincidence of her birth and the Sunday morning praise activities in the nearby Baptist church may have accounted for her intense religious devotion as a child and for her love of "God and Nature with a passion nearing fanaticism."[2] She also wrote of the significance of her native Kansas in African American history as a "refuge for the runaway slave," emphasizing her upbringing in the context of a strong tradition of struggle for freedom and equality. From her origins in these black religious and activist cultures, Jessye went on to have a career as a self-described "dramatist of Negro music" which spanned much of the twentieth century, with credits in the "race records" industry of the 1920s and appearances on film and television. She staged and conducted plays and operas, enjoyed a thriving career on the concert scene, and participated, through the arts, in civil rights activism.[3]

Jessye's work as a "dramatist of Negro music"—which involved arranging,

composing, and conducting religious music in ensemble and choral contexts—
serves as a starting point to raise broad questions about how African American
women have used the arts to do theological work and to put their theologies into
play in public arenas that included but were not limited to religious institutions.
Jessye's career, carried out largely outside of churches, calls us to interrogate and
reformulate simple understandings of a boundary between sacred and secular
in African American life (generally configured along the lines of church or
nonchurch).[4] Various scholars of gospel music have argued that the emergence
of this musical form opened avenues to religious authority for black women, particularly in Christian denominational contexts in which they were denied access
to ordination and the pulpit. In exploring the politics of gender, religion, and music in African American history, scholars have tended to limit themselves to institutional contexts, understanding the pulpit as the primary locus of religious authority and the formal sermon or published treatise as the primary religious
discourse.[5]

Jessye was dedicated to the Christian message throughout her long life, but
she did not locate her religious experience or work in a particular denominational
or church context. The implications of this commitment raise significant methodological questions for the study of African American women's religious history.
In an interview late in her life, she expressed pride in her work with the National
Council of Churches and said, "[of] course I work for all churches. And I'm interested in so many things. Anything that makes a man better, that's the right
church."[6] Moreover, it seems clear that Jessye understood her work as a choral
conductor as a religious vocation that allowed her to promote Christianity in ways
that contravene clear distinctions between the secular and the sacred.[7] The academic tendency to limit the investigation of questions about black women and religious authority to traditional denominational contexts is challenged by the theological and cultural work in which Jessye and others engaged in using the arts
to express their religious commitments.[8]

Jessye entered the scene as an arranger and interpreter of black religious
music during a period of heightened contestation over the means of collecting
and preserving spirituals, the communally produced religious music that began
emerging from black communities in the antebellum period. In addition to raising a variety of issues about preservation, African American intellectuals in the
1920s and 1930s debated the appropriate and authentic styles and venues for
singing spirituals and the relationship between black religious musical traditions
and contemporary black cultural politics. Black intellectuals including W. E. B.
Du Bois, Alain Locke, and Zora Neale Hurston weighed in, each proposing differ-

ent approaches to preserving black folk culture, but all agreed that "the progress of the New Negro depended on a successful recuperation and elucidation of the long-maligned black cultural inheritance."[9]

Precisely how to formulate and represent the relationship between the cultural products of the black folk and the modern, urban future of black America remained a fraught question throughout the 1920s and 1930s when Jessye was particularly active in preserving and performing traditional black music. Spirituals and other black folk music often figured prominently in these debates. While Du Bois, Locke, Hurston and others engaged vigorously the question of how best to transmit cultural memory within African American communities and represent it to others, they did not generally see the preservation and presentation of spirituals as an explicitly religious endeavor. Whereas Du Bois saw spirituals as "redemptive fragments of a fading stage of folk life" that needed to be given a place of distinction in African American memory, Jessye believed their dramatic performance to be a critical tool in the social, political, and spiritual development of African Americans.[10] Jessye approached the issues that were raised in the context of the Harlem Renaissance from a perspective deeply informed by religious commitment, but she did not see her faith as placing her outside the scope of the movement. Indeed, she was acquainted with many of the literary and artistic figures of the Harlem Renaissance, and she composed music and rehearsed her choirs in Harlem studios during the movement's heyday.[11] Although she understood the desire of generations born in freedom to distance themselves from the cultural products of slavery, she nevertheless criticized "those who inherited this great musical birthright" for coming to despise that cultural legacy.[12] Through her writings about and performances of spirituals, Jessye argued forcefully for the centrality of these cultural products in the religious lives and political activism of African Americans.

In addition to dedicating herself to the preservation and transmission of distinctively black religious music, Jessye made the case throughout her career that spirituals could be used to illuminate and illustrate biblical stories and texts from Western literature and that placing these materials alongside one another could highlight or recast theological elements of the spirituals. In composing her own oratorios and folk oratorios—works that combined spirituals and European classical music with biblical, literary, and folk texts—she put forth powerful interpretations of major Christian theological tenets and demonstrated a commitment to using music and drama to promote a vision of human equality.[13] Jessye endorsed an approach to African American religious aesthetics that valued music and performative styles that emerged from black communities, but did not understand African American religious experience as facilitated *only* by arts from African American contexts.[14]

Interpreting and Performing Spirituals

Eva Jessye recalled two encounters that motivated her to devote her career to arranging and interpreting African American spirituals. First, as a young student at the African Methodist Episcopal (AME) Church–affiliated Quindaro State Normal School in Quindaro, Kansas, she met the African American composer and conductor Will Marion Cook, whose work the music historian Eileen Southern characterizes as nationalist in orientation because of its reliance on black folk music and black performance practices.[15] Cook encouraged and mentored Jessye for a number of years, helping her to make important professional connections, including in the publishing world, and she counted as transformative this meeting with such an important figure in American music. Jessye was also influenced by Booker T. Washington, who spoke at Quindaro about the importance of preserving spirituals for the generations of African Americans born after the end of slavery.[16] In taking up this charge, Jessye turned to familiar sources, particularly to the spirituals and other folk music she heard growing up among the descendants of runaway slaves and of Exodusters.[17]

Throughout her career, Jessye emphasized the importance for performance purposes of appreciating the social and historical contexts from which spirituals emerged. While she saw them as available to anyone for enjoyment and spiritual encouragement, she felt that the presentation of the songs needed to be placed in the hands of someone who felt the context deeply. Fifty years after she first began performing black religious folk music, Jessye wrote, "Understanding of spirituals is very involved . . . dependent on one steeped in the traditional interpretation. It is impossible for anyone else to get from them the flavor that I, thru [*sic*] long experience, can."[18] In the preface to her collection *My Spirituals* (1927), she emphasized her experiential authority in interpreting the songs and leveled an implicit critique at folklorists and anthropologists to whom this culture was unfamiliar, writing that "collecting these songs has not been a difficult task. I was not obliged to delve in remote corners of the South or coax them from reluctant elders. They are the songs of my childhood and of my people. I have sung them all my life."[19] Indeed, choosing a small subset of these spirituals for publication was difficult because of the host of songs that "surge[d] at the door of [her] memory" as she reflected on her childhood experiences. In the end, Jessye selected sixteen songs that she hoped would "spread a message of Humility, Love and Faith."[20]

Her only major publication, *My Spirituals* became influential among musicians, in part because it preserved songs that were not contained in the growing body of published collections of spirituals, but also because of the beauty of Jessye's arrangements.[21] Jessye stressed that she wished to focus on the songs themselves rather than on music theory or history, which she found well covered in the existing literature, so she included little discussion of what she took to be the distinctive components of black religious music.[22] Indeed, the arrangements for solo voice and piano accompaniment are simple and straightforward; according to Dr. Melville Charlton, a well-known organist in New York City at the time, they "can be comprehended and executed by any tyro."[23] Paul Robeson wrote to Jessye to congratulate her on the publication and told her that he found the "melodies most interesting, and different from the usual type of spiritual." He informed her that he planned to add two of her selections, "Who is Dat Yonder?" and "Gwine to March Down to Jordan," to his recital program.[24]

Jessye seems to have striven for simplicity in her arrangements and compositions in an effort to provide performers with latitude for improvisation. After surveying the entirety of Jessye's published and unpublished works, Doris Wilson determined that Jessye achieved this simplicity through a variety of means, including limiting instructions about dynamics and other elements of expression in performance and emphasizing a straightforward stanza and refrain structure, as well as call and response between a soloist and the ensemble. In her own compositions, Jessye employed the sounds most characteristic of African American spirituals, tying herself closely to this musical tradition. Wilson notes that in these works, Jessye's "melodies are based chiefly on the tones of the major and pentatonic scales. Her text setting is declamatory in style, with a single note for each syllable; she always aims for economy of expression."[25]

Jessye's arrangements and original works were also simple and straightforward in that her accompaniments generally followed the melody rather than providing contrasting counterpoint. This economical approach to arranging, which is evident in *My Spirituals* and her other works, did not result in bland or uninteresting accompaniment. Instead, Wilson argues, Jessye employed "coloration devices to display her originality."[26] In addition to emphasizing tonal connections between her compositions and arrangements and the traditional spirituals, Jessye brought rhythm to the fore. Jessye herself pointed out that the piano settings she wrote for the spirituals, which were originally developed in worship communities as a cappella songs, emphasized the syncopated rhythms characteristic of this black folk music. In her own compositions, Jessye also made frequent use of triplets as a way of creating heightened drama within the syncopation.[27] In a review of *My Spirituals* for the National Urban League's *Opportunity* magazine, the poet and teacher Gwendolyn Bennett characterized the arrangements as "quite exquisite," asserting that, "now and again, we have a truly immortal chord." She continued, "For me there was a keen joy in playing these spirituals over on the piano and hammering out the words as I went along. Most of the songs I had never heard before and I was delighted to find them charged with a wistful beauty that should make them as popular as many of the old favorites."[28]

While Jessye insisted that *My Spirituals* was not meant to be "a story of the quaint folk among whom I was born and the melody that poured from their un-tutored lips" and sought to resist any attempt to romanticize the people from whom she learned the songs, her decision to place each song in the context of the life of an individual in her community lends particular power to her presentation. In her introduction to each song, Jessye recreated elements of life in the Coffey-ville of her childhood, focusing on its religious communities and the women whose devotion dominated them. She associated "Bles' My Soul an' Gone" with the summers she spent with her Aunt Harriet, in whose frail body "a glorious voice dwelt." Jessye recalled that "she sang the first two lines, 'I wouldn't be a sin-nah, I tell you de reason why,' with a weird distant tone that seemed to travel on the night wind to the furthest roll of the plain. It was the most beautiful singing of Spirituals I have ever heard."[29] In the most poignant section of the book, Jessye tied the well-known spiritual, "I've Been 'Buked an' I've Been Scorned," to Sister Fannie Watts, "the personification of Christian piety and humility."

> The intense fervor of her trembling voice raised in prayer reaches through the years and warms my heart. Her prayers would meet the most obdurate sinner and were solicited as the last resort when "mourners" were having a hard time "coming through." She was the preacher's right hand helper in the Amen corner and never let the spirit lag in the meeting . . .
>
> Sister Fannie Watts was beloved and respected by all who knew her and no one ever forgot the sweet nobility of her face. She had the mien of one who had suffered deeply and surmounted many obstacles. She was a person of broad and deep sym-pathies, a product of her own sorrows.
>
> Born a slave in Saint Augustine, Texas, she was about seventeen years of age when freedom was declared. The indignities heaped upon her girlish shoulders during slavery left wounds that were never healed and to hear her doleful singing of "I've Been 'Buked" was to be haunted for days by the pity of it all.[30]

Sister Watts, Aunt Charlotte Ellis, and Aunt Lizzie Buckner together "formed the 'Amen' triumvirate of the Baptist Church in which all three were charter members."[31] Although Jessye's introductions mention the pastor and a deacon of Macedonia Baptist Church, it was clearly the women of the church community who most influenced her religious sensibility.

Charlton, who reviewed the book for New York City's *Amsterdam News*, argued that these stories helped to move the book beyond a simple collection of songs and into the realm of "a music-drama." Gwendolyn Bennett wrote that Jessye "has done more than the mere gathering together of a collection of spirituals; she has given them character, 'body.'"[32] From this very early publication, Jessye's interest in preserving the history of African American musical traditions becomes clear, as does her deep commitment to crafting a narrative of African American history and cultures through the use of spirituals. These twin concerns remained at the center of her work, regardless of the genre or venue in which she performed.

Although Jessye sought to make some of her favorite spirituals available through published arrangements, she saw the work of the performing groups she led as much more important in spreading the songs' messages.[33] She began her career as a choir director when, at the age of twelve, she formed a girls' quartet that performed in Coffeyville.[34] After completing normal school at Quindaro State, Jessye obtained a teaching certificate from Langston University in Oklahoma. In her study of African American women composers, Helen Walker-Hill argues that Quindaro, which later became Western University, was an extremely important institution for black female musicians. "The music department offered a rigorous four-year course of theory, harmony and analysis, and composition, as well as applied piano and voice, marching band . . . , orchestra, and the Jubilee Singers. At its peak in 1912 it had 153 music students."[35] Jessye spent a short time teaching school in Oklahoma before moving to Baltimore in 1919, where she worked for part of that year as music director at Morgan College. She then returned to Oklahoma, where she taught at the AME Church–affiliated Flipper Key Davis School in Tullahassee.[36] When Jessye returned to Baltimore in 1925, she became associated with the Dixie Jubilee Singers, a group that specialized in spirituals and black folk songs, and soon she became its director.[37] By the summer of 1925 Jessye and the Dixie Jubilee Singers had moved to New York City and were regularly performing a repertoire of spirituals and other black folk songs.

Beginning with her experience with the Dixie Jubilee Singers, Jessye established dramatic performances as her most significant means of propagating the religious message of the spirituals and established patterns for the types of venues and concert programs that would best support her project. Jessye's Dixie Jubilee Singers quickly became well known in New York City in the late 1920s through appearances in the stage show at the Rivoli and Capitol movie theaters and on the Capitol Theatre show's later incarnation as the *Major Bowes Family Radio Hour.* The audiences for these performances were likely working-class immigrants as well as native-born whites and African Americans. The group also appeared in its own radio programs, *Aunt Mandy's Chillun* and *Four Dusty Travelers,* both on WOR, and at a number of public events such as the annual celebrations of Lincoln's birthday.[38] In all of these contexts the group performed religious and secular songs, including recently composed works by African American composers and arrangers like Will Marion Cook, Hall Johnson, Harry T. Burleigh, R. Nathaniel Dett, and Jessye herself.[39] On some occasions, the Dixie Jubilee Singers included in the program humorous sketches, presentations of folklore, and readings of poems by Jessye and Paul Laurence Dunbar.[40]

In the early 1930s, Jessye collaborated with Ismay Andrews to create the Eva Jessye Folk Ensemble, which specialized in "Negro dances of America."[41] In its earliest years the group generally featured eight to ten members, but in the 1930s it grew to have as many as thirty singers in its incarnation as the Eva Jessye Choir.[42] In a typical program Jessye presented some works with a trio of women, others with a male quartet or mixed quartet, and yet others with the entire choir.[43] The Dixie Jubilee Singers recorded on Brunswick, Columbia, and Cameo records in the 1920s, making available to a national audience recordings of well-known spirituals like "Roll, Jordan, Roll" and "Good News," as well as at least two less familiar songs from Jessye's *My Spirituals,* "Stand Steady" and "Who Is That Yonder."[44] The Four Dusty Travelers, the male quartet that Jessye directed, also recorded both secular and religious songs and, in 1929 recorded "Marching Down to Jerdon," one of the distinctive pieces Jessye arranged for *My Spirituals.*[45]

Jessye's choral groups reached a broader audience through a number of significant stage and screen appearances in the 1920s and 1930s. Through the Dixie Jubilee Singers' appearances at the Capitol Theatre and on the *Major Bowes Family Radio Hour,* Jessye's work came to the attention of Metro-Goldwyn-Mayer movie director King Vidor, who engaged the singers to appear in *Hallelujah,* the second "all-black cast" feature film to be released by a major Hollywood studio.[46] By the early 1930s she had renamed her group the Eva Jessye Choir and directed it in Virgil Thomson and Gertrude Stein's opera *Four Saints in Three Acts,* which premiered on Broadway in 1934, and in George Gershwin and DuBose Heyward's *Porgy and Bess,* which was staged by Rouben Mamoulian and premiered on Broadway in 1935.[47] In the case of Vidor's *Hallelujah,* Jessye's contributions to the musical selections are readily apparent, as the film includes black leisure folksongs ("E-I-O"), religious songs ("I Belong to That Band"), and contemporary compositions (Dvořák's "Goin' Home"), all of which had been in the Dixie Jubilee Singers' repertoire for some time.[48]

In addition to these various commercial appearances, the Dixie Jubilee Singers and the Eva Jessye Choir functioned as a religious choir in explicitly religious venues. Some events, such as the evening performances at predominantly or exclusively white churches like Rev. John Roach Straton's Calvary Baptist Church, St. John's Episcopal Church, and Second Presbyterian Church, at black churches like Mt. Olivet Baptist Church, and at synagogues like Temple Adath Israel in the Bronx, were engagements meant primarily to generate income for the choir, but the audiences were likely composed of members of these congregations.[49] The Dixie Jubilee Singers occasionally functioned as the congregational choir during these visits, as when they participated in a Sunday night service in 1931 at the Madison Avenue Presbyterian Church, a liberal church known for its social service and missionary work.[50]

In the mid- to late 1920s, the singers began to participate occasionally in services at the Rescue Society, an interdenominational mission on Doyers Street in New York's Chinatown. Founded in 1895, the mission announced its field as "people in trouble" and promised services that were "Evangelistic, Enthusiastic, Extraordinary." The Rescue Society extended a special invitation to "drunkards, drug addicts, the homeless and friendless," and it was for this constituency that Jessye's singers participated in Thanksgiving and Easter services.[51] Jessye was extremely impressed with the Rescue Society's work and considered it to have "sheltered more unfortunates" than any other institution with which she had worked.[52] Jessye's understanding of many of the choir's performances as worship is borne out by her outrage at the group's treatment by the members of the nondenominational Church of the Strangers in New York City. According to Jessye, the church, which had been founded by a white native of Maryland, held fast to the segregationist practices of the South. "I remember we sang there one night, and the moment we sang they gave us some money and said to go. They were Southerners and they didn't want us worshipping with them. Come entertain them, yes, but worship with them, no."[53] Part of Jessye's mission in presenting spirituals and other religious music at a variety of religious institutions, many of them predominantly or exclusively white in membership, was to use the music to bridge racial divides. She was particularly proud of the occasions on which her singers were successful at doing so, as when their appearance at the Fitchburg Church of Christ in Fitchburg, Massachusetts, ended the church's policy of racial segregation.[54]

Although the Dixie Jubilee Singers and the Eva Jessye Choir often performed in religious venues, many of their concerts took place in secular settings, a practice that raised the ire of some black cultural critics. African American journalist Cleveland G. Allen was incensed by the commercialization of spirituals and singled out for particular attention groups that sang "spirituals in theatres and other undesirable places for no other reason than commercial gain." Given the Dixie Jubilee Singers' prominence, it is difficult to imagine that Allen did not have them in mind when he wrote to the *New York Times* to complain about the "cheapening of negro songs." "The exploitation of these songs is doing a great deal to rob them of their real religious beauty and value and is making them too common," Allen wrote. "Those who have made anything of a study of these songs will agree with me when I say that the tragic conditions under which they were born, in which the soul of a people expressed its yearning, were not meant to be commercialized. These songs were sacred to the negro, and were the weapons by which he expressed his faith, sorrow, hope, courage, and joy. These things must forever be kept in mind."[55] He lauded the concert presentations of spirituals by the Fisk Jubilee Singers and the famed tenor Roland Hayes because they always kept in mind the original sacred context for the production of the spirituals. Although the Dixie Jubilee Singers and the Eva Jessye Choir continued to perform spirituals in concert venues, in theaters, and on the radio as well as in religious venues, the group discontinued working in movie theater stage shows sometime after 1927. Throughout her career Jessye remained committed to the perspective that spreading the message of the spirituals did not require that they be sung in churches, but it seems likely that she came to agree with Cleveland G. Allen that the highly commercialized venue and her lack of control over the content of the stage shows and the films exhibited made movie theaters an inappropriate environment for the singing of spirituals.

The performance style that Jessye adopted for some of the spirituals her groups presented occasionally made her the object of criticism. Her work placed her in hotly contested terrain; issues regarding the preservation and transmission of black religious folk music were highly politicized. While Allen found the concert versions of spirituals presented by the Fisk Jubilee Singers and Roland Hayes admirable, other African American commentators argued that, taken out of their proper contexts, these could not be said to represent authentic spirituals. Zora Neale Hurston never named Jessye in particular, but in 1934 she wrote in opposition to what she dubbed decidedly inauthentic "neo-spirituals," black religious songs performed for an audience. "There has never been a presentation of genuine Negro spirituals to any audience anywhere," Hurston contended. "What is being sung by the concert artists and glee clubs are the works of Negro composers or adaptors *based* on the spirituals . . . But with all the glee clubs and soloists, there has not been one genuine spiritual presented."[56] Particularly problematic for Hurston was that performed spirituals fixed the character of the presentation from one occasion to the next, whereas with authentic congregational singing, "no two times singing is alike, so that we must consider the rendition of a song not as a final thing, but as a mood. It won't be the same thing next Sunday."[57] For Hurston, the formalized performances of spirituals arranged and adapted by Harry T. Burleigh, J. Rosamond Johnson, Nathaniel Dett, Hall Johnson, and John W. Work—all of whom were Jessye's acquaintances or working colleagues— erased the unique musical qualities of black church singing, particularly "the harmony and disharmony, the shifting keys and broken time that make up the spiritual."[58]

While Alain Locke agreed with Hurston that many formalized and stream- lined concert versions were "travesties of the real folk singing," he felt strongly that there was a place for choral renditions of spirituals. Writing in 1936 about "the Negro and his music," Locke placed Jessye's work among the most success- ful at preserving an authentic performance character.

> Only recently have we recaptured in any art organization the true flavor and man- ner of these songs. But a record of the Eva Jessye Choir or the Hall Johnson Singers will give us our closest reproduction of the genuine Negro way of singing these songs. Both of them, it will be noticed, have the actual mechanics of improvised Ne- gro choral singing, with its syllabic quavers, off-tones and tone glides, improvised interpolations, subtle rhythmic variation. In most conventional versions of the spir- ituals there is too much melody and formal harmony. Over-emphasize the melodic elements of a spiritual, and you get a sentimental ballad à la Stephen Foster. Stress the harmony and you get a cloying glee or "barber-shop" chorus. Over-emphasize, on the other hand, the rhythmic idiom and instantly you secularize the product and it becomes a syncopated shout, with the religious tone and mood completely evap- orated. It is only in a subtle fusion of these elements that the genuine folk spiritual exists or that it can be recaptured.[59]

Jessye shared Locke's interest in how to maintain the unique compositional and performative elements of the spirituals and yet allow for dynamic development and engagement with other musical traditions, particularly European classical music.[60] Neither saw a conversation between African American and other musi- cal traditions as necessarily destructive of the distinctiveness of black music, and neither imagined the political impact of the music to be diminished by locating it in broader musical or social contexts.[61]

Jessye was quite conscious of this problem of rendering in the context of a concert performance songs that should be sung, in Hurston's words, by "a group bent on expression of feelings and not on sound effects" and, certainly, not on the concert stage by a trained chorus.[62] In much of her promotional literature for the choir, Jessye emphasized that "overdirection is studiously avoided so the quality of spontaneity may be retained," and her group's recordings from the 1920s provide a clear sense of how she attempted to accomplish this.[63] The published arrangements render the lyrics in dialect, and, despite Jessye's failure to comment on this element of her work, it seems clear that she understood dialect to be an important element of authentic performance. Although Jessye's published arrangements of the spirituals have piano accompaniment, as do some of the recorded performances, the Dixie Jubilee Singers most often presented the songs a cappella as they would have been in their original contexts. Jessye's arrangements also emphasized the call and response between a lead singer or singers— in the recordings, most often male—and the chorus, a performance style often used as part of a standard of authenticity by black cultural critics of the day. It is certainly possible that, in live performance, the emphasis on call and response also allowed the audience to participate in the music.

Along with finding ways to present the music within a structure that resembled the traditional contexts in which spirituals were sung, Jessye sought to create a choral tone that would reflect the spontaneous and cooperative context for the production of the spirituals and avoid the "cloying" effect that Locke identified with excessive attention to harmony. In order to achieve what one scholar has called the "Jessye full-throated sound," she selected singers who brought different vocal talents to the group. While she trained them to sing as a choir, she did not attempt to eradicate each singer's unique sound. In a description of her process for selecting singers to perform in a later choral ensemble, Jessye wrote that each singer "must provide a distinct color for the vocal canvas. One projects humor, another conveys deeply religious feeling, another for down-to-earth expression, others for hearty, neighborly vocal tone, light modern or heavy jazz interpretation. All are then utilized so that a perfect balance is maintained."[64] Although Jessye spent considerable time training her choirs to perform the repertoire she selected, her commitment to preserving the individuality of the varied voices resulted in a performance with a vernacular quality that, in many ways, erased her own hard work in its production. Her success at achieving this spontaneous quality in performance and its consequent deemphasizing of the craft of the choir conductor has, no doubt, contributed to the lack of attention to Jessye's work in the scholarship on African American religious cultures, but it is clear that this style was part of a thoughtful approach to conveying the message of the spirituals.[65]

While Jessye sought to minimize signs of her own intervention in the choir's vocal delivery, she did make her work clear in the physical expressions the choir used. Dramatic presentation was a central element of the performances under Jessye's direction, and she noted its importance in the process of selecting members, indicating that singers were "selected not only for vocal qualifications, but for imagination, originality and dramatic expression."[66] In addition to educating her choir members about the history and contexts for the creation of spirituals, she tutored them in dramatic presentation and understood this embodied approach to be critically important in assisting the choir in conveying theological complexity. In her notes on the performance of the song "Three Tears of the Spirit," for example, she wrote, "There are three periods in the Christian experience which are recognized in the verses of THREE TEARS. First . . . The period of Doubt . . . second . . . Period of Conviction . . . third . . . of ANTICIPATION."[67] Jessye instructed the singers to present the first verse facing the audience in a posture of "self-analysis" and to appear to shed tears of "self-condemnation." The second verse, representing the realization of God's purpose for the individual's life, was to be presented with "head up . . . hands tightly clasped . . . up to chest . . . as in delight . . . the tears are of joy." Finally, in anticipation of a future time in heaven, the singers were to turn to the side with their arms reaching out and palms together, "almost as in supplication." Many reviewers noted the importance of these dramatic elements, as in a 1939 review by Russell McLaughlin, who wrote that, "the chorus 'acted.' The verse was usually given out by a solo voice. There were shouted interruptions. There was rhythm of body as well as of voice."[68] Like Jessye's approach to choral tone, which seemed designed to expose the composite and spontaneous nature of the choir's work even as she cultivated a tightly structured and well-rehearsed presentation, Jessye's instructions on dramatic performance often emphasized spontaneity within an overall unity.[69]

At the same time that Jessye sought through her publications and performances to underscore her authority as an arranger and interpreter of Negro spirituals and worked with her choirs to render the songs in a way that audiences would take to be "authentic," she also felt secure enough in her depth of understanding to set spirituals within classical European musical genres, particularly the oratorio, and alongside major works of Western music and literature. Jessye believed that African American artists should not be limited to singing spirituals or other black folk music and, in fact, resigned her position as music director at Morgan College in Baltimore because its president circumscribed the choral repertoire. Years later she recalled, "Dr. Spencer, the President, was a white Southerner. He had the idea, like so many did at the time, that Black people's ability should be concentrated only on their own music, nothing else."[70] She was particularly proud that she left the school's community with a strong sense of the varied talents of black singers. At the final chapel service that she conducted at Morgan, she led the choir in Charles Gounod's "Unfold, Ye Portals Everlasting" from his 1882 oratorio *The Redemption.*

Jessye felt strongly about the importance of the thorough and wide-ranging musical education she had received at Quindaro. She required her chorus to be equally well trained and placed her singers in contact with broadly trained conductors and musicians as frequently as possible.[71] In the 1920s Jessye became friends and colleagues with Eugene Ormandy, who conducted the orchestra at the Capitol movie theatre in New York City and went on to serve as music director of the Philadelphia Orchestra for more than forty years. She corresponded with the composer and music theorist Percy Goetschius, who suggested readings and shared his writings with her; he read and responded enthusiastically to *My Spirituals.* The choir worked with Leopold Stokowski, conductor of the NBC Symphony Orchestra, on a 1942 radio performance of William Grant Still's cantata, "And They Lynched Him on a Tree."[72] As firmly as Jessye located herself in African American religious communities that sang spirituals in worship and among black musicians who arranged and interpreted this music, she also saw herself as situated within a broader musical context that included European classical music as well as more recently composed American music.[73]

Spirituals in New Contexts

Jessye created several dramatic pieces that combined spirituals, European classical music, and specially composed music, which the Eva Jessye Choir performed widely in churches, concert halls, and schools and on radio.[74] Through these works Jessye exercised the authority to interpret biblical texts and to present central topics in Christian theology in ways that more conventional religious contexts—particularly the many black Protestant churches that excluded women from their pulpits—might not have allowed. In addition, she used spirituals, biblical, and religious literary texts in the context of her own compositions to negotiate questions about the relationship between Christianity, the Bible, and African American history. Jessye promoted a cosmopolitan artistic vision that incorporated materials from a wide range of contexts and a universal view of Christianity that utilized art to bridge racial divides. In approaching her work in this way,

Jessye insisted that peoples of the African diaspora were the rightful heirs of the African and European cultural streams that combined in unique ways in diasporic contexts, and she did not hesitate to claim a connection to both. Jessye's bold interpretations of the Bible, of Christian theology, and of major works of Western literature explicitly challenged narrow definitions of African American culture and implicitly defied gendered constructions of religious work that denied women access to platforms for public leadership.

In her 1936 piece *The Chronicle of Job,* subtitled "The Story of the Most Patient Man in Biblical History," Jessye employs a strategy common in African American religious thought, exploring the metaphoric connections between the experiences of biblical characters and those of African Americans.[75] In this piece to be performed in "speech, mime, music, and dance," Jessye presents a biblical story to which she cannot directly connect African Americans but, through dialogue and musical choices, she makes clear the applicability of Job's story to black life and history.[76] Her narrative, like the biblical text, emphasizes Job's loss of wealth and property, of family and health, and it is difficult to imagine, especially given Jessye's intention that the piece be performed by African American singers, that audiences would not understand Job's trials to resemble the hardships experienced by Africans in America. Near the narrative's end, for example, when Satan has taken everything from him, Job calls out to God:

> If I have been sinful, Lord, tell me . . . (Choir repeats "tell me.")
> If I have been deceitful, Lord, tell me . . .
> If I have been scornful, Lord, tell me . . .
> If I have in any way displeased you, Lord, tell me. Tell me![77]

Jessye might well have intended to encourage audience members, of whatever background, to imagine enslaved Africans beseeching God for an explanation for their loss of home, family, and freedom. Moreover, in using Job, who God and Satan agree is a good man and who clearly does not merit his difficulties, Jessye emphasizes the unjustness of African slavery in America.

Jessye presents Job's story largely through narration spoken along with a piano instrumental composed by Reginald Beane, known as an accompanist for Ethel Waters.[78] Although she sometimes notated the rhythm of such narration, as in her "Negro story song" "Simon the Fisherman," Jessye's scripting of the narrator's part and of the spoken choral responses in the *Chronicle of Job* generally are not fixed but structured simply by the measures of the accompaniment in 4/4 time. Once near the end of the piece she provides both tone and rhythm for the narrator and directs that this section be presented "in half tone."[79] Job's first-person sections are performed by a baritone solo and, although they represent a remarkably small part of the piece, they emerge powerfully following the long sections of spoken narrative. Jessye supports and emphasizes Job's words with a sung choral echo. When the narrator tells the audience that Job's wife has given up on God, Jessye presents Job's response to her in the first person as he sings "The Lord may have his way with me," and the choir echoes his assertion.[80] Job remains steadfast through the loss of family, wealth, and health and finally declares of God, "Though he slay me, yet will I trust him."[81] At the chronicle's conclusion, the chorus, which has functioned throughout to comment on the action and as a stand-in for the audience, sings ("with gusto," in Jessye's stage directions),

> I'm gonna pray like Job (solo)
>
> pray to my Lord (chorus)
>
> I'm gonna trust like Job (solo)
>
> trust in the Lord (chorus)
>
> I'm gonna wait like Job (solo)
>
> wait on the Lord (chorus)
>
> Wait till my change comes (solo)
>
> wait on the Lord (chorus)
>
> I'm gonna bear my afflictions, jes' like Job! (chorus)[82]

In this antiphonal section, characterized by call and response, Jessye moves the solo part from baritone to soprano to bass, an approach she had used earlier in the oratorio for "Blessed Be the Name of the Lord," the only other section performed by the chorus alone. The alternation of the solo part in the promise to follow Job's model affirms the chorus's position as representative of the contemporary audience and emphasizes the accessibility of this level of spiritual dedication to anyone.[83]

In a manner typical of black Christian identification with the trials and tribulations of figures from the Hebrew scriptures, Jessye presents Job as a model for behavior and as a figure whose experiences of God's blessings assures African Americans of a similar outcome.[84] Job may have been the most patient man in biblical history, but Jessye's work insists that since the biblical age others have borne their afflictions like Job and live in expectation of God's blessing. Although the conclusion of the piece could be read as counseling patient acceptance of the difficulties of this life in favor of rewards in heaven—a common stereotype of African American Protestant theology—Jessye's selection of Job, who is rewarded for his faith in his lifetime, works against the stereotype. Immediately before the concluding exclamation by the choir that they will "wait like Job," the narrator tells the audience, "the Lord blessed the latter end of Job more than his beginning. Job had seven sons and three daughters. He also had fourteen thousand sheep, and six thousand camels, and a thousand yoke of oxen, and a thousand she-asses. And after this Job lived an hundred and forty years, and saw his sons, and his son's sons, even four generations. So Job died, being old and full of days."[85] The connections Jessye draws between Job's patience and the faith and patience of African Americans do not, then, seem to be in service of passivity in the face of oppression but emphasize the possibilities of faith as an agent in social change.

In *The Story of Baltasar, The Black Magus,* which was written for an NBC Radio (WBZ New York) Christmas broadcast in 1932 and survives only in fragmentary form, Jessye moves beyond common metaphoric identification and takes up one of relatively few biblical stories in which African American audiences would be able to see themselves as literal participants in Christian sacred history.[86] In the small surviving portion of the drama, Jessye's Baltasar of Ethiop emerges as a man willing to believe in a prophecy that comes out of "a faith not [his] own."[87] "For years did I keep a constant vigil," Baltasar tells the audience, "lest His sign appear, trusting the holy watch to none. One night I slept, soundly . . . forgetful." Baltasar continues, "Suddenly a host of voices awakened me. I sprang from my couch, summoned servants and hastily prepared for a long journey." Jessye tells the story from Baltasar's perspective as he encounters the other kings also in search of the child and, in placing him at the center, provides a means for African Americans to take full possession of Christian sacred history. African peoples were there from the beginning of Christian history, *The Story of Baltasar* asserts, and, represented in the person of Baltasar, they recognized the significance of the combination of divinity and humanity in the infant whom Christians believe was the Messiah.[88] Jessye's use of spirituals also connects African American history and biblical history in a less literal but no less powerful way. As Baltasar embarks on his journey, the choir sings "Rise, Shine the Light is a Comin'."

O, rise! shine! for thy light is a-coming
Rise! Shine! For thy light is a-coming
O, rise! shine! for thy light is a-coming
My Lord says He's coming by an' by
This is the year of Jubilee
My Lord says He's coming by an' by
My Lord has set His people free.

As is typical in Jessye's use of spirituals in her oratorios, this song draws a connection between Baltasar's experiences and those of black Americans in its deliberate association of the liberation of humanity from sin that Christians understand Jesus' birth to have effected with the liberation of African Americans from slavery.

In Jessye's portrayal of his experience, Baltasar recognizes that the Christ child is human and, therefore, not entirely different from Baltasar himself or black people as a whole. The narrator establishes this unique contribution in the drama's foreword, beginning, "The whole world today worships at the manger of the Christ Child. There also reverently knelt three kings who first saw His Sign. They were far wiser than we, these men from the east, where men read the stars. They came not empty-handed, but bore Gracious gifts: Melchior, the eldest, offered gold in acknowledgement of His Sovereignty. Gaspar, young and beardless, offered frankincense in recognition of the Christ's divinity; *but* Baltasar, the black Ethiop and King of Egristula, offered myrrh to Jesus' humanity [emphasis added]."[89] While the gifts of the other kings are of significance, the narrator's description clearly privileges Baltasar's gift and highlights Jessye's particular interest in the significance of Christian belief in Jesus' simultaneous divinity and humanity.

Jessye moved from considering the implications for human equality of Jesus' divinity and humanity to an exploration of Jesus' experience of human existence in her piece *The Life of Christ (in Negro Spirituals)*, which her choir performed in churches and on the radio in the early 1930s.[90] A composite of music by Gounod, Bach, Handel, Malotte, and spirituals arranged by Jessye, Edward Boatner, and J. Rosamond Johnson, *The Life of Christ* focuses more on music than on narrative, with Jessye providing short introductory texts for the spirituals that make up the bulk of the work. Although likely an engaging work when performed, particularly given the variety of musical styles and the interesting collection of spirituals, Jessye's *The Life of Christ* is not a coherent piece in which she pursues a clear line of theological investigation, an achievement that is evident in *The Chronicle of Job* or in the fragments of *The Story of Baltasar*. Certainly, the Christian belief in the redemptive sacrifice of Jesus lies at the core of the narrative, but Jessye's selection of events in Jesus' life appears to have been driven by the availability of appropriate spirituals rather than the significance of the events. Although Jessye presented this work on a number of occasions, she did not retain it as a regular part of her choir's repertoire beyond the early 1930s. Given her repeated use of such compositions as the secular "Simon, The Fisherman" and songs from *Hallelujah* and *Porgy and Bess,* as well as a variety of spirituals throughout her long career, it seems possible that Jessye was not satisfied with *The Life of Christ* from either an artistic or religious perspective and consequently did not keep it in the repertoire.[91]

Sometime around 1936 Jessye adapted John Milton's 1667 and 1671 poems *Paradise Lost* and *Paradise Regained* as a folk oratorio with spirituals and two songs she composed herself.[92] The original version, broadcast on the Eva Jessye Choir's NBC radio show (WJZ New York), was thirty minutes long, but Jessye later expanded it to a longer work under the title *Paradise Lost and Regained: A Folk Oratorio.*[93] In explaining her decision to use Milton, Jessye often told of finding a box of discarded books in front of Wanamaker's department store in Manhattan, among them a copy of *Paradise Lost*. "I had read it, of course, in school before this," Jessye recalled many years later, "but you know school, we all thought, oh that Milton, so dry; so dry. So I read it again, and it was marvelous, and suddenly I thought there's spirituals on every subject here. And it really works well."[94] Indeed, Jessye created a powerful work by seamlessly integrating spirituals and Milton's text; the result was much more successful than *The Life of Christ*. Praising Milton's work, Jessye wrote in her notes for a production that "*Paradise Lost* is one of the finest narratives ever written, excelled only by the Holy Bible and Shakespeare."[95] The inclusion of spirituals and original music, in her view, "introduces, emphasizes and extends the thought . . . and even clarifies some of the most complex passages penned by the immortal Milton." In her review of the 1972 production at the Washington Cathedral, Joan Reinthaler wrote, "Dr. Jessye has perceived the unexpected affinity between Milton's elegant and purple poetry and the personalized romanticism of the idiom. Within a rather conventional oratorio framework she has brought these two expressions together in a way that makes each one more itself."[96]

As much as she respected the beauty of Milton's poem, Jessye's intimate knowledge of the text and her confidence in her own theological commitments authorized her to rework the narrative so that she could explore themes of interest to her, particularly the meaning of human suffering and the experience of Jesus in humanity. Jessye's *Paradise Lost and Regained* dramatically reduces the roles of Lucifer and Adam, the leading figures in Milton's version, and focuses the drama instead on the decision of God's Son to "be mortal to redeem Man's mortal crime."[97] Midway through Jessye's oratorio, God calls to the heavenly powers for an intercessor on humanity's behalf, and the Son accepts that role, singing "Prepare me a body, I'll go down and die," and "These bones shall rise again," as well as reciting from Milton's *Paradise Lost:*

Father, thy word is passed. Man shall find grace.

Behold Me, then, Me for him, life for life

I offer, on Me let thine anger fall;

Account Me man; I for his sake will leave

Thy bosom, and this glory next to Thee

Freely put off, and for him lastly die

Well pleased . . .[98]

Concluding her *Paradise Lost and Regained* with a section near the end of Milton's *Paradise Regained,* Jessye presses the theological theme she emphasized in her earlier *Story of Baltasar:* the Christian belief in the revolutionary significance of the human incarnation of God's son for the purpose of redeeming humanity's loss of paradise. Following the choir's singing of "Ride on, King Jesus," the narrator concludes:

In the bosom of bliss, and light of light

Conceiving, or remote from Heaven, enshrined

In fleshly tabernacle, and human form,

Thou hast regained lost Paradise . . .

A fairer Paradise is founded now

For Adam and his chosen sons.[99]

The Christian understanding of Jesus' redemptive sacrifice forms the core of the oratorio, but Jessye's version also highlights metaphoric connections between African Americans and biblical history as in *The Chronicle of Job.* In reorganizing Milton's narrative Jessye transforms the story of humanity from one of prophecy (as told to Adam and Eve by Raphael in Milton's *Paradise Lost*) to one of history (recounted as a prelude to Jesus' triumph over Satan). Using spirituals including "Go Down, Moses," "Joshua Fit the Battle of Jericho," and "By the Waters of Babylon" in conjunction with carefully selected portions of Milton's text, Jessye focuses the audience's attention on the experiences of the Israelites in prosperity, in bondage, and in exile. In doing so, she participates in a theological tradition that draws connections between the travails of Israelites and those of African Americans as a means of affirming a belief in the certainty of God's commitment to his suffering people. As in earlier works, Jessye is especially attentive to questions about African American history, using biblical narratives to locate black people in Christian sacred history and to emphasize the social implications of the Christian belief that God's son took on human frailty and suffering in the cause of human redemption and equality.[100]

Although Jessye was principally concerned with theological and social issues particular to African American history, she composed these dramas and oratorios with the hope of forging connections across denominational and racial boundaries. In her notes for a 1978 production of *Paradise Lost and Regained,* she wrote that she intended these dramas to appeal "to persons of all classes, faiths, and levels of intelligence." Jessye was likely overly optimistic about the appeal of explicitly Christian material to people from other religious backgrounds (beyond aesthetic enjoyment), but her interest in creating dialogue among members of different Christian denominations bore fruit. Audience members and sponsors of productions of *Paradise Lost* in particular concurred with Jessye on the possibilities of the work to foster dialogue. Rev. George A. Ackerly, Executive Secretary of the Greater Lawrence Council of Churches in Massachusetts, which sponsored performances of a number of Jessye's works, wrote that *Paradise Lost* "was the most inspiring event of my sojourn in Lawrence. It was a demonstration of how churches of all denominations can cooperate and people of different cultural backgrounds contribute to the amity of community, country and world."[101] It was, perhaps, this perspective on the possibilities of African American music to assist in social transformation that led the organizers of the 1963 March on Washington to select Jessye's group as the event's official choir.[102]

Art as Religious Praxis

It is difficult to assess how the members of the diverse audiences that attended performances of Eva Jessye's works over the years responded to the theological concerns evident in her compositions. The absence of such information does not diminish the potential critical value of examining Jessye's career, however. A number of interests and themes in her work point to significant lacunae in the study of African American women's religious history and African American religious history more broadly and challenge scholars to find new conceptual models that can incorporate Jessye and other black female artists' approaches to expressing their religious commitments. Jessye operated with absolute confidence that her arrangements of spirituals, as well as her unique compositions that combined spirituals and European classical music, spoke *from* and *to* particularly African American religious contexts. In entering into the 1920s and 1930s debates over the authenticity of choral versions of spirituals and in continuing to perform these songs in varied contexts throughout her long life, she decisively resisted attempts by blacks and whites to narrow the religious and artistic possibilities for African Americans. Although she believed that her experiences growing up in a black community in Kansas in the early years of the twentieth century provided her with privileged access to the musical and emotional complexities of spirituals, she did not accept the contention that spirituals (or, in later years, gospel music) represented the only means by which African Americans could or should express themselves religiously through music. Through her promotion of an individual identity and an identity for her choirs that stressed both rootedness in poor black communities and the achievements of college-educated African Americans, Jessye worked to bridge class divides in twentieth-century religious communities.[103] She charted a similar path in the content of her art, using black vernacular cultures to help interpret and amplify the power of biblical and other religious texts and placing her classical training in service of spreading the message of the spirituals to a broad audience. Clearly, the definition of authentic and appropriate religious music for African Americans, while contested, was broad enough to include Jessye's work. Jessye's success and popularity across so many years requires scholars of African American religious history to allow cultural productions like *Paradise Lost and Regained: A Folk Oratorio* to help set the terms for understanding the aesthetics of African American religious life.

That Jessye did not address gender explicitly in her religious works, when many prominent black Baptist women did, should not deter us from exploring the implications of her compositions and performances for the gendering of African American religious cultures.[104] Rather than creating oratorios that highlighted female biblical figures or provided interpretations of scripture emphasizing the possibility of expanded roles and authority for women in churches, Jessye chose instead to focus on other issues in Christian theology in her work. It remains important, nevertheless, to take account of how African American women helped to shape religious discourse in institutions and in the broader culture, even if the content of that discourse was not explicitly feminist. Jessye used the arts to assert her authority regardless of gender, to act as an interpreter of scripture and as a Christian evangelist within and outside of church institutions and before racially diverse audiences. There is evidence in some of her writings of her sense of the arts as accomplishing feminist goals. In an early journalistic piece about the increasing presence of African American "chorus girls" on the New York stage, for example, Jessye argued that "the chorus girl has forced recognition on the beauty and charm of the colored woman, not only from the outside, but has awakened the Negro woman herself to her own possibilities, which feat may be considered the greater accomplishment."[105]

Jessye's confident expression of her religious beliefs through her dramatic performances, a stance no doubt influenced by the women of her family and the churches of Coffeyville, provided audiences and church members with an opportunity to engage the theological concerns she identified as most significant for African American Christians and Christians more broadly. Jessye understood her talent to be a divine gift but also insisted on the importance of her own agency in accounting for her success as an interpreter and promoter of spirituals and other religious music. She was fond of insisting that "talent comes from God. God be praised and the artist congratulated."[106] Similarly, on a photograph that she inscribed to singer Marian Anderson in 1929, Jessye combined a saying of Jesus with her own philosophy of hard work, writing "All things are possible to the deserving." Although she did not explicitly confront gender restrictions within black religious institutions through her biblical exegesis, Jessye's interpretations of the meaning of Jesus' embodiment in humanity for Christians and the relationship of Christianity to African American history constituted a challenge to anyone who would deny women the right to engage in similar religious work.

For Jessye, music, particularly the oratorios she composed, provided a productive avenue to present the biblical arena as one to which everyone has equal access and to present audiences and performers with an opportunity to imagine and engage a shared history. The phrase that serves as this chapter's title, "Truths that Liberate the Soul," is drawn from Jessye's poem "The Singer," in which she writes of the divine gift of music to African Americans. Nature, she writes, taught the enslaved singer "truths that liberate the soul / From bonds more galling than the slaver's chain."[107] Art was political and religious praxis for Jessye. In an interview late in her life, she mused: "Well, I was thinking, if anything is going to bring this world together, nation to nation, it is going to be music . . . The arts have great and inestimable potential here because art is a communication of the spirit. We in the black American music community will help bring about the day when all individuals' feelings are influenced by art. We've done it in the past and will continue doing it through the unique ways we practice art!"[108]

CHAPTER TWELVE

Shopping with Sister Zubayda

African American Sunni Muslim Rituals of Consumption and Belonging

CAROLYN ROUSE

"We're okay [with toys]. I get her the Barbie and the Hello Kitty.
I make dolls, so every time she gets a Barbie I'm sewing *hijab* for
her, and a little dress. I love Hello Kitty, I grew up on Hello Kitty. I
read in a *hadith* that Aisha played with dolls. And it was in Bukhari
which is sound, so I said, 'Okay, she can play with dolls'."
—*Sister Zubayda, an African American Sunni Muslim, and the
mother of a seven-year-old girl and a five-year-old boy*

Zubayda lives in an ethnically and economically diverse community in Los Angeles. The main streets of this sprawling suburb feature stores owned by the region's conglomerates, from Rite Aid drug stores and Vons grocery stores to a heart-stopping array of fast-food restaurants. From the four- and six-lane highways that crisscross the region, it is difficult to observe community life. The city is organized for people to spend efficiently in the privatized space of malls and minimalls and then drive a short distance back to their houses, cocooned on fairly lifeless blocks designated by traffic engineers as neighborhoods. Zubayda's block is no different. Just a hundred yards off a major highway zoned for commerce and industry, squat one-story stucco houses, mostly rentals, line her dusty but well-kept street.

Inside Zubayda's rented two-bedroom house, the full story of life in Los Angeles is made visible. Zubayda successfully transforms objects purchased at Wal-Mart or Rite Aid into signs of her and her husband's beliefs and values. The beige carpet and white walls contrast with the black furniture and framed Islamic art, enhancing the rooms' appearance of order and cleanliness. Two comfortable couches fill a third of the small living room and face shelves full of children's videos, toys, a music system, and a television. From the couch in the living room, one can peer into Zubayda's daughter's room overflowing with colorful toys. The interior signifies that this devout Muslim family engages in mainstream forms of consumption.

In contemporary American culture, consumption is often conflated with individual agency, as most consumer goods are sold as tangible expressions of authentic, unadulterated free will.[1] Advertising slogans—including Nissan's "Everything you want, nothing you don't"; Nike's "If it feels good then just do it"; and the Cattlemen's Beef Board's simple and direct "Beef. It's what you want"— cast consumption as agentive, even liberating. The current social-scientific literature seems to mirror the message of product advertisers who proclaim that one becomes empowered through consumption, but is consumption agentive? In a city where the relationship between entertainment (desire), commerce, and politics are iconically instantiated in the Staples Center, a sports and entertainment arena, what potential exists for religiously committed Angelenos to transform their lives and communities through well-considered acts of consumption?[2] Consumption is a particularly interesting site for the study of lived religion. African American Sunni Muslim women in Los Angeles struggle to practice moral forms of consumption and exchange in an economy controlled by powerful multinational corporations. For some observant Muslims, being able to transcend the control of multinationals who dictate fashion becomes an important expression of faith. Religious belief, and local articulations of Islamic exegesis, and consumption are imbricated, which means that exchange has moral significance. Most importantly, the act of policing consumption and the act of policing the borders of the community are almost indistinguishable.

For Muslims living in secular Los Angeles, however, religious sincerity alone is insufficient to overcome the power of capitalist logics. Through unrelenting control of public space in the interest of private capital, the city directs not only how people shop and move throughout Los Angeles but also how they imagine and create themselves as consumers. In *City of Quartz,* a fascinating exegesis of Los Angeles, Mike Davis observes, "The designers of malls and pseudo-public space attack the crowd by homogenizing it . . . They enclose the mass that remains, directing its circulation with behaviorist ferocity. It is lured by visual stimuli of all kinds, dulled by musak, sometimes even scented by invisible aromatizers. This Skinnerian orchestration, if well conducted, produces a veritable commercial symphony of swarming, consuming monads moving from one cash-point to another."[3] In an effort to promote the *concept* of security in the 1980s, Los Angeles's elite waged a relentless battle to control the use of public and private space. Developers, redevelopers, and city officials continued to privatize democratic spaces, including parks, walking streets, and cruising streets, while allowing for the erection of metaphorical and literal walls around middle- and upper-middle class "communities."

Given the spatial policing instituted to generate particular monetary and social transactions, what consumer interventions are possible for Sister Zubayda? Like most Americans, Muslims want to be able to consume themselves, meaning that they want to buy and eat things that reflect their sense of identity. The absence of markets and goods reflecting Muslim values and beliefs makes it difficult to perform their faith and proclaim their identity in daily transactions. Given these limits, individuals either redefine the symbolic significance of mainstream consumer goods, dressing Barbie in *hijab*, or they consume within the miniscule borders of the Muslim-owned economy of Los Angeles. Ultimately, how Muslims choose to shop, the quality of their consumer activism, is predicated on different interpretations of *halal* which determine the purity of different city spaces and the lawfulness of particular forms of consumption.

Through a discussion of Zubayda's consumption practices, I articulate the political meaning and personal and social potential expressed in the current consumption practices of Muslim women in Los Angeles. I focus on Zubayda because within her community she is revered as the ideal Muslima, Muslim woman. Her commitment to wearing *hijab*, her successful marriage, her knowledge of the faith, and her regular attendance at Friday services have empowered her with a unique authority within the community. Zubayda mentioned in a 2003 interview that Muslim women who have seen her drive have remarked with astonishment and awe, "You drive! I didn't think you drove," voicing the belief that the most devout Muslimas do not drive. Zubayda says, "And if they ask me if I vote, I'm going to tell them I vote too!" Zubayda recognizes that she has the power to shape women's praxis by example, and she takes this authority seriously by trying to perform her faith to the best of her ability. Rather than reject the values she held before converting to Islam, Zubayda blends what she considers the best of both worlds. Zubayda's charisma as a devout Muslima draws from a number of embodied dispositions familiar to most African American Muslims in Southern California, dispositions that generate a similar but not determinate set of consumption practices.

Islam

Before exploring the connection between Islamic exegesis and women's forms of consumption, let me first describe some aspects of Islam and some general characteristics of the African American Muslim community in Los Angeles. Given the extreme diversity within the *ummah*, the world community of Muslims, the thing that makes them all part of one religious tradition is the *shahadah*, the witness of faith. The *shahadah* is one of the five pillars of the faith; it is recited in prayers and spoken aloud when someone converts to Islam. It states:

La ilaha ill-Allah
(There is no deity but Allah)
Muhammad-ur-rasoolullah.
(Muhammad is the Messenger of Allah.)

The other four pillars of the faith are *salat* (prayer), *zakat* (charity), *syam* (fasting), and *hajj* (pilgrimage). It is difficult to inscribe a border around the community based upon adherence to the five pillars because some committed Muslims, both Sunni and Shi'a, do not perform these four pillars of *ibaadat* (worship) with any regularity. Therefore, I argue, what unites all Muslims is their belief in Allah and the prophet Muhammad. With the exception of the *shahadah*, there is considerable room for interpretation—not an exegesis that denies the validity of the other pillars of the faith but one that legitimates being Muslim and neglecting regular worship.

Moving out from the five pillars of *din* (faith), there are injunctions for daily living which are often organized into five broad categories: *ibaadat* (worship), *eimaaniyat* (belief), *mu'amalat* (personal relationships), *mu'asharat* (community relationships), and *akhlaqiyyat* (good manners).[4] These spheres of *din* are informed by Islamic sources including the Qur'an, which has been subjected to numerous interpretations, and the *sunnah* (the words and deeds of the prophet), which have questionable legitimacy. The words and deeds of the prophet were transmitted orally before being preserved in written *hadith,* and uncertainty about the validity of these traditions means that they receive serious scrutiny and challenge. These standards of behavior suggest an ideal social order, which explains, in part, why they are subject to intense contestation.

In order to understand Zubayda's agency, it is necessary to understand how she interprets her faith. Most African American Muslima consider Islam to be the first monotheistic faith to canonize women's equality. The women I worked

with described how they read the Qur'an and the sunnah against what they know
to be the spirit of Islam as embodied in the practices of the prophet Muhammad.
The prophet's first wife Khadijah represents for many African American Muslim
women an ideal type, as the Virgin Mary represents an ideal type for many Christians. She was a successful businesswoman when she proposed to the future
prophet.[5] Throughout their monogamous marriage, she supported her husband
financially, politically, and personally. Eventually she became his first convert. For
many African American Muslims, Khadijah embodies women's essential power,
and, perhaps more so than Africa, she represents an imagined point of origin and
commonality that is gendered rather than racialized.

Asserting a hermeneutic reading of the text, the women compare the prefer-
ence for men in one *ayat* (Sura 4:34) against accounts of the prophet's participation in domestic chores, his equal and kind treatment of his wives, and his un-
ambiguous acceptance of his wives' careers.[6] Currently, the African American
Sunni community embraces Islam as a liberatory faith that fosters equality by
making women's rights, social welfare, and economic redistribution a part of worship. This idealized ethic is often described as a Muslim brotherhood or sisterhood, or wanting for your sister what you want for yourself.

Stepping into the *ummah* by accepting the *shahadah* means that one can participate in Islamic exegesis, in defining what comprises legitimate worship, practice, and faith. The chapter's epigraph exemplifies this process. Zubayda discovered through a *hadith* preserved by Ismail al-Bukhari that dolls are allowed. Using
legitimated primary and secondary sources, Muslim women author an exegesis
that subverts oppressive cultural practices, including patriarchy and economic
disempowerment. Converting to Islam is generally not based upon a need to challenge sexism or mainstream forms of consumption. However, women who do
convert find ways to use the faith to challenge common forms of racial, class, and
gender oppression. These women believe Islam frees them from ways of thinking about self and others that contribute to a lack of initiative, substance addic-
tion, personal disempowerment, and community disenfranchisement. This
framing of the liberatory power of Islam is, importantly, a communal exegesis.

From the Nation of Islam to Sunni Muslim Orthodoxy

Before the African American Sunni Muslim community began a sustained period of growth in 1975, the Nation of Islam authored the meaning of Islam for
most African American Muslims. During that time, the founder Elijah Muhammad articulated in his weekly journal *Muhammad Speaks*, and his books *Message*

to the Blackman in America and *How to Eat to Live,* what he perceived to be the sacred connection between consumption, religious and race purity, and economic
empowerment. Purchasing goods in black- or Nation-owned stores and ingesting
healthy and lawful foods was for most Nation members a method of redemption
through consumption.[7] The current African American Muslim community rejects
the need for a separate state free from the pollutions of the white Christian majority. The Nation of Islam's goals of purity and economic self-sufficiency have not
disappeared entirely. Instead, they have been displaced, at least in part, onto the Islamic notion of *halal* (lawful) and the Islamic ideal of brotherhood and sisterhood.

The explicit rejection of race-conscious religious praxis by African American
Sunni leader Imam W. Deen Mohammed (Elijah Muhammad's son), coupled
with the goal of social and economic integration into the mainstream, makes the
effectiveness of the religiously motivated consumer agency available to Muslims
like Zubayda subtle and uncertain. While the Nation of Islam's binary divisions—
us and them, black and white—have been replaced by a more nuanced critique
of oppression, the African American Sunni community continues to acknowledge that racism nourishes and sustains black urban poverty. As a result, Imam
W. Deen Mohammed's desire for economic mainstreaming is appreciated in theory, but at a pragmatic level the community understands that secularizing all
forms of consumption could lead to their continued disempowerment. In this
case, I refer to secular consumption as exchange premised upon neoliberal principles of individualism and utility; it is clearly distinguishable from consumption
guided by religious understandings of sacred and profane, purity and pollution,
safety and danger, and order and chaos.[8]

Zubayda would like to control her consumption for religious and social reasons, but how successful can she be, given the power of global markets to secu-
larize not just the state but the body as well?[9] The secularizing power of these capital forces affects not just Zubayda but the entire *ummah,* the world community
of Muslims, which is currently developing a taste, if not for McDonald's hamburgers, then for *halal* McDonald's hamburgers. Consumption often expresses
religious identity, but does purchasing a *halal* hamburger constitute an act of religious faith, or a secular rite orchestrated through a symbolic sleight of hand?
Or is the distinction irrelevant? The Nation of Islam discouraged forms of consumption that did not take into account the "purity of production," which meant
that every phase of manufacture had to be black owned for a product to be considered pure. By turning the focus to consumption rather than production and
the material relations embedded in consumer goods, the current Sunni Muslim
community accepts the purchase of goods that in the past would have been con-

sidered questionable, possibly *haram*. The mouthless Pochacco character Hello Kitty and hypersexualized Barbie are not, after all, paragons of Muslim women's virtue and their purchase is not a means to community empowerment.

Recognizing the limits placed upon all Muslims by space, time, and capitalism, the Los Angeles community tolerates these symbolic sleights of hand. But, rather than cede defeat, the community turns these conceptual impasses into opportunities to articulate what signifying practices matter to the community and its future viability. Countenancing *halal* hamburgers is currently regarded as appropriate, given the community's desire to be taken seriously as "orthodox" *and* American. Based upon American ideals of multiculturalism and individualism, the Sunni community encourages Muslims to individualize their exegesis and orthopraxy. This ethic, however, exists in tension with a desire to be recognized as orthodox by Muslims worldwide. In Zubayda's narrative of her conversion, her marriage, and her choices, the reader will see that current consumption practices are not the product of free will but reflect the community's disposition toward faith, city, nation, race, and gender. Zubayda demonstrates that signifying practices related to consumption are not the product of free agents but are part of a dialogic process that precedes the individual. The power Zubayda has is the power to recast worn metaphors through resignification.

CAROLYN: How old were you when you converted?

ZUBAYDA: I was about twenty. I was in junior college. I was dating a young man [Kamal]. Half of his family was Muslim. So I would see them pray and I would see them recite the Qur'an and I was curious. I kind of was one foot in and one foot out. I never read the Qur'an until after I took my *shahada*. When I started reading the Qur'an, it was like, "this is it." It was in my heart. It made so much sense, and after that I just jumped in both feet.

Zubayda eventually married Kamal.

The conversion narratives of African Americans who accepted Islam before the mid-1980s often describe explicit political motivations. Akbar, who now belongs to the Sunni Muslim community, described to me how he was moved to join the Nation of Islam in 1965 after hearing reports that the police deliberately burned down a Nation temple during the Watts Riot. He reasoned that the only way that the police could feel threatened by the Nation was if the organization was empowering the black community. Another member of the Sunni community, Aida, appreciated the Nation of Islam's goal of black economic self-sufficiency, and she joined the Nation in 1974, even though she never accepted the legitimacy of Elijah Muhammad's status as the Messenger of Allah.

While the Nation of Islam encouraged followers to draw a connection between personal practices and therapeutic healing, it focused on revitalizing the community rather than on empowering the individual. In *Muhammad Speaks*, Elijah Muhammad listed demands for justice, freedom, education, and a separate state. Elijah Muhammad never envisioned Africa as the future homeland for black Americans, but he did want to reproduce an ideal social system that he believed existed in Africa before slavery. This system he imagined, built upon patriarchal families, capitalism, and the Protestant work ethic, seemed to be more American than African, but for Elijah Muhammad and his followers, embracing that history was the first step toward *liberation*. Even after Elijah Muhammad's death in 1975 and during the subsequent transition from the Nation of Islam to Sunni Islam, converts continued to emphasize Islam's potential as a counterdiscourse to Eurocentrism, colonialism, and social inequality.[10] Hawaa, for example, was inspired to become a Shi'a Muslim in 1981, believing that the courage of Iranians to challenge American imperialism emanated from their faith.

Zubayda's conversion was different. Like many of the newer converts, Zubayda was moved by the promise that Islam could strengthen social bonds and produce a sense of peace through worship and discipline. From the mid-1980s on, African American female converts began to recognize new possibilities in Islam beyond its potential as a political counterdiscourse. For these newer converts, Africa was never understood to be a utopia, but because Islam has deep historical roots in Africa, their claims to Islam were as legitimate as those of Middle Easterners and South Asians. Azizah, for example, described to me how converting to Islam felt like a return home. For these women—many of whom were dealing with single parenthood, racism, poverty, sexism, and/or problems with substance abuse—the orthopraxy of Sunni Islam offered a means through which to cultivate and embody healthy dispositions. This devotional labor, a term I borrow from Rachel Harding, is informed by past experiences with race and gender oppression but inflected by modern interpretations of Islam and new diasporic possibilities. Since the 1980s, orthodox Islam has been used to author different understandings of the relationship between Islam, history, and self, a relationship mediated not by a charismatic leader but by Islamic exegesis.

Disputes over what constitutes authentic orthopraxy occur as frequently within Orisha as they do within the African American Muslim community, and, like Tracy Hucks, I observed that it is the women who often determine the outcome of these disputes. At the level of the everyday, converts like Zubayda rely on authoritative sunnah and the Qur'an to decide if it is acceptable to buy a Barbie. As the community's reliance on textual interpretations to understand issues of race and economic empowerment grows, the adherents' social practices, including consumption, continue to change.[11] In the Nation of Islam, what one wore, where one shopped, and what one ate signified a person's race consciousness and community solidarity. Now these actions signify how Muslims position themselves with respect to various readings of the faith, which indicates the community's openness to individualism. From Zubayda's perspective, her consumption practices are informed by her God consciousness, but she feels she is forced to make compromises because of the cultural, economic, social, and geographic make-up of Los Angeles.

Zubayda gave several examples of how she draws a line between her family practices and prevailing social norms.

CAROLYN: So, how do you make Islam bigger than your house?

ZUBAYDA: Try to practice it in everything we do.

CAROLYN: What about TV?

ZUBAYDA: I limit the shows. Nickelodeon . . . if the cartoon that's on now the little girl is in love with this little boy and they're kissing we talk about it. She knows that little girls and little boys don't need to be kissing each other. I'm always telling her, "Sweetie, you're going to see stuff on TV that we don't do." As long as *they* know that this is something *we* don't do, then we are okay. She already has that foundation in her where she's shy about it. She'll say, "Mommy, turn the channel, they're kissing." She knows that we prefer you wait until you're married to get involved with all that.

Zubayda believes strongly that an embodied God consciousness is more powerful than television and advertisers. African American Muslims in the city face the temptations of secular life, and in response some choose to insulate themselves and their children from any contact with Los Angeles's expressive culture. Others, like Zubayda, do not fear the choices her children might make. After all, she and her husband grew up in the same area and have never been lured by drugs or crime. She does not classify the secular material world as evil but rather as something other and separate from her and her family's emotional life.

CAROLYN: In terms of the shopping, where do you shop for food?

ZUBAYDA: Well, there's a *halal* (lawful) meat market, actually two of them that are pretty close by. I go to the regular grocery store and I buy my fish and my juice and everything else. Of course, we read labels. I just found I couldn't eat gelatin. We were kind of bummed out about that. The kids like the pop tarts and stuff like that. As far as the labeling goes, if it says gelatin, I won't buy it. We stay away from the marshmallows. They have *halal* marshmallows now, so . . . Then we get the meat from the *halal* meat market. Now some people say you have to have your meat from the *halal* meat market or it's *haram* (unlawful). Every now and then I'll pick up chicken from Vons, or ground beef. It depends because, honestly, *halal* meat is a little bit more expensive.

CAROLYN: Who owns the *halal* store?

ZUBAYDA: There's one Indian-owned one that's close by, and there's another one, but I don't know who it's owned by. But, my husband was telling me that when you cook it, you say a *dua* over it, when you eat it, you say a *dua* over it if it's not bought from the *halal* meat market. *Halal* just means that when they killed it they said a *dua* over it. And it's probably cleaned a lot better than the stuff from the grocery store. So, my husband is like, "You're not going to be thrown into the hell fire for buying chicken from Vons." When we first converted I was stressing because I couldn't get to the *halal* meat market, or I didn't have enough money. My husband's like, "Don't stress over it, it's not a sin. You're not going to burn in hell from buying chicken from Vons. Just say a prayer over it, and cook it, and we'll be fine." So, I don't stress over it as much as I used to. We still read the labels, and we do the best we can. We try to be more healthy and buy more organic, and go to the farmers' market and get the fresh fruit and the fresh vegetables. But, you know, we were brought up on candy, chips and junk. Honestly. But as a whole, we're just trying to be more healthy.

In practice, financial and time constraints often overwhelm Zubayda's desire to buy and eat *halal*. The feeling of obligation to purchase lawful meats and foods competes with patterns of consumption learned as children and challenges any lower-middle-class family's budget. Having to purchase goods in multiple stores can add stress and expense by increasing distances traveled for shopping trips. Fortunately, increasingly available organic foods and farmers' markets are considered by most women in the community to be acceptable alternatives. Both the manufacture and consumption of organic and locally grown foods emphasize the community's economic and physical health over corporate enrichment and therefore fit within these women's current understandings of *halal*.

Zubayda's and her husband Kamal's liberal understanding of *halal* makes one wonder: is their Islamic exegesis facilitating acquiescence to social inequality? These potentially *haram* markets are not entirely disinterested in facilitating Zubayda's agency and empowerment as a consumer. Even fast-food chains accept, to some degree, the moral burden of reciprocity by making available to customers food that fulfills the needs of Muslim consumers.

CAROLYN: How about McDonald's, Burger King . . . ?

ZUBAYDA: Every now and then we go to McDonald's. We do fast food but most of the time it's chicken. We'll go to Popeye's Chicken. It doesn't bother me. Overseas they have McDonald's and KFC. It's *halal* there. You just say a prayer and if you're going to eat it, you know the consequences. It's hard living in California and say[ing], "I'm not going to do any fast food ever, at all," when you have kids. As a matter of fact, her school on Thursdays, they eat KFC. It's *halal* KFC. There's a *halal* store right across the street from her school and they'll do *halal* KFC.

A number of restaurants in southern Los Angeles will fry meat or fish brought in by the customer; however, sensitivity to this subpopulation could be read quite cynically. Whether it is empowering to eat fatty, fried food, *halal* or not, is open for debate. Nevertheless, the existence of this form of reciprocity indicates that Muslim acquiescence to non-Muslim markets is altering material relations at some level. Even in fast-food restaurants, exchange involves some element of symbolic, rather than merely monetary, interaction across group boundaries. My impression is that this shift in many mainstream businesses' disposition toward their Sunni clientele speaks to the emerging public acceptance of Islam, as well as the increasing number of Muslim entrepreneurs in Los Angeles.

For African American Muslims, an ethic of purchasing from Muslim or black-owned producers has been replaced by a more indeterminate value associated with purchasing from manufacturers promoting social justice. This liberalization advances a multicultural vision of Los Angeles which indirectly benefits the African American Muslim community. Given the increased uncertainty about the effectiveness of this form of consumption, why is it preferred? One explanation is that the African American Sunni community accepts Islam as a faith that does not tax the faithful. To demand a cessation of partaking in all things non-Muslim would facilitate the fulfillment of ideals of purity, but it would place barriers in the way of achieving other goals, including education, career, family, and a higher standard of living. Many Muslims encourage the liberal crossing between secular and religious domains because they feel that the strength of the Muslim community is proportional to the success of each individual member within, or even outside, mainstream society.

The adoption of orthodoxy in 1975 increased the acceptance of varied approaches to Islam among African Americans. Despite the seeming paradox implicit in these terms, Sunni Muslim orthodoxy is less restrictive in its range of practices than was the code of behavior promulgated by the Nation of Islam. This liberalization is evident in the discourses and practices related to consumption.

Women like Zubayda allow themselves to indulge in mainstream forms of consumption but alter the significance by modifying the objects or acts of consumption (making a head scarf for a Barbie, saying a *dua* over a non-*halal* hamburger). Choosing to make Islam easy by allowing oneself the luxury of crossing the border into the secular domain is expressed in African American Islamic exegesis and social dispositions.

During my interview, Zubayda acknowledged her liberal orthopraxy.

ZUBAYDA: I'm not as strict as I want to be as far as discipline. And I know the difference between strict and extremism, and where the line is and where not to cross. But I don't get intimidated when I meet people who are very strict, because I pretty much understand where they're coming from . . .

CAROLYN: Where are they coming from?

ZUBAYDA: They're coming from—at least the people I know—wanting to follow what they know pretty much to the "T," not waver to the best that they can, and at the same time not be extreme. It's more of a feeling of preserving and protecting and guarding their Islam. I say "their" Islam because everyone's level of faith is different. Where I am in my Islam is not the same place where my sister-in-law is with her Islam, or the same place my husband is with his Islam. That's one thing my husband always says, "Islam is perfect, Muslims aren't." If we were to all follow the perfect religion perfectly, we would be perfect, but we're human beings and we can't. And God knows that.

CAROLYN: So, what keeps you from being as strict as you would like to be?

ZUBAYDA: Laziness. Uh . . . complacency sometimes. Sometimes just coming home feeling like, "Okay, I've done enough, I'm okay." Knowing in the back of my head that I can always do better, and I can always improve.

CAROLYN: What could you do, though?

ZUBAYDA: When I'm at home and the alarm clock goes off, instead of just saying, "Let me just finish this last dish," and then, after that last dish, I end up putting clothes in the laundry and doing something else and then thirty minutes later, "Oh, I was supposed to make *salat*," and then rushing to make *salat*. Or, when someone angers me and I shout . . . well, not shout, I never shout, but you know . . . I say something not very nice. I can control that and not say anything at all. So, there's always ways to strive to reach perfection.

CAROLYN: You were saying that you're learning a lot from your husband who is a "constant seeker of knowledge who is always trying to learn and improve."

ZUBAYDA: Yeah, in terms of my actions, because he's always telling me, "You know when the Prophet, peace be upon him, will do anything, he will always seek to do it the best that he can." A lot of us don't do that. We'll do just enough to get by, just enough to turn it in, or whatever the case is. I wash dishes sometimes, I just wash them to get them out of the way. My husband will pick up a glass and go, "What happened here?" You know . . . just simple things like that. One thing that my husband said to me that really stuck in my head is, "As Muslims we have to beware of Satan because he's not going to try and get us on the big things if we're strong in faith, because he can't. He's going to try to get us on the little things like being angry and saying something like 'stupid woman.'" That one little comment could affect that woman, make her sad for that day, and she'll take it out on her kids. One little comment that if I would have just kept to myself and not said it. And, that's where I would like to improve. Simple things like that.

Zubayda's conceptual engagements continually foster the development of dispositions that encourage particular practices, feelings, and consumption choices.

Acquiescence or Empowerment?

At this point, I am impelled to confront a dilemma that R. Marie Griffith accurately describes in the introduction to her book on evangelical Christian women, *God's Daughters:* "I have struggled against the temptation to romanticize resistance, that is, to read all forms of resistance as ultimately liberating rather than simply 'a diagnostic of power' that illuminates the ways in which people are caught up in various forms of power, discipline, and control."[12] Thus far I have portrayed Zubayda, and by extension the African American Sunni Muslim community, as authors of their personal dispositions and agents in control of their own choices. However, this conclusion could easily be turned on its head. I could argue that Islamic exegesis facilitates acquiescence to social inequality and authorizes acts that reproduce disempowerment. This sort of conformity is unmistakably expressed in the forms of consumption practiced by Zubayda and Kamal. The African American Sunni Muslim community of Los Angeles tries not to divide their city according to race, but as a result whatever economic potential existed in race consciousness has vanished.[13] These women's acceptance of KFC or McDonald's could indicate simply that they have been beaten into submission by powerful corporations.[14] With respect to social practice, shouldn't the fact that Zubayda is overwhelmed by the geography of Los Angeles and the financial burdens of being in the lower-middle class encourage less inward thinking about the level of God consciousness expressed in a washed glass and more consideration of the effort required to overturn economic sys-

tems that generate inequality? The shift in priorities from promoting black economic self-sufficiency to seeking religious purity and authenticity has changed
the community's social potential.

I posed these questions of race consciousness and economic solidarity directly
to Sister Zubayda.

CAROLYN: Do you ever think in terms of race? When you go out shopping in
black neighborhoods, buying from black stores, do you think about those things?
ZUBAYDA: Yeah, yeah. We still try to support the black community because
that's part of who we are. Granted, once you become Muslim, you're Muslim first.
Faith is before race, but race is still second. We're still proud to be black or African
American. I worked for four years in a black community on Crenshaw. I was very
in touch and aware. We still try to support black businesses.

Since we live in the South Bay, we try to support a Muslim or a black-owned,
African American business, or whatever we can. But, we're still aware of things
that are going on that have to do with our community. If there's something to vote
on, we try and vote. We can't afford to donate money, but we still try to be aware of
what's going on as far as financially. Certain schools in certain neighborhoods are
suffering. We've seen it working with the preschool kids. When I was working in
Watts it was very evident. My husband and I talk about how as African Americans
you have the Muslim community as a whole, and then the African American Muslim community. Sometimes we're still African Americans in that Muslim community. You know, we're still our own group, almost. It's hard to explain.

My husband was reading something . . . it might have been a newspaper . . . it
was saying how in the Jewish community, a dollar will circulate seven times before it leaves the community.[15] In our community, it will circulate once or twice.
And, we were like, "Wow, that's terrible."

We were talking about a lot of the communities. See, they know how to support each other. We don't know how to support each other. We really don't. [Saudi
Muslims] will seek money from Saudi Arabia and build a school, and a masjid.
The Pakistanis, they will seek money from Pakistan. Not only will they seek it,
they will get it. We have nobody to seek it from but ourselves, and we don't have
much to begin with. We don't know how to support each other. For example, my
husband is a barber, and it absolutely amazes him how many brothers *don't* come
to him. He's like "I'm a Muslim barber, support me as a Muslim, as a black man,
as something, but support me." Now, he's just like, "Whatever," but at first it really
used to bother him and he used to be like, "Why are they going here and there to
Joe Bob's barber shop over here, when they could come to me?"

The ideal of black economic self-sufficiency has not disappeared entirely, but there is considerable uncertainty about how to achieve it. The determination to deessentialize religion, race, and nation—that is, to make each of these terms subject to individual as well as group interpretation—powerfully subverts a number of problematic discourses and practices that have marginalized groups. But the subtlety and complexity of Zubayda's orthopraxy and that of her Muslim sisters precludes the development of the kinds of essentialist discourses of solidarity that empowered Muslims in the Nation. Strategic essentialism, which emphasizes the common interests and values that people share because of their racial position and promotes forms of collective action, continues to be used effectively to ratify social activism in African American Christian communities and Louis Farrakhan's Nation of Islam. The Sunni Muslim community has deliberately abandoned that ethic as racist, sexist, and ultimately anti-Islamic.[16]

Given the seemingly intractable urban poverty that disproportionately affects blacks, the black community could conceivably reembrace strategic essentialism. For now, however, Muslims like Zubayda continue to interpret their faith and attempt to discipline their bodies and desires accordingly. Rather than being separatist or ascetic, their interpretation of Islam connects them in particular ways to the political and economic exigencies and opportunities of Los Angeles and the world. Their agency is tied to a faith that good intentions lead to rewards in the hereafter, regardless of how compromised they may be by the city's spatial and consumerist logics.

I asked Zubayda about her decision-making process, given the demands of her faith.

CAROLYN: How do you decide what to let go? Where do you draw those lines?

ZUBAYDA: If it's something that's not going to affect my faith and my belief system, like the chicken. If it's not a clear-cut sin . . . like the issue of the *hijab*. Some of my friends and family members differ because it doesn't say in the Qur'an it's a sin not to wear a *hijab*. But, it does . . . you know, so we differ. And I know it doesn't say it's not a sin, but I'm still going to wear it every day. If Allah says in the Qur'an, "This is what you do, this is how you behave," then that's what I'm going to try to do, and that's how I'm going to try to behave. I do the best I can. I'm only human, I falter. But, I don't try to add extra, or overinterpret, or try to read between the lines. If it says "do this," I try to do it. If it says "don't do that," I try to stay away from it. And there was a *hadith* that pretty much in a nutshell said, "if you doubt it, if you're not sure if it's *haram*, stay away from it." Be safe. That's what I try to do.

While I have portrayed Zubayda's choices as determined by the parameters set by multinational corporations and the postmodern city, community censorship and control also shape her consumption decisions. The sign function of *hijab,* for example, is entangled in the tensions resulting from the African American Muslim community's increasing desire to be recognized as both Muslim and American. Theoretically, social scientists and critical observers trace the desire for McDonald's or the latest fashion accessory to producer and retailer manipulation, but rarely do we critique the commodity aesthetics of new social movements.[17] For example, Zubayda's choice to dress in flowing African print robes or plain *jilbab* and traditional Middle Eastern head coverings has a political economy of its own, situating her in a particular configuration with respect to the Muslim *ummah* and beliefs about religious authenticity.

At a women's fashion show in the summer of 2002, the combined use of African, South Asian, and American styles, accented with mud-cloth lapels or a tie-dyed scarf, revealed the women's complex self-positioning. The fashion show was held in a red-brick community college in a seemingly deserted middle-class black neighborhood of one-story pastel stucco houses. Several African and African American women had purchased space from the organizers to set up booths outside the hall, where they sold the clothing exhibited in the show, along with African-inspired art objects, skin creams, perfumes, and gift baskets. The organizers divided the fashion show into daily mother's wear, business attire, and mosque and evening wear. The clothing honored diverse subjectivities and presented numerous ways to perform race, gender, and nation, thereby enabling the women to cross back and forth across the borders between the Muslim community, secular Los Angeles, and the non-Muslim black community. By not fetishizing the head scarf as *the* symbol of Muslim womanhood and modesty, the lead organizer attempted to expand the borders of the religious community as well.

The playful signification through fashion of a relationship between race and Islam, two distinct diasporas, was threatening to some women, who felt that the clothing displayed was not properly Muslim. Two women I spoke with expressed pleasure that the audience turnout was extremely low, which in their view meant that other women were rejecting any identity other than Muslim. The low turnout, which some interpreted as a boycott, reinscribed the borders of Muslim consumer space more narrowly, and the result was the devaluation of the associated fashion aesthetic. I do not want to overstate the influence of this so-called boycott, because the women who did attend the fashion show included some of the most dynamic leaders in the community. Nevertheless, the negative responses spoke to a continuing contest over the community's borders, which are symbolically and substantively marked by fashion and consumption.

Zubayda wanted to go to the fashion show but was unable to attend because the thirty-five-dollar entrance fee was prohibitive. The women who objected to the fashion show were poorer than the women who organized the show. For the wealthier Muslimas, *hijab* places limits on career advancement, and this fashion show was an attempt to inscribe themselves within the borders of the Sunni community and secular Los Angeles. For the poorer Muslimas who acquire status within the community through their religious asceticism, redefining women's covering as optional or even inauthentic was socially displacing.

At this intricate intersection of consumption and desire, I insert my analysis of what it means to be an African American Sunni Muslim in Los Angeles. Consumption signifies one's identification with a particular set of beliefs, peoples, cultures, and even nation-states, and as such consumption delineates structural and ideological borders between groups. In light of these relationships, Zubayda's consumption must be understood as her passport across a number of different domains: Muslim, African American, woman, Los Angelina, mother, wife. The Muslim community continues to reconsider the meaning of various forms of consumption practices and social performances relative to new developments in African American citizenship, gender consciousness, economic class, faith, and the group's acceptance by the *ummah*, the international Muslim community. Desire has multiple origins, but the choices Zubayda makes about how she dresses, what food she consumes, and what household items she purchases and displays are related to how these consumption patterns and performances situate her within the domains in which she and her community seek to identify.

Regardless of the strength of Zubayda's religious convictions, she resists adopting the strictest orthopraxy because secular Los Angeles overwhelms. The city contributes to the what and why of Zubayda's consumption, including the use of television; reliance on fast food, given the distances that must be traversed by car; the purchase of *haram* meats for convenience and cost; the inconsistent support of Muslim-owned businesses; serendipitous exposure to a secular expressive culture generated in mediascapes; and necessary reliance on two incomes. It is difficult to know how she would author her consumption practices if she could exercise greater control over her space, time, and resources. Zubayda, however, does not recognize these as limits but instead attempts through her faith to make peace with practices that situate her and the community within rather than outside multicultural and secular Los Angeles. Compromise, in this case, is not read as compromise but as the necessary means to a particular end.

My initial interest in the African American Sunni community, which began in the mid-1980s, arose out of a desire to know how Islam represented a resistance discourse to economic and social disenfranchisement. The community has since developed a new focus and identity, and new discursive methods for discovering "truth." In the process, what has been lost is a plan for economic empowerment tied to race consciousness. The prophet Muhammad envisioned a world united by faith rather than divided by race or tribe, and the current African American Sunni community fervently promotes that ethic. In the United States, particularly since 9/11, individualism has increasingly been accepted as the community encourages members to develop their own, informed exegesis. This very democratic approach has opened the door for diverse and indeterminate forms of agency and orthopraxy which have no resolute social purpose other than the embodiment of *taqwa,* or God consciousness. This is positive and negative. On the one hand, the community has a sophisticated understanding of race, class, and gender that accepts all three as attributes rather than absolutes. In addition, the fashion show demonstrated the possibilities of female economic empowerment in the marketing of these complex identities.[18] On the other hand, the material relations of Los Angeles overwhelm subtle (individualized) attempts to redirect capital flows, and making peace with Barbie and Hello Kitty can have unintended economic and social consequences.

The consumption practices of Sister Zubayda demonstrate the continuities and discontinuities between secular and religious forms of exchange. While secularism, or, more aptly, secularisms (which come in distinct varieties, as American secularism differs from French secularism), are difficult to separate from religion, expectations of reciprocation frame religious transactions, whereas expectations of compensation frame secular transactions.[19] Religious forms of reciprocity— whether an act is done in hopes of receiving a blessing from Allah or for the sake of recognition as a true believer within the community—are signifying practices that identify group membership and instantiate ideology in material relationships.[20] Muslims are advised to conduct regular worship, to eat only permitted foods, to engage in particular exchange relationships, and to channel their desires in religiously sanctioned ways. Converts, in short, must elucidate their relationship with the material constraints and social temptations of secular Los Angeles such that their actions do not compromise their understanding of their faith.

In her recent expositions of consumption in Japan, anthropologist Dorinne Kondo demonstrates how, through a playful engagement with notions of the essential Japanese subject, Japanese designers subvert particular racialized and gendered stereotypes. Rather than positioning consumption as revolutionary,

Kondo suggests that this symbolic playfulness often connects authorized discourses with counterdiscourses. Through these linkages, fashion has the power to inform new social dispositions through the artful manipulation of desire.[21]

For many African American converts to Islam, faith authorizes new personal narratives and engenders new social dispositions and possibilities.[22] Zubayda's story demonstrates the potential of Islamic conversion to facilitate interventions in the structural and capital flows that otherwise rigidly position her racially and economically. Can the social dispositions engendered as a result of Zubayda's conversion to Islam, however, actually alter the Faustian logics of a class war waged through the totalitarian arrangement of consumerist space? In arguing for the possibility of an oppositional culture in Los Angeles, Mike Davis says that "a radical structural analysis of the city can only acquire social force if it is embodied in an alternative experiential vision."[23] Fundamental structural change, Davis contends, is contingent on an alternative vision of space and capital. The limits imposed by the multiple panopticons that impose capitalist order at the expense of quality of life and class integration are powerful; nevertheless, in Los Angeles the emphasis on consumption has generated its own counterlogic, which is expressed by the everyday practices of people like Zubayda.[24]

Zubayda's agency, or her belief about the way the universe works, is informed by multiple sources, from the Qur'an to the constraints imposed by the material relations of Los Angeles.[25] Since the African American Muslim community burgeoned in the 1970s, converts and their children, who now comprise the second and third generation, have been deeply engaged in *tafsir*. In the 1980s and 1990s, their major regret was that other Muslim communities in the United States rarely acknowledged them as practitioners of orthodox Islam. Many leaders worked to change that image, and in large measure the Los Angeles African American Sunni community has been successful locating themselves within the *ummah*. Like Zubayda, the majority of African American converts now put their religion ahead of their race as a chosen marker of identity, and this dynamic has changed how the community is viewed by others and how the community views itself.

The African American Muslim community of Los Angeles still struggles with high rates of male incarceration and unemployment, lack of educational opportunities, poverty, and a lowered life expectancy, but it deals with these conditions less directly and less collectively than it did thirty years ago. At present, the community wants to witness the potential of orthopraxy to raise the social status of individuals, who in turn will pass their success on to the rest of the Muslim brotherhood and sisterhood. The community believes that economic integration into the mainstream is important for community development.

Zubayda's consumption practices speak to that ethic. For Muslims like Zubayda, who are educated, live free of Jim Crow, purchase cheap goods in discount chains, and have a comfortable couch, TV, and stereo, the question of liberation is a matter of degrees. From the Nation of Islam's inception in the 1930s until it peaked politically in the 1960s, the material deprivation of the black community was much more acute than it is now. For the Nation, the act of consuming had material as well as symbolic meaning, and reciprocal exchange and the recirculation of wealth within the black community was understood as a moral obligation. The obligations felt by Muslims with respect to consumption at the turn of the twenty-first century relate to orthodox forms of signification: wearing proper gendered clothing, displaying Islamic art, maintaining an orderly house. For Zubayda, the act of purchasing is not in itself meaningful. Instead, Islam brings new meaning to her established patterns of consumption. With some modifications— *hijab* on Barbie, a *dua* said over non-*halal* meat—Zubayda validates her own subjectivity relative to the *ummah*. The discourses she generates through Islamic exegesis empower her to validate the purchase and consumption of the things she desires and to maintain a position of authority within the community. Zubayda's consumption reveals, most importantly, that she gives equal weight to her Muslim and American identities.

Both the Nation of Islam and the Sunni community encouraged women to adopt a set of social dispositions that would situate the women and the group as a whole in a particular configuration with respect to faith, family, marriage, work, education, the local Muslim community, and the *ummah*. African American Muslim women's sense of power and purpose are disconnected from dominant discourses about race, gender, or class in the United States. For them, the dispositions and practices they have chosen are informed by a community-wide Islamic exegesis that is not necessarily related to a need to accumulate wealth, earn an income, or even get married and have children. These women are fashioning a sense of purpose that does not fit neatly into social-scientific models of empowerment. Many people in the community oppose affirmative action at the same time that they recognize that race matters. The women support institutionalized male leadership roles at the same time that they believe in gender equality. Finally, the community promotes economic redistribution in a capitalist context. The consumption of *halal* McDonald's hamburgers beautifully signifies the current ethic.

The Muslim community and secular Los Angeles frame Zubayda's agency. Women have some flexibility with respect to interpretation, but, short of abrogation, they are confined by a validated set of Islamic discourses and traditions. Islam has been and will continue to be interpreted in varied and socially relevant ways. Religious aporia generates a cascade of *tafsir* and engenders a renewed sense of agency. In the meantime, Zubayda's beliefs do not alter her race, gender, or economic status, but through Islamic exegesis she makes peace with the material limits imposed by the city by turning Barbie and Hello Kitty into objects that she feels she owns rather than objects that own her.

CHAPTER THIRTEEN

"But, It's Bible"

African American Women and Television Preachers

MARLA FREDERICK-MCGLATHERY

> I think T. D. Jakes, Paula White, Prophetess Bynum, Rod Parsley, I
> think God has a mission for them for people that have a heart that
> wants to change. And God will open up an avenue for you to get
> what He wants you to get, because it says in Matthew 5: "Blessed
> are those who hunger and thirst after righteousness, for they shall
> be filled." And God says, "My word will not return unto me void."
> And I think that's why I'm being aimed at so much because now
> I have the Word living inside of me and at one point I didn't . . .
> I have always known the Word, but never lived the Word.
>
> —*Gail Thomas, Halifax County, North Carolina*

As I turned onto the gravel road, Gail Thomas's new home came into full view. Our conversation the night before had hinted at her pride in first-time home ownership.[1] When I heard her excitement, I thought immediately of fine brick walls, a landscaped yard, and a two-car garage. When I arrived, her home appeared much humbler than I had imagined it, a doublewide trailer underpinned by brick, with two cars parked at random in an unmanicured yard. As Gail welcomed me inside the immaculate home, decorated in white and ivory, I noticed immediately the doves aligned along the wall and the open Bible neatly placed in the center of the glass-topped coffee table. The place, comfortable enough for two, accommodates her disabled father on one end and her on the other.

Gail's home is located among a row of similar structures at the edge of one of Halifax County's newest trailer-home communities. The rural area boasts nearly 56,000 people, the vast majority of whom are originally from Halifax County or adjacent rural areas in North Carolina. African Americans dominate the area where Gail lives, while white people are predominantly located in the cities where the jobs are and the tax base is traditionally higher. The history of slave plantations and sharecropping in this area exerts lingering effects upon the community's economic, political, and social development. Halifax County seems to have been relatively untouched by the "New South" and the recent "Sunbelt" boom, except for its access to modern media. By contemporary national standards, these rural residents are relatively poor in a region that remains isolated from expanding employment opportunities and other engines of economic development. Black women here live in an environment that is quite different from that of their counterparts in the inner cities, but they face similar constraints on their upward class mobility. Nevertheless, to Gail and the other African American women whom I interviewed, this place is home. Trailer parks like this one are a step up for many families who aspire to home ownership.

The recent purchase of property solidifies Gail's roots here. Buying a home is one in a series of experiences that Gail believes God has "placed in order" in her life. Her newfound commitment to living her faith is "manifesting fruit" in many aspects of her life: physical, mental, spiritual, and financial. She is forty pounds lighter, has been celibate for the past two years, and enjoys being free of unproductive relationships. As she tells her story, the television ministries of T. D. Jakes, Paula White, and Rod Parsley play an important role in her ongoing transformation. Some scholars see this turn toward faith as a postmodern move toward religion among the American populace at the turn of the twenty-first century. According to prevailing views in religious studies, modernity, postmodernity, and the accompanying questions of authoritative truth undergird contemporary spiritual revivals, which center on reclaiming faith and biblical authority in a secular and skeptical age.[2]

For many Christian believers, the power of the "Word" mediates personal praxis, social interactions, and politics.[3] Articulating and magnifying this power is the staple of American religious television. Asked why they watch television preachers, any group of viewers is likely to render the same response regardless of race, gender, or socioeconomic background: "Because they preach the Word!"[4] While it is important to consider the entertainment value, relationship advice, and comedic relief that many televangelists provide, allegiance to scripture by far outweighs other reasons for watching television preachers. According to adherents, direct application of the text to everyday life turns the television "preacher" into a "teacher" of the Word. This type of exegetical preaching moves away from what is seen as reverence for tradition and liturgy toward an expression of faith based upon more or less literal interpretations of the Bible which are put into practice in the most challenging realms of everyday life.

A cursory analysis of televangelist programming might assume that each viewer receives and interprets the same information in the same way. However, the message that is preached is expressed through an already established, although not static nor monolithic, set of cultural meanings and values. Similarly, the message is received through a comparatively established set of cultural meanings and values. Viewers bring their own predispositions, ideas, and aspirations to the act of viewing. Scholars argue that for most viewers, religious television does not convert them to the faith but rather serves as a means of reinforcing previously established Christian beliefs. This caveat is certainly true of the black women I studied; they had been raised in the deeply rooted traditions of black Baptist churches and continue to belong to their local congregations. Yet this presumption that televangelists reinforce viewers' faith does not begin to account for their varied responses to television preachers.[5] While a variety of people may hold the same desire for the Word, social positions that are marked by race, class, gender, and locale influence how they receive and interpret the Word.

Social location, for example, informs the types of religious imaginations and identities that emerge. Anthropologist Lila Abu-Lughod suggests that "television makes obvious the fact that the same cultural texts have different imports in different contexts."[6] Across diasporic boundaries, women view and appropriate the messages of television ministers differently.[7] Yet, the task of interpreting audience reception is difficult at best. The "thorniest questions" in reception studies arise, according to Faye Ginsburg, Abu-Lughod, and Brian Larkin not only because of the diversity within the medium itself but also because of the multiple influences upon individuals.[8] Television is one among a number of cultural texts, including worship services, bible studies, and social and political club meetings, that people experience daily. Electronic media filters in at varying levels of importance. Nevertheless, according to Abu-Lughod, "the effects of media on what Appadurai calls the 'work of the imagination' and 'self-fabrication' are worth tracing to particular configurations of power, education, and wealth in particular places."[9] What, then, are "the configurations of power, education and wealth" at play in African American women's reception of religious television in Halifax County, North Carolina? And, how do the messages emanating from religious television inform women's constructions of self, their organization of their lives, and their sense of social efficacy?

For anthropologist Roger Silverstone, we must be conscious that people "live in different overlapping but not always overdetermining spaces and times: domestic spaces, national spaces; broadcasting and narrowcasting spaces; biographical times; daily times; scheduled, spontaneous but also socio-geological times."[10] The ability of religious broadcasting to simultaneously travel to transnational locations, meeting women at various diasporic locations, raises numerous questions about the power of the medium for transforming local communities, reconstituting individual religious identities, and penetrating national economic and political discourses. This chapter explores how religious television, operating within a rural North Carolina community, informs women's everyday life decisions.

Reading Texts

While Ginsburg, Abu-Lughod, and Silverstone are anthropologists working to make sense of diverse audiences' receptions of television media, biblical scholar Renita Weems makes a similar claim about the need for contextualization in understanding how African American women read the biblical text. For Weems, "texts are read not only within contexts; a text's meaning is also dependent upon the pretext(s) of its readers."[11] "In fact," she argues, "one's socio-cultural and economic context exerts enormous influence upon not only how one reads, but what one reads, why one reads and what one reads for. Thus, what one gets out of a text depends in large measure upon what one reads into it."[12] According to Weems, while the biblical text has been associated with the historical oppression of African American people and of women in particular, women's readings of the text open it up to new and alternative interpretations which form liberatory patterns. Just as over the centuries African American Christianity has emphasized the Old Testament's stories of liberation from slavery and the New Testament's promises of universal redemption, so women actively read the biblical text against others' interpretations in subversive and empowering ways.

Vincent Wimbush, editor of a comprehensive volume titled *African Americans and the Bible: Sacred Texts and Social Textures*, similarly asserts that the context in which biblical interpretation and exegesis emerges is as important as the exegesis itself. "The African American engagement of the Bible is too much a rupture, a disruption, a disturbance or explosion of the Europeanized and white Protestant North American spin on the Bible and its traditions not to begin with the fundamental and open questions that can inspire the most nuanced intellectual work."[13] Contributors to that volume examine how black readers have used the Bible not only to address and resolve questions of personal morality but also to confront and militate against forms of racial and class oppression that confront them in everyday life. According to James Shopshire, "The Bible continues to help Black people in their encounters with an environment that is, in many aspects, still dominated by the institutionalized hostilities of white people. It is the subtle instrument of hope of many African American people who populate the bottom tier of the socio-economic system, even those crushed under the system called the "underclass."[14] While it cannot be presumed that African Americans as a group excavate one collective message of liberation from the biblical text— especially given the plurality of religious denominations and doctrines within African American faith traditions—the complicated readings of the text that have emerged often have been written against otherwise historically hegemonic and oppressive readings. The importance of contextual analysis to understanding African Americans' uses of the Bible applies as well to their interpretations of the messages offered by television ministers who present what they preach as the authoritative Word. Black women, too, construe what they hear in ways that speak to their deeply gendered and raced social position and the dilemmas they face every day.

In his study of audiences and television media, Shaun Moores argues that contemporary scholarship on television has focused primarily on textual analysis— what the media create—to the exclusion of audience analysis—how it is interpreted by viewers.[15] He posits a need for "reception ethnographers," researchers who "attend to the media's multiple significances in varied contexts of reception as opposed to focusing on quantification through measurement" (i.e., the numbers of viewers of a particular show or station). Such ethnographers would "engage with the production of meaning in everyday life" in order to understand how "settings and dynamic social situations of consumption" inform how consumers read, interpret, and incorporate media messages.[16] I embraced that suggestion in designing the methodology for this research.

Given the social contexts and experiences of black women in Halifax County, how do they evaluate the messages transmitted to them through the medium of religious television? How does hearing these interpretations of and testimonies about the Word challenge women's established personal praxis? How does it inform their religious identities? How might the changes that result from their engagement with televangelism influence women's social and political interaction with the world, given the conservative political and theological leanings of evangelical television? Through interviews and roundtable discussions, I examine the various ways in which women negotiate the benefits of their experience with televangelism, as well as the concerns they express regarding this rapidly expanding phenomenon. These women embrace television ministries as a means of mediating complicated personal concerns while simultaneously resisting the often spoken or otherwise implied political concerns of these same ministers. While the black women I interviewed empathize with many of the concerns that tele-vangelists articulate regarding family values, abortion, and same-sex unions (matters that fall squarely within the political domain of the religious right), the social context in which they experience and express their faith causes them to look beyond these assiduously defined moral considerations in outlining their political praxis. More often, the broader concerns that they express politically are articulated as class issues that manifest themselves in racial form. Given the long and pervasive sharecropping history of Halifax County, women understand that their class position is necessarily influenced by their race position. Some of the women that I interviewed did not merely describe themselves as "black women," but as "*poor* black women." By emphasizing their class position in relation to their raced and gendered position, they insist upon the simultaneity of class, race, and gender in making sense of their world. Class, as the emphasized first descriptor, draws attention to the social context of their lives. The conditions of Halifax County schools, public works, and neighborhoods necessitate an accounting of the real economic challenges that these women face within the context of a state and national discourse that presumes economic prosperity.

These women's experiences, viewpoints, and clearly articulated perspectives require social scientists to reconsider the agency of viewers in the process of media reception, as well as the ways in which African American women translate popular evangelical messages into their own social and economic contexts. Furthermore, their experiences with televangelists require scholars to examine the diversity of religious figures emerging on television since the heydays of Oral Roberts, Billy Graham, Pat Robertson, and Jerry Falwell. Some television ministries, especially those of African American male preachers like T. D. Jakes and white and black female preachers like Joyce Meyer and Juanita Bynum, offer different messages and are received differently than the well-known white male televangelists of the past.

Televangelism's History

Long before African American televangelists like Creflo Dollar and T. D. Jakes assumed positions of influence within popular religious broadcasting, Rev. Frederick Eikerenkoetter (commonly referred to as Rev. Ike) was the most widely known African American minister on television.[17] With familiar and comedic gestures, older women in Halifax recall the days when Rev. Ike would admonish his congregants *not* to place anything in the offering plate that "makes noise"; he preferred the silence of dollar bills. His emphasis upon material prosperity—of his parishioners, as well as his church—set him apart as one of the earliest media proponents of the prosperity gospel. Images of him, along with those of the more evangelically inclined Billy Graham, stand as these women's earliest recollections of religious television. Most studies of religious television, however, fail to mention the pioneering work of Rev. Ike. Historians focus primarily on white male television preachers, who were perceived as more charismatic and who may have in fact been more fundamentalist in orientation.

The history of televangelism begins with the official launching of religious television on Easter Sunday, 1940, in New York City. The growth of evangelical television is a story of survival, revival, and transformation. While evangelical Protestantism had experienced unprecedented growth during the Great Awakening of the nineteenth century, the Scopes trial of the 1920s and the expansion of American modernism, along with the influx of Catholic immigrants, forced evangelicalism to the fringes of American culture.[18] The Federal Council of Churches (later the National Council of Churches), an ecumenical organization representing over twenty Protestant denominations, dominated religious airwaves with the expansion of radio in the 1920s. The emergence of religious television in the 1940s allowed the liberal Federal Council of Churches, along with other mainstream religious groups, to enjoy the benefits of technological progress and widespread popular and financial support.

The Communications Act of 1934 brought to a halt "indiscriminate use of the airwaves," insisting that "broadcasters operate 'in the public interest, convenience and necessity.'"[19] This ruling secured the place of the Federal Council of Churches in broadcasting decisions. After that time, religious television programs fell into two main groups: "sustaining-time programs, where the network or local station meets all or part of the costs of producing and broadcasting the program; and paid-time programs, where the broadcaster himself meets all the costs of producing and broadcasting the program, mainly by raising money from viewers."[20] The Federal Council of Churches enjoyed the lion's share of the sustaining-time programs because major radio and television stations were comfortable with the "well-organized" and "predictable" efforts of mainstream churches. Other prominent groups, such as the U.S. Catholic Conference, the New York Board of Rabbis, and the Southern Baptist Convention, later enjoyed the perquisites of sustaining-time programs.[21]

Feeling shut out of broadcasting efforts, a group of evangelicals organized the National Association of Evangelicals (NAE) in 1942 and the National Religious

Broadcasters (NRB) in 1944. The NRB was formed out of the NAE as a separate association charged with investigating the possibilities for evangelical broadcasting. In 1946 this group drew clear lines between itself and the liberal Federal Council of Churches with a resolution sent to radio and television broadcasters throughout the country: "One misconception is that American Protestantism is one unified religious group, whereas in fact there are two distinct kinds of Protestants in America today. Each adheres to a particular form of teaching—the one the antithesis of the other. One group believes the Bible to be the infallible rule for belief and conduct whereas the other does not."[22] The NAE encouraged evangelicals to purchase airtime in furtherance of the gospel and as a means of asserting its version of biblical truth on the airwaves. Audience reception and support of paid-time religious television grew to a point where the Federal Communications Commission decided to reconsider the allotment of religion-based sustaining-time programs. In 1960 the Federal Communications Commission decided to end the distinction between sustaining-time and paid-time religious broadcasting, arguing that "there is no public interest basis" for such a distinction. Stations could meet the public interest and earn a profit. This decision saw an effective decline in sustaining-time programming from 47 percent in 1959 to a mere 8 percent in 1977, ushering in the new wave of paid-time religious programming and the beginning of the "electronic church" phenomenon.[23] "By 1977, 92 percent of all programming was paid time."[24]

During the 1980s, according to Mimi White, "The most visible religious programs that emerged on American television in this context did not represent mainstream Protestant religious practice; instead they featured evangelical Protestantism with a fundamentalist or Pentecostal emphasis. In this sense, the conservative religious doctrine purveyed by the programs embraces a popular, conservative religious subculture."[25]

Many scholars have focused on the intersection of politics and religious media, especially given the rise of the Christian Right in the 1980s during the presidential candidacies of Ronald Reagan and George H. W. Bush.[26] In question has been the political influence of such men as Pat Robertson, who ran for president during the 1980s, and Jerry Falwell, who organized the Moral Majority, a conservative political action group that some credit for the national success of the Republican Party in the 1980s.[27]

With evangelicals and fundamentalist groups dominating the airwaves, the return to the biblical message has become central to religious broadcasting. The emergence of cable television broadcasting via satellite has furthered the spread of evangelical and fundamentalist teachings across the globe. Neoconservative televangelists have sought to return to a time like the Great Awakening of the nineteenth century, when "evangelicalism was 'Bible-centered' and had a theology of the Word," even as they utilize the most up-to-date communication technologies.[28]

Because of its meaning for conservative Christians and its value in orienting their lives, the Bible is the central symbol found in televangelism. The telecasts began as Bible-oriented preaching, and although sermonizing has changed greatly with shifts in format, televangelism has never taken its emphasis off the Bible and biblical fundamentals as authoritative for Christians. All of the television programs make frequent reference to the Bible, reading directly out of it, selling it, and giving it away. Ministers and others who appear on their shows tirelessly quote it, preach out of it, and display it. Bible passages are frequently printed on the screen. A great deal of the music on the program makes reference to it. The Bible and fundamentalist belief are the bedrock of televangelism.[29]

In this context Christian programming has multiplied in airtime, and its viewership now reaches from the United States to South America, Africa, Asia, and Europe.[30] The Christian Broadcasting Network (CBN) founded by Pat Robertson and the Trinity Broadcasting Network (TBN) of Paul and Jan Crouch have become world-famous satellite-transmitted programs.[31] In addition to these stations, the Inspirational Channel (INSP), Daystar, and Black Entertainment Television (BET) have been host to a number of ministers who seek out technology as a means of sharing the gospel with the world. In 1997 and 1998 INSP was added as one of the first twenty-four-hour Christian stations in northeastern North Carolina. While residents have been able to watch television ministers on stations such as BET on Sunday mornings and evenings for years, INSP was the first all-day station of its kind in Halifax County.

The reliance of television preachers on what they discern as biblical truth and revelation is not simply an outgrowth of television antics but has deep roots in the rebirth of evangelicalism and the successful battle over the airwaves. According to media scholar Stewart Hoover, the "struggle for America's soul" manifest in the contemporary neoevangelical movement is accompanied by a "crisis in meaning," as people feel that contemporary social practice is wandering further and further away from the beliefs and values with which they were raised and which they still profess to hold. Hoover analyzes this growth in conservatism and allegiance to biblical authority on an individual as well as social level, pointing to the crisis moments in individual lives when people have experienced trauma (death of a child, divorce, loss of a parent) and have found that they need to rediscover a connection with spiritual values. This same type of crisis occurs on a social level. For evangelicals, the increase in crime rates, the rise in AIDS cases, the ban on prayer in public schools, the movement away from creationism and the advancement of science, the passing of prochoice legislation, and a host of other social "ills" have all been seen as signs of societal crisis. These changes further emboldened evangelicals to plead that the United States go "back to the Bible."

Women Headed "Back to the Bible"

Like women one hundred years ago who traveled the nation in Bible bands, African American Christian women today still hold affinity for the biblical text with all of its complexity and seeming contradictions. In Halifax County, alongside local pastors and religious leaders, television ministers contribute significantly to some black women's understanding of scripture. Many who desire to study the "Word" seriously and seek to grow in their relationship with God turn to television ministers. They watch programs and order tapes, books, and other material that might satisfy their thirst for knowledge. Their desire for the Word in televised evangelical form has arisen not only within the broad historical context that marks the rise of evangelicalism within American culture but within the specific context of the black church tradition.

The idea of returning to the Word has particular resonances for African American women. Contemporary debates about the future of American society have taken place within the context of a black church tradition already seeking to identify its mission in the post–civil rights era.[32] As a diverse though shared institution whose recent history is informed by the civil rights movement, the traditional black church has been forced to reconcile its prophetic engagement as a movement for social justice with its priestly responsibility to care for the individual souls of its flock.[33] The current influence of evangelical television reinforces the priestly, more individualist direction in the redefinition of its mission.

In his exploration of evangelicalism and fundamentalism in the African American biblical tradition, historian A. G. Miller speculates that televangelism will produce a growing evangelical influence among African American religious communities. In his estimate, scholars have not fully grasped the historical development of evangelicalism in African American churches, often overlooking the powerful roles of Bible colleges, para-church organizations, and media influences.[34] According to Miller, the critical articulation of black evangelicalism as otherworldly and compensatory that was put forward in the 1930s by Benjamin E. Mays and Joseph W. Nicholson, along with St. Clair Drake and Horace Cayton, has proven insufficient to the study of black evangelicalism in the early twenty-first century. As Drake and Cayton put it in *Black Metropolis,* "Lower class ministers lean heavily upon 'prophecy'. They thunder away at 'Sin' and remind their congregations of the destruction of Sodom and Gomorrah and of Noah's flood. Their choirs sing ominously that 'God's gonna move this wicked race, and raise up a nation that will obey.' Seizing upon the eschatological tradition in Christianity, they claim insight into God's 'plan of the ages.' They teach that we are living in the 'last dispensation.'"[35] Such an otherworldly orientation may never have prevailed in black evangelical churches to the degree that these social scientists believed, and in any case such eschatological hopes have almost entirely given way to this-worldly solutions to everyday problems among evangelicals. The phenomenon of religious self-help, coupled with positive thinking and prosperity preaching, heavily influences the consciousness of black believers. Furthermore, evangelicalism is no longer confined to the lower class (if it ever was). Today, evangelical teaching lies squarely in the center of middle-class America, regardless of race. For the women I interviewed, television ministries not only help to increase their sense of spiritual connection but also validate their economic pursuits. Like many viewers of religious television, African American women in Halifax County watch primarily as a means of achieving spiritual growth and resolving personal concerns.

According to women viewers, television ministries have not necessarily changed their beliefs as much as they have influenced behavior. As Gail Thomas explained, "I have always known the Word, but never lived the Word." Watching televangelists encourages her to "live the Bible." For her, this has meant practicing the conservative teachings of her childhood years—abstinence from nonmarital sexual relationships and "guarding her tongue"—along with a new emphasis on daily prayer and Bible study. These changes are important because, as Miller points out, the growth of evangelicalism in the twentieth century among African Americans has meant focusing on premillennial theology, which maintains a concern for personal sin and salvation. As the women bear out in their testimonies, however, the contemporary expansion of evangelicalism also means identifying solutions to everyday personal problems, which in mainstream black congregations have often been subsumed by conversations about larger structural issues of social inequality.[36] Furthermore, the advance of evangelicalism, coupled with the gains made by the women's movement, have placed at center stage women's issues that were formerly officially silenced or relegated to the margins of the institutional church.

Televangelists' conservative messages center on their quest to restore biblical order and save the "traditional family," although that tradition is more often imagined than actually remembered. Women in general, and black women in particular, interpret these ideas to suit themselves. When manipulated by individuals to fit into their own lives, conservative family values provide a framework for women trying to live up to their responsibilities as wives and mothers, which for black women have always included providing financially for the family.[37] The broadcasts of such personalities as T. D. Jakes and Creflo Dollar, as well as Joyce Meyer, a white traveling evangelist, and Juanita Bynum, an African American "prophetess" who received her initial national exposure with T. D. Jakes ministries, promise that individual social and economic advancement are possible along with the benefit of eternal life for those who trust in Jesus. These messages of material prosperity in this life and the enjoyment of perfect happiness in the world to come are at the heart of contemporary televangelism. Black women in Halifax County who watch these ministers see themselves as moving from the margins of society, from a place of "being bound" to a place of freedom as their faith is renewed. In deepening and living consistently by their faith, Jakes assures them, "woman thou art loosed," a biblical phrase that calls upon all the resonances that bondage and freedom have for women whose foremothers were enslaved. The black women I interviewed see the teaching that they receive as liberating them from destructive and abusive relationships, low self-esteem, and financial instability. They adopt sexual abstinence outside of marriage for their own reasons, albeit with biblical justification. In compelling ways the new discourse on sexual purity, marital fidelity, and economic prosperity provides them with a subversive, even feminist discourse that confronts the conundrums of their personal lives. They come to respect themselves more deeply and to demand respect from men, rather than compromise their integrity for the sake of public appearances or financial support. Black women use the perimeters of biblical conservatism to catapult them into spaces of social, economic, and emotional freedom.

Marriage and Sexuality

Religious television for numerous viewers is about the reconstruction of religious identity. For Annette Taylor, whose marriage to her college sweetheart almost came to an abrupt end after her extramarital affair, television ministries offer hope and restoration not only for her family life but also for her own spiritual life. Although she describes herself as a Christian who has participated religiously in her local church, she decided to seek attention and fulfillment from another man when the stress of her husband's long hours of work and their lack of communication reached its peak. Despite her commitment and her position as the church's choir director, she justified her relationship as a response to the disappointment she felt in her marriage. She never felt guilty about her decision until one day, while driving down the street, "God told me, 'Tell your husband. Stop running . . . Tell your husband.'" The fear of telling him overwhelmed her to the point that she came close to an emotional breakdown. Confronting him meant confronting the contradiction in her own constructed religious identity. Although she was a leader in the church, she was still corroborating in sin. The inconsistency of her act proved a disruption of social respectability as well as personal holiness. Late one evening after he returned from work, she decided to tell him and simply endure the pain that would come from his well-justified anger. Surprisingly, the turmoil only lasted about "two or three days." When her husband recovered, they vowed to make their relationship better. Reconstituting authenticity in their relationship and her own religious identity became her central goal. "Obedience to God" would no longer be for her a matter only of performance but actual practice.

The explanation Annette gives for the quick climax and resolution of this difficult period in her marriage is the instruction she and her husband receive from television ministers. Juanita Bynum in particular—and not coincidentally, a black woman like Annette herself—encouraged her to "be obedient to God." "Juanita Bynum was ministering to me. It wasn't one particular thing that she said to me, but just her ministry. And, she was just talking about how we have to be obedient to God. And, just different things that affected different aspects of my life." Soon after listening to Bynum and exposing her secret to her husband, Annette went to a Christian bookstore and purchased *A Woman After God's Own Heart* for herself and *A Man After God's Own Heart* for her husband. Their renewed commitment to their marriage would be worked out in obedience to God, she determined. Annette even attributes her husband's immediate turnaround after her affair at least in part to the ministry of televangelists. He would watch the ministers in the afternoon while she was at work. "He would tell me . . . he would call and tell me about a ministry that he watched that touched him and how he just cried [about their relationship] . . . And, of course I was really broken hearted. I felt bad. You know sometimes you just allow the flesh to take control of you . . . But, right now, I thank God He allowed us to go through that, because I can truly say my marriage has never been as good as it is now." Annette believes that these ministries and their insistence upon her authentic and even painful obedience to God saved her marriage.

Television ministries have played a key role in how other women I interviewed interpret and experience their relationships. For Sandra, a mother of two grown children who is now in her third marriage, the ministries of people like T. D. Jakes and Joyce Meyer help her understand how to "make a marriage work." While she admits that she stayed in one abusive marriage long enough for her husband to finish paying for her daughter's college education, she says that she vowed to get out once her daughter graduated. Without a college degree and few opportunities for sustained labor in a small community, Sandra compromised her personal safety as well as her self-respect in order to ensure her daughter's future as she explains. However, she believes that if she had been "in the Word" then, she would not have stayed in that relationship so long. The Word, presumably mediated through televangelists, would have granted her the faith necessary to walk away from the abusive relationship. Contrary to popular perceptions that conservative religiosity binds one to marriage without recourse, Sandra believes that had she received faith *sooner,* she would have left her marriage sooner. She would have simply trusted God to provide the finances needed for college. Now, married to a man she believes God has sent into her life, she intends on taking what she has learned from the preachers and applying it to her new marriage.

> I really did not know how to be married . . . I just didn't know how to be married. And, now listening to T. D. and him telling, you know, this is how you walk with your husband, this is what you do with your family . . . Giving you steps. And Joyce Meyer also does that too. But, T. D. Jakes does tell you. You know. You walk with your husband. You discuss things with your husband. You don't just walk and do what you want to do and then come back later and say, "Hey, look I did this and you have to go along with it" . . . He's just influenced my life showing me things that I need to do in a godly way. And, I like that . . . I like that . . . This marriage will work, and it's going to work according to the way God would have it to work.

Televangelists through their consistent attention to matters of personal morality, especially in marriage, challenge women to construct new models for interpreting and engaging in marital relationships. In numerous ways Sandra is reconstructing her views of marriage, but she is also restructuring her ideas about her "role" as a woman in relationship to masculine leadership in the home. These ideas are constantly negotiated against her history as a single mother, her husband's commitment to similar religious doctrines, and her awareness of contemporary models of gender equality. That her husband also watches religious television assists in their efforts to reconstruct their marriage. When I asked Sandra whether her husband watches the ministries with her, she explained that "He likes Gilbert Earl Patterson [Presiding Bishop of the Church of God in Christ, COGIC] and he does like T. D. His least favorite is Creflo Dollar, and he says that's because Creflo focuses on money so much and finances. And he doesn't particularly care about focusing on that so much." Sandra's husband's discrimination among ministers reflects the constant work that people engage in to tailor the messages they receive to their ideas as well as their circumstances. Nevertheless, that her husband watches the ministries, often with her, communicates their shared desire to live according to "the Word." For her, this commitment is what will sustain the marriage and make it better than either of her previous relationships.

Television ministries play a major role in other women's decisions to remain celibate outside of marriage. After Gail Thomas's divorce over ten years ago, she sought sexual fulfillment outside of the context of marriage. Recently, after attending a "Woman Thou Art Loosed Conference" in New Orleans sponsored by T. D. Jakes, she made a commitment to disengage in nonmarital sex. The conference, according to her account, changed her life. Since the Jakes conference she has sought spiritual guidance from coworkers who she says "knew more about salvation and sanctification and purging and cleansing." This language of "purging and cleansing" carries with it the connotation that her previous relationships were dirty, if not toxic, and so left her in need of "cleansing." In many ways her language of sexual purity departs from liberal feminist notions of sexual freedom and liberal Protestant notions of sexual expression. Nevertheless, Gail's approach to sexuality provides her with a faith-induced sense of renewal, as well as a sense of discipline and accomplishment. Recently she enrolled in a "Purity with Purpose" course taught at a local white nondenominational church, where they study a notebook on sexual purity that requires them to keep a journal about their sexual experiences and establish accountability partners who periodically check in with them. The course also asks that participants memorize certain scriptures and apply what they describe as biblical principles in their relationships with the opposite sex. For Gail, it has now been two years since she has been involved with anyone sexually, and every day she is "learning how to discipline myself." This discipline is connected not only to understanding that God is "a jealous God" but also to understanding how valuable her study of the Bible is to her newfound commitment. "He [God] likes the first fruits. I used to always study the Word at night and I'd be tired. And, the enemy knows when you're tired and you go to sleep. So now I tried this morning at 5, but I got 5:30, quarter to 6. And, when I get into it, it's like I'm really into it. And, I do my journal and I write and talk to the Lord and He speaks back to me."

Key in remaining on the right track sexually and in every other area of her life, including controlling her weight, is the study of God's word. Her spiritual reawakening causes her to reimagine herself as "pure" and free of toxic relationships. While notions of social respectability inevitably inform women's negotiations of their sexual encounters, because they are "watched" by other church members and because they could bear the physical mark of sexual activity on their bodies through pregnancy, Gail's decision to remain celibate seemed less about the performance of holiness for others as much as the actualization of holiness for herself. Her incessant study of scripture, along with her efforts to rise early in the morning to pray, read, and journal, indicate that much of her transformation is personal and not necessarily for public presentation. For African American women at the turn of the twenty-first century, the intersection of race and respectability factor less publicly in their decisions about sexuality than it did for women at the turn of the twentieth century. Unlike earlier discussions of sexuality which publicly ridiculed black women as sexually deviant (as evidenced in the work of Wallace Best), contemporary discussions of sexuality are much less overt even if the implications of earlier models still exist. Televangelists in particular do not talk in racial terms when discussing sexuality. Instead, "sexual purity" is an idea that is prescribed for all viewers, across race and gender lines. America as a nation, however, is seen as sexually deviant and morally depraved. In reconstructing their sexual identities, women like Gail are using evangelical models of sexuality in order to redeem their own shattered pasts. For Gail, Bible study brings discipline and keeps her focused on what is really important. Television preachers only serve to reinforce this emphasis. She is determined, however, not to make a false god or idol out of anything, "not even television ministries." Sometimes, she says, "I even have to turn them off." While she maintains this critical distance from the ministries, they are still an important part of her spiritual diet.

In a place like Halifax County, where a growing number of people have returned to the South for retirement, the number of senior citizens living alone for the first time after the death of a spouse or living alone following the relocation of their children is considerably high. For Ms. Canty, a widow and returnee to the South who now lives with her daughter, dating is not an option. Very attractive and still interested in participating in the community and the church, she laments the effort needed to engage in dating. While she is committed to living the Bible and religiously watches television ministries, she finds it hard to find a like-minded male companion. When I asked her whether or not the ministries assist in decisions she makes about her family, relationships, and finances, she insisted that, at her age, those kinds of issues do not arise any more.

MS. CANTY: I don't have any of those problems now. And, you see I didn't know T. D. Jakes when I had those problems. You know, I just met T. D. Jakes about four or five years ago and I didn't have any of those problems . . . And when a man gets in my face, I tell him right in front, "Ain't nothin' shakin' here for you brother." You see because it's nothing wrong 'bout having a friend and going out to dinner, go to church together, but these men want you to go to the hotel. And, I'm not sending my soul to hell.

MARLA: Really?

MS. CANTY: Yeah, because, you see, you're not suppose to do that. You're not suppose to do that and I know I'm not suppose to be doing it and I'm not doing it.

MARLA: Right, unless you're married.

MS. CANTY: That's right.

MARLA: So, even older men want you to go to the hotel! It's not just the younger ones?

MS. CANTY: Oooh chile! [Much laughter.] And, you be wondering, "what they gonna do," Marla?

MARLA: Well, they're going to try.

MS. CANTY: Not with me . . . The last man at my church . . . you know, he kept on . . . You see, I wouldn't mind going to dinner. You see, I told him. I thought he was very nice. And, I told him, "Listen, I'm on a special diet. If you want me to go to dinner with you . . . I could bring my lunch when I leave home. Then we could leave church and go on and have lunch. You'll have lunch and I'll have my lunch." But, see, I found out that wasn't the way he wanted it. We were going to eat lunch and then we were going to the hotel.

MARLA: Really?!

MS. CANTY: Uhhm hmm, yes indeed. So you know what? I got right up and walked out the restaurant. Got me a cab and came home.

MARLA: Did you?

MS. CANTY: Yes ma'am, because you see, I wasn't going to no hotel with him.

MARLA: Right. Right . . . How old was he?

MS. CANTY: Well, both of us was in our eighties. [Laughs.] Do you see where I'm coming from, Marla? Do you see where I'm coming from? And, do you understand? . . . So, he told all the fellas. He said, "I don't know who she thinks she is." See, you see, because a lot of the women do that.

MARLA: Really.

MS. CANTY: Some women will do anything to have a man. I learned that. And, you'd be surprised who does it . . . But you see that's not me. Because I believe that Word I read in the Bible. That's what I'm living by, Marla. And, I ain't lettin' nobody . . .

Ms. Canty's determined decision not to "go to the hotel" speaks to the influence of television ministries and the "Word" in how older women make decisions about their sexuality.

Given statistics which indicate that HIV/AIDS is increasing dramatically among older, heterosexual women who, like Ms. Canty and Gail, live in the rural South, it is important to note that a number of women are making alternative decisions about their sexual practices postmarriage based at least in part upon their adherence to television messages. Johnnetta B. Cole and Beverly Guy Sheftall in their work *Gender Talk: The Struggle for Women's Equality in African American Communities* are correct in lamenting the silence of the black church in addressing sexuality, especially given that black women "make up 56 percent of the total female HIV/AIDS cases."[38] However, we must consider the alternative religious spaces where women are gaining knowledge about sex and relationships. While local black churches may hedge on the subject, television ministries eagerly seek to address the personal concerns of their constituencies. Their collective effect on how people interpret their personal lives invites sociological analysis. If television ministries are influencing women's sexual practices, then it is important to consider how their behavior is actually changing and whether this change decreases their risk of contracting diseases. Women like Ms. Canty and Gail, who are opting for celibacy as a means of honoring God, are simultaneously making decisions about their physical health. Nevertheless, the haunting question remains whether women like Ms. Canty and Gail are more susceptible to contracting diseases if they are unprepared for sexual activity when or if they fail to hold to their own standards.

Finances

The popular television messages of personal fulfillment and spiritual growth inform women's decisions about their financial situations as well as their sexual lives. For Ms. Canty, T. D. Jakes is a blessing. "I think he's just wonderful. I don't see anything wrong with what he does. A lot of people criticize him, but you know, people are going to criticize you, I don't care what you do. But, I don't have nothing to criticize about T. D. Jakes." His ministry to women and his constant encouragement that they get their personal lives together and become "leading ladies" is exactly what women need to hear. According to Ms. Canty, black women especially need to hear Jakes's teachings because they have not been exposed to this type of encouragement, certainly not from a minister. "Black women didn't have that before. Who tried to encourage you to have anything? I never had one encourage me. No, not my pastor . . . One thing, they didn't think women should do this and do that, didn't think women should have their own business, you know. See, but that's where T. D. Jakes came in at. He got on up there and he let people know what the women can do. Yeah. Do you know of a black minister that did it? [Laughs.]" To Ms. Canty, black women are working against a set of historical assumptions made not only by white people but also by black male preachers, who did not believe women capable of establishing successful and independent business careers. "He's different from local pastors. They do not encourage women . . . Mine don't, at least." That Ms. Canty remains in a church where she recognizes the pastor's inadequate affirmation of women's abilities demonstrates that she selectively reads not only televangelistic texts but also the texts that come weekly from her pastor. Jakes offers a corrective to her pastor. The encouragement she receives from him and the transformation she sees in the lives of other women is exactly what women today need, she concludes.

Several women in the roundtable discussions indicated that before watching television ministers they adamantly opposed women in ministry. One even walked out of a revival service when she realized that a woman was the guest preacher. However, since seeing Joyce Meyer and Prophetess Bynum preach on television and hearing the teachings of T. D. Jakes and witnessing his support for women ministers, she believes that her earlier convictions were misinformed. Other women testified to a similar transformation in their viewpoint. Ms. Canty, like these women, believes T. D. Jakes to be a liberator of women. "He has a lot of leading ladies now. And, them ladies is something else! He's training them and they're doing all right as far as I'm concerned . . . I just enjoy him and those ladies enjoy him too . . . And they're doing good . . . T. D. Jakes is all right in my book."

Jakes's "Leading Lady" conference is a spinoff from his "Woman Thou Art Loosed" conferences. While the first set of conferences encouraged women to leave situations and people that were keeping them "bound," this next series of conferences is designed to assist women in coming into their financial, social, and spiritual abundance. The emphasis among contemporary television ministers upon finding a fulfilling earthly life, instead of waiting on the next life, is a departure from early evangelical teachings.[39] These ministers unapologetically place at the center the abundance that they believe to be the inherited right of God's children.[40] Annette and Sandra indicated that these ministries have encouraged them to handle their finances differently. Annette resolved to get out of debt and "save differently, invest in a 401K . . . to invest and bank some of that money." Hearing from Creflo Dollar taught her a great deal about investing, though she doesn't want to go overboard.

> With Creflo, I used to listen to him a lot . . . and I know that God wants us to prosper . . . but I don't want to get that much into it that I lose focus. You know some people are blessed with these things until they forget where it comes from . . . I don't think He wants us to be poor, you know, and always struggling. No. [Laughs.] And, I'm not complacent where I am. You know . . . If I could just get me—not if, but when, because we are going to prosper and we're going to get some more money. Because, right now we're trying to get a new home, so we are going to prosper. I'm not worried about that . . .

Currently living in a new doublewide trailer on her family's land, Annette wants to move into a modular home, which is more permanent. While both types of homes are popular among lower-middle-class families in Halifax, a prefabricated home is a step up. While popular television ministers might boast of multimillion dollar homes, women in the viewing audience, like Annette, often must negotiate their interpretations of prosperity against the limited resources of their communities. Based upon their personal "rags to riches" narratives, ministers on television encourage Annette to save and invest so that she too will accumulate the necessary funds to advance socially. According to Annette, this logic produces practical results. Before she would "simply spend" money and not be able to account for where it went. Now, she pays special attention to how the money is used and the types of investments that she makes. Among all the women I interviewed, Annette is the only one who actually sends money in support of television ministries. She does not send money to any particular personality, but now that she has extra money she sends eighty dollars per month to the INSP station. As a public school teacher whose husband also works full time, she believes that this contribution is not a stretch in her budget and could help other people benefit from the message. Although Annette remains critical of Creflo Dollar's emphasis upon money, she attributes her new consciousness about her money to the teachings she received from him.

Similarly, Sandra sees the ministry of Creflo Dollar as important to how she has come to think about finances. "I like to listen to him [Dollar] because . . . I think I can learn something from any of them as long as they do it by the Bible. Maybe they see something in there about finances that they read that I don't see. So, I'll watch it and hope, maybe I can learn something . . . He does say something maybe about mutual funds and that kind of thing. Something I don't know a lot about, but you know my husband. He's a true . . . He's not going to go in the stock market whereas I will." While her husband remains critical of Dollar, Sandra embraces his teachings about finances because she believes that he has something to say. Outside of the cosmopolitan mainstream of financial markets, investments, and *Wall Street Journal* reports, Dollar offers Sandra information on a subject about which she knows very little. His messages, while offering advice for succeeding within the mainstream, do not, however, challenge the very practice of free-market capitalism, the heart of America's economic system.

Sandra's critical distance is established through her giving practices. While she does not demand of Dollar a critique of free-market capitalism, she is aware that ministries on television are often lucrative and removed from her own reality. Like most of the women I interviewed, she does not send money to his ministry, but she does listen and glean from what he teaches. Others, like Annette, send in money to support the ministry when they feel they have extra funds. Of the twenty women and seven men with whom I conducted interviews, only Annette stated that she sends money to religious broadcasters. Others have purchased books or tapes periodically, but most simply watch the ministries in the privacy of their homes at their leisure. Like Sandra's husband, Gail has ceased watching Creflo Dollar because she has grown weary of his teachings on finances. "I don't listen to him anymore. There's nothing different. You know every time I hear him, it's the same thing . . . You know sometimes you need to hear something more than prosperity. You know you're going through some things and there's some other things that you're dealing with in your life . . . You know, something spiritual . . . You know, not just always prospering. So, that's why I stopped listening to him . . . But, it's not that I didn't like his ministry. It's just that at different times in your life you need other Word coming forth."

The messages that television preachers give are ultimately personal, focusing on a renegotiation of self that leads to a type of spiritual and personal liberation. These biblical messages are, however, filtered through a powerful set of cultural lenses. The conservative teaching of evangelical religion stresses the need for sexual abstinence before marriage without exception regardless of the various conditions under which people remain single. The emphasis upon financial blessing is also deeply rooted in American middle-class values, a belief in 401Ks and mutual funds as opposed to critiques of unbridled free-market capitalism and challenges to excessive consumerism. These values coincide with the shift in popular evangelical discussions from life in the next world to the contemporary rewards of faith. Under this new guise the message of prosperity is fully affirmed.

Embedded Political Praxis

In his study of religious television viewers in the United States, Bobby Alexander suggests that, aside from a desire for personal spiritual growth, viewers are attracted to televangelism as a means of establishing community with a like-minded group of social and political conservatives. Televangelists such as Pat Robertson and Jerry Falwell give this "marginalized group" entrée into the political mainstream as conservative Christians who, amid growing secularization in America, can locate a "common sense of self" among the religious right of the Republican Party. However, Alexander's study focuses primarily upon a presumably (but questionably) race-neutral white audience. While moving into the political mainstream of conservative religious politics may help establish community for many (although not all) white viewers, moving into such arenas would alienate many black viewers from their established political communities. While one set of viewers negotiates political community around the idea of being "marginalized" as a religious group, another negotiates political community as members of a raced group already marginalized within American society. As a result, while the African American women whom I interviewed in Halifax County hold similar religious convictions about personal morality, they identify other concerns, especially their lack of access to material resources, as motivating their selection of a political community. While their reading of the "Word" preached by televangelists inspires them to concentrate on issues of personal morality, the context in which the Word is received means that they look beyond televangelism to define their political praxis. In my research it appears that African American women's alternative contextualized readings of religious television allow them to dissent from the politically conservative messages of televangelists while adopting the more biblically conservative tenets of evangelical Christianity. In many instances their individual appropriation of certain elements of conservative Christianity resonates with a different type of feminist social consciousness as they work toward building and sustaining their own and other women's physical and emotional health. At the same time, their reading of the political messages of religious television demonstrates the race- and class-based differences between them and religious broadcasters.

The women who watch the ministries of Joyce Meyer, T. D. Jakes, Paula White,

Juanita Bynum, and John Hagee are constantly filtering the messages they receive. The messages are all "Bible based," which gives them a veneer of neutrality, especially when it comes to political issues and political affiliations. Jerry Falwell is no longer pushing the Moral Majority and has vowed to leave the type of political activism in which he engaged in the 1980s. Pat Robertson, though still visibly involved in politics, is not among these women's favorite evangelists. Politics, it seems, has become less central to the ministries of televangelists since the heyday of right-wing televangelism in the 1980s. Or has it? People want *Bible*, not politics. They want to restore their families, establish sound financial futures, and build their marriages, not engage in politics.

The ministers women tend to watch give such attention to the personal matters of faith and everyday life experiences—marriage, relationships, and finances—that politics appears to become a secondary interest. Women consistently indicate in their interviews that they do not watch televangelists in order to gain an understanding of national politics. Unlike the viewers in Bobby Alexander's study of the ritual of televangelism, black women in Halifax County are not seeking a type of political community that brings the concerns of conservative Christians to the fore in American politics. They are listening primarily for spiritual and personal reasons.

Nevertheless, the ministries that they watch are not politically neutral. The subtle push toward political conservatism remains entrenched in the messages of contemporary television personalities. Their political bent is seen not so much in what is discussed as in what is not discussed. Issues of social justice are not discussed. America, as "a nation founded by Christians," becomes central to the establishment of Christian identity, while unquestioning patriotic support of the nation-state becomes central to a person's profession of faith. While Republican and Democratic partisan allegiances are rarely mentioned by televangelists, allegiance to the Republican Party agenda is clearly expressed.

Beyond the use of television as a means to promote political goals, many of the televangelists affirm their political positions through the use of Internet web sites, which are often more explicit about the ministers' support of particular political parties and candidates.[41] Although she generally refrains from advocating for the Republican Party during her sermons, Joyce Meyer has clearly affirmed her support for the party as a representative from the Christian Coalition. During her conference in Atlanta, Meyer had ushers distribute literature encouraging participants to join the "Road to Victory 2002" conference to be held in Washington, D.C.[42] Among the speakers for the conference were Tom Delay, Pat

Robertson, and J. C. Watts. President George W. Bush and Vice President Dick Cheney were listed as invited speakers.

In contrast to Meyer, Jakes does not openly align himself with a specific political party. When asked about his political affiliation, he expresses a complex and ambivalent viewpoint that bespeaks his African American identity and his identification with the poor. "Politics pose a dilemma for me because some politicians who embrace my concerns—pro-life and other issues—seem to have great compassion for unborn children and no interest in feeding them after they're born. If I line up with people who are interested in feeding people in need and who attack racism and discrimination, then they often also support abortion, homosexuality and other things I see as unscriptural."[43] Jakes's concerns align him with the heart of the popular evangelical critique of abortion and homosexuality and yet simultaneously with poor and minority communities concerned with feeding hungry children and fighting racial discrimination. Privileged by the presumption of race and class neutrality that accrues to her whiteness, Joyce Meyer is not compelled to address the contradictions that Jakes outlines in declaring allegiance to either party. She addresses the issues defined as primary to the majority of white, middle-class evangelicals: abortion and homosexuality.

Opposition to abortion, support of conservative judges, opposition to Bill Clinton based upon his marital problems, early support for the war in Iraq, uncritical allegiance to Israel, and a host of other agenda items clearly demarcate political affiliations without an explicit discussion of politics. These ideas permeate the milieu of popular religious programming and are rarely called into question, given the decidedly neutral positions of those who stand to offer alternative perspectives. For many televangelists, a Republican commitment to family values and unquestioned support of America as a Christian nation-state are the primary concerns that true Bible believers should maintain. Under these conditions, it seems only plausible that women would adopt the biblical teachings of these ministers in relationship to every area of their lives.

This research and other scholarship attests to a more complex reality. According to Alexander, "It is well known that the general television viewer is not a passive viewer. Television viewers reflect on the ideas or views of the world presented by television and reconfirm or question their own ideas, making the television message meaningful for themselves. There is give and take between television programs and their viewers."[44] In the experience of African American women viewers in Halifax County, there is clear "give and take" when it comes to embracing the messages presented by television ministers.

The women I interviewed consistently indicate that they share the televangelists' concerns about personal morality and abortion, but they remain Democrats because of their conviction that "Republicans are for the rich." Throughout the interviews, even women who remained loyal to the Democratic Party simply out of "tradition" indicated that they hesitate to switch to the Republican Party because of their understanding that Republicans generally operate in the interest of the wealthy. When asked, "Do you consider yourself a Republican, Democrat, or an Independent?" Elaine, one of the women in the roundtable who faithfully watches television ministers, responded that she's "down as a Democrat." When prompted to explain, she clarified, "Well, I guess originally we started out being a Democrat because of, I guess the appreciation for what Roosevelt did for the American [people], blacks in particular, and you always ended up voting that way. So far the Republicans have shown us that they're really not for the poor people . . . They just seem to be for power. Not for what is best for individuals. And, so far, I've found the Democrats to be more, you know, what is best for the individual person." For Elaine, the marginalization of poor people, and particularly black people, from access to material resources forms her primary set of concerns when it comes to determining her political allegiances. Furthermore, that Republicans "seem to be for power" directly challenges the image created by the religious right of Republicans acting on behalf of ordinary people. Elaine's social context forces her to read beyond the perimeters of religious association established by other conservative Christian television viewers.

Sandra Washington explained that her allegiance to Democratic politics has more to do with class than anything else. "To me democracy means that everybody gets a fair chance at being heard, a fair chance at doing things correctly, and to me that's what democracy is suppose to be." She identified democratic rights with a small *d* and the Democratic Party with a capital *D*. When I pressed her about her position, asking how she viewed Republicans, she replied, "I see the Republicans as for the rich." In Sandra and Elaine's constructions, the Republican Party is "for power" and "for the rich," attributes that immediately locate Sandra and Elaine outside of the Republican mainstream. These ideals further challenge the populist image of Republicans constructed by the religious right. When asked whether or not she is influenced by the political beliefs of television ministers, Sandra insists that she pays no attention to their politics.

> No. They don't influence me . . . And, I used to watch the 700 Club at one time and they were totally Republican too. I don't let it influence me any at all, because when they get to talking about politics, then that's when I go out and go do whatever I've

got to do. Whether they're talking and it's for Democrats or Republicans, either way . . . I don't listen to it. Because that cannot influence what I know I need to do. I know Republicans are not for me. I don't have no money. I am just a poor, black, hard-working woman. [Chuckles.] With a strong mind to do exactly what I need to do. And, they're not. That's not for me.

Sandra is clearly aware of the political affiliations of religious television personalities and continues to watch them as a source of inspiration. She distinguishes between what she chooses to absorb and what she chooses to reject, at times physically turning her attention away from the television. For Sandra, doing what needs to be done despite what others may say about her decisions is at the core of her identity as a black woman.

Many other viewers construct and maintain a similar distinction in how they respond to the ministers' messages. They simply turn off the television or filter out John Hagee's lamentations about the poor lifestyle choices of Bill Clinton. It's not that they disagree with Hagee regarding Clinton's moral failings; they simply see Hagee performing an exercise in politics as well as religion. These black women conduct this type of filtering as an ongoing process while they watch television ministers. In a place like Halifax County where African Americans are every day reminded of the burdens of poverty, the social context in which these women experience faith mediates how religion informs their sense of political community. They and their church communities, after all, were instrumental in the grassroots campaign that secured Representative Eva Clayton's position in the U.S. Congress. As one of the first African Americans to represent her district and as a politician who did not receive major contributions from large corporations, Clayton ran her campaign as one that would address the social conditions of poor people in Halifax County. She, along with her successor former Representative Frank Balance, traveled the county conducting town hall meetings to bring to light the concerns facing their rural region. Women who read the Bible, watch televangelism, and vote in Halifax County are equally aware of their social class positioning and the democratic tradition that supports them as they are of the conservative political messages that come to them via the television. They are not passive viewers of religious dogma but rather active participants in the construction of their own religious reality.

The invisible spirit that joins women viewers and televangelists in biblical faith does not necessarily transcend the cultural markers that divide them when it comes to politics. Preaching the Bible is as much a marker of cultural positioning as it is spiritual inspiration. Women who adopt the Bible-centered orientations of televangelists engage in a sifting process when determining who they will watch and which messages they will apply to their everyday lives. As they seek to better adhere to their religious convictions, messages relating to marital relationships, sexual practices, and finances fit into an established set of social beliefs and address problems that many experience firsthand. Contrarily, the televangelists' subtle and not-so-subtle messages about politics do not resonate with their experiences as African Americans living in a poor community. This tension propels them to filter even the authoritative biblical messages that come from favored televangelists.

Introduction

1. Hortense J. Spillers, "Who Cuts the Border?: Some Readings on 'America,'" in *Comparative American Identities: Race, Sex, and Nationality in the Modern Text*, ed. Hortense J. Spillers, 1–25 (New York: Routledge, 1991); Kwame Anthony Appiah, *In My Father's House: Africa in the Philosophy of Culture* (New York: Oxford University Press, 1992); Paul Gilroy, *The Black Atlantic: Modernity and Double Consciousness* (Cambridge, MA: Harvard University Press, 1993); Katherine Clay Bassard, *Spiritual Interrogations: Culture, Gender, and Community in Early African American Women's Writing* (Princeton, NJ: Princeton University Press, 1999); Brent Hayes Edwards, *The Practice of Diaspora: Literature, Translation, and the Rise of Black Internationalism* (Cambridge, MA: Harvard University Press, 2003).

2. Brent Hayes Edwards, "The Uses of *Diaspora*," *Social Text* 66, vol. 19, no. 1 (Spring 2001): 64; Bassard, *Spiritual Interrogations*, 5.

3. Sandra Gunning, Tera W. Hunter, and Michele Mitchell, "Introduction: Gender, Sexuality, and African Diasporas," *Gender and History* 15, no.3 (November 2003): 398.

4. Noted examples of historical, sociological, and anthropological works include Evelyn Brooks Higginbotham, *Righteous Discontent: The Women's Movement in the Black Baptist Church, 1880–1920* (Cambridge, MA: Harvard University Press, 1993); Judith Weisenfeld, *African American Women and Christian Activism: New York's Black YWCA, 1905–1945* (Cambridge, MA: Harvard University Press, 1998); Judith Weisenfeld and Richard Newman, ed., *This Far By Faith: Readings in African-American Women's Religious Biography* (New York: Routledge, 1996); Cheryl Townsend Gilkes, *If It Wasn't For the Women: Black Women's Experience and Womanist Culture in Church and Community* (New York: Orbis Books, 2000); Jualynne E. Dodson, *Engendering Church* (Lanham, MD: Rowman and Littlefield, 2002); Marla Frederick, *Between Sundays: Black Women and Everyday Struggles of Faith* (Berkeley: University of California Press, 2003); Carolyn Moxley Rouse, *Engaged Surrender: African American Women and Islam* (Berkeley: University of California Press, 2004). This literature is not so extensive as that emerging from feminist and womanist theologians and ethicists.

Chapter 1. É a Senzala

1. The Petro *lwa* (deities) are one of the spiritual lineages of Haitian Vodou and are recognized as particularly aggressive, even vehement, energies, representing a kind of cosmic rage. Maya Deren describes the Petro rite as having been born out of the ire of Africans against the suffering they experienced in displacement and enslavement. These deities and their ceremonies symbolize "the violence that rose out of that rage, to protest against it"; see Deren, *Divine Horsemen: The Living Gods of Haiti* (1953; reprint, New York: Documentex, 1983), 61–62.

2. The growth of Candomblé in Brazil and internationally, among ethnically and racially diverse populations, has elicited several alternative perspectives on the nature of connection between *orixás* and devotees. One approach suggests that because the *orixás* are as much natural energies of the universe (wind, water, fire, etc.) as ancestral forces, they exist in some form in all beings, and cultivating relationship with the *orixás* is open to anyone. Another point of view suggests that because all human beings share an ancient African progenitor (the first mother), we are all children of the *orixás* because we are all, ultimately, children of Africa. These various perspectives coexist in the lived experience of Candomblé devotees and *terreiros*.

3. Although women have had (and continue to have) chief sacerdotal responsibilities at Casa Branca and Ilê Axé Opô Afonjá, two *babalawos* (male priests of Ifá) are widely recognized as having been major contributors to the establishment of these *terreiros*: Bamboxê Obitico at Casa Branca, founded in the mid-nineteenth century, and Martiniano Eliseu do Bomfim at Ilê Axé Opô Afonjá, founded in the early twentieth century. While the tradition of female leadership of Candomblé *terreiros* is very common in Bahia, men have become more prominent among religious leaders as Candomblé has spread elsewhere in Brazil, especially to such cities as Rio de Janeiro and São Paulo. Male leadership is also more common in the Fon and Congo/Angola traditions of Candomblé (known as *Jêje* and *Angola*, respectively) than in the Yoruba (*Nagô*) tradition.

4. Charles H. Long, "Perspectives for a Study of African-American Religion in the United States" in *African-American Religion: Interpretive Essays in History and Culture*, ed. Timothy Fulop and Albert Raboteau (New York: Routledge, 1997), 27.

5. The combination of these various regional, linguistic, and ethnic elements created an essentially pan-African synthesis in Candomblé, a more nuanced and foundational commingling than the Afro-Catholic "syncretism" also associated with the religion.

6. On women as heavy manual laborers, see Katia Mattoso, *Bahia, a cidade do Salvador e seu mercado no século XIX* (São Paulo: HUCITEC, 1978). On women as water carriers, see Luis Viana Filho, *O negro na Bahia*, 3d ed. (Rio de Janeiro: Nova Fronteira, 1998), photo portfolio.

7. Ana de Lourdes Ribeira da Costa, "Ekabó!: trabalho escravo, condições de moradia e reordenamento urbano em Salvador no século XIX" (Master's thesis, Universidade Federal da Bahia, 1989), 58–60; also, Rachel E. Harding, *A Refuge in Thunder: Candomblé and Alternative Spaces of Blackness* (Bloomington: Indiana University Press, 2000), 119–20.

8. Harding, *Refuge in Thunder,* 116.

9. Raimundo Nina Rodrigues, *Os africanos no Brasil,* 7th ed. (Brasilia: Editora Univer-

sidade de Brasilia, 1988), 102. Nina Rodrigues, a forensic physician, studied Candomblé in the late nineteenth century. His published essays and books were among the first to attempt to document and analyze the developing Afro-Brazilian religion.

10. Cecilia Moreira Soares, "As ganhadeiras: mulher e resistencia negra em Salvador no seculo XIX," *Afro-Asia* 17 (1996): 64–65.

11. Harding, *Refuge in Thunder*, 118.

12. Two letters from J. A. A. F. Henriques to the Subdelegate of São Pedro, July 25 and 26, 1862, Capitães Mores, maço 5754, Policia: Registro de Correspondencia Expedida com Subdelegados 1862–1863, Arquivo Público do Estado da Bahia. Also, Pompílio Manuel de Castro to the Chief of Police, July 27, 1862, which includes Report of Search and Items Found, July 25, 1862, Capitães Mores, maço 6234, Policia: Delegados 1861–1862, Arquivo Público do Estado da Bahia. My thanks to Alexandra Brown for bringing the items from maço 6234 to my attention.

13. *O Alabama*, November 8, 1864, 3–4, cited in Dale Graden, "So Much Superstition among These People! Candomblé and the Dilemmas of Afro-Bahian Intellectuals, 1864–1871," in *Afro-Brazilian Culture and Politics*, ed. Hendrick Kraay (Armonk, NY: M. E. Sharpe, 1998), 68–69.

14. In addition to these women, seven men with ritual responsibilities were mentioned in the journal article: six drummers and a "man at the door who guides the ceremony." Of the five who were identified by color or ethnicity, two were *crioulos*, one was an African, and the other was a *pardo*. One of the *crioulos* is identified as a slave, and the *pardo* is identified as "a guard in the 4th battalion." Graden, "So Much Superstition among These People!" 68–69.

15. Harding, *Refuge in Thunder*, 111.

16. Where space is at a premium, a group of related *orixás* may share a room or house. When access to the natural environment is available, a well, a waterfall, a tree, or some other natural element may be consecrated to the deity and considered its residence.

17. Harding, *Refuge in Thunder*, 151.

18. Raimundo Nina Rodrigues, *O animismo fetichista dos negros bahianos* (Rio de Janeiro: Civilização Brasileira, 1935), 101.

19. Pierre Verger, *Orixás: deuses iorubás na Africa e no novo mundo* (Salvador: Corrupio, 1981), 33.

20. Karen McCarthy Brown, *Mama Lola: A Vodou Priestess in Brooklyn* (Berkeley: University of California Press, 1991), 252–53.

21. Publicly acknowledging and valuing the religion of Candomblé is a relatively new phenomenon in Brazil, dating from around the mid-twentieth century. Prior to that time, Candomblé was seen as a vice, if not a contagion, and certainly a liability in the "civilizing" mission of Brazilian elites. Because of its long association with blacks and slaves, the religion suffered great marginalization and persecution. Even today, many observers of and participants in the religion consider the public acceptance and embrace of Candomblé (and Afro-Brazilian religious and cultural expressions more generally) problematic and incomplete. One of the principal concerns is that Candomblé, for all of its profound influence in contemporary Brazilian cultural life, is still "exoticized" or "folklorized," which is another form of marginalization, and rarely understood or respected in the fullness of its meaning

and import. In places like Salvador and Rio de Janeiro, Candomblé *terreiros* have become major tourist attractions, and the Afro-Brazilian religious culture is increasingly commercialized, with little benefit for black Brazilians as a whole.

22. These are Yoruba language terms for "mother of the orixá" and "father of the orixá"; having the same meaning as mãe-de-santo and pai-de-santo.

23. Maria Salete Joaquim, *O papel da lideranca religiosa feminina na construção da identidade negra* (Rio de Janeiro: Pallas, 2001), 106.

24. Salete Joaquim, *O papel da liderança religiosa feminina,* 44.

25. Salete Joaquim, *O papel da liderança religiosa feminina,* 135.

26. Other scholars of Afro-Brazilian religion have written about the exponential growth of Candomblé *terreiros* in the industrial cities of Brazil, especially Rio de Janeiro and São Paulo. Many of these newer communities have significant participation by white Brazilians, some of whom formerly practiced other popular Brazilian religions such as Spiritism and Umbanda and who appear to be attracted to what they perceive as Candomblé's greater "authenticity" and "depth" of connection to ancestral energies. Reginaldo Prandi writes that there were virtually no Candomblé *terreiros* in São Paulo until the 1960s, but by the 1980s there were approximately 2,500, and by the year 2000 there were close to 4,000, sharing the city with 40,000 Umbanda *terreiros*. See Reginaldo Prandi, *Os Candomblés de São Paulo: A velha magia na metrópole novo* (São Paulo: Hucitec and Edusp, 1991), 20–22, and Reginaldo Prandi, "African Gods in Contemporary Brazil: A Sociological Introduction to Candomblé Today," *International Journal of Sociology* 15, no. 4: 644, cited in Paul Johnson, *Secrets, Gossip and Gods: The Transformation of Brazilian Candomblé* (Oxford: Oxford University Press, 2003), 156. In Bahia, most Candomblé communities remain overwhelmingly black.

27. Personal conversation with author, 1994, Salvador, Bahia.

28. The *tronco* (stocks) was used as an instrument of torture during slavery. "Nos só saimos do tronco. Estamos ainda na senzala." Personal conversation with author, August 2003, Salvador, Bahia.

29. Personal conversation with author, July 1999, Salvador, Bahia.

30. Harding, *Refuge in Thunder,* 130.

31. Johan B. von Spix and Karl von Martius, *Atraves da Bahia* (Salvador: Imprensa Official do Estado, 1916), 90, and Jean Baptiste Debret, *Viagem pitoresca e histórica ao Brasil,* 2 vols., 4th ed. (São Paulo: Livraria Martins, n.d.), 1:252.

32. Muniz Sodré, *O terreiro e a cidade: a forma social negro brasileiro* (Petropolis: Vozes, 1988), 123.

33. Luc de Huesch, quoted in Sheila Walker, "African Gods in the Americas: The Black Religious Continuum," *The Black Scholar* 1980 (November–December): 30.

34. Rosamaria Susanna Barbara, "A Dança Sagrada do Vento," in *Faraimará-O Caçador traz Alegria: Mãe Stella, 60 Anos de Iniciação,* orgs. Cléo Martins and Raul Lody (Rio de Janeiro: Pallas Editora, 2000), 155.

35. Sodré, *O terreiro e a cidade,* 124–25.

36. The longer an individual has been initiated, or the longer an item has been in the possession of the *terreiro*, the more *axé* or spiritual force is said to be contained therein.

37. Ruth Landes, *The City of Women* (New York: Macmillan, 1947; 2d ed., Albuquerque: University of New Mexico Press, 1994).

38. Martiniano Eliseu de Bomfim's parents were Yoruba *libertos* (freed slaves) in Bahia. As a teenager, he became one of an influential group of returnees of the Yoruba diaspora when he was sent to his parents' homeland for eleven years where he was trained to be an Ifá diviner and educated at a Presbyterian school by African Anglophone professors. See J. Lorand Matory, "The English Professors of Brazil: On the Diasporic Roots of the Yorùbá Nation," in *Comparative Studies in Society and History* 41, no. 1 (1999): 79.

39. Iansã is a female warrior orixá, patroness of stormy winds, lightning, and transformational energy. She is also associated with cemeteries and the dead.

40. Landes, *City of Women*, 215–16.

41. Bomfim was interviewed in 1936 by the newspaper *O Estado da Bahia*, quoted in Julio Braga, *Na gamela do feitiço: repressão e resistencia nos candomblés da Bahia* (Salvador: EDUFBA, 1995), 45.

42. Charles H. Long, "African-American Religion in the United States of America," in *The Charles Long Reader* (Princeton: Charles H. Long Imagination of Matter Project, Moses Mesoamerica Archive, Princeton University, 1995), 505–6. The phrase "what is the case" is a reference to Wittgenstein—"the world is what is the case."

43. Valdina Pinto, public lecture at Brother Jeff's Cultural Center and Café, May 10, 2003, Denver, Colorado.

Chapter 2. *"I Smoothed the Way, I Opened Doors"*

1. For a formal definition, see Tracey E. Hucks, "Trinidad, African-Derived Religions," in *The Encyclopedia of African and African American Religions*, ed. Stephen D. Glazier (New York: Routledge, 2001), 342.

2. David V. Trotman, "The Yoruba and Orisha Worship in Trinidad and British Guinea: 1838–1870," *African Studies Review* 19, no. 2 (September 1976): 1–2.

3. Maureen Warner-Lewis, *Yoruba Songs of Trinidad* (London: Karnak House, 1994), 7; Trotman, "The Yoruba and Orisha Worship," 8.

4. J. D. Elder, "The Yoruba Ancestor Cult in Gasparillo," *Caribbean Quarterly* 16 (3) (September 1970): 6–8.

5. Warner-Lewis, *Yoruba Songs of Trinidad*, 22.

6. Maureen Warner-Lewis, *Trinidad Yoruba: From Mother Tongue to Memory* (Tuscaloosa: University of Alabama Press, 1996), 2. Warner-Lewis conducted ethnographic fieldwork from 1966 to 1972, recording songs, poems, and folktales that were retained in the dialect she called "Trinidad Yoruba" by the descendants of liberated Africans, who ranged from age 60 to 103. In addition, she analyzed the recordings of Yoruba songs made in Trinidad thirty years before by the anthropologists Melville Herskovits and Frances Herskovits. She also consulted indigenous Yoruba speakers from Nigeria in order to assist in the translation of her linguistic samples. On the basis of ethnographic fieldwork, historical data, and careful cross-checking with Yoruba speakers from Africa, Warner-Lewis concludes that there was a strong African cultural impression in Trinidad which was largely

Yoruba. Finally, within the wider context of cultural and linguistic creolization, Warner-Lewis demonstrates the detailed ways in which Afro-Trinidadians engaged in complex code-switching among languages, phonological innovation, and the effective use of religious ritual and ceremony as a means of resisting language death. She concludes that "conditions *did* exist for the survival of African languages and culture patterns on this side of the Middle Passage. The assumption that African languages died out once a slave was "seasoned" derives ultimately from racist premises that dissociate Africans from culture, cultural loyalty, an affective being, and intellect."

7. Warner-Lewis, *Trinidad Yoruba*, 22.

8. Laws of Trinidad and Tobago, Summary Offences Act, Chapter 11:02, 24.

9. Laws of Trinidad and Tobago, Summary Offences Act, Chapter 11:02, 24.

10. Proclamation, Trinidad No. 9, 1889.

11. Trotman, "The Yoruba and Orisha Worship," 224.

12. Dianne Stewart, "Womanist Theology in the Caribbean Context: Critiquing Culture, Rethinking Doctrine, and Expanding Boundaries," *Journal of Feminist Studies in Religion* 20, no. 1 (Spring 2004): 81–82.

13. Rudolph Eastman and Maureen Warner-Lewis, "Forms of African Spirituality in Trinidad and Tobago," in *African Spirituality: Forms, Meanings, and Expressions,* ed. Jacob K. Olupona (New York: Crossroad Publishing, 2000), 405. Funso Aiyejina and Rawle Gibbons, "Orisa (Orisha) Tradition in Trinidad," *Caribbean Quarterly* 45, no. 4 (December 1999): 44.

14. Aiyejina and Gibbons, "Orisa (Orisha) Tradition in Trinidad."

15. "Mother of the Orisas," *Trinidad Express*, August 1, 1988, p. 25.

16. Pearl Eintou Springer, "Orisha and the Spiritual Baptist Religion in Trinidad and Tobago," in *At the Crossroads: African Caribbean Religion and Christianity,* ed. Burton Sankeralli (Trinidad and Tobago: Caribbean Conference of Churches, 1995), 96.

17. Ibid.

18. Maureen Warner Lewis, *Guinea's Other Suns* (Dover, MA: Majority Press, 1991), xvii.

19. Marta Vega, *Yoruba Philosophy* (Ph.D. diss., Temple University, 1995). Springer, "Orisha and the Spiritual Baptist Religion in Trinidad and Tobago," 96.

20. Aiyejina and Gibbons, "Orisa (Orisha) Tradition in Trinidad," 42.

21. Contest over the role and authority of Africa and African ritual orientations figures prominently in current Orisha discussions. The controversy is influenced by a number of factors that define the complex meanings of Africanness in contemporary Trinidad: the inherited ideologies of Trinidad's Black Power Movement of 1970; the island's distinct ethnocultural diversity, with a substantial East Indian population that dates back to 1845 adding a third element to the dynamic of European colonialist and African-Trinidadian identities; the prominence of national public holidays, such as Emancipation Day, which commemorate Trinidad's African presence; and the recent expansion of the Orisha initiation landscape to include Africa. Only a few decades removed from the legal limitations of Iya Rodney's era, a younger generation of Orisha practitioners has emerged in a more tolerant social context, advocating de-Christianization and Africanization of the religion.

22. Tape-recorded interview conducted by author with Rawle Gibbons, University of the West Indies, St. Augustine, Trinidad, July 2001.

23. Tape-recorded interview conducted by author with Iyalorisha Sangowunmi, Santa Cruz, Trinidad, August 2001.

24. Interview with Rawle Gibbons, July 2001.

25. Charles Long, *Significations: Signs, Symbols, and Images in the Interpretation of Religion* (Philadelphia: Fortress Press, 1986), 176.

26. Paul Gilroy, *The Black Atlantic: Modernity and Double Consciousness* (Cambridge, MA: Harvard University Press, 1993), 199.

27. Springer, "Orisha and the Spiritual Baptist Religion in Trinidad and Tobago," 90.

28. Pearl Eintou Springer, "Black Power, Religion and Spirituality," (Unpublished paper, the Heritage Library, Port of Spain, Trinidad, no date), 1.

29. Ibid., 2.

30. Springer, "Orisha and the Spiritual Baptist Religion in Trinidad and Tobago," 91.

31. Tape-recorded interview conducted by author with Pearl Eintou Springer, the Heritage Library, Port of Spain, Trinidad, August 2002.

32. Because ritual offerings to Orisha deities at times include animals, practitioners have often been stereotyped in Trinidad public lore and practitioners deemed "blood drinkers."

33. Interview with Pearl Eintou Springer, August 2002.

34. Minutes of the Trinidad House of Representatives, July 30, 1999, p. 556.

35. Springer, "Orisha and the Spiritual Baptist Religion in Trinidad and Tobago," 91.

36. Gilroy, *The Black Atlantic*, xi.

37. Tape-recorded interview conducted by author with Iyalorisha Molly Ahye, Petit Valley, Trinidad, August 2002.

38. Minutes of the Trinidad House of Representatives, July 30, 1999, p. 567. *Trinidad Guardian*, March 23, 1999.

39. Minutes of the Trinidad House of Representatives, July 30, 1999, p. 567, 568.

40. Interview with Pearl Eintou Springer, August 2002.

Chapter 3. Joining the African Diaspora

I would like to thank the Center for the Study of Religion at Princeton University, especially the Program on Women and Religions of the African Diaspora coordinated by R. Marie Griffith and Barbara Dianne Savage. Funding from the center supported the writing of this essay in fall 2003. My immense thanks also to Geneviève Zubrzycki, who read, edited, and helped rethink its structure and argument. Finally, Richard Kieckhefer's questions in response to my presentation of a shorter version of this paper at Northwestern University in January 2004 were helpful in thinking through the issue of multiple "diasporic horizons" in the final section.

1. The term most felicitously condensing such processes and exchanges was the neologism *transculturation,* an intellectual product of the Caribbean which first appeared in Fernando Ortiz's 1940 book, *Contrapunteo cubano del tabaco y el azúcar,* published in English as *Cuban Counterpoint: Tobacco and Sugar,* trans. Harriet de Onís (Durham: Duke University Press, 1995). Ortiz proposed the new word as superior to *acculturation,* a term especially associated with Melville Herskovits, because it did not imply a unilinear process of

adopting a new culture, or the idea that the former slate is completely erased before the new one is written. Rather, it suggested the nuances of culture-loss, or "deracination," as such losses and the responses to them continue to inform the experience of the new situation. It also connoted the partial and fragmentary assimilation of a new culture, as well as the completely novel creations that were bound to arise in what Ortiz called *neo-culturation*. More important than this semantic dexterity was the way Ortiz wrote about "culture" in the history of Cuba, as the process of human interaction with, and thinking through, the material resources at hand. Ortiz presented tobacco and sugar as nothing less than a total semiotic system of contrasts through which people experienced the world. In Ortiz's view, the material products of the island provided the lens through which issues of race and religion were perceived, contemplated, and worked—that is, *transcultured*.

2. I specify "within a given temporal frame" because, if we expand the temporal frame broadly enough, all human beings stem from the African diaspora. A category that excludes nothing has no classifying utility.

3. This definition of culture is especially influenced by William H. Sewell Jr., "The Concept(s) of Culture," in *Beyond the Cultural Turn: New Directions in the Study of Society and Culture*, ed. Victoria E. Bonnell and Lynn Hunt (Berkeley: University of California Press, 1999), 35–61. As a comparative analytical concept, a diaspora culture is a semiotic repertoire carried by a population with a relatively shared self-understanding of origins dispersed in enduring fashion to two or more sites separated from an agreed-upon homeland. See especially William Safran, "Diasporas in Modern Societies: Myths of Homeland and Return," *Diaspora* 1 (1991): 83–99; James Clifford, "Diasporas," *Cultural Anthropology* 9 (1994): 302–38; Khachig Tölölyan, "Rethinking Diaspora(s): Stateless Power in the Transnational Moment, *Diaspora* 5 (1996): 3–33; Robin Cohen, *Global Diasporas* (Seattle: University of Washington Press, 1997); Nicholas Van Hear, *New Diasporas: The Mass Exodus, Dispersal and Regrouping of Migrant Communities* (Seattle: University of Washington Press, 1998); and Kobena Mercer, "A Sociography of Diaspora," in *Without Guarantees: In Honour of Stuart Hall*, ed. Paul Gilroy, Lawrence Grossberg, and Angela McRobbie (London: Verso, 2000), 233–45. Economic, cultural, and social remittances maintain contacts between the homeland and the new communities. Nevertheless, migrants feel a degree of alienation in the new place, so that aspirations of return, or minimally a collective consciousness of the homeland as the repository of identity and a degree of commitment to it, termed *geopiety*, are sensed, at least but not only as an imagined community. See Benedict Anderson, *Imagined Communities: Reflections on the Origin and Spread of Nationalism* (London: Verso, 1983); Arjun Appadurai, *Modernity at Large: Dimensions of Globalization* (Minneapolis: University of Minnesota Press, 1996); Cohen, *Global Diasporas;* Thomas A. Tweed, *Our Lady of the Exile: Diaspora Religion at a Cuban Catholic Shrine in Miami* (New York: Oxford University Press, 1997); Clifford, "Diasporas"; George Gmelch, *Double Passage: The Lives of Caribbean Migrants Abroad and Back Home* (Ann Arbor: University of Michigan Press, 1992); Paul Gilroy, *The Black Atlantic: Modernity and Double Consciousness* (Cambridge, MA: Harvard University Press, 1993); Peggy Levitt, *The Transnational Villagers* (Berkeley: University of California Press, 2001); and Gabriel Sheffer, *Diaspora Politics: At Home Abroad* (Cambridge: Cambridge University Press, 2003). This definition does not necessarily require a temporal reach toward an idealized past.

4. Raymond Williams, *The Country and the City* (London: Chatto and Windus, 1973); Gilroy, *The Black Atlantic*, 110; Sewell, "The Concept(s) of Culture"; Martin Baumann, "Diaspora: Genealogies of Semantics and Transcultural Comparison," *Numen* 47 (2000): 313–47; Kim D. Butler, "Defining Diaspora, Refining a Discourse," *Diaspora* 10 (2001): 189–219; Edmund T. Gordon, *Disparate Diasporas: Identity Politics in an Afro-Nicaraguan Community* (Austin: University of Texas Press, 1988).

5. Clifford, "Diasporas," 315.

6. Andrea Klimt and Stephen Lubkemann, "Argument across the Portuguese-Speaking World: A Discursive Approach to Diaspora," *Diaspora* 11 (2002): 147.

7. Sidney Mintz and Richard Price, *The Birth of African-American Culture: An Anthropological Perspective* (1976; reprint, Boston: Beacon, 1992), 47.

8. Alexander Anderson, *Geography and History of St. Vincent*, ed. and transcribed by Richard A. and Elizabeth S. Howard (Arnold Arboretum: Cambridge, MA, 1983), written in 1798, quoted in Peter Hulme and Neil L. Whitehead, ed., *Wild Majesty: Encounters With Caribs from Columbus to the Present Day, An Anthology* (Oxford: Clarendon, 1992), 229.

9. Stuart Hall, "New Ethnicities," in *Critical Dialogues in Cultural Studies*, ed. David Morley and Kuan-Hsing Chen (London: Routledge, 1996), 447.

10. Edmund T. Gordon and Mark Anderson, "The African Diaspora: Toward an Ethnography of Diasporic Identification," *Journal of American Folklore* 112/445 (1999): 282–96; Stephan Palmié, *Wizards and Scientists: Explorations in Afro-Cuban Modernity and Tradition* (Durham: Duke University Press, 2002); Pnina Werbner, "Introduction: The Materiality of Diaspora—Between Aesthetic and 'Real' Politics," *Diaspora* 9 (2000): 5–20.

11. As James H. Sweet details, specific ethnic groups from the continent of Africa only became "Africans" as a shared identity with the transit to the Americas; in a sense, then, "Africanness" is an American phenomenon. James H. Sweet, *Recreating Africa: Culture, Kinship and Religion in the African-Portuguese World, 1441–1770* (Chapel Hill: University of North Carolina Press, 2003). "The African diaspora" did not exist under that nomenclature before the 1950s, or as a political project of generating sentiments among black peoples of shared African origins before the end of the nineteenth century. See George Shepperson, "African Diaspora: Concept and Context," in *Global Dimensions of the African Diaspora*, ed. Joseph E. Harris (Washington, D.C.: Howard University Press, 1982); George Shepperson, "The African Abroad or the African Diaspora," *African Forum: A Quarterly Journal of Contemporary Affairs* 2 (1996): 76–93; Kwame Anthony Appiah, *In My Father's House: Africa in the Philosophy of Culture* (New York: Oxford University Press, 1992); and Gilroy, *The Black Atlantic*. These various movements assumed very different political objectives of "unity," ranging from Marcus Garvey's separatism to Brazil's national assimilationism; see Michael George Hanchard, *Orpheus and Power: The Movimento Negro of Rio de Janeiro and São Paulo, Brazil, 1945–1988* (Princeton, NJ: Princeton University Press, 1994); "Race and the Public Sphere in Brazil," in *Racial Politics in Contemporary Brazil*, ed. Michael Hanchard (Durham: Duke University Press, 1999), 59–82. The transfusion of the Herskovitses' work in the United States, the francophone *négritude* movement of Léopold Senghor and Aimé Césaire, and the U.S. civil rights movement of the 1960s established "the African diaspora" as a political and cultural artifact of the public domain, systematized in international conferences, university departments, and other institutional venues. In the wake of the new, post-1960

migration wave and the theorizations that followed, contingencies and fissures appeared in that united front. With the variety of Caribbean groups that arrived en masse in the United States and Europe bearing disparate ethnic, racial, and religious self-understandings and the sudden copresence and confrontation between lusophone, hispanophone, francophone, and anglophone groups, all presenting claims on or resistance to the category, the African diaspora's heavy links to a monolithic primordial Africa were strained. They were replaced by the notion of imagined communities of hybrid "black" and "African" identifications as relatively floating or at least fluid signifiers, adapted differently in distinct nation-state venues; putative genetic and organic bonds were replaced by late-modern "signifying chains." The African diaspora was redefined as a derivative of shared suffering under slavery and subsequent racist regimes and as a common political project of resistance, which, while not essentialized in race, ethnicity, or territory, nevertheless has a relative stability based in shared experiences of subjugation under regimes of racial terror, though not always slavery (the Garífuna were never enslaved). On these shifting notions, see Mintz and Price, *The Birth of African-American Culture;* Appiah, *In My Father's House;* Gilroy, *The Black Atlantic;* Clifford, "Diasporas"; Michelle M. Wright, *Becoming Black: Creating Identity in the African Diaspora* (Durham: Duke University Press, 2004); Cornel West, *Race Matters* (1993; reprint, New York: Vintage, 2001). Membership in the African diaspora is therefore not an identification that is merely given through racial or ethnic essences but is rather acquired through cultural processes—what Max Weber called "conscious monopolistic closure" around certain features—which entail a conversion of consciousness. See Livio Sansone, *Blackness Without Ethnicity: Constructing Race in Brazil* (New York: Palgrave Macmillan, 2003), 10; Arlene Torres and Norman E. Whitten Jr., "To Forge the Future in the Fires of the Past: An Interpretive Essay on Racism, Domination, Resistance and Liberation," in *Blackness in Latin America and the Caribbean,* ed. Arlene Torres and Norman E. Whitten Jr. (Bloomington: Indiana University Press, 1998), 3–36; and Mary C. Waters, *Black Identities: West Indian Immigrant Dreams and American Realities* (New York and Cambridge, MA: Russell Sage Foundation and Harvard University Press, 1999).

12. In the early twentieth century, Weber and Boas redefined *ethnicity* and *race* as cultural categories, a contention that has since been widely reinforced. It should follow that the adoption of cultural practices, including religion, may variously reify, modify, or transform one's ethnicity or race. Yet as Michael Hanchard points out, it is the nondiscursive structural parameters of race, that which "goes without saying," that strongly delimit the range of race malleability; see Hanchard, "Race and the Public Sphere in Brazil," 73–74; Sansone, *Blackness Without Ethnicity,* on "hard" versus "soft" arenas of racial closure; Nancy Foner, "Race and Color: Jamaican Migrants in London and New York City," *International Migration Review* 19, no. 4 (Winter 1985): 708–27; Philip Kasinitz, Juan Battle, and Inés Miyares, "Fade to Black? The Children of West Indian Immigrants in Southern Florida," in *Ethnicities: Children of Immigrants in America,* ed. Rubén Rumbaut and Alejandro Portes (Berkeley: University of California Press, 2001), 267–301; and Isar P. Goudreau, "Changing Space, Making Race: Distance, Nostalgia, and the Folklorization of Blackness in Puerto Rico," *Identities* 9 (2002): 281–304.

13. Compare Elizabeth McAlister, "Sacred Stories from the Haitian Diaspora: A Collective Biography of Seven Vodou Priestesses in New York City," *Journal of Caribbean Stud-*

ies 9 (Winter 1993): 10–27; David H. Brown, "Altared Spaces: Afro-Cuban Religions and the Urban Landscape in Cuba and the United States," in *Gods of the City,* ed. Robert A. Orsi (Bloomington: Indiana University Press, 1996), 155–231; and Karen McCarthy Brown, "Staying Grounded in a High-Rise Building: Ecological Dissonance and Ritual Accommodation in Haitian Vodou," in Orsi, *Gods of the City,* 79–103.

14. Santería or Lukumi intercedes with a condensed Yoruba pantheon of *orishas* in terms of petition and exchange. Palo summons the force of the dead, called *nkisi,* represented in "sticks" (*palos*) kept in iron caldrons (*calderon, nganga,* or *prenda*). To follow Stephan Palmié (see note 10), the systems are calibrated in relation to one another: the *orishas* refer to deep African roots and kinship relations; Palo refers to mercenary "contracts" and the commodification of humans under enslavement and colonization. The *nkisi* spirit of the dead is not petitioned but rather commanded and even brutalized, and the themes of warfare, military conquest, and the need to "tie" and "bind" enemies and defend one's own territory are central.

15. Paul Christopher Johnson, *Secrets, Gossip, and Gods: The Transformation of Brazilian Candomblé* (New York: Oxford University Press, 2002). The notion of immigration as a "theologizing" experience was proposed by Raymond Brady Williams, in *Religions of Immigrants from India and Pakistan: New Threads in the American Tapestry* (Cambridge: Cambridge University Press, 1988).

16. Columbus first misheard in 1492 the word *Carib,* which was used by Arawakan peoples to refer to the fierce "man-eaters" of distant islands. This event is recorded in the shreds we have of Bartolomé de Las Casas's biography, a third-hand account written sixty years after the fact. Columbus's journals were lost, as were his brother's copy and the Spanish royal scribes' copies. *Garifuna* is actually the name of this group's language. That it is commonly used as the ethnic group's name bespeaks the centrality of language in defining Garifunaness. The current proper name for the ethnic group is Garinagu, a transformation of the actual name of the "Carib," whose name for themselves was *Kalipuna,* if a woman was speaking (in Arawakan languages), or *Kalinago,* if a man was speaking (in the Carib form). *Garifuna* may be the commonly used form since it is closer to the female (Arawak) title and women have been the primary carriers of culture. This name has only been standardized since the 1970s. The recent development of Garifunas' self-consciousness as an ethnic group, which accelerated during the 1980s, is noted in Nancie L. Gonzalez, *Sojourners of the Caribbean: Ethnogenesis and Ethnohistory of the Garifuna* (Urbana: University of Illinois Press, 1988), xiii, 70; and Virginia Kerns, *Women and the Ancestors: Black Carib Kinship and Ritual,* 2d ed. (Urbana: University of Illinois Press, 1997), 202.

17. Thomas Young, *Narrative of a Residence on the Mosquito Shore* (London: Smith, Elder, and Co., 1847), cited in Kerns, *Women and the Ancestors,* 13.

18. Gonzalez, *Sojourners of the Caribbean;* Kerns, *Women and the Ancestors.*

19. Mary Helms refers to this process for the Garifuna as the creation of a "colonial tribe"; see Helms, "The Cultural Ecology of a Colonial Tribe," *Ethnology* 8 (1969): 76–84.

20. Douglas Taylor, *The Black Carib of British Honduras* (New York: Wenner Gren, 1951), cited in Kerns, *Women and the Ancestors,* 15.

21. Gonzalez, *Sojourners of the Caribbean,* 5. This occurred also, presumably, as a form

of revitalization movement. See Margaret Sanford, "Revitalization Movements as Indicators of Completed Acculturation," *Comparative Studies in Society and History* 16 (1974): 504–18.

22. Kerns, *Women and the Ancestors,* 12.

23. Armando Cristano Meléndez, *El enojo de las sonajas: Palabras del ancestor,* 2d ed. (Tegucigalpa, Honduras: Editorial Cultura, 2002).

24. Sarah England, "Negotiating Race and Place in the Garifuna Diaspora: Identity Formation and Transnational Grassroots Politics in New York City and Honduras," *Identities* 6/1 (1999): 5–53; Gordon and Anderson 1999, "The African Diaspora."

25. The phenomenon is noted especially by John Lloyd Stephens, *Incidents of Travel in Central America, Chiapas, and Yucatan,* vol. 1 (New York: Harper and Brothers, 1841), quoted in Kerns, *Women and the Ancestors,* 34. Gonzalez notes that ninety percent of contemporary Garífuna consider themselves "Catholic" and that this is not in any way regarded as contradictory with ancestor rituals; see Gonzalez, *Sojourners of the Caribbean,* 97. I have observed the same phenomenon in the Honduran villages where I have worked, with the key proviso that the number of converts to the new wave of evangelical Protestantism (*evangélicos*) is much higher today. *Evangélicos* aggressively resist and denounce practices invoking ancestral spirits as primitive and diabolical.

26. While it is possible to consider contemporary African consciousness-raising among the Garífuna as a reactivation of suppressed collective memories, it is also important to recognize the creative agency of such recoveries. For example, the most common source of African identity referred to is Yoruba, although the mid-seventeenth-century dates of the initial shipwrecks that delivered Africans to St. Vincent would suggest Central African rather than exclusively West African origins.

27. Garífuna migration to the United States can be schematized into three stages. The first large influx occurred during the 1940s, as Garífuna men flocked to the United States to fill jobs vacated by soldiers and employment by Central American fruit companies declined. A second wave began with the reform of immigration law under the 1965 Hart-Celler Act, which expanded and diversified the immigrant stream. A third stage was triggered by the economic boom of the service economy during the late 1980s and 1990s. By this time, many Garífuna families had migration paths in place: relatives in the United States, a roof overhead, and potential job-referral networks for new arrivals. What is more, a mythology had grown up around the idea of migration to the United States, so that the traditional male model of adventuring to find a livelihood at sea was replaced by a migratory leap made by entire families. See Gonzalez, *Sojourners of the Caribbean;* and Linda Miller-Matthei and David A. Smith, "Women, Households, and Transnational Migration Networks: The Garífuna and Global Economic Restructuring," in *Latin America in the World-Economy,* ed. Roberto Patricio Korzeniewicz and William C. Smith (Westport, CT: Greenwood Press, 1996), 133–50.

28. Miller-Matthieu and Smith, "Women, Households, and Transnational Migration Networks"; England, "Negotiating Race and Place"; Gordon and Anderson, "The African Diaspora"; Paul Christopher Johnson, "Migrating Bodies, Circulating Signs: Brazilian Candomblé, the Garífuna of the Caribbean, and the Category of 'Indigenous Religions,'" *History of Religions* 41 (2002): 301–28.

29. England ("Negotiating Race and Place," 8) notes that "autochthonous" and "African" origins vary, depending on the issues in play and the location of their invocation. In Central America, "autochthonous" origins are strategic because they emphasize land rights; in the diaspora, "African" origins are forwarded because they generate networks of political claims. The third possible site of origin, St. Vincent, mediates these two claims.

30. Walter Benjamin, *Illuminations* (New York: Schocken, 1968); Richard Handler and Jocelyn Linnekin, "Tradition, Genuine and Spurious," *Journal of American Folklore* 97 (1984): 273–90; Eric J. Hobsbawm, "Introduction: Inventing Traditions," in *The Invention of Traditions,* ed. Eric J. Hobsbawm and Terence Ranger (Cambridge: Cambridge University Press, 1983), 1–14; Stuart Hall, "Gramsci's Relevance for the Study of Race and Ethnicity," "New Ethnicities," and "What is This 'Black' in Black Popular Culture?" in *Critical Dialogues in Cultural Studies,* ed. David Morley and Kuan-Hsing Chen (London: Routledge, 1996), 411–42, 441–50, 465–76.

31. Gilroy, *The Black Atlantic,* 193, 221; Palmié, *Wizards and Scientists;* Johnson, *Secrets, Gossip, and Gods.*

32. The Palo god named Lucero is also called Tata Elegua, or Exu Pavena, for example. Palo Zarabanda is sometimes described as "like Ogun" and Palo Centella as Oya.

33. Thomas Young, *Narrative of a Residence on the Mosquito Shore* (London: Smith, Elder, and Co., 1847).

34. For Cubans, this dates to the massive exodus following the 1959 revolution.

35. Mintz and Price, *The Birth of African-American Culture,* 10, 45, 51; see also Roger Bastide, *The African Religions of Brazil: Toward a Sociology of the Interpenetration of Civilizations,* trans. Helen Sebba (Baltimore: Johns Hopkins University Press, 1978).

36. Following Michel Foucault (*The History of Sexuality,* vol. 1, trans. Robert Hurley [New York: Vintage, 1980]), I think this drive to discourse always accompanies entrance into the public sphere; see Johnson, *Secrets, Gossip, and Gods.* The transfer from unvoiced ritual meaning to explicit discursive meaning occurs as part and parcel of the Garífuna becoming a known "player" in the politics of identity characteristic of U.S. society. Practically speaking, this development occurs in interviews, artistic displays in museums, folkloric presentations in restaurants, festivals, and other venues, and the competition for limited semiotic and physical space and the funding required to maintain them. See Rubén G. Rumbaut and Alejandro Portes, "Ethnogenesis: Coming of Age in Immigrant America," in *Ethnicities: Children of Immigrants in America,* ed. Rubén G. Rumbaut and Alejandro Portes (Berkeley: University of California Press, 2001), 1–21.

37. Johnson, "Migrating Bodies, Circulating Signs."

38. Melville Herskovits and Frances Herskovits, *Trinidad Village* (New York: Alfred A. Knopf, 1947); Ruth Landes, *The City of Women* (New York: Macmillan, 1947). For a critical view, see Patricia Birman, *Fazer estilo criando gêneros: Possessão e diferenças de gênero em terreiros de umbanda e candomblé no Rio de Janeiro* (Rio de Janeiro: Editora Universidade do Estado do Rio de Janeiro, 1995).

39. Ruy Coelho, "The Black Carib of Honduras: A Study in Acculturation" (Ph.D. diss., Northwestern University, 1955), cited in Kerns, *Women and the Ancestors,* 142.

40. Taylor, *The Black Carib of British Honduras,* cited in Kerns, *Women and the Ancestors,* 187.

41. Byron Foster, "Body, Soul and Social Structure and the Garifuna *Dugu*," *Belizean Studies* 9, no. 4 (1981): 1–11; Gonzalez, *Sojourners of the Caribbean;* Cynthia Bianchi, "Gubida Illness and Religious Ritual among the Garifuna of Santa Fe, Honduras: An Ethnopsychiatric Analysis" (Ph.D. diss., Ohio State University, 1988); Kerns, *Women and the Ancestors.*

42. Young, *Narrative of a Residence on the Mosquito Coast* (1847), cited in Kerns, *Women and the Ancestors,* 186.

43. Carol L. Jenkins, "Ritual and Resource-Flow: The Garifuna *Dugu*," *American Ethnologist* 10 (1983): 432; Gonzalez, *Sojourners of the Caribbean,* 113; Kerns, *Women and the Ancestors,* 51.

44. Kerns, *Women and the Ancestors,* 51.

45. Gonzalez, *Sojourners of the Caribbean,* 183. On the new freedoms created through migration for women among West Indians, which also apply to the Garifuna, see Waters, *Black Identities,* 92–8,

46. To be more specific, it is not simply Yoruba hegemony that is reproduced but rather the familiar Yoruba/Kongo opposition. The Yoruba pantheon is rendered emblematic of "authentic Africa," and the Kongo repertoire becomes emblematic of adaptation to human commodification in the Americas. The two symbol sets mutually construct each other's signifying domains. See Palmié, *Wizards and Scientists,* 159–201.

47. England, "Negotiating Race and Place."

48. Hall, "What is This 'Black' in Black Popular Culture?"; Gilroy, *The Black Atlantic.*

49. Kwame Anthony Appiah, "Race," in *Critical Terms for Literary Study,* 2d ed., ed. Frank Lentricchia and Thomas McLaughlin (Chicago: University of Chicago Press, 1990), 274–88; Gilroy, *The Black Atlantic.*

50. Sidney Mintz, "Slave Life on Caribbean Sugar Plantations: Some Unanswered Questions," in *Slave Cultures and the Cultures of Slavery,* ed. Stephan Palmié (Knoxville: University of Tennessee Press, 1995), 19–20.

51. Albert J. Raboteau, *Slave Religion: The "Invisible Institution" in the Antebellum South* (New York: Oxford University Press, 1978); Palmié, "Introduction," in *Slave Cultures and the Cultures of Slavery,* xxv.

52. Reginaldo Prandi, *Os Candomblés de São Paulo* (São Paulo: Hucitec/EDUSP, 1991); Vagner Gonçalves da Silva, *Orixás da Metrópole* (Petrópolis: Editora Vozes, 1995); Antônio Flávio Pierruci and Reginaldo Prandi, "Religious Diversity in Brazil: Numbers and Perspectives in a Sociological Evaluation," *International Sociology* 15 (2000): 629–41; Beatriz Góias Dantas, *Vovó Nagô e Papai Branco: Uso e abuso da África no Brasil* (Rio de Janeiro: Graal, 1988); Johnson, *Secrets, Gossip, and Gods.* For Cuba, see Palmié, *Wizards and Scientists,* 197–98; David H. Brown, *Santería Enthroned: Art, Ritual, and Innovation in an Afro-Cuban Religion* (Chicago: University of Chicago Press, 2003), 96.

Chapter 4. *Women of the African Diaspora Within*

1. In the Hebrew Bible, the "chosen people" are redeemed from slavery in Egypt and yearn to return from exile to the Promised Land. Christian theologians in the West define redemption as personal salvation through the death and resurrection of Jesus. According to the Masowe Apostles, all people suffer and die, and all may be restored to well-being

through healing while on earth, in the hope of ultimately becoming united with God. In their view, Christ was exemplary in his suffering and was blessed with resurrection beyond the grave.

2. For example, the introduction to *The African Diaspora* by Okpewho, Davies, and Mazrui makes general remarks about Africans who were transported to the Americas since the advent of slavery and describes the economic, social, political, and cultural processes that characterize the African diasporic condition. Despite the rapid rise of spiritualities by which slaves resisted their oppression and constructed concepts of Africa as the lost homeland to the east, there is hardly any discussion of the religious dimension of the diaspora. See Isidore Okpewho, Carole Boyce Davies, and Ali A. Mazrui, eds., *The African Diaspora: African Origins and New World Identities* (Bloomington: Indiana University Press, 1999), xi–xxviii.

3. Bengt Sundkler observed that the conquest of Africa, which the Portuguese began in the fourteenth century, was also seen as opening doors for European missionaries to spread the gospel, a purpose that extended through the heyday of European colonialism, evangelical Christian revivals, and the end of the slave trade in the nineteenth century. See B. Sundkler and C. Steed, *The History of the Church in Africa* (Cambridge: Cambridge University Press, 2000), 42–123.

4. Gerrie ter Haar, *Religious Communities in the Diaspora* (Nairobi: Acton Press, 2001).

5. D. Beach, *The Shona and Their Neighbors* (Oxford: Oxford University Press, 1994), 1–30.

6. Ibid.

7. I. Phiri, *Proclaiming Political Pluralism: The Transformation of an Age* (Westport, CT: Praeger, 2001).

8. Ibid.

9. R. Shaw, *Memories of the Slave Trade: Ritual and the Historical Imagination in Sierra Leone* (Chicago: University of Chicago Press, 2002).

10. T. O. Ranger, "Taking on the Missionary's Task: African Spirituality and the Mission Churches of Manicaland in the 1930s," *Journal of Religion in Africa* (Leiden, Brill), 28, no. 4 (1999): 1–31; C. Dillon-Malone, *The Korsten Basketmakers: A Study of the Masowe Apostles, An Indigenous African Religious Movement* (Manchester: University of Manchester Press, 1978); B. Jules-Rosette, "Women as Ceremonial Leaders in an African Church: The Apostles of Johane Maranke," in *The New Religions of Africa*, ed. B. Jules-Rosette (Norwood, NJ: Ablex Publishing, 1979), 127–44; B. Jules-Rosette, *African Apostles: Ritual and Conversion in the Church of John Maranke* (Ithaca: Cornell University Press, 1975); R. Werbner, "The Argument of Images: From Zion to the Wilderness in African Churches," in *Theoretical Explorations in African Religion*, ed. Wim van Binsbergen and Matthew Schoffeleers (London: Routledge and Kegan Paul, 1985), 253–86.

11. In the 1970s, Dillon-Malone estimated that there were 1.5 million Masowe Apostles dispersed in southern, central, and east Africa; see Dillon-Malone, *The Korsten Basketmakers*, inside front cover. Three million is my own conservative estimate thirty years later. The Apostles remain very popular, and their numbers continue to grow. They are difficult to count because of their migrations and the rise of offshoot groups who prefer to remain anonymous. The proportion of women at the Apostles' gatherings is substantial enough to lead me to con-

clude that women contribute to the Masowe thought pattern in a significant way. See I. Mukonyora, "Marginality and Protest: The Role of Women in Shaping the Masowe Thought Pattern," *Southern African Feminist Review* 4, no. 2, and 5, no. 1 (2001–2001): 1–21.

12. Werbner, "The Argument of Images," 253–86.

13. According to Clive Kileff and Margaret Kileff, Johane Masowe was born in 1915; see C. Kileff and M. Kileff, "The Masowe Vapostori of Seki: Utopianism and Tradition in an African Church," in *New Religions in Africa*, ed. Jules-Rosette, 151–67. Nengomasha, one of Johane Masowe's immediate followers, stated that he was born in 1914; see Dawson Munjeri's interview with Amon Nengomasha and Jeremiah Dvuke, National Archives of Zimbabwe, File AOH/4. Dillon-Malone concluded that his date of birth is unknown because records included only those who were educated enough to submit details of vital events to colonial authorities, see Dillon-Malone, *Korsten Basketmakers*, 15.

14. Ranger, "Taking on the Missionary's Task."

15. In Shona culture, women would often adopt new names for themselves or their children to communicate their anxieties or joys and, occasionally, to ensure that the community was aware of injustices. *Tapera* and *Muchazviona* are typical pessimistic names; *Rudo* and *Tatenda* are typical names by which outsiders are assured that the family is happy. When Europeans came, English words such as Sixpence gained currency as names by which Africans related their understanding of the new world of white masters and black servants. See Peter Godwin, *Mukiwa: A White Boy in Africa* (London: MacMillan, 1996), 23.

16. Ranger, "Taking on the Missionary's Task," cited by Dillon-Malone, *Korsten Basketmakers*, 6.

17. According to Angela Cheater, "Individual members of the Pioneer column claimed large tracts of potential farming land, while the British South Africa Company laid general claim to both mineral and land rights in Mashonaland and Matebeleland in terms of the Rudd and Lippert Concessions." See A. P. Cheater, *Idioms of Accumulation* (Harare: Mambo Press, 1984), 1–6.

18. A. S. Cripps, *An Africa for Africans: A Plea on Behalf of Territorial Segregation Areas and of Their Freedom in a South African Colony* (London: Longmans, Green and Co., 1927).

19. Cheater, *Idioms of Accumulation*, 1. Cf. N. Bhebhe, "The Ndebele and Mwari before 1893: A Religious Conquest of the Conquerors by the Vanquished," in *Guardians of the Land*, ed. J. M. Schoffeleers (Gweru: Mambo Press, 1979), 278–95.

20. Ranger, "Taking on the Missionary's Task," 1–31.

21. Dillon-Malone, *Korsten Basketmakers*, 15.

22. Werbner described the sacred wilderness, or *masowe*, as places that are "indefinite" and "temporary" because Johane Masowe characteristically wandered from place to place, and his followers followed his rules. See Werbner, "The Argument of Images," 254.

23. Dillon-Malone, *Korsten Basketmakers*, 12.

24. See Munjeri's interview with Nengomasha, February 17 and March 3, 1977, National Archives of Zimbabwe, File AOH/4.

25. Although there is nothing to stop this development overseas, the tendency of Zimbabweans to call all those who dress in white robes and pray outdoors "Masowe Apostles" can be misleading.

26. R. Werbner, "The Argument of Images: From Zion to the Wilderness in African

Churches," *Theoretical Explorations in African Religion,* ed. Wim Van Binsbergen and M. Schoffelers (London: Routledge, 1985), 253–86.

27. N. Bhebhe, *The ZAPU and ZANU Guerilla Warfare and The Evangelical Lutheran Church in Zimbabwe* (Gweru: Mambo Press, 1999), 131.

28. Werbner, "The Argument of Images," 269–71. Some of the Maranke Apostles resist the word *masowe,* lest they be mistaken for Johane Masowe's followers.

29. Jules-Rosette, *African Apostles.*

30. Dillon-Malone, *Korsten Basketmakers,* 132; Sundkler and Steed, *The History of the Church in Africa,* 47; C. Oosthuizen, *Post-Christianity in Africa: A Theological Anthropological Study* (London: C. Hurst and Co., 1968), 132, 164. See also I. Mukonyora, "The Fulfillment of African Religious Needs Through the Bible," in *Rewriting the Bible: The Real Issues,* ed. I. Mukonyora et al. (Gueru: Mambo Press, 1992), 249–62.

31. I. Mukonyora, "The Dramatization of Life and Death by Johane Masowe," *University of Zimbabwe Humanities Journal* (Zambezia) 25, no. 2 (1988): 192–207, and republished as "Johane Masowe's Life and Death Dramatizations," *Swedish Missiological Themes* 88, no. 3 (2000): 409–30.

32. E. Schmidt, *Peasants, Traders, and Wives: Shona Women in the History of Zimbabwe 1870–1939* (London: James Currey, 1992), 14–70.

33. Schmidt, *Peasants, Traders, and Wives,* 11.

34. Mukonyora, "Marginality and Protest," 1–21.

35. D. Lan, *Guns and Rain: Guerrillas and Spirit Mediums in Zimbabwe* (London: James Currey, 1988), 31; M. Bourdillon, *The Shona Peoples: Ethnography of the Contemporary Shona with Special Reference to Their Religion* (Gweru: Mambo Press, 1987). Cf. M. L. Daneel, *God of the Matopo Hills: An Essay on Mwari* (The Hague: Mouton, 1970).

36. Bourdillon, *The Shona Peoples,* 21–22.

37. I. Mukonyora, "Women and Ecology in Shona Religion," *Word and World Journal* 19 (1999): 276–84.

38. Daneel, *God of the Matopo Hills,* 22.

39. Daneel, *God of the Matopo Hills,* 24. This photograph of a shrine shows a small cave that serves as an enclosure for a pool surrounded by shrubs.

40. Dillon-Malone, *Korsten Basketmakers,* 63.

41. Mukonyora, "Women and Ecology in Shona Religion," 176–84.

42. Dillon-Malone, *Korsten Basketmakers,* 63.

43. Ibid.

44. Dillon-Malone, *Korsten Basketmakers,* 1–47. Rozvi kings and family trees of chiefs instill a strong sense that *Mwari* is, as Gelfand describes, a deity arising for the expansionism of kingdoms. As these rulers, such as the Rozvi dynasty, extended their power over vast territories, a language of praise and veneration was used for their ancestors, putting them so high that they became "the high God (*Mwari*) who reaches such exaltation to fill people with awe." I have not heard anthropomorphism described so aptly in literature on *Mwari.* M. Gelfand, "The Religion of the Mashona," *Journal for the Native Affairs Department* (NADA) 5, no. 33 (1956): 27–31.

45. Interview with the evangelist Philemon at a Masowe Apostles healing ceremony in Rusape, Zimbabwe, July 24, 1999.

46. Zimbabweans are so accustomed to buying huge sacks of fertilizers each growing season that it has become common to pour fertilizers on all soils, even the good soil, before planting crops. Colonial settlers profited from pushing people to grow crops on poor soil by creating big factories and outlets for selling fertilizer, in addition to making profits from the huge commercial farms on which Africans worked as cheap labor. The violence in Zimbabwe is often blamed on President Mugabe's selfish desire to stay in power for as long as he can. Mugabe himself speaks about colonial history to arouse a feeling of justifiable anger among the poor masses, who are now being encouraged to take back the lands of their ancestors. Violence is common because the method of redistributing the land has become politically divisive and comes with no guarantees that families return to the homelands of their forefathers. Mugabe's supporters come first, and the migrant workers from Mozambique and Malawi have to run for their lives because they are not considered Shona.

47. Interview with evangelist Philemon in Dowa near Rusape in Zimbabwe, September 2000.

48. According to Daneel, *Mwari* as a male deity with a female dimension was part of the composite picture of Shona religion. See Daneel, *God of the Matopo Hills,* 16.

49. In patriarchal societies, it is common to find such contradictions, and even a deliberate avoidance of aspects of popular religious belief and practice that appear to promote women. When I asked my students at the University of Zimbabwe about the popular feminine names for *Mwari* that Daneel mentions, they responded with skepticism. "He must be distorting our past," said one student. "*Mwari* is of our forefathers as taught in the Bible, the Father of Creation." However, I managed to show them what I meant, and they agreed with me that perhaps it was true that *Mwari* has a female dimension after all. Every year, when Shona traditionalists go the shrines of *Mwari* to pray for rain, they use the most appropriate praise names of *Mwari* in their prayers, our Great Mother (*Mbuya*) and *Dzivaguru*. It is also common knowledge that women speak in the shrines of the high god so authoritatively that Daneel, who observed proceedings at Matonjeni during the 1960s, concluded that "she who speaks from these shrines" mediates so powerfully that "she represents God." See Daneel, *God of the Matopo Hills,* 44. Missionaries used the word *Mwari* to translate the word *god* into Shona in the many places where the Bible portrays God as male. Hence there was confusion among my Zimbabwean students from missionary schools where no lessons were provided to encourage the persistence of traditional Shona beliefs and practices.

50. M. L. Daneel, *Zionism and Faith Healing in Rhodesia: Aspects of African Independent Churches* (The Hague: Mouton, 1970), shows that healing ceremonies are very common. I focus here on movements in and out of places where healing ceremonies are held, rather than on what goes on there.

51. This summary is based on my extensive research into healing ceremonies. Being of a quiet temperament, I met many who, like me, remained calm throughout these ceremonies. Masowe Apostles recognize that, when handling the ailments that arise from frustrations with life, healing means different things to different people. When I was not watching participants' varied responses to prayers for healing, I meditated quietly and sometimes managed to think about my findings. I never had to quiver to show my empathy as a participant observer.

52. Daneel, *Zionism and Faith Healing in Rhodesia*.

53. Matthew Engelke, "Live and Direct: History, Ritual, and Biblical Authority in an African Christian Church" (Ph.D. diss., University of Virginia, 2002).

54. I was shocked by the many misogynistic remarks Nzira made publicly to hundreds of women to assert his authority. Women at this gathering shrugged their shoulders, arguing that, if the Holy Spirit judged Nzira's claims to authority, he would soon wake up and find his gift of healing gone—and the hundreds of women attending his meetings gone, too. Field work notes from July to September 2000. Nzira is now in jail on six charges of rape; see the *Herald* (Zimbabwe), March 27, 2003.

55. M. Gelfand, *The African Witch* (Edinburgh: Edinburgh University Press, 1967), 27.

56. Gordon Chavhunduka argues that, in debates about the merits of Western medicine in modern Shona society, Europeans condemned "traditional" healers as "witchdoctors," confusing the antisocial or immoral behavior of witches with the work of healers. Indigenous healers treated physical ailments by providing herbal medicines and included the social and psychological problems of individuals within their families and communities in the diagnosis of illness. G. Chavhunduka, *Traditional Healers and the Shona Patient* (Gweru: Mambo Press, 1978).

57. Interview with Ezra Chitando, University of Zimbabwe, 2000.

58. For stories that still circulated in popular culture, see Chavhunduka, *Traditional Healers and the Shona Patient*.

59. M. Gelfand, "The Shona Mother and Child," *Journal for the Native Affairs Department* 191 (1969) 76–80.

60. Interview with evangelist Philemon, Harare, 1997. Philemon grew up in a family whose members joined different faiths, including the Catholic, Methodist, and Masowe Apostle churches. He enjoyed theological debate, so he was quite happy to find out that the beliefs and practices he took for granted raised questions about gender.

61. H. Aschwanden, *Karanga Mythology: An Analysis of the Consciousness of the Karanga in Zimbabwe* (Harare: Mambo Press, 1989), 13.

62. Diana Jeater, *Marriage, Perversion, and Power: The Construction of Moral Discourse in Southern Rhodesia, 1894–1930* (Oxford: Clarendon, 1992), 21–22; Theresa Barnes and T. E. Win, *To Live a Better Life: An Oral History of Women in the City of Harare, 1930–1970* (Harare: Baobab, 1992).

63. Jeater, *Marriage, Perversion, and Power*.

64. M. Hinfelaar, *Respectable and Responsible Women: Methodist and Roman Catholic Women's Organizations in Harare, Zimbabwe (1919–1985)* (Zoetermeter, Netherlands: Boekencentrum, 2001). When my friend Marja traveled to do her research on women members of the first established African township in Harare, called *Mbare*, her main challenge was the crowded houses and the big terminus where busses converged from every corner of the country, marketers shouted to lure her to buy their goods, and pickpockets lurked, until she arrived in the environs of the Roman Catholic Church. I studied the map of Harare looking for marshes, forests behind factory buildings, and other waste places. We came across each other asking the clerks at the National Archives for the same material on colonial history and missionary Christianity.

65. Dillon-Malone, *Korsten Basketmakers*, 49. Johane Masowe was called "the messen-

ger of God to Africa," or *nhume yevatema*, literally, messenger to black peoples. The male leaders of the Masowe Apostles stress that they are black and are speaking only to black people; the salvation of white people is their own business in whatever lands God speaks to them. Matthew Engelke, despite being made welcome as a researcher, often heard racially exclusive points of view expressed by the group's leaders; see Engelke, "Live and Direct."

Chapter 5. "Power in the Blood"

Epigraph: Cheryl Johnson-Odim and Margaret Strobel, "Series Editor's Introduction: Conceptualizing the History of Women in Africa," in *Women in Sub-Saharan Africa,* ed. Iris Berger and E. Frances White (Bloomington: Indiana University Press, 1999, xxvii.

1. Rosemary N. Edet, "Christianity and African Rituals," in *The Will to Arise,* ed. Mercy Oduyoye and M. R. A. Kanyoro (Maryknoll, NY: Orbis, 1995), 27–29, 31, 39; Mary Douglas, *Purity and Danger: An Analysis of the Concepts of Pollution and Taboo* (London: Routledge and Kegan Paul, 1966), 1–5, 113; Thomas C. T. Buckley and Alma Gottlieb, "A Critical Appraisal of Theories of Menstrual Symbolism," in *Blood Magic: The Anthropology of Menstruation,* ed. Thomas C. T. Buckley and Alma Gottlieb (Berkeley: University of California Press, 1988), 23–50.

2. Deidre H. Crumbley, *Spirit, Structure and Flesh: Institution-Building and Gender Practices In Three African Instituted Churches* (forthcoming, University of Wisconsin Press); "On Being First: Dogma, Disease, and Domination in the Rise of an African Church," *Religion* 30 (2000): 169–84; "Impurity and Power: Women in Aladura Churches," *Africa* 62, no. 4 (1992): 505–22; "Indigenous Institution-Building in an Afro-Christian Movement: The Aladura as a Case Study" (Ph.D. diss., Northwestern University, 1989); "Even a Woman: Sex Roles and Mobility in an Aladura Hierarchy," *West African Journal of Archaeology and Anthropology* 16 (1985): 133–50.

3. Isabel Mukonyora, "The Complementarity of Male and Female Imagery in Theological Language: A Study of the Valentinian Masowe Theological Systems" (Ph.D. diss., Oxford University, 1997).

4. In her study of India's *hijra,* a third gender of persons born as anatomical males who assume the dress and manners of women, Nanda notes that the major distinction between them and "real women" is the absence of menstruation and the associated inability to give birth. Serena Nanda, *Neither Man nor Woman: The Hijras of India* (Belmont, CA: Wadsworth, 1990), 18–19.

5. *Church of the Lord Constitution Year 2000: Revised Constitution of the Church of the Lord Aladura World Wide* (Shagamu, Nigeria: Grace Enterprises, 2001), 62. (This cite is referred to hereafter as *CLA Constitution.*)

6. For an explanation of this conceptual framework, see Richard Newbold Adams, *Energy and Structure: A Theory of Social Power* (Austin: University of Texas Press, 1975), 36–52.

7. Oyeronke Olajubu, *Women in the Yoruba Religious Sphere* (Albany: State University of New York Press, 2003), 55.

8. Rosalind I. J. Hackett, "Sacred Paradoxes: Women and Religious Plurality in Nigeria," in *Women, Religion and Social Change*, ed. Y. Y. Haddad and E. B. Findley (Albany: State University of New York Press, 1985), 260–69.

9. Bennetta Jules-Rosette has written extensively on the roles of women in African Instituted Churches, investigating the influence of traditional gender practices on these new religious expressions; see "Privileges Without Power: Women in African Cults and Churches," in *Women in Africa and the African Diaspora*, ed. Roslyn Terborg-Penn et al. (Washington, DC: Howard University Press, 1987), 99, 104, 115. Also see Bennetta Jules-Rosette, "Women in Indigenous African Cults and Churches," in *The Black Woman Cross-Culturally*, ed. F. C. Steady (Cambridge, MA: Schenkman, 1981), 185–207; "The Arcadian Wish: Toward a Theory of Contemporary African Religion," in *The New Religions of Africa*, ed. Bennetta Jules-Rosette (Norwood, NJ: Ablex, 1979), 219–29; and "Women as Ceremonial Leaders in an African Church: The Apostles of John Maranke," in *New Religions of Africa*, 127–44.

10. Douglas, *Purity and Danger*, 35; Buckley and Gottlieb, "A Critical Appraisal of Theories of Menstrual Symbolism," 4–5.

11. Douglas, *Purity and Danger*, 3–4, 35, 113. Ian Hogbin, *The Island of the Menstruating Men: Religion in Wogeo, New Guinea* (Prospect Heights, IL: Waveland, 1970), 85–91, 120–21.

12. Buckley and Gottlieb, "A Critical Appraisal of Theories of Menstrual Symbolism," 4–33; Alma Gottlieb, "Menstrual Cosmology among the Beng of Ivory Coast," also in *Blood Magic*, 55–70, 74.

13. Emile Durkheim, *The Elementary Forms of the Religious Life* (New York: Free Press, 1965), 338.

14. Douglas, *Purity and Danger*, 3, 94, 104, 114–15.

15. Dr. Olabiyi Yai, interviewed by the author in Gainesville, Florida, April 24, 1989.

16. Dr. Abraham Akrong of the University of Ghana, Legon, interviewed by the author in Hirschluch, Germany, September 13, 2003.

17. Ibid.

18. For a feminist study from within the Jewish tradition, see Rachel Adler, "In Your Blood, Live: Revisions of a Theology of Purity," *Tikkun* 8, no. 1 (1993): 38–41.

19. Philip Jenkins, *The Next Christendom: The Coming of Global Christianity* (Oxford: Oxford University Press, 2002).

20. Allan Anderson, *African Reformation: African Initiated Christianity in the 20th Century* (Trenton, NJ: African World Press, 2001), 10; Rufus O. Ositelu, *African Instituted Churches* (New Brunswick, NJ: Transaction Publishers, 2002), 74–75. The CLA website includes "Missio Africana! The role of an African Instituted Church in the Mission's Debate: Remissionization—Mission Reversed," in which the current primate, Dr. Rev. Rufus Ositelu, encourages African missionaries in the diaspora to propagate the gospel, and not their own "particular culture," around the world, thereby avoiding the errors of earlier European missionaries in Africa; see www.aladura.de/artikel.htm (accessed May 29, 2004).

21. Ositelu, *African Instituted Churches*, 201.

22. United States Department of Homeland Security, *Yearbook of Immigration Statistics, 2002* (Washington, DC: U.S. Government Printing Office, 2003), 12–14, 17–18.

23. D. O. Olayiwola, "Church and the Healing Ministry in Nigeria," *Asia Journal of Theology* 4, no. 2 (1990), 417–18; J. D. Y. Peel, *Aladura: A Religious Movement among the Yoruba* (London: Oxford University Press, 1968), 60–62, 73, 101–2, 292.

24. Peter Probst, "The Letter and the Spirit: Literacy and Religious Authority in the History of the Aladura Movement in Western Nigeria," *Africa* 59, no. 4 (1988), 486–87; H. Turner, *History of an African Independent Church: The Church of the Lord (Aladura)*, 2 vols. (London: Oxford University Press, 1967), 1:24, 41–45, 48; E. S. Sorinmade, *Lecture Delivered to Mark the 10th Anniversary of the Death of Dr. J. O. Ositelu* (Ake, Abeokuta, July 15, 1977), 76, 13–20; Ositelu, *African Instituted Churches*, 128–29. The founder, Josiah Olunowo Ositelu, remained primate until his death in 1966. He was succeeded by his follower, Dr. E. O. A. Adejobi. Primate Adejobi was succeeded first by the founder's older son, Gabriel Olusenun Ositelu, in 1991, and then by a younger son, Dr. Rufus O. O. Ositelu, in 1998, each assuming the primacy on the death of his predecessor. See Ositelu, *African Instituted Churches*, 171–73.

25. Ositelu, *African Instituted Churches*, 130.

26. Turner, *History of an African Independent Church*, 1:vii.

27. E. O. A. Adejobi, *The Authentic Traditions, Customs, and Early Practices of the Church of the Lord-Aladura* (Mushin, Lagos: Olufayo Industrial Enterprises, n.d.), 23.

28. Turner, *History of an African Independent Church*, 1:197–98.

29. For a discussion of the life and work of the second primate, see a CLA church document by Jacob A. Sofolahan, "A Short Sketch on Dr. E. O. Adeleke Adejobi" (n.p., n.d.).

30. According to Primate Adejobi, on September 14, 1930, eight men became CLA disciples. The next year eight more men became disciples. The first seven church wardens, appointed in the 1930s and 1940s, also were male. E. O. A. Adejobi, *The Early Diary of the Church of the Lord* (Munshin, Lagos: Olufalyo Industrial Enterprises, n.d.), 16–18. For information about the women, as well as the men, who were trained at the CLA seminary, see E. O. A. Adejobi, "Lest We Forget," in *Who is Who at the Aladura Theological Seminary and Prophet and Prophetess Training Institute* (Somolu, Lagos: Printer Mosobalaje and Brothers, n.d.).

31. On dual-sex and gender systems, see Nkiru Nzegwu, "Gender Equality in a Dual Sex System: The Case of Onitsha," *Canadian Journal of Law and Juris Prudence* 7, no. 1 (1994): 73–95; Cheryl Townsend Gilkes, "The Politics of Silence: Dual-Sex Political Systems and Women's Traditions of Conflict in African-American Religion," in *African-American Christianity*, ed. Paul E. Johnson (Berkeley: University of California Press, 1994), 80–109; Ifi Amadiume, *Re-Inventing Africa: Matriarchy, Religion, and Culture* (New York: Zed, 1977), Ifi Amadiume, *Male Daughters, Female Husbands: Gender and Sex in an African Society* (London: Zed Books, 1987). On gender relations in this region more generally, see N. Sudarkasa, "Female Employment and Family Organization in West Africa," in *The Black Woman Cross-Culturally*, 49–55; N. Sudarkasa, "The 'Status of Women' in Indigenous African Societies," in *Women in Africa and the African Diaspora*, 25–39; J. S. Eades, *The Yoruba Today* (Cambridge: Cambridge University Press, 1980), 37–38, 49–50; and J. D. Y. Peel, *Ijeshas and Nigerians: Incorporation of a Yoruba Kingdom, 1890s–1970* (Cambridge: Cambridge University Press, 1983), 51–52.

32. O. Oyewumi, *The Invention of Women* (Minneapolis: University of Minnesota Press, 1997), 84–91; Eades, *The Yoruba Today*, 99.

33. Judith Hoch-Smith, "Radical Yoruba Female Sexuality: The Witch and the Prostitute," in *Women in Ritual and Symbolic Roles*, ed. J. Hoch-Smith et al. (New York: Plenum, 1978), 245–67, 295.

34. K. Barber, *I Could Speak Until Tomorrow: Oriki, Women, and the Past in a Yoruba Town* (Washington, DC: Smithsonian Institution Press, 1991), 103, 288–89; Oyewumi, *The Invention of Women*, 136–42; M. Oduyoye, *Daughters of Anowa: African Women and Patriarchy* (Maryknoll, NY: Orbis, 1995), 173–80; J. D. Y. Peel, *Religious Encounter and the Making of the Yoruba* (Bloomington: Indiana University Press, 2000), 119; Turner, *History of an African Independent Church*, 2:42; D. Badejo, *Osun Seegesi: The Elegant Deity of Wealth, Power, and Femininity* (Trenton, NJ: Africa World Press, 1996), 175–77; M. T. Drewal, *Yoruba Ritual: Performers, Play, and Agency* (Bloomington: Indiana University Press, 1992), 172–77, 180–86, 190; Olajubu, *Women in the Yoruba Religious Sphere*, 21–42.

35. For a discussion of the contemporary implications of these constraints for development, see Philomena Okeke, "Reconfiguring Tradition: Women's Rights and Social Status in Contemporary Nigeria," *Africa Today* 47 (2000): 49–63.

36. Badejo, *Osun Seegesi*, 1, 77, 80; Andrew Apter, *Black Critics and Kings* (Chicago: University of Chicago Press, 1992), 111–14; J. L. Matory, *Sex and the Empire That Is No More: Gender and the Politics of the Metaphor in Oyo Yoruba Religion* (Minneapolis: University of Minnesota Press, 1994), 73–77; J. L. Matory, "Government by Seduction: History and Tropes of 'Mounting' in Oyo-Yoruba Religion," in *Modernity and Its Malcontents: Ritual and Power in Postcolonial Africa*, ed. Jean Comaroff and John Comaroff (Chicago: University of Chicago Press, 1993), 57–88.

37. Badejo, *Osun Seegesi*, 179.

38. Ann Neil, interviewed by author, Wake Forest, N.C., July 6, 2001. Mrs. Neil offered these observations from the perspective of a foreign white woman who taught and lived as part of the Southern Baptist mission in Nigeria and Ghana. Cognizant of the privileges of her race and class, Mrs. Neil reports a comparable resistance to female ordination in her church back in the United States where, as in Nigeria, Baptist women could "speak" but not "preach" the gospel. It was not until March 2000, almost fifty years after she began her life and work in Nigeria during the 1950s, that Mrs. Neil was ordained at the Millbrook Baptist Church in Raleigh, North Carolina, on the Sunday before she turned eighty years old. Mrs. Neil has been a visiting scholar in residence at Garrett Theological Seminary. In "The Role of Women in Traditional Religion in Yoruba Traditional Society," Neil documented and analyzed field observations on the interplay of missionary outreach, church building, and gender dynamics (unpublished paper, Garrett Evangelical Seminary, Evanston, IL, 1987).

39. Badejo, *Osun Seegesi*, 178; Eades, *The Yoruba Today*, 123–25, 167; Matory, *Sex and the Empire That Is No More*, 37, 110, 117–18; H. Drewal, D. Drewal, and M. Thompson, *Gelede Art and Female Power Among the Yoruba* (Bloomington: Indiana University Press, 1983), 234; Barber, *I Could Speak Until Tomorrow*, 234–36, 277, 325; A. Apter, "Atinga Revisited: Yoruba Witchcraft and the Cocoa Economy, 1950–1951," in *Modernity and Its Malcontents*, 111–28.

40. For the perspectives of African women on polygamy in contemporary Africa, see S. Arndt, "African Gender Trouble and African Womanism: An Interview with C. Ogunyemmi and W. Muthoni," *Signs* 25, no. 3 (2000): 709–26; M. R. A. Kanyoro, "Interpreting Old Testament Polygamy through African Eyes," in *The Will to Arise*, 87–100; and A. Nasimiyu-Waskie, "Polygamy: A Feminist Critique," also in *The Will to Arise*, 101–18.

41. Oyewumi, *The Invention of Women*, 130–34, 150–52; L. Denzer, "Domestic Science Training in Colonial Yorubaland, Nigeria," in *African Encounters With Domesticity*, ed. Karen T. Hansen (New Brunswick, NJ: Rutgers University Press, 1992), 116–17, 121; L. Denzer, "Yoruba Women: A Historiographical Study," *International Journal of African Historical Studies* 27, no. 1 (1994), 19–20, 25–28; A. Mama, *Women's Studies and Studies of Women in Africa during the 1990s* (Senegal: Codesria, 1996), 4, 28, 37, 61–66; Hackett, "Sacred Paradoxes," 260–63, 268; Oduyoye, *Daughters of Anowa*, 104, 172.

42. JoAnne Marie Terrell, *Worterbuch der Feministischen Theologie* (Redaktion Beate Wehn Gutershloher Verlagshaus, 1991), 90. Since I am neither a biblical scholar nor versed in Greek and Hebrew, I have drawn upon the scholarship of those with such expertise. During an extended telephone interview, Dr. Terrell explicated the meanings of ritual impurity in Hebrew scripture and New Testament texts, noting that the word *daveh*, translated as a "menstrous cloth" in Isaiah 30:22 (KJV), refers to a woman who is ill, menstruating, or has just given birth. I also benefited from discussions with Prof. Obgu Kalu, Dr. Jenny Everts-Powers, and audience participants in the parallel session of the Society of Pentecostal Studies (April 14, 2004, Marquette University, Marquette, Michigan), where I presented an earlier version of this essay. These scholars provided insights into early Christian gender practices, in particular the New Testament provision that widows must be sixty years of age before being "taken into the number" (1 Timothy 5:9, KJV). Especially helpful was the linguistic expertise of Dr. Raachel Jurovics, rabbi at Temple Beth Orr in Raleigh, North Carolina, for her insights into ancient Jewish menstrual practices and for referring me to the work of Rachel Adler, which informed the interpretive framework of this study.

43. James White, "Church Missionary Society (CMS) Journal Extracts for the Quarter Ending 25 March 1865," paraphrased by John D. Y. Peel, School of African and Oriental Studies, London, United Kingdom, personal communication via e-mail, June 1, 2004.

44. "The Blessed Virgin Mary took her Son to the temple to do what the law prescribed after childbirth . . . Occupying just three pages of the *Book of Common Prayer* we have the form of the 'Thanksgiving of Women after Childbirth' commonly called 'Churching.' The rubric speaks of the woman accompanied by her husband coming into church. The preamble then speaks of God in his great goodness giving safe deliverance and the future is committed to God's care . . . It was a regular feature of parish life when I began as a priest. Seldom, if ever, is this ministry asked for today" (newsletter, St. Michael's Parish, Great Torrington, UK, February 2, 2003, available at www.gtorrington.freeserve.co.uk/oldnews.htm [accessed May 29, 2004]). In the United States, Rector Marilyn Minns of Truro Episcopal Church in Fairfax, Virginia, addressed the presentation of the boy Jesus at the Temple in Jerusalem (Luke 2:2–40), in similar terms. "It was an ancient custom that had its origin in the Book of Leviticus (chap. 12) where we are told that a woman was considered ceremonially unclean after childbirth and so had to wait forty days before she could go to the temple or touch anything sacred . . . We may not be able to relate to some of the ceremo-

nial details but the idea of thanksgiving after childbirth is something to which we can all relate . . . There is even a service in the 1662 Prayer book called the 'Churching of Women.'" See Rev. Marilyn Minns, Rector, "The Presentation: A sermon given February 2, 2003, Luke 2: 22–40," available at www.trurochurch.org (accessed May 29, 2004).

45. Edet, "Christianity and African Rituals," 36, 38fn.

46. Olajubu, *Women in the Yoruba Religious Sphere*, 49, 54.

47. Neil, "The Role of Women," 11.

48. Peel, *Religious Encounter and the Making of the Yoruba*, 103, 114–15, 233–38, 244–47, 374; J. D. Y. Peel, "Gender in Yoruba Religious Change," *Journal of Religion in Africa* 32, no. 2 (2002): 11–13, 18, 22–25.

49. Ida B. Robinson, quoted in Felton O. Best, "Breaking the Gender Barrier: African-American Women and Leadership in Black Holiness-Pentecostal Churches, 1890–Present," in *Flames of Fire: Black Religious Leadership From the Slave Community to the Million-Man March*, ed. Felton O. Best (New York: Edwin Mellen, 1998), 158–61, 168. Ida B. Robinson founded Mount Sinai Holiness Church (MSHC) after she migrated to Philadelphia in 1917. She was active in the United Holiness Church of America (UHCA) until she broke from it over church leaders' resistance to the public ordination of women. A skilled administrator, she set up eighty-four MSHC branches, establishing missions in Guyana and Cuba. Despite a heavy load of administration and preaching, she did not cease mentoring other women, ordaining 125 women out of 140 church elders and putting female elders in charge of new converts. All subsequent Mount Sinai bishops have been women.

50. Teresia Hinga, "Jesus Christ and the Liberation of Women," in *The Will to Arise*, 183–94.

51. E. Schmidt, "Patriarchy, Capitalism, and the Colonial State in Zimbabwe," *Signs* 16, no. 4 (1991): 734, 741, 753–56.

52. Turner, *History of an African Independent Church*, 2:44. This remark alludes to Genesis 2:18.

53. Turner, *History of an African Independent Church*, 2:43–44. Although the taboos arising from this belief do not preclude female ordination, the popular notion that the smell of menstrual blood offends the angels is echoed in the rationale Primate Adejobi provided for CLA menstrual practices: "It does not indicate that this natural act of Nature . . . is sinful unto God. It does not mean that the transcendent and immanent God can be defiled. It does not mean that the spirit of the risen Christ and Lord at such period of time departs from every woman during her menstrual period . . . Unlike the God Almighty, the angels abhor to be present and to join the believer at such period (in order to avoid physical pollution). It is therefore to retain the fellowship of the Angels in God's worship, to avoid physical pollution that this practice is strictly observed (Leviticus 19:15)." See E. O. A. Adejobi, *The Observances and Practices of the Church of the Lord (Aladura) in the Light of Old Testament and New Testament* (Nigeria: Enterprise Du Chez, 1976), 13.

54. Turner, *History of an African Independent Church*, 1:48.

55. Adejobi, *The Early Diary of the Church of the Lord*, 16–18.

56. Turner, *History of an African Independent Church*, 2:45.

57. Adejobi, *The Authentic Traditions, Customs, and Early Practices of the Church of the Lord-Aladura*, 15.

58. Turner, *History of an African Independent Church*, 2:46, 48.

59. *CLA Constitution*, 10–18, 60–61. The parallel offices are:

Primate: The "constitutional and spiritual head of the church" . . . "he shall preside over the International Church Executive Council."

Provisional Head: Administrative link between the dioceses and the primate, undertaking duties "delegated to him by the Primate."

Apostle/Reverend Mother Superior: Appointed to function as provincial head or diocese overseer; oversees all ranks of ministers in lower offices and performs the sacraments.

Bishop/Reverend Mother: Administrative diocesan overseer within a province; performs sacraments.

Archdeacon/Archdeaconess: Zonal superintendent with sacramental duties.

Senior Prophet/Senior Prophetess—Senior Evangelist/Senior Pastor: Performs pastoral functions and assigned administrative duties.

Prophet/Pastor/Prophetess—Evangelist/Pastor/Lady Evangelist (Grades I): Performs sacraments; responsible for local parish clergy.

Prophet/Pastor/Prophetess—Evangelist/Pastor/Lady Evangelist (Grades II): Holds "iron staff of office," heads parish, evangelizes; performs sacraments.

Probationary Ministers: Performs pastor duties under a senior minister but not the four sacraments of baptism, communion, marriage, and funeral service.

Disciples: Seminarian ministers-in-training.

60. *CLA Constitution*, 60.

61. Ibid., 16.

62. Ibid., 18.

63. *CLA Constitution*, 18. At the CACDE conference in Germany, I raised this proviso that female ministers must be sixty years old and thus postmenopausal with the current CLA primate, Dr. Rufus Ositelu (who holds doctorates in computer sciences and religion). He pointed out that age also informs when a male aspirant is assigned to high office, bringing to mind Oyewumi's methodological caveat to consider the intersection of age and gender when assessing Yoruba gender practices; see Oyewumi, *The Invention of Women*, ix–xiii, 13–15, 29, 31, 46–49, 58–62. Yet Primate Ositelu agreed that physiological changes in body function do not inform clerical duties for men as they do for women. The primate also pointed out that the sixty-year minimum age is not a key factor; what matters most is that the woman is postmenopausal (interview by author, September 13, 2003). This sixty-year-old provision is in line with 1 Timothy 5:9 (KJV): "Let not a widow be taken into the number under threescore years old."

64. Adejobi, preface to *Observances and Practices of the Church of the Lord (Aladura)*.

65. Episcopal Church Women's Ministries, "A Chronology of Events Concerning Women in Holy Orders in the Episcopal Church, USA and The Worldwide Anglican Communion," www.episcopalchurch.org (accessed May 28, 2004); *The Virginia Report*, www .anglicancommunion.org/documents/virginia/english/origin.html (accessed May 29, 2004); Emily Hewitt and Suzanne Hiatt, "Appendix A: Chronology of Major Anglican Documents and Actions Concerning Women in Holy Orders, 1862–1872," in *Women Priests:*

Yes or No?, ed. Emily Hewitt and Suzanne Hiatt (New York: Seabury, 1973), 102–4, www.womenpriests.org (accessed May 29, 2004); Christopher T. Cantrell, "The Ordination of Women to the Priesthood and Episcopate: Where Are We?" The Episcopal Diocese of Fort Worth, www.fwepiscopal.org/resources/resources.html (accessed May 2, 2004); "Women Priests in the World Wide Anglican Communion," www/religioustolerance.org .femclrg3.htm (May 29, 2004).

66. Currently based in the Washington, D.C. area, Cline-Smythe has been living in the United States for the last ten years. As a leader in the Sierra Leonean branch of CLA, Senior Prophetess Cline-Smythe worked closely with Primate Adejobi and his two successors. Her deep Christian devotion and administrative acumen, coupled with her reputation as an articulate and moving preacher, made her a logical choice for such an important foreign post.

Chapter 6. *"The Spirit of the Holy Ghost is a Male Spirit"*

1. Richard Wright, *12 Million Black Voices* (1941; reprint, New York: Thunder's Mouth Press, 1988), 93.

2. Jacqueline Grant, "Black Women and the Church," in *All the Women Are White, All the Blacks Are Men, But Some of Us Are Brave*, ed. Gloria T. Hull, Patricia Bell Scott, and Barbara Smith (Old Westbury, NY: Feminist Press, 1982), 141; Anne Braude, "Female Experience in Religion," *Religion and American Culture* 5 (Winter 1995): 9.

3. C. Eric Lincoln and Lawrence Mamiya, *The Black Church in the African American Experience* (Durham, NC: Duke University Press, 1990), 289; Elaine J. Lawless, "Writing the Body in the Pulpit: Female-Sexed Texts," *Journal of American Folklore* 107 (Winter 1994): 56.

4. Kathleen Canning, "The Body as Method? Reflections on the Place of the Body in Gender History," *Gender and History* 11 (November 1999), 499.

5. Stephanie M. H. Camp, "The Pleasure of Resistance: Enslaved Women and Body Politics in the Plantation South, 1830–1861," *Journal of Southern History* 68 (August 2002): 535.

6. Anthony B. Pinn, "Black Theology, Black Bodies, and Pedagogy," *Cross-Currents* 50 (Spring-Summer 2000): 196–202; E. Patrick Johnson, "Feeling the Spirit in the Dark: Expanding Notions of the Sacred in African American Gay Communities," in *The Greatest Taboo: Homosexuality in Black Communities*, ed. Delroy Constantine Simms (New York: Alyson Books, 1999), 89.

7. "Mrs. Williams (Pastor of the Royal Prayer Band)," "All Nations Assembly" folder, Box 185, Federal Writers' Project Records, Illinois State Historical Library, Springfield.

8. Caroline Walker Bynum, *Jesus as Mother: Studies in the Spirituality of the High Middle Ages* (Berkeley: University of California Press, 1984); Evelyn Brooks Higginbotham, *Righteous Discontent: The Women's Movement in the Black Baptist Church, 1880–1920* (Cambridge, MA: Harvard University Press, 1993), 142. On "muscular Christianity," see note 34.

9. See Caroline Walker Bynum, " ' . . . And Woman His Humanity': Female Imagery in the Religious Writing of the Later Middle Ages," in *Gender and Religion: On the Complexity of Symbols*, ed. Caroline Walker Bynum, Stevan Harrell, and Paula Richman (Boston: Beacon, 1986), 273.

10. Paul E. Johnson, *A Shopkeeper's Millennium: Society and Revivals in Rochester, New York, 1815–1837* (New York: Hill and Wang, 1978), 7; Charles E. Sellers, *The Market Revolution: Jacksonian America, 1815–1846* (New York: Oxford University Press, 1991).

11. Nancy F. Cott, *The Bonds of Womanhood: "Woman's Sphere" in New England, 1780–1835* (New Haven, CT: Yale University Press, 1977); Ann Douglas, *The Feminization of American Culture* (New York: Knopf, 1977), 1–143; Barbara Welter, "The Feminization of American Religion: 1800–1860," in *Clio's Consciousness Raised: New Perspectives in the History of Women,* ed. Mary S. Hartman and Lois Banner (New York: Harper and Row, 1974), 137–57.

12. Higginbotham, *Righteous Discontent,* 190; "Experiences of the South. By a Southern White Woman," *Independent* 56 (March 17, 1904); Anne Stavney, " 'Mothers of Tomorrow': The New Negro Renaissance and the Politics of Maternal Representation," *African American Review* 32 (Winter 1998): 534–35.

13. Catherine Brekus, *Strangers and Pilgrims: Female Preaching in America, 1740–1845* (Chapel Hill: University of North Carolina Press, 1998), 272. Zilpha Elaw, "Memoirs of the Life, Religious Experiences, Ministerial Travels, and Labors of Mrs. Zilpha Elaw," in *Sisters of the Spirit: Three Black Women's Autobiographies of the Nineteenth Century,* ed. William L. Andrews (Bloomington: Indiana University Press, 1986).

14. James T. Campbell, *Songs of Zion: The African Methodist Episcopal Church in the United States and South Africa* (Chapel Hill: University of North Carolina Press, 1998), 45; Brekus, *Strangers and Pilgrims,* 179; Jarena Lee, *Religious Experiences and Journal of Mrs. Jarena Lee: A Preachin' Woman* (reprint; Nashville, TN: African Methodist Episcopal Church Sunday School Union/Legacy Publishers, 1991), 22, 8, 14; Brekus, *Strangers and Pilgrims,* 259; Jeane B. Williams, "Loose the Woman and Let Her Go! Pennsylvania's African American Women Preachers," *Pennsylvania Heritage* 21 (Winter 1996): 4–9.

15. Brekus, *Strangers and Pilgrims,* 280; Maria Stewart, *Productions of Mrs. Maria Stewart, Presented to the First African Baptist Church and Society of Boston,* reprinted in *Spiritual Narratives,* ed. Sue E. Houchins (New York: Oxford University Press, 1988), 7, 3; Maria Stewart, "Mrs. Stewart's Farewell Address to her Friends in the City of Boston," in *Maria W. Stewart: America's First Black Woman Political Writer: Essays and Speeches,* ed. Marilyn Richardson (Bloomington: Indiana University Press, 1987), 68.

16. Brekus, *Strangers and Pilgrims,* 185; Elaw, "Memoirs," 82, 136.

17. Brekus, *Strangers and Pilgrims,* 185, 220; Lee, *Religious Experiences,* 18.

18. Hazel V. Carby, "Policing the Black Woman's Body in an Urban Context," *Critical Inquiry* 18 (1992): 739; Kimberley Roberts, "The Clothes Make the Woman: The Symbolics of Prostitution in Nella Larsen's *Quicksand* and Claude McKay's *Home to Harlem,*" *Tulsa Studies in Women's Literature* 16 (Spring 1997): 108.

19. Deborah Gray White, *Ar'n't I a Woman: Female Slaves in the Plantation South* (New York: W. W. Norton and Co., 1985), 161.

20. James Baldwin, *The Amen Corner* (1968; reprint, New York: Vintage, 1998), 36–37.

21. Stephen Ward Angell, "The Controversy over Women's Ministry in the African Methodist Episcopal Church During the 1880s: The Case of Sarah Ann Hughes," in *This Far By Faith: Readings in African-American Women's Religious Biography,* ed. Judith Weisenfeld and Richard Newman (New York: Routledge, 1996), 101.

22. Linda S. Schearing, "Double Time . . . Double Trouble? Gender, Sin, and Leviticus

12," in *Book of Leviticus,* ed. Robert A. Kugler and Rolf Rendtoff (Boston: Brill, 2003), 429–50; Joanne M. Pierce, " 'Green Woman' and Blood Pollution: Some Medieval Rituals for the Churching of Women after Childbirth," *Studia-Liturgica* 29 (1999), 191–215; Natalie Knodel, "Reconsidering an Obsolete Rite: The Churching of Women and Feminist Liturgical Theology," *Feminist Theology* 14 (January 1997), 106–25; G. L. C. Frank, "Menstruation and Motherhood: Christian Attitudes in Late Antiquity," *Studia Historiae-Ecclesiasticae* 19 (1993): 185–208; William Coster, "Purity, Profanity, and Puritanism: The Churching of Women, 1500–1700," in *Women in the Church* , ed. W. J. Sheils and Diana Woods (Oxford: Basil Blackwell, 1990), 377–87; Walter von Arx, "The Churching of Women after Childbirth," *Liturgy and Human Passage* (New York: Seabury, 1979), 63–72; David H. Tripp and William James Cameron, "Churching: A Common Problem of the English Churches," *Church Quarterly* 3 (October 1970): 125–33.

23. *Mahalia Jackson—The Power and the Glory: The Life and the Music of the World's Greatest Gospel Singer,* dir. by Jeff Scheftel (1997; New York: Xenon Entertainment, 2003), DVD.

24. Cathi M. Falsani, "On the Verge of Ideological Mutiny: Celibacy and the Roman Catholic Priesthood," *Daughters of Sarah* 22 (Winter 1996): 16–19; Douglas Laudenschlager, "In Persona Christi," *Angelus* 1 (April 1978): 1, 8.

25. Michael Eric Dyson, *Race Rules: Navigating the Color Line* (Reading, MA: Addison Wesley, 1996), 88; D. Dance, *Shuckin' and Jivin': Folklore from Contemporary Black Americans* (Bloomington: Indiana University Press, 1978), 55; James Robert Saunders, *The Wayward Preacher in the Literature of African American Women* (Jefferson, NC: McFarland, 1995); Marvin McMicle, "Film Portrayals of the Black Preacher" (Ph.D. diss., Case Western Reserve University, 1997); J. Ronald Green, "Oscar Micheaux's Interrogation of Caricature as Entertainment," *Film Quarterly* (Spring 1998): 16–31; bell hooks, "Micheaux: Celebrating Blackness," *Black American Literature Forum* 25 (Summer 1991): 351–60; Roberts, "The Clothes Make the Woman," 116–18.

26. Baldwin, *The Amen Corner,* 84.

27. Bureau of the Census, *Fifteenth Census of the United States* (Washington, DC: 1930).

28. Alice Walker, *In Search of Our Mother's Garden: Womanist Prose* (New York: Harcourt Brace and Jovanovich, 1983), xi.

29. Carroll Smith-Rosenberg, "The Female World of Love and Ritual: Relations Between Women in Nineteenth Century America," *Signs* 1 (1975): 1–30; John D'Emilio and Estelle B. Freedman, *Intimate Matters: A History of Sexuality in America* (New York: Harper and Row Publishers, 1988), 192.

30. Caroll Hibler, "Historical Encyclopedia of Chicago Women Project: Entry Assignment: Reverend Mary G. Evans: Informant Interview Summary," 2, 14. All project interview transcripts are in the possession of this author and used by permission.

31. Hibler, "Historical Encyclopedia of Chicago Women Project," 22.

32. Ibid., 8.

33. Samuel Strong, "Social Types in the Negro Community of Chicago: An Example of the Social Type Method" (Ph.D. diss., University of Chicago, 1940), 206–7; "Sunday Service," Box 186, Federal Writers' Project, Illinois State Historical Library, Springfield.

34. "Muscular Christianity" was the religious aspect of a broader cultural movement known as the "cult of masculinity," which lasted into the late 1920s. The first religious or-

322 *Notes to Pages 116–119*

ganization to express the masculinist claims of this movement was the Men in Religion Forward Movement, with the motto "More Men for Religion, More Religion for Men." Gail Bederman, "'The Women Have Had Charge of the Church Work Long Enough': The Men and Religion Forward Movement of 1911–1912 and the Masculinization of Middle-Class Protestantism," *American Quarterly* 41 (1989): 432–65; Michael S. Kimmel, "The Contemporary 'Crisis' of Masculinity in Historical Perspective," in *The Making of Masculinities: The New Men's Studies*, ed. Harry Brod (Boston: Allen and Unwin, 1987), 121–54; Joe L. Dubbert, "Progressivism and the Masculinity Crisis," in *The American Man*, ed. Elizabeth H. Pleck and Joseph H. Pleck (Englewood Cliffs, NJ: Prentice Hall, 1980), 303–20; Donald E. Hall, ed., *Muscular Christianity: Embodying the Victorian Age* (New York: Cambridge University Press, 1994); Bruce Barton, *The Man Nobody Knows: A Discovery of the Real Jesus* (New York: Grossett and Dunlap for Bobbs-Merrill, 1924), iv; James A. Nuechterlein, "Bruce Barton and the Business Ethos of the 1920s," *South Atlantic Quarterly* 76 (Summer 1977): 303; Leo P. Ribuffo, "Jesus Christ as Business Statesman: Bruce Barton and the Selling of Corporate Capitalism," *American Quarterly* 33 (Summer 1981): 206–31.

35. "God's Saintly Servant," *Now!* January 6, 1962.

36. Caroll Hibler, interview by author, Harry S. Truman College, Chicago, IL, December 26, 1996.

37. George Chauncey, *Gay New York: Gender, Urban Culture, and the Making of the Gay Male World, 1890–1940* (New York: Basic, 1994).

38. Jean McMahon Humez, ed., *Gifts of Power: The Writings of Rebecca Jackson, Black Visionary, Shaker Eldress* (Amherst: University of Massachusetts Press, 1981), 9, 17.

39. Hibler, "Historical Encyclopedia of Chicago Women Project," 11, 19.

40. Ibid., 10.

41. "In Testimony of the Faith of the Reverend Mary G. Evans, D.D.," Marjorie Stewart Joyner Papers, Vivian G. Harsh Collection, Carter G. Woodson regional branch, Chicago Public Library; "The Cosmopolitan Community Church," Federal Writers' Project Files, Container A125, "Illinois Religion" folder, Library of Congress, Washington, DC.

42. Cheryl Townsend Gilkes, *If It Wasn't for the Women* (Maryknoll, NY: Orbis, 2001): 61–75; C. Eric Lincoln and Lawrence Mamiya, *The Black Church in the African American Experience* (Durham, NC: Duke University Press, 1990), 75.

43. Marina Warner, *Alone of all Her Sex: The Myth of the Cult of the Virgin* (New York: Vintage, 1983); Yaroslav Pelikan, *Mary Through the Centuries: Her Place in the History of Culture* (New Haven, CT: Yale University Press, 1998); Mary F. Foskett, *A Virgin Conceived: Mary and Classical Representations of Virginity* (Bloomington: Indiana University Press, 2002).

44. Stavney, "Mothers of Tomorrow," 538–47; Claudia Tate, *Domestic Allegories of Political Desire: The Black Heroine's Text at the Turn of the Century* (New York: Oxford University Press, 1992), 97; W. E. B. Du Bois, "The Black Mother," *Crisis* 5 (December 1912), 78.

45. Stavney, "Mothers of Tomorrow," 553; Nella Larsen, *Passing*, 1929 (New York: Modern Library, 2002), 88, 124.

46. Nell Irvin Painter, "Representing Truth: Sojourner Truth's Knowing and Becoming Known," *Journal of American History* 81 (September 1994): 461–92.

47. "Church Amens Stop; Too Much Truth is Told: Bobbed Haired Evangelist Rips into the Hypocrisy of So-Called Christians," *Chicago Defender*, December 2, 1922.

48. Strong, "Social Types," 274.

49. I consider *From Farm to Pulpit* a biography rather than an autobiography because it is not clear that Elder Smith could actually read and write proficiently enough to produce such a work. It is also not clear who assisted her and for what purpose. One of the two editions of the biography appears as an appendix to Samuel Strong's 1940 dissertation; that is the one used for this essay. See Strong, "Social Types."

50. Strong, "Social Types," 394.

51. The 1920 census lists William Smith as living with his wife. They had a son, Henry, who was born in Illinois in 1912, two years after Lucy Smith came to the city, so William must have followed Lucy to Chicago within a year or so. Bureau of the Census, *Fourteenth Census of the United States*, vol. 23 (Washington, DC: 1920), E. D. 96, Sheet 7, Line 23.

52. "William Smith Obituary, 1938," Lucy Smith Collier Papers, Vivian G. Harsh Collection, Carter G. Woodson regional branch, Chicago Public Library.

53. Francis Foster, *Written By Herself: Literary Production by African American Women, 1746–1892* (Bloomington: Indiana University Press, 1993).

54. Interview by author with "Little Lucy" Collier at her home in Chicago, December 1996.

55. Herbert M. Smith, "Three Negro Preachers: A Study of Religious Leadership" (M.A. thesis, University of Chicago, 1935), 12; Horace Cayton and St. Clair Drake, *Black Metropolis: A Study of Negro Life in a Northern City* (1945; reprint, New York: Harper and Row, 1962), 643; "Tour—Lucy Smith's Pentecostal Church," Folder 36, Box 182, Federal Writers' Project Files, Illinois State Historical Library, Springfield.

56. "Church of All Nations 3825 South Dearborn," Box 185, Federal Writers' Project Files, Illinois State Historical Library, Springfield.

57. Allan Spear, *Black Chicago: The Making of a Negro Ghetto, 1890–1920* (Chicago: University of Chicago Press, 1967), 176; Smith, "Three Negro Preachers," 17–19.

58. "All Nations Pentecostal Church," Box 185, Federal Writers' Project Files, Illinois State Historical Library, Springfield.

59. Interview with "Little Lucy" Collier, December 1996.

60. Bureau of the Census, *Fifteenth Census of the United States*.

61. Hibler, "Historical Encyclopedia of Chicago Women Project," 6.

62. Wright, *12 Million Black Voices*, 93.

63. Smith, "Three Negro Preachers," 11.

64. Telephone interview by author with "Little Lucy" Smith Collier, October 26, 1999; "Interview with Elder Lucy Smith," "General Survey," Box 185, Federal Writers' Project Files, Illinois State Historical Library, Springfield.

65. Molly Hite, "Writing—and Reading—The Body: Female Sexuality and Recent Feminist Fiction," *Feminist Studies* 14 (Spring 1988): 120–42. See also Helene Cixous, "The Laugh of Medusa," trans. Keith Cohen and Paula Cohen, in *New French Feminisms: An Anthology*, ed. Elaine Marks and Isabelle de Courtivron (New York: Schocken, 1981), 245–64.

66. *Chicago Defender*, March 31, 1917.

67. "Churches to Hear Actress Now Evangel," *Chicago Defender*, November 28, 1936; Miles Mark Fisher, "Organized Religion and the Cults," *Crisis* 44 (January 1937): 10; *Chicago Defender*, March 1, 1941, November 29, 1941, July 25, 1942.

68. "First AME Bishop in 213 Years (Vashti Murphy Mckenzie of the African Methodist Episcopal Church)," *Ebony* (September 2000); "African Methodist Episcopal Church Elects First Woman Bishop," *Christianity Today* (July 2000); Vashti McKenzie, *Not Without Struggle: Leadership Development for African American Women in Ministry* (Place: United Church Press, 1996); Lincoln and Mamiya, *Black Religion in the African American Experience*, 295.

Chapter 7. *"Make Us a Power"*

1. Gardner quoted in William J. Walls, *The African Methodist Episcopal Zion Church: Reality of the Black Church* (Charlotte, NC: AME Zion Publishing Co.), 392–93. "The Mite Missionary Society: Women's Missionary Society," *Christian Recorder*, May 28, 1874.

2. See chapter 6 in this volume.

3. The term *public culture* is, in one sense, intended to suggest that antebellum free black people shared a private sphere of deliberation through which they arrived at notions of the common good and challenged their standing vis-à-vis the state—a public sphere in Habermasian terms; see Jurgen Habermas, *The Structural Transformation of the Public Sphere: An Inquiry Into a Category of Bourgeois Society*, trans. Thomas Burger with Frederick Lawrence (Cambridge, MA: MIT Press, 1989). More precisely, this community of activists may be said to have comprised a subaltern counterpublic, to borrow Nancy Fraser's rereading of Habermas. Fraser, along with numerous other feminist, progressive, and antiracist social theorists, critique Habermas for setting forth an idealized model of the public sphere which does not fully account for the extent to which race, class, and gender necessarily exclude some from liberal, bourgeois publicity, and thus from that powerful mode of democratic political practice. Fraser argues that beyond Habermas's idealized public sphere lie nonliberal, nonbourgeois, competing public spheres, one of which was created through the discursive practices of antebellum free black people. See Nancy Fraser, "Rethinking the Public Sphere: A Contribution to the Critique of Actually Existing Democracy," in *Habermas and the Public Sphere*, ed. Craig Calhoun (Cambridge, MA: MIT Press, 1992), 109–42. This essay argues that for African Americans, the public realm was constructed not merely through discursive practices but also through the materiality of African American life, hence my adoption of the term *culture* rather than *sphere*. While this study considers the discursive dimension of black publicity, it also argues that the public engagement of African Americans was shaped through the conditions of everyday life: poverty, displacement, violence, labor, and law. For one discussion of African Americans and the public sphere, see Thomas C. Holt, "Afterword: Mapping the Black Public Sphere," in *The Black Public Sphere: A Public Culture Book*, ed. the Black Public Sphere Collective (Chicago: University of Chicago Press, 1995), 325–28.

4. Recent works that take up the intellectual dimension of nineteenth-century African American culture include Mia Bay, *The White Image in the Black Mind: African-American Ideas About White People, 1830–1925* (New York: Oxford University Press, 2000); Leroy T. Hopkins, "Spiritual Fatherland: African-American Intellectuals and Germany, 1850–1920," *Yearbook of German-American Studies* 31 (1996): 25–35; Emma Jones Lapsansky, "'Discipline to the Mind': Philadelphia's Banneker Institute, 1854–1872," *Pennsylvania Magazine of History and Biography* 117 (1–2) (1993): 83–102; David W. Blight, "In Search of

Learning, Liberty, and Self-Definition: James McCune Smith and the Ordeal of the Ante-bellum Black Intellectual," *Afro-Americans in New York Life and History* 9, no. 2 (1985): 7–25; and Patrick Rael, *Black Identity and Black Protest in the Antebellum North* (Chapel Hill: University of North Carolina Press, 2002).

5. Numerous black antislavery activists were deeply engaged with the transatlantic dimension of the abolitionist movement. See Richard J. M. Blackett, *Building an Antislavery Wall: Black Americans in the Atlantic Abolitionist Movement, 1830–1860* (Baton Rouge: Louisiana State University Press, 1983); and Alan Rise and Martin Crawford, eds., *Liberating Sojourn: Frederick Douglass and Transatlantic Reform* (Athens: University of Georgia Press, 1999).

6. Historians have worked to restore African American women to the narrative of the nineteenth-century women's movement. Rosalyn Terborg-Penn has uncovered the many long-overlooked African American activists who took part in the movement led by Stanton and Anthony. Others have pointed to numerous nineteenth-century black feminists, including Frances Ellen Watkins Harper, Mary Ann Shadd Cary, Josephine St. Pierre Ruffin, and Ida B. Wells, who did much of their public work outside of a women's movement. Evelyn Brooks Higginbotham has argued for a churchwomen's movement among black Baptists late in the century. Higginbotham's work demonstrates that, while putting black women at the center of the narrative is essential to our understanding, equally important is analyzing their struggles in the context of the public spaces in which they lived and worked. One culmination of the black Baptist women's movement, Higginbotham argues, was the founding of the denomination's Women's Convention in 1900. Here, women's rights are not read as abstract aspirations, nor were they identical to those rights sought by middle-class white women. The communities and the institutions in which black Baptists made their lives defined the parameters of women's quests for rights. See Evelyn Brooks Higginbotham, in *Righteous Discontent: The Women's Movement in the Black Baptist Church, 1880–1920* (Cambridge, MA: Harvard University Press, 1993). Regarding those African American who took part in the movement led by white women, see Rosalyn Terborg-Penn, *African American Women in the Struggle for the Vote, 1850–1920* (Bloomington: Indiana University Press, 1998). Biographies of early black feminists include Melba Joyce Boyd, *Discarded Legacy: Politics and Poetics in the Life of Frances E. W. Harper* (Detroit, MI: Wayne State University Press, 1994); Jane Rhodes, *Mary Ann Shadd Cary: The Black Press and Protest in the Nineteenth Century* (Bloomington: Indiana University Press, 1998); Maude T. Jenkins, "She Issued the Call: Josephine St. Pierre Ruffin, 1842–1924," *Sage: A Scholarly Journal on Black Women* 5, no. 2 (1988): 74–76; and, Patricia Ann Schechter, *Ida B. Wells-Barnett and American Reform, 1880–1930* (Chapel Hill: University of North Carolina Press, 2001).

7. For a discussion of the founding of the Order of the Eastern Star among black Masons, see Elizabeth L. Davis, *The History of the Order of the Eastern Star Among Colored People/Mrs. Joe S. Brown* (1922; reprint, New York: G. K. Hall, 1997).

8. See Ellen Du Bois, *Feminism and Suffrage: The Emergence of an Independent Women's Movement in America, 1848–1869* (Ithaca, NY: Cornell University Press, 1978), 53–78.

9. The U.S. Senate accepted the Fifteenth Amendment, in its final form, on February 26, 1869, by a vote of 39 to 13. Xi Wang, *The Trial of Democracy: Black Suffrage and Northern Republicans, 1860–1910* (Athens: University of Georgia Press, 1997), 46.

10. "Proceedings of the Colored National Labor Union," reprinted in *Organized Labor and the Black Worker*, ed. Philip D. Foner (New York: Praeger, [1974]), 173.

11. "Proceedings of the National Convention of the Colored Men of America, Washington, D.C.," reprinted in *Proceedings of the Black State Conventions, 1840–1865: Volume I: New York, Pennsylvania, Indiana, Michigan, Ohio*, ed. Philip S. Foner and George E. Walker (Philadelphia: Temple University Press, 1979), 367.

12. For an extensive analysis of African Americans in post–Civil War women's suffrage campaigns, see Terborg-Penn, *African American Women in the Struggle for the Vote*.

13. A. A. Taylor, "The Negro in South Carolina During the Reconstruction," *Journal of Negro History* 9, no. 4 (October 1924): 381.

14. Terborg-Penn, *African American Women in the Struggle for the Vote*, 45.

15. Elsa Barkley Brown, "Negotiating and Transforming the Public Sphere: African American Political Life in the Transition from Slavery to Freedom," *Public Culture* 7 (1994): 107–46.

16. *The Elevator* (San Francisco, CA), October 11, 1865, reel 3, Misc. Negro Newspapers, Wisconsin Historical Society, Madison.

17. W. E. B. Du Bois, *The Negro Church. Report of a Social Study Made Under the Direction of Atlanta University; Together with the Proceedings of the Eighth Conference for the Study of the Negro Problems, Held at Atlanta University, May 26th, 1903* (Atlanta, GA: Atlanta University Press, 1903).

18. Du Bois, *The Negro Church*, 123–37, 153.

19. Eric Foner, *Freedom's Lawmakers: A Directory of Black Officeholders During Reconstruction* (Baton Rouge: Louisiana State University, 1996), xxi, 35–36, 108, 203–4.

20. "Bishop Haven Has Been Elected," *Christian Recorder*, November 5, 1874; "The Ballot for Women," *Christian Recorder*, December 23, 1875.

21. B. F. Grant, "A Few Sparks: No Use to Kick Because a Woman Has Been Ordained an Elder," *Star of Zion*, March 23, 1898, 6; *Daily Journal of the Sixteenth Quadrennial Session of the General Conference of the A.M.E. Zion Church, of America, Held at Montgomery, Alabama, May, A.D., 1880* (New York: Book Concern of the A.M.E. Zion Church, 1880).

22. *The Fifteenth Quadrennial Session of the General Conference of the African Methodist Episcopal Church. Place of Session, Nashville, Tennessee. May 6, 1872.*

23. W[illiam] N[ewton] Hartshorn, *An Era of Progress and Promise, 1860–1910* (Boston: Priscilla Publishing Co., 1910), 440; Elizabeth Cazden, *Antoinette Brown Blackwell: A Biography* (Old Westbury, NY: Feminist Press, 1983); Andrea M. Kerr, *Lucy Stone: Speaking Out for Equality* (New Brunswick, NJ: Rutgers University Press, 1992).

24. *The Sixteenth Session, and the Fifteenth Quadrennial Session of the General Conference of the African Episcopal Methodist Church. Place of Session, Atlanta, Georgia, from May 1st to 18th, 1876.*

25. Walls, *The A.M.E. Zion Church*, 111.

26. Rev. Mark M. Bell, *Daily Journal of the Sixteenth Quadrennial Session of the General Conference of the A.M.E. Zion Church, of America, Held at Montgomery, Alabama, May, A.D., 1880* (New York: Book Concern of the A.M.E. Zion Church, 1880), 71.

27. Bell, *Daily Journal of the Sixteenth Quadrennial Session of the General Conference of*

the A.M.E. Zion Church, of America, 71; Terborg-Penn, *African-American Women and the Struggle for the Vote*, 38.

28. *The Fifteenth Quadrennial Session of the General Conference of the African Methodist Episcopal Church. Place of Session, Nashville, Tennessee. May 6, 1872.*

29. Walls, *The A.M.E. Zion Church*, 111.

30. Othal H. Lakey, *The History of the C.M.E. Church* (Memphis, TN: C.M.E. Publishing House, 1996), 272.

31. Lakey, *History of the C.M.E. Church*, 272.

32. Walls, *The A.M.E. Zion Church*, 111. Cicero R. Harris, *Zion's Historical Catechism* (Charlotte, NC: AME Zion Publishing House, 1922), 17; *Minutes, Eleventh Session, South Carolina Annual Conference, 1876,* 9.

33. Lakey, *History of the C.M.E. Church*, 272.

34. *The Fifteenth Quadrennial Session of the General Conference of the African Methodist Episcopal Church. Place of Session, Nashville, Tennessee. May 6, 1872.*

35. "Primitive Deaconate," *Christian Recorder*, July 8, 1875 (reprint from the *Christian Union*).

36. H[enry] M[cNeil] T[urner], "Communications. How the Stewardesses System Operates in the A.M.E. Church," *Christian Recorder*, May 15, 1873.

37. Lawrence S. Little, *Disciples of Liberty: The African Methodist Episcopal Church in the Age of Imperialism, 1884–1916* (Knoxville: University of Tennessee Press, 2000), 10.

38. Walls, *The A.M.E. Zion Church*, 376, 388.

39. Lakey, *History of the C.M.E. Church*, 303.

40. Walls, *The A.M.E. Zion Church*, 376, 388; Little, *Disciples of Liberty*, 10.

41. "The Mite Missionary Society: Women's Missionary Society," *Christian Recorder*, May 28, 1874.

42. "West Tennessee and Miss. Conference," *Star of Zion*, December 19, 1884.

43. "Mississippi," *Star of Zion*, October 24, 1884, 8; "Mississippi: Synopsis of the Minutes of the Second District Meeting," *Star of Zion*, November 28, 1874. Throughout the mid-1880s numerous women were reported as being elected delegates, appointed agents, and speakers before black Methodist conferences at all levels.

44. "Baltimore District Conference." *Star of Zion*, July 3, 1885.

45. Rev. Benjamin W. Arnett, B.D., *Journal of the 17th Session and the 16th Quadrennial Session of the General Conference of the African Methodist Episcopal Church in the United States, Held at St. Louis, Missouri, May 3–25, 1880* (Xenia, OH: Torchlight Printing Co., 1882).

46. *Minutes of the Thirteenth Session of the Georgia Annual Conference of the AME Church Held in Campbell Chapel, Americus, Georgia, January 21, 1880.*

47. Quoted in Walls, *The A.M.E. Zion Church*, 391.

48. Ibid.

49. Ibid., 392.

50. Rev. Joseph H. Morgan, *Morgan's History of the New Jersey Conference of the A.M.E. Church, From 1872 to 1887. And of the Several Churches, as Far as Possible From Date of Organization, with Biographical Sketches of Members of the Conference* (Camden, NJ: S. Chew, Printers, 1887).

51. Morgan, *Morgan's History of the New Jersey Conference*.

52. Rev. C. R. Harris, *Daily Proceedings of the Seventeenth Quadrennial Session of the General Conference of the A.M.E. Zion Church in America, Held in New York City, May, 1884* (New York, NY: A.M.E. Zion Book Concern, 1884).

53. Walls, *The A.M.E. Zion Church*, 392–393; *Scott v. Sanford*, 60 U.S. 393 (1857), 407.

54. Quoted in Walls, *The A.M.E. Zion Church*, 392–93.

55. Adrienne M. Israel, *Amanda Berry Smith: From Washerwoman to Evangelist* (Lanham, MD: Scarecrow, 1998), 60.

56. National Association of Colored Women (U.S.), *A History of the Club Movement Among the Colored Women of the United States of America: As Contained in the Minutes of the Conventions, Held in Boston, July 29, 20, 31, 1895, and of the National Federation of Afro-American Women, Held in Washington, D.C., July 20, 21, 22, 1896* (n.p., 1902).

57. Rayford W. Logan, *The Negro in American Life and Thought: The Nadir, 1877–1901* (New York: Dial, 1954); *The Betrayal of the Negro: From Rutherford B. Hayes to Woodrow Wilson* (New York: Collier, 1965).

58. Evelyn Brooks Higginbotham, "The Black Church: A Gender Perspective," in *African-American Religion: Interpretive Essays in History and Culture*, ed. Timothy E. Fulop and Albert J. Raboteau (New York: Routledge, 1997), 205–6. For a general discussion of this period, see Joel Williamson, *A Rage for Order: Black/White Relations in the American South Since Emancipation* (New York: Oxford University Press, 1986), 117–51. For instances of white-on-black violence throughout the South during this era, see the essays contained in *Black Freedom / White Violence, 1865–1900*, ed. Donald G. Nieman (New York: Garland, 1994).

59. Miss May M. Brown, "A Woman's Views on Current Topics," *A.M.E. Zion Quarterly Review*, 1891.

60. Little, *Disciples of Liberty*, 10.

61. See Elizabeth E. Grammar, "Female Itinerant Evangelists in Nineteenth Century America," *Arizona Quarterly* 55 (Spring 1999): 67–96; and Jualynne E. Dodson, "Nineteenth-Century A.M.E. Preaching Women," in *Women in New Worlds*, ed. Hilah F. Thomas and Rosemary S. Keller (Nashville, TN: Abingdon, 1981), 276–92.

62. On Turner, see Stephen Angell, *Bishop Henry McNeil Turner and African-American Religion in the South* (Knoxville: University of Tennessee Press, 1992); and John Dittmer, "The Education of Henry McNeal Turner," in *Black Leaders of the Nineteenth Century*, ed. Leon Litwack and August Meier (Urbana: University of Illinois Press, 1988), 253–74.

63. Stephen W. Angell, "The Controversy Over Women's Ministry in the African Methodist Episcopal Church During the 1880s: The Case of Sarah Ann Hughes," in *This Far By Faith: Readings in African-American Women's Religious Biography*, ed. Judith Weisenfeld and Richard Newman (New York: Routledge, 1996), 94–109. See also Dodson, "Nineteenth-Century A.M.E. Preaching Women"; Jualynne E. Dodson, "Power and Surrogate Leadership: Black Women and Organized Religion," *Sage* 5, no. 2 (Fall 1988): 37–42; Jualynne E. Dodson and Cheryl T. Gilkes, "Something Within: Social Change and Collective Endurance in the Sacred World of Black Christian Women," in *Women and Religion in America*, vol. 3, *1900–1968*, ed. Rosemary Radford Reuther and Rosemary Skinner Keller (San Francisco: Harper and Row, 1986), 80–89; Cheryl T. Gilkes, "The Politics of 'Silence': Dual-

Sex Political Systems and Women's Traditions of Conflict in African-American Religion," in *African-American Christianity: Essays in History*, ed. Paul E. Johnson (Berkeley and Los Angeles: University of California Press, 1994), 80–110; Catherine Peck, "Your Daughters Shall Prophesy: Women in the Afro-American Preaching Tradition," in *Diversities of Gifts*, ed. Ruel W. Tyson, James L. Peacock, and Daniel W. Patterson (Urbana: University of Illinois Press, 1988); and Jeanne B. Williams, "Loose the Woman and Let Her Go! Pennsylvania's African American Women Preachers," *Pennsylvania Heritage* 22, no. 1 (1996): 4–9.

64. Rt. Rev. J. P. Campbell, D.D., and Rt. Rev. John M. Brown, D.D., "The Ordination of Women; What Is the Authority For It?" *A.M.E. Church Review* (April 1886).

65. Angell, *Bishop Henry McNeil Turner*, 183.

66. Campbell and Brown, "The Ordination of Women," 454–55. Brown might also have had in mind the case of Mrs. Margaret Wilson. Wilson had been called to the ministry in 1870 and served as missionary until 1883. See Morgan, *Morgan's History of the New Jersey Conference*, 51.

67. David W. Wills, "Womanhood and Domesticity in the A.M.E. Tradition: The Influence of Daniel Alexander Payne," in *Black Apostles at Home and Abroad: Afro-Americans and the Christian Mission From the Revolution to Reconstruction*, ed. Richard Newman and David Wills (Boston: G. K. Hall, 1982), 133–46; Charles Killiam, "Daniel A. Payne and the A.M.E. General Conference of 1888: A Display of Contrasts," *Negro History Bulletin* 32, no. 7 (1969): 11–14.

68. *The Doctrines and Discipline of the A.M.E. Church* (Philadelphia: A.M.E. Book Concern, 1912), 208; Little, *Disciples of Liberty*, 11.

69. *Star of Zion*, June 2, 1898, 2.

70. Evalina H. Badham, "Woman's Place in the Church," *A.M.E. Zion Quarterly Review*, 7, no. 1 (April 1897): 21.

71. Mrs. Bishop C. C. [Sarah] Pettey, "Woman's Column: Signs of the Times," *Star of Zion*, October 28, 1897. See also Glenda E. Gilmore, "Gender and Jim Crow: Sarah Dudley Pettey's Vision of the New South," *North Carolina Historical Review* 68, no. 3 (July 1991): 261–85.

72. Rev. J. Harvey Anderson, "Searchlight Scenes: Ordination of Women and the General Conference," *Star of Zion*, September 29, 1898.

73. Rev. J. J. Adams, "Something Will Drop Yet," *Star of Zion*, October 6, 1898.

74. Eliza A. Gardner, "From Boston, Mass," *Star of Zion*, February 16, 1899.

75. "Cannot Frighten Her," *Star of Zion*, November 23, 1899.

76. Rev. R. A. Morrisey, "Female Preachers: Objections Answered—Scripture Proofs," *Star of Zion*, September 22, 1898.

77. Mrs. Clarissa Betties, "Let Rev. Mrs. Small Alone," *Star of Zion*, December 22, 1898.

78. Bishop J. W. Hood, "The Woman Question: Woman Originally Was Man's Equal and Will Be Again," *Star of Zion*, January 12, 1898.

79. Rev. S. A. Chambers, "Cannon Balls: Reply to Rev. J. H. Gilmer, Jr.," *Star of Zion*, July 21, 1898.

80. "Physically Unfit," *Star of Zion*, August 18, 1898.

81. Rev. S. A. Chambers, "Redhot Cannon Ball: No Authority in Scripture for the Ordination of Women," *Star of Zion*, June 16, 1898, 1.

82. "Don't Need Women Elders," *Star of Zion*, August 11, 1898, 4.

83. See Best, "The Spirit of the Holy Ghost is a Male Spirit."

84. Deborah Gray White, *Too Heavy a Load: Black Women in Defense of Themselves, 1894–1994* (New York: W.W. Norton and Company, 1999).

85. Randall B. Woods, "C. H. J. Taylor and the Movement for Black Political Independence, 1882–1896," *Journal of Negro History* 67, no. 2 (Summer 1982): 122–35.

86. See Best, "The Spirit of the Holy Ghost is a Male Spirit."

87. *Star of Zion*, July 28, 1898, 4; reprinted from the *Pee Dee (NC) Herald*.

88. Bishop J. B. Small, "Mrs. Small's Case: Bishop Small Speaks," *Star of Zion*, June 16, 1898, 6.

89. Rev. S. A. Chambers, "Cannon Balls: Reply to Rev. B. J. Bolding," *Star of Zion*, July 28, 1898, 2, 7.

90. Rev. S. A. Chambers, "Cannon Balls: Reply to Rev. J. H. Gilmer, Jr.," *Star of Zion*, July 21, 1898, 3.

91. "Physically Unfit," 4.

92. Betties, "Let Rev. Mrs. Small Alone," 6.

93. Mrs. Rev. W. L. Moore, "Eyes of Jealousy," *Star of Zion*, July 28, 1898, 5.

94. Grant, "A Few Sparks," 6.

95. Anderson, "Searchlight Scenes," 1.

96. Bishop J. W. Hood, "Female Elders: Not Until There is a Call for Female Pastors Will There be a Necessity for Female Elders," *Star of Zion*, October 27, 1898, 5. See also John H. Satterwhite, "An Interpretation of History: Henry Evans, James Walker Hood, and Bishop James Wesley Wactor," *A.M.E. Zion Quarterly Review* 96, no. 3 (1984): 28–31.

97. Rev. J. H. McMullen, "Bishop Small Errs: The General Conference Never Dreamed of Women Elders," *Star of Zion*, June 30, 1898, 1.

98. Rev. F. M. Jacobs, "Topics of the Times: Star—Dream—Woman Ordination—Paul's Advice," *Star of Zion*, July 21, 1898, 1.

99. Grant, "A Few Sparks," 6.

100. Jacobs, "Topics of the Times," 1.

101. Anderson, "Searchlight Scenes," 1. Anderson reports after an informal poll of the bishops that four of the eight—Pettey, Walters, Small, and Hood—publicly endorsed women's ordination. Bishops Lomax and Harris later publicly endorsed Mary Small's elevation to the station of bishop. Bishop T. H. Lomax, "Episcopal Visits," *Star of Zion*, July 28, 1898, 3; Bishop C. R. Harris, "Episcopal Dots: Women Elders—Railroad Discrimination—Coleman Factory," *Star of Zion*, August 4, 1898, 2.

102. Harris, "Episcopal Dots," 2.

103. Michele Mitchell, " 'The Black Man's Burden': African Americans, Imperialism, and Notions of Racial Manhood, 1890–1910," *International Review of Social History* 44 (1999): 77–99; Lawrence S. Little, *Disciples of Liberty*; James T. Campbell, *Songs of Zion* (New York: Oxford University Press, 1995).

104. Mrs. Maggie Hood-Banks, "The Missionary Department: Shall the Women or Men Control It," *Star of Zion*, April 19, 1900.

105. Miss S. J. Janifer, "A Woman's Plea: Let the Women Control the Missionary and Church Extension Departments," *Star of Zion*, November 23, 1899; James Harvey Ander-

son, *Biographical Souvenir Volume of the Twenty-Third Quadrennial Session of The General Conference of the African Methodist Episcopal Zion Church* (n.p., 1908), 28.

106. Terborg-Penn, *African American Women in the Struggle for the Vote,* 65.

107. Rev. J. N. Manly, "Let the Women Have the Missionary Department," *Star of Zion* (1900).

108. See Glenda E. Gilmore, *Gender and Jim Crow: Women and the Politics of White Supremacy in North Carolina, 1896–1920* (Chapel Hill: University of North Carolina Press, 1996). Gilmore's history, while principally focused on female activists in the secular realm, carefully examines black churchwomen's work within it. See, Glenda E. Gilmore, "Gender and Jim Crow: Sarah Dudley Pettey's Vision of the New South," 261–85.

Chapter 8. *"Only a Woman Would Do"*

1. Joanna P. Moore is a figure who has been lost in obscurity, yet she links many of the Baptist and Holiness networks in the South. See her autobiography *In Christ's Stead* (Chicago: Women's Baptist Home Mission Society, 1902); see also Grace M. Eaton, *A Heroine of the Cross: Sketches of the Life and Work of Miss Joanna P. Moore* (n.p.: American Baptist Home Mission Society, 1934); Louise A. Cattan and Helen C. Schmitz, *One Mark of Greatness* (Philadelphia: Judson, 1961), 88–107. For context, see Evelyn Brooks Higginbotham, *Righteous Discontent: The Women's Movement in the Black Baptist Church 1880–1920* (Cambridge, MA: Harvard University Press, 1993); and David D. Daniels III, "The Cultural Renewal of Slave Religion: Charles Price Jones and the Emergence of the Holiness Movement in Mississippi" (Ph.D. diss., Union Theological Seminary, 1992).

2. Moore, *In Christ's Stead,* 170.

3. Men were members of Bible Bands as well.

4. Cheryl T. Gilkes, *If It Wasn't For the Women: Black Women's Experience and Womanist Culture in Church and Community* (Maryknoll, NY: Orbis, 2001), 50–51.

5. For further discussion, see Higginbotham, *Righteous Discontent,* 100–03. Most of the discourse on the ideal of domesticity pertained to white women; however, there was also a considerable religiously based discourse on domesticity, which had greater currency among black women. Missionary work spread these ideals, and educational institutions and leaders such as Anna Julia Cooper supported ideals of womanhood and domestic life coupled with religiosity.

6. *Hope* 24, no. 3 (November 1908): 347, microfilm, ATLA serials preservation program, ATLA film 2005-So.

7. Both the National Baptist Women's Convention and the Women's Work department of the Church of God in Christ had their foundational roots in the Bible Band movement. See Virginia Broughton, *Twenty Years' Experience of a Missionary* (Chicago: Pony Press, 1897), 100–101. See also "Mother" Lizzie (Woods) Robinson, "History of the Bible Band," *Hope* (April 1937), which was reprinted in the 7th Annual Women's Convention booklet of the Church of God In Christ (1998), 334.

8. As women became more organizationally savvy, male pastors who had once lauded the Bible Bands' work began to criticize it. See Broughton, *Twenty Years Experience,* 34–39; and Lizzie Robinson, "Women's Page," The Whole Truth, February 1968, p. 3.

9. Kevin Gaines, *Uplifting the Race: Black Leadership Politics and Culture in the Twentieth Century* (Chapel Hill: University of North Carolina Press, 1996), 139; see also Higginbotham, *Righteous Discontent*, 113–14.

10. See Higginbotham, *Righteous Discontent*, 14. Higginbotham contends that women of the black Baptist church felt certain that "respectable" behavior in public would earn their people a measure of esteem from white America, and hence they strove to win the black lower class's allegiance to temperance, industriousness, thrift, refined manners, and Victorian sexual morals. However, these values are also attached to certain biblical admonitions and beliefs to which these women referred far more than to the search for respect from whites.

11. Eaton, *Heroine of the Cross*, 18–23, 25; Moore, *In Christ's Stead*, 20, 22, 23, 25. Moore does not identify the missionary by name.

12. Higginbotham, *Righteous Discontent*, 98; Moore, *In Christ's Stead*, 26–28, *Tidings* (Chicago: American Baptist Home Mission Society), September 1897, 4.

13. Moore, *In Christ's Stead*, 49–58, 73.

14. Ibid., 81. Moore's reference to the colored people is not pejorative; rather, it is in keeping with the New Orleans convention regarding the people of color or Creoles, those of French descent in Southern Louisiana.

15. Ibid., 81.

16. Ibid., 253.

17. Ibid., 249–50.

18. Ibid., 165, 163, 161, 159–66.

19. The process of oral storytelling of scripture has some implications for how the hermeneutic process of understanding scripture takes place.

20. Moore, *In Christ's Stead*, 174.

21. Ibid., 219.

22. On race mixing and other prohibitions, see Moore, *In Christ's Stead*, 217.

23. This method was designed to insure they could actually find the scripture verses being studied. See Moore, *In Christ's Stead*, 173–74.

24. *Hope* 18, no. 20 (December 1902).

25. *Hope* 1, no. 5 (February 1886).

26. I suspect that Moore may have corrected the grammar in the letter, although this is purely conjecture on my part. Bible Band participants were at all levels of the educational spectrum, so it is difficult to place individual letters.

27. Numerous letters to the magazine described being freed from "sinful activities," and Moore was an advocate and worker for the Women's Christian Temperance Union. "They Needed a Woman's Help," *Missions* 23, no. 10 (December 1932): 598.

28. Eaton, *Heroine of the Cross*, 64.

29. *Hope* 2, no. 12 (August 1886).

30. Ibid.

31. Ibid.

32. Broughton, *Twenty Years' Experience of a Missionary*, 8, 9.

33. Ibid., 14.

34. Ibid., 10, 12.

35. Ibid., 15.

36. Ibid., 32–33.

37. Ibid., 35.

38. Moore, *In Christ's Stead*, 191, 203.

39. Broughton, *Twenty Years' Experience of a Missionary*, 83–84; "Miss Moore's Booth at the Tennessee Centennial Exposition," *Tidings*, September 1897, 27–28; *Hope* 13, no. 141 (October 1897): 30.

40. Broughton, *Twenty Years' Experience of a Missionary*, 100.

41. A more detailed narrative about this quest for a separate women's convention is found in Higginbotham, *Righteous Discontent*, 47–80. Higginbotham downplays what I believe is the significant role of Bible Bands and other existing organizations in establishing a network of women; through these groups, women became organized enough to push for a separate organization for women within the Baptist convention. Broughton's account confirms this connection; see Broughton, *Twenty Years' Experience as a Missionary*, 100–107.

42. See Higginbotham, *Righteous Discontent*, 150–64. However, I argue that the organizational efforts of women in the Bible Bands helped pave the way for the formation of the Baptist women's convention.

43. Moore, *In Christ's Stead*, 221–22.

44. Susie Stanley, *Holy Boldness: Women Preachers' Autobiographies and the Sanctified Self* (Knoxville: University of Tennessee Press, 2003), 2; and Donald W. Dayton, *Theological Roots of Pentecostalism* (Peabody, MA: Hendrickson, 1987), 15–19.

45. Women involved in the Holiness movement included Phoebe Palmer, Elizabeth Mix, and Joanna P. Moore. Holiness camp meetings were attended by Christians from many denominations.

46. The definitive work on the black Holiness movement, which traces how the inception and reception of holiness beliefs split local and state black Baptist conventions, is Daniels, "The Cultural Renewal of Slave Religion."

47. Moore's understanding of sanctification came from a Reformed theological viewpoint more than a Wesleyan standpoint. Moore emphasized service and the power of the Holy Spirit to do that service, rather than perfection as freedom from sin, which the Wesleyan adherents of the Holiness movement espoused. See Daniels, "The Cultural Renewal of Slave Religion," 163–66. Moore developed many of her Holiness connections through work with the state Baptist conventions, specifically in Arkansas, and was intimately involved in the Holiness network of camp meetings throughout the South. There she worked with C. P. Jones, one of the founders of the Church of God in Christ, and Harrison Woodsmall, who was also teaching sanctification in his work with some Baptist conventions in the South. See Daniels, "The Renewal of Slave Religion," 155–56.

48. For more on camp meetings, see Daniels, "The Renewal of Slave Religion," 163–66.

49. Broughton, *Twenty Years' Experience of a Missionary*, 79. In a previous chapter, Broughton talks about her experience of healing, which usually was part of the teachings on sanctification. Although Broughton did not leave the Baptist fold, she did subscribe to Holiness teachings, which sheds an interesting light on previous assessments of Broughton's role in Baptist women's work.

50. Donald W. Dayton, "Yet Another Layer of the Onion: or, Opening the Ecumenical Door to Let the Riffraff In," *Ecumenical Review* 40 (January 1988): 87–110, 108.

51. "Mother" Lizzie (Woods) Robinson, "History of the Bible Band," reprinted from *Hope* (April 1937), in the 37th Annual Women's Convention booklet of The Church of God In Christ (1988), 334.

52. *Hope* 17, no. 192 (January 1902): 499. Numerical changes in volume numbers represent the change in the publisher of *Hope*.

53. Dayton, "Yet Another Layer of the Onion," 115–38.

54. *Hope* 24, no. 3 (November 1908): 25.

55. *Hope* 18, no. 203 (December 1902): 726; *Hope* 22, no. 7 (September 1906): 23.

56. *Hope* 23, no. 3 (November 1907): 63; *Hope* 24, no. 3 (November 1908): 25.

Chapter 9. Exploring the Religious Connection

Epigraph: Words spoken by Harriet Tubman to Mary Talbert a month before her death in 1913, quoted in Marc Ferris, "Aunt Harriet's Home," *American Legacy* (Summer 2004): 68.

1. Catherine Clinton, *Harriet Tubman: The Road to Freedom* (New York: Little Brown and Company, 2004). Clinton points to the importance of abductors as well as conductors on the Underground Railroad. Tubman was the only black person and the only woman who was an abductor—someone who went into the South specifically to extract people from slavery.

2. Alice Walker, *In Search of Our Mothers' Gardens: Womanist Prose* (New York: Harcourt Brace Jovanovich, 1983), 242.

3. Mary Patillo-McCoy, *Black Picket Fences: Privilege and Peril Among the Black Middle Class* (Chicago: University of Chicago Press, 1999).

4. Definition of *fortitude, Webster's Seventh New Collegiate Dictionary,* 328.

5. Mary Frances Berry and John W. Blassingame, *Long Memory: The Black Experience in America* (New York: Oxford University Press, 1982); John W. Blassingame, *The Slave Community: Plantation Slavery in the Antebellum South* (Oxford: Oxford University Press, 1972); Herbert G. Gutman, *The Black Family in Slavery and Freedom, 1750–1925* (New York: Random House, 1976).

6. Deborah Gray White, *Ar'n't I A Woman: Female Slaves in the Plantation South* (New York: W. W. Norton and Co., 1985).

7. See also Thomas L. Webber, *Deep Like the Rivers: Education in the Slave Quarter Community, 1831–1865* (New York: W. W. Norton and Co., 1978).

8. For an understanding of Nat Turner's apocalyptic worldview and its importance for his revolutionary action, see Stephen B. Oates, *The Fires of Jubilee: Nat Turner's Fierce Rebellion* (New York: New American Library, 1975).

9. Michelle Cliff, "I Found God in Myself and I Loved Her Fiercely," *Journal of Feminist Studies in Religion* 2 (Spring 1986): 7–39.

10. William L. Andrews, ed., *Sisters of the Spirit: Three Black Women's Autobiographies of the Nineteenth Century* (Bloomington: Indiana University Press, 1986).

11. Bettye Collier-Thomas, *Daughters of Thunder: Black Women Preachers and Their Sermons, 1850–1979* (San Francisco: Jossey-Bass, 1998).

12. Dorothy Sterling, *We Are Your Sisters: Black Women in the Nineteenth Century* (New York: W. W. Norton and Co., 1984).

13. Nell Irvin Painter, *Sojourner Truth: A Life, A Symbol* (New York: W. W. Norton and Co., 1996).

14. Clinton, *Harriet Tubman*, 66–67, 213.

15. Tera Hunter, *To 'Joy My Freedom: Southern Black Women's Lives and Labors After the Civil War* (Cambridge, MA: Harvard University Press, 1997).

16. Evelyn Brooks Higginbotham, *Righteous Discontent: The Women's Movement in the Black Baptist Church, 1880–1920* (Cambridge, MA: Harvard University Press, 1993).

17. Collier-Thomas, *Daughters of Thunder*.

18. Cheryl Townsend Gilkes, *If It Wasn't for the Women: Black Women's Experience and Womanist Culture in Church and Community* (Maryknoll, NY: Orbis, 2001).

19. W. E. B. Du Bois, *The Gift of Black Folk: The Negro in the Making of America* (1924; reprint, New York: Washington Square Press, 1972).

20. Joyce A. Hanson, *Mary McLeod Bethune and Black Women's Political Activism* (Columbia: University of Missouri Press, 2003).

21. Belinda Robnett, *How Long? How Long? African American Women in the Struggle for Civil Rights* (New York: Oxford University Press, 1997).

22. For explicit discussions of black women's political activism as prophetic, see Cornel West, *Prophetic Fragments* (Grand Rapids, MI, and Trenton, NJ: William B. Eerdmanns Publishing Co. and Africa World Press, 1988); Marcia Y. Riggs, *Awake, Arise, and Act: The Womanist Call for Black Liberation* (Cleveland, OH: Pilgrim Press, 1994); Rosetta Ross, *Witnessing and Testifying: Black Women, Religion, and Civil Rights* (Minneapolis, MN: Augsburg Fortress Publishers, 2003); Judith Weisenfeld, *African American Women and Christian Activism: New York's Black YWCA, 1905–1945* (Cambridge, MA: Harvard University Press, 1998).

23. I have discussed their approach to providing human services in Cheryl Townsend Gilkes, "Successful Rebellious Professionals: The Black Woman's Professional Identity and Community Commitment," *Psychology of Women Quarterly* 6 (Spring 1982): 289–311; and Cheryl Townsend Gilkes, "Going Up for the Oppressed: The Career Mobility of Black Women Community Workers," *Journal of Social Issues* 39 (1983): 115–39.

24. For a more extended discussion of the role of missionary and evangelist in the Church of God in Christ, see Cheryl Townsend Gilkes, "'Together and in Harness': Women's Traditions in the Sanctified Church," *Signs* 11 (1985): 678–99; "The Roles of Church and Community Mothers: Ambivalent American Sexism or Fragmented African Familyhood?" *Journal of Feminist Studies in Religion* 2 (Spring 1986): 41–59; and "The Role of Women in the Sanctified Church," *Journal of Religious Thought* 43, no. 1 (Spring-Summer 1986): 24–41.

25. I later learned that she was part of a group of women who founded the church where she was a member. Although it was a Baptist church, its spiritual style was that of a Sanctified Church.

26. Du Bois, *The Gift of Black Folk*.

27. Elaine Brown, *The Condemnation of Little B* (Boston: Beacon, 2001).

Chapter 10. The Arts of Loving

A warm thanks to Lee Bernstein, Anthea Butler, R. Marie Griffith, Tracey Hucks, Barbara Dianne Savage, Valerie Smith, Margaret Vendryes, and Judith Weisenfeld for their inspiring scholarship, wise commentary, and encouragement. I am also indebted to Alison Saar, whose art never fails to summon me.

1. Gertrude "Ma" Rainey, "Louisiana Hoodoo Blues," Paramount #2138–1, recorded May 1925; reissued on *Ma Rainey: Complete Recorded Works*, vol. 2, Document Records, 1997.

2. Muddy Waters, "(I'm Your) Hoochie Coochie Man," Chess Single #1560, recorded January 7, 1954; reissued on *Muddy Waters: The Anthology*, MCA Records, 2001.

3. The Clovers, "Love Potion No. 9," United Artists Single #180, recorded August 1959; reissued on *The Very Best of the Clovers*, Rhino Entertainment Co., 1998.

4. Alison Saar, "Artist's Statement," in *New Visions: James Little, Whitfield Lovell, Alison Saar* (New York: Queens Museum, 1988), 15.

5. John Michael Vlach, *The Afro-American Tradition in Decorative Arts* (Cleveland, OH: Cleveland Museum of Art, 1978; reprint, Athens: University of Georgia Press, 1990), 108. See also "Negro's Art Lives in His Wrought Iron," *New York Times Magazine* (August 1926): 14–15; reprinted in *The Other Slaves: Mechanics, Artisans, and Craftsmen*, ed. James E. Newton and Ronald L. Lewis (Boston: G. K. Hall, 1978), 227–31. For a discussion of metal work in Africa, see Patrick McNaughton, *The Mande Blacksmiths: Knowledge, Power, and Art in West Africa* (Bloomington: Indiana University Press, 1988).

6. Vlach, *The Afro-American Tradition in Decorative Arts*, 111.

7. Judith Weisenfeld, "Marie Laveau," in *Encyclopedia of African-American Culture and History*, ed. Jack Salzman et al. (New York: Macmillan, 1996), 1581.

8. Judith Wilson, "Hexes, Totems and Necessary Saints: A Conversation with Alison Saar," *Real Life* 19 (Winter 1988–1989): 40.

9. Saar, "Artist's Statement," 14.

10. Karen McCarthy Brown, "Voodoo," in *Encyclopedia of African-American Culture and History*, 2751. Brown suggests that there may have been three generations of women called Marie Laveau, an enslaved woman brought from Haiti to Louisiana, followed by her Louisiana-born daughter and granddaughter.

11. Michel Laguerre, "Haitians," in *Encyclopedia of Southern Culture*, ed. Charles Reagan Wilson and William Ferris (Chapel Hill: University of North Carolina Press), 433.

12. Saar, "Artist's Statement," 15.

13. Zora Neale Hurston, "High John de Conquer," *American Mercury* 57 (October 1943): 452; reprinted in *The Sanctified Church: The Folklore Writings of Zora Neale Hurston* (Berkeley, CA: Turtle Island, 1981), 71. In her provocative article, Hurston argues that the slave trickster John (a.k.a. High John de Conquer) also took the form of Brer Rabbit, his animal analogue.

14. Hurston, "High John de Conquer," *The Sanctified Church*, 71–72.

15. Samella Lewis, *African American Art and Artists* (Berkeley: University of California Press, 1990), 284–85.

16. *Betye and Alison Saar: Conjure Women of the Arts,* prod. by Linda Freeman and dir. by David Irving (Chappaqua, NY: L & S Video Enterprises, 1994), videocassette.

17. Ronica Sanders Smucker, "Interview: Alison Saar," *Art Papers* 18, no. 4 (July–August 1994): 19.

18. Regenia A. Perry, "African Art and African-American Folk Art: A Stylistic and Spiritual Kinship," in *Black Art—Ancestral Legacy: The African Impulse in African-American Art,* ed. Robert Rozelle et al. (Dallas, TX: Dallas Museum of Art, 1989), 47.

19. Ibid.

20. Shari Cavin Morris, "Bessie Harvey: The Spirit in the Wood," *Clarion* 12, nos. 2–3 (1987): 45.

21. Ibid.

22. Smucker, "Interview: Alison Saar," *Art Papers,* 16.

23. Wilson, "Hexes, Totems and Necessary Saints," *Real Life,* 41.

24. *Betye and Alison Saar: Conjure Women of the Arts.*

25. Saar, "Artist's Statement," *New Visions,* 15.

26. Ibid.

27. Ibid.

28. Ibid.

29. Donna May Hatcher, "Alison Saar," *Q* (May 1991), 38.

30. Mary Nooter Roberts and Alison Saar, "Conversing Forms," in *Body Politics: The Female Image in Luba Art and the Sculpture of Alison Saar* (Los Angeles: University of California Los Angeles Fowler Museum of Cultural History, 2000), 36–38.

31. Lisa Gail Collins, *The Art of History: African American Women Artists Engage the Past* (New Brunswick, NJ: Rutgers University Press, 2002), 62. For more on Kongo *minkisi,* see Wyatt MacGaffey, "The Eyes of Understanding: Kongo *Minkisi,*" in Wyatt MacGaffey and Michael D. Harris, *Astonishment and Power: Kongo Minkisi and the Art of Renée Stout* (Washington, DC: National Museum of African Art, 1993). See also Robert Farris Thompson, "Kongo Civilization and Kongo Art," in *The Four Moments of the Sun: Kongo Art in Two Worlds,* ed. Robert Farris Thompson and Joseph Cornet (Washington, DC: National Gallery of Art, 1981).

32. The heart pierced with nails also evokes Ezili Freda, the goddess of love and ardor in *Vodou,* for Ezili is often associated with images of the heart-pierced Mater Dolorosa. See "Ezili Freda" in *Sacred Arts of Haitian Vodou,* ed. Donald J. Consentino (Los Angeles: University of California Los Angeles Fowler Museum of Cultural History, 1995), 240.

33. Kongo *minkisi* are a likely source for the related set of spirit-activated objects known in Haitian *Vodou* as *pakèt-kongo.* See Robert Farris Thompson, *Flash of the Spirit: African and Afro-American Art and Philosophy* (New York: Random House, 1983), 125–27. See also Robert Farris Thompson, "From the Isle Beneath the Sea: Haiti's Africanizing *Vodou* Art," in *Sacred Arts of Haitian Vodou,* 108–14.

34. Rusty Freeman et al., *The Art of William Edmondson* (Nashville, TN: Cheekwood Museum of Art, 1999), 196.

35. During the fall of 1937, William Edmondson became the first African American artist to have a solo show at the Museum of Modern Art.

36. Edmund L. Fuller, *Visions in Stone: The Sculpture of William Edmondson* (Pittsburgh, PA: University of Pittsburgh Press, 1973), 15–16.

37. Ibid., 14.

38. Chiori Santiago, "Private Dialogues, Shared Visions," *Museum of California* 15, no. 3 (Summer 1991): 10.

39. Thomas W. Talley, *The Negro Traditions* (1923), ed. Charles K. Wolfe and Laura C. Jarmon (Knoxville: University of Tennessee, 1993), 314.

40. Bobby L. Lovett, "From Plantation to the City: William Edmondson and the African-American Community," in *The Art of William Edmondson*, 21–22.

41. Fuller, *Visions in Stone*, 3.

42. Mark Van Proyen, "A Conversation with Betye and Alison Saar," *Artweek* 22, no. 26 (August 15, 1991): 15.

Chapter 11. *"Truths that Liberate the Soul"*

I would like to thank archivist Randy Roberts of the Special Collections and Archives Division, Leonard H. Axe Library, Pittsburg State University, for invaluable assistance with this project; and my colleagues Lisa Gail Collins, Margaret Vendryes, Valerie Smith, and Timea Szell for their comments on earlier drafts of this work. I am also grateful for Grey Osterud's insightful comments and fine editorial work on this essay.

1. Eva A. Jessye, *My Spirituals* (New York: Robbins-Engel, 1927), preface.

2. Jessye, *My Spirituals*, preface. The family name was originally spelled Jesey, but Eva changed her name to Jessye in the 1920s. Her father, Albert Jesey, was born in Texas and her mother, Julia Buckner Jesey, was born in Coffeyville, but her family had been enslaved by the Buckners in Kentucky. After her parents divorced, Jessye spent time with family members in Seattle and St. Louis. Donald Fisher Black, "The Life and Work of Eva Jessye and Her Contributions to American Music" (Ph.D. diss., University of Michigan, 1986), 18–19.

3. Jessye billed herself as such in many of her publicity materials. See "The Eva Jessye Choir: Dramatists of Negro Music," Columbia Artists, Inc., Columbia Lecture Bureau brochure, n.d., Alexander Gumby Collection of Negroania, Rare Book and Manuscript Library, Columbia University.

4. Cheryl Townsend Gilkes raises similar interpretive issues in her discussion of women's religious activism and its relationship to the institutional church in chap. 9.

5. Notable exceptions include Gayle Wald, "From Spirituals to Swing: Sister Rosetta Tharpe and Gospel Crossover," *American Quarterly* 55, no. 3 (September 2003): 387–416; Jerma Jackson, *Singing in My Soul: Black Gospel Music in a Secular Age* (Chapel Hill: University of North Carolina Press, 2004); and Rosalind Hinton, "'There Will be a Grand Concert Tonight': Alma Lillie Hubbard, the New Orleans Years, 1895–1932, Making a Life, Building a Community" (Ph.D. diss., Northwestern University, 2001).

6. Jacob U. Gordon, *Narratives of African Americans in Kansas, 1870–1992: Beyond the Exodust Movement* (Lewiston, ME: Edwin Mellen Press, 1992), 106.

7. In an interview about how she came to be hired as the choral director for the Broadway premiere of *Porgy and Bess*, Jessye described the successful audition in which she di-

rected her choir in singing "Plenty Good Room," which she characterized as "a little shout song." Jessye spoke first of having been "called" to the position of choral director as a result of the audition, indicating a sense of vocation but then said simply that she was "named" choral director. The change in terminology may have been in recognition that her listeners may not have known how to interpret her understanding of the religious import of her performance work. *Porgy and Bess: An American Voice,* written by Gloria Naylor and Nigel Noble, directed by Nigel Noble, produced by the University of Michigan in collaboration with Vanguard Films and Mojo Working Productions, 1997.

8. Additional work needs to be done on such figures as Florence Price, who arranged spirituals in addition to composing symphonic pieces; Margaret Bonds, who also arranged spirituals and collaborated with Langston Hughes on the oratorio *The Ballad of the Brown King* (1954); Evelyn Pittman, who arranged spirituals and wrote the folk opera *Cousin Esther* (1956); and Undine Smith Moore, known as an arranger of spirituals and composer of *Daniel, Daniel Servant of the Lord* (1953). See Mildred Denby Green, *Black Women Composers: A Genesis* (Boston: Twayne, 1983).

9. Paul Allen Anderson, *Deep River: Music and Memory in Harlem Renaissance Thought* (Durham, NC: Duke University Press, 2001), 2.

10. Anderson, *Deep River,* 114.

11. Jessye had rehearsal studios for her choir on West 133rd Street and on Edgecombe Avenue at 155th Street at various points during the 1920s and 1930s. She later moved her choir's headquarters briefly to Sumter, South Carolina, and then to Lawrence, Massachusetts, in both cases to follow husbands in short-lived marriages, which she apparently preferred not to discuss. The recently rediscovered James P. Johnson vocal score for Langston Hughes' 1940 blues opera *De Organizer* was found among Jessye's papers at the University of Michigan. Jessye rehearsed the choir for the sole performance at Carnegie Hall, and the only evidence that remains of Johnson's composition is Jessye's copy of the working score of the vocal lines. In 2002, James Dapogny, a music professor at the University of Michigan, used Jessye's vocal score to reconstruct Johnson's full score. See *Chicago Tribune,* December 6, 2002; *Los Angeles Times,* December 6, 2002; *New York Times,* December 28, 2002. Doris Louise Jones Wilson, "Eva Jessye: Afro-American Choral Director" (Ed.D. diss., Washington University, 1989), 47, 50.

12. "The Spiritual Heritage," n.d., folder 188, Scripts Series, Eva Jessye Collection, Axe Library Special Collections, Pittsburg State University, Pittsburg, Kansas.

13. The oratorio is a musical setting of a sacred but nonliturgical text, usually in a dramatic narrative format. The folk oratorio uses literature other than scripture for the narrative.

14. Tracing the broader implications of Jessye's contribution to the Harlem Renaissance lies beyond the scope of this short essay, but it seems clear that locating her fully within this broad cultural movement would force a reevaluation of its scope as well as interrogate the marginalization of black engagements with European classical music in scholarly studies of the Harlem Renaissance. That Jessye's work has attracted so little scholarly attention speaks not only to the small group of African Americans who receive attention in the study of American history but also to the entrenchment of particular understandings of black cultural authenticity in the field of African American studies which categorize black classical music as inauthentic.

15. Eileen Southern, *The Music of Black Americans: A History,* 2d ed. (New York: W. W. Norton and Co., 1983), 266.

16. Black, "The Life and Work of Eva Jessye," 22, 24.

17. *Exoduster* is a term for African Americans who migrated from the South to Kansas in the late 1870s. See Nell Irvin Painter, *Exodusters: Black Migration to Kansas Following Reconstruction* (Lawrence: University of Kansas Press, 1986).

18. Eva Jessye to Gene DeGruson, August 3, 1977, quoted in Wilson, "Eva Jessye: Afro-American Choral Director," 117.

19. Jessye, *My Spirituals,* preface. Despite the strong case that Jessye made for the possibility of locating "authentic" spirituals in black communities outside the Deep South, some were not so easily persuaded. When Dr. Hugo Riesenfeld, music director at the Rialto and other New York movie theaters and later music director for various Hollywood studio films, asked Jessye, as an "authority on negro music," to help him with the score for the Universal Pictures 1927 production of *Uncle Tom's Cabin,* he asked her to go South to "unearth" songs. The *New York Times* reported that "in the course of her visits among negro cotton field workers Miss Jessye heard them chanting unfamiliar songs, which on investigation she learned had been handed down by their parents and grandparents." Riesenfeld used Jessye's arrangement of "Sold Away to Georgia" as the film's theme song, and her choir later performed this song on a regular basis (*New York Times,* October 30, 1927).

20. Jessye, *My Spirituals,* preface. The songs she included in the volume are "Who is Dat Yondah?," "Spirit o' the Lord Done Fell on Me," "An' I Cry," "Bles' My Soul an' Gone," "I Been 'Buked an' I Been Scorned," "Stan' Steady," "Ain't Got Long to Stay Heah," "March Down to Jerdon," "John Saw de Holy Numbah," "I'm a Po' Li'l Orphan," "When Moses Smote de Water," "So I Can Write My Name," "I Can't Stay Away," "Tall Angel at the Bar," "Got a Home at Las'," and "I'se Mighty Tired."

21. That the singer Rufus Gibson used Jessye's arrangements of spirituals alongside songs by Beethoven, Brahms, and Fauré in a 1941 program at Carnegie Hall gives some sense of the impact of her published collection. See *New York Times,* October 12, 1941. There are conflicting accounts about what led Jessye to publish *My Spirituals.* Doris Wilson writes that, when seeking advice on compositional theory, Jessye shared a draft of her arrangements with the music theorist and composer Percy Goetschius in 1926. Wilson also indicates that Will Marion Cook used his influence in 1927 to persuade the music publisher Robbins-Engel to commission Jessye to do a collection, a job she was happy to take because she was in desperate need of money. Wilson reports that Jessye completed the work in a few weeks. It is not clear whether the material Jessye shared with Goetschius is the same as what was published as *My Spirituals* the following year. See Doris Louise Jones Wilson, "Eva Jessye: Afro-American Choral Director," 27–28.

22. Influential collections of spirituals that preceded Jessye's include John Wesley Work, *Folk Songs of the American Negro* (Nashville, TN: Fisk University Press, 1914); Harry T. Burleigh, *Negro Spirituals Arranged for Solo Voice* (New York: C. Picardi, 1917–1925); and James Weldon Johnson and J. Rosamond Johnson, *The Book of American Negro Spirituals* (New York: Viking, 1925). On the distinctiveness of African American folk songs, John W. Work wrote: "The very foundation of this music is of the Negro's building. The scale is peculiarly his own, and consequently satisfies his nature. Through it this nature manifests it-

self to the world. The spirit of music is a common possession which takes outward form according to the nature of the possessor. The Negro in his primitive nature expressed his musical scale 1-2-3-4-5-6. Why? That was all the world meant to him. But the American Negro has gone one step further and added one more note, flat seven, an addition which goes a long way toward expressing the effect of added experience brought to him by a new life in a New World. This flat seven expresses a wild and overwhelming surprise at the utter strangeness of things . . . The folk song of the American Negro, then, is characterized by the elements of religion, rhythm, syncopation, spontaneity, and the sexatonic scale with the flat seven expressing surprise and the absence of any feeling of hatred or revenge" (*Folk Songs of the American Negro,* 42).

23. Dr. Melville Charlton, review of *My Spirituals, New York Amsterdam News,* June 8, 1927. By this time, Charlton, a graduate of City College in New York and Howard University, had served as organist at Union Theological Seminary and at a number of synagogues in the city. He was the first African American to pass the examinations to become a member of the American Guild of Organists. See Joseph J. Boris, ed., *Who's Who in Colored America* (New York: Who's Who in Colored America Corp., 1927), 40.

24. Paul Robeson to Eva A. Jessye, September 21, 1927, f. 11, Correspondence Series, Eva Jessye Collection. The Special Collections and Archives Division of Emory University's Robert W. Woodruff Library holds Robeson's personal copy of *My Spirituals,* which contains his annotations on "An' I Cry." The Eva Jessye Choir performed with Robeson and the New York Philharmonic at Lewisohn Stadium in 1941, where they presented "And They Lynched Him on a Tree" and "Ballad for Americans"; reports indicate that 14,000 people attended the concert. The choir, Robeson, and the New York Philharmonic also performed together in Newark in a program featuring "Ballad For Americans," which was attended by 23,000. See *New York Times,* April 6, 1941; June 24, 1941.

25. Wilson, "Eva Jessye: Afro-American Choral Director," 130–31. The major scale has eight notes separated by a whole step, with the exception of the III–IV steps and the VII–VIII steps, which are separated by a half step. In the key of C, for example, the major scale contains C-D-E-F-G-A-B-C. The pentatonic scale is made up of five notes spread across an octave and may be major or minor. Typically, the major pentatonic scale differs from the major scale in that the IV and VII degrees are absent. The minor pentatonic scale consists of I bIII IV V bVII VIII (with b representing a flat note).

26. Here, Wilson has identified a number of strategies that Jessye used, including: "mild dissonances, chords foreign to the usual I, IV, V progressions, a tone added to a chord, chromatic alteration, or the juxtaposition of both raised and lowered third" ("Eva Jessye: Afro-American Choral Director," 136).

27. Syncopated rhythms place the accent on the weak beats of the measure. Triplets are three notes of equal length that are performed within the time of two beats.

28. *Opportunity* (November 1927). Jessye's collection was reviewed in the *New York Times* along with James Weldon Johnson's poetic sermons in *God's Trombones* (New York: Viking, 1927). Both Bennett and the *Times* reviewer noted the contribution to the book's success of the illustrations by "Millar of the Roland Company." I have been unable to find any biographical information on the artist (*New York Times,* June 19, 1927).

29. Jessye, *My Spirituals,* 19. Jessye does not provide any additional information about

her parents' disinterest in religion, or about the apparent religious interests of members of her extended family. In talking about her upbringing in an interview later in life, she emphasized the community context of religious life. "From the time I was a child, I was surrounded by church people. You sang religious songs; we condoned only religious practices. And we did not gamble; we did not swear—one thing we did though, we did dance. We did dance and sing" (Gordon, *Narratives of African Americans in Kansas*, 106).

30. Jessye, *My Spirituals*, 23.

31. Ibid., 69.

32. *Opportunity* (November 1927).

33. Membership in Jessye's groups shifted a great deal over the years, as she employed anywhere from four to more than fifteen singers. In some promotional material, she characterizes the group's members as "for the most part Southern born and college bred." The following singers appear most frequently in programs and newspaper clippings about Jessye's groups in the 1920s through 1940s: Roger Alford, Edward Nathaniel Broadnax, Viviande Carr, Lucille Dixon, Jester Hairston, Pernell Hall, G. Willard MacLean, Helen Dowdy (Moore), William O'Neill, Philip Patterson, Annabell Ross, Carl Taylor, Eloise Uggams, and James Watkins. Helen Dowdy was a featured singer in the original Broadway production of *Porgy and Bess* and in a number of revivals, and had parts in the original Broadway productions of *Mamba's Daughters* (1939), *Cabin in the Sky* (1940), and *Kiss Me, Kate* (1950). See, e.g., the program for "Negro Lore in Music and Dance" by Eva Jessye and Her Eva Jessye Choir and Folklore Ensemble with Ismay Andrews, March 3, 1933, Clipping File, Schomburg Center for Research in Black Culture, New York; *New York Times*, February 11, 1928; program for a performance at Calvary Baptist Church, New York City, June 7, 1927, and program for "Negro Music of Three Centuries," n.d., reproduced in Wilson, "Eva Jessye: Afro-American Choral Director," 172–73.

34. Wilson, "Eva Jessye: Afro-American Choral Director," 13.

35. Helen Walker-Hill, *From Spirituals to Symphonies: African-American Women Composers and Their Music* (Westport, CT: Greenwood, 2002), 18.

36. Black, "The Life and Work of Eva Jessye," 25; Wilson, "Eva Jessye: Afro-American Choral Director," 18–20.

37. See, e.g., *New York Times*, October 11, 1925. Many recent biographical sketches list Jessye as the founder of a group called the Original Dixie Jubilee Singers, but, with few exceptions, contemporary references refer to it as the Dixie Jubilee Singers. There was an early twentieth-century group that performed on the Chautauqua circuit under the name Williams' Original Dixie Jubilee Singers, but Jessye had no connection to it. Jessye also worked as a proofreader and then writer for the *Baltimore Afro-American* during this period.

38. On the Capitol Theatre appearances, see *New York Times*, February 28, 1926; March 21, 1926; April 10, 1927. Impresario Major Edward Bowes managed New York City's Capitol Theatre and, beginning in 1922, presented the *Family Radio Hour*. This show later became the *Major Bowes Original Amateur Hour* radio show and launched a number of new stars, including Frank Sinatra. On *Aunt Mandy's Chillun* and *Four Dusty Travelers*, see *New York Times*, July 14, 1929; August 18, 1929; September 8, 1929; October 11, 1929; December 26, 1929; January 16, 1930; January 23, 1930; April 4, 1930; and the *Pittsburgh*

Courier, April 23, 1932. In 1934 New York City's WOR became the flagship station for the newly launched Mutual Broadcasting System.

39. The *Pittsburgh Courier,* September 15, 1928, published a drawing by Aaron Douglas that celebrated the work of Jessye and the Dixie Jubilee Singers. Douglas's image represented the three principal genres in which the singers worked: blues, spirituals, and work songs. The group used this image on some of its publicity materials in this period.

40. Jessye wrote and published poetry throughout her career. A number of her poems are included in Robert T. Kerlin, *Negro Poets and Their Poems* (Washington, DC: Associated Publishers, 1923), in a chapter with other female poets, including Alice Dunbar-Nelson, Georgia Douglas Johnson, Angelina W. Grimké, Anne Spencer, and Jessie Fauset. One of these poems, "The Singer" (from which the title of this essay is taken) was reproduced in Jessye's *My Spirituals.*

41. Program for "Negro Lore in Music and Dance"; *New York Times,* February 23, 1933. The program describes Andrews as "a native of Lagos, Nigeria, and of pure African extraction. She has spent practically all her life in America and is highly educated. Forsook career as trained nurse for the stage. An artist in Negro folk expression." Prior to her collaboration with Jessye, Andrews appeared in *The Black King,* directed by Bud Pollard (Southland Pictures, 1932), a satire of Marcus Garvey's activities in Harlem. Zora Neale Hurston had produced a similar theatrical review, *The Great Day,* which premiered on Broadway in 1932 and which she later revised as *From Sun to Sun.* The production featured Bahamian dances, in addition to African American spirituals and secular songs.

42. Over the years various configurations of the group also performed under the names Lincoln Jubilee Singers, the Ebonnaires, and the American Concert Ensemble.

43. See, e.g., *New York Times,* April 10, 1927; June 4, 1927. Program for a performance at Calvary Baptist Church, New York City, June 7, 1927, and program for "Negro Music of Three Centuries," n.d., reproduced in Wilson, "Eva Jessye: Afro-American Choral Director," 172–73.

44. See *Dixie Jubilee Singers: Complete Recorded Works in Chronological Order, 1924–1928* (Document Records, 1996); *Dixie Jubilee Singers: Complete Recorded Works in Chronological Order, 1928–1931* (Document Records, 1996). These recordings contain all releases in this period by groups under the name Dixie Jubilee Singers. According to the producers of this compilation, there is evidence that not all of these were Jessye's groups and that tracks by the Birmingham Jubilee Singers were released under the name Dixie Jubilee Singers. Part of the confusion arises from the varied styles in the arrangements of the spirituals, but the producers of the collection concede that Jessye may have been versatile enough as an arranger and conductor to have directed most of these recordings. Having had access to other textual materials about Jessye's career and to some of her published and unpublished compositions and arrangements, I am convinced that she did not seek to present a uniform style in the performances of her ensembles and choruses.

45. Some of the recordings of the Four Dusty Travelers have been collected on *Vocal Quartets, Vol. 2: D/E/F/G* (Document Records, 1997) and *Black Secular Vocal Groups, Vol. 3: 1923–1940* (Document Records, 1998).

46. *Hallelujah,* dir. by King Vidor (MGM, 1929). The other film with an all-black cast released earlier that year was Fox's *Hearts in Dixie,* directed by Paul Sloane.

47. Wilson, "Eva Jessye: Afro-American Choral Director," 22–39; Black, "The Life and Work of Eva Jessye," 29–47.

48. Jessye published her arrangement of "E-I-O" for SATB (soprano, alto, tenor, and bass) with piano accompaniment in 1965 and wrote that she had learned the song in Oklahoma ("E-I-O," adapted by Eva Jessye, edited by Julian Work [New York: Skidmore Music Company, 1965]). The lyrics and Negro spiritual arrangement of the Largo movement from Antonin Dvořák's 1893 *Symphony From the New World* was published by William Arms Fisher in 1922.

49. *New York Times,* June 4, 1927; February 19, 1928; March 4, 1928; February 14, 1934; *Pittsburgh Courier,* February 21, 1931. On Straton and the cultural politics of religion in New York City in this period, see J. Terry Todd, "New York, the New Babylon? Fundamentalism and the Modern City in Reverend Straton's Jazz Age Crusade," in *Faith in the Market: Religion and the Rise of Urban Commercial Culture,* ed. John M. Giggie and Diane H. Winston (New Brunswick, NJ: Rutgers University Press, 2002).

50. *Pittsburgh Courier,* February 21, 1931.

51. Thomas J. Noonan, known as "the Bishop of Chinatown," served as the society's superintendent from 1904. Beginning in the fall of 1926, the Rescue Society broadcast its services as a "Radio Mass Meeting" on WMCA, featuring choirs and ministers from a variety of churches, including a number of African American congregations, including Abyssinian Baptist Church and Salem Methodist Episcopal Church. See, e.g., *New York Times,* December 6, 1914; April 26, 1919; January 10, 1925; November 25, 1925; October 2, 1926; October 30, 1926; November 7, 1926; April 16, 1927.

52. Jessye, *My Spirituals,* 4.

53. Gordon, *Narratives of African Americans in Kansas,* 107.

54. Wilson, "Eva Jessye: Afro-American Choral Director," 51.

55. *New York Times,* January 17, 1926.

56. Zora Neale Hurston, "Spirituals and Neo-Spirituals," in *Negro: An Anthology,* ed. Nancy Cunard, abridged by Hugh Ford (1934; reprint, New York: Continuum, 1996), 224.

57. Hurston, "Spirituals and Neo-Spirituals," 224.

58. On Hurston, spirituals, and folk culture, see, e.g., Hazel Carby, "The Politics of Fiction, Anthropology, and the Folk: Zora Neale Hurston," in *History and Memory in African American Culture,* ed. Geneviève Fabre and Robert O'Meally (New York: Oxford University Press, 1994); John Trombold, "The Minstrel Show Goes to the Great War: Zora Neale Hurston's Mass Cultural Other," *MELUS* 24, no. 1 (Spring 1999): 85–107; Leigh Ann Duck, "'Go there tuh *know* there': Zora Neale Hurston and the Chronotype of the Folk," *American History* 13, no. 2 (Spring 2001): 265–94.

59. Alain Locke, *The Negro and His Music* (Port Washington, NY: Kennikat Press, 1968), 22–23.

60. About the potential of Jessye's work to assist with such a project, Locke wrote: "The younger Negro musicians [including] Eva Jessye, while they have written effective solo versions, are turning with increasing interest to the choral form. Herein lies the significance of the newer types of Negro choral choir that are beginning to appear or re-appear, among them the excellent choral organizations led by Eva Jessye and Hall Johnson. They have

about restored the spirituals to their primitive choral basis and their original singing style. Developed along the lines of its own originality, we may expect a development of Negro folk song that may equal or even outstrip the phenomenal choral music of Russia" (*The Negro and His Music,* 24). See Anderson, *Deep River,* chap. 3, for more on Locke and African American music.

61. Tracey Hucks (chap. 2) addresses debates about religious authenticity in Trinidad, exploring the contested relationship between Yoruba traditions and Roman Catholicism. Although Jessye's work and that of women in contemporary Trinidad are separated by time and space, both reveal complex negotiations of diasporic religious identities.

62. Hurston, "Spirituals and Neo-Spirituals," 223.

63. The Eva Jessye Choir, Town Hall Program, October 28, 1948. Alexander Gumby Collection of Negroania, Rare Book and Manuscript Library, Columbia University.

64. Souvenir Program for Eva Jessye's American Concert Ensemble, March 17, 1957, Clipping File, Schomburg Center for Research in Black Culture, New York.

65. As part of his dissertation research, Donald Black sent questionnaires to forty-seven of Jessye's friends, colleagues, students, and choir members to obtain a sense of her working style and received twenty-seven responses. Black reported that, as he began his research, he "speculated on how difficult it must have been for Jessye to work with solo caliber voices to achieve any kind of vocal blend and uniformity of tonal production, as well as many other aspects which lead to successful choral singing . . . The majority of respondents (50 percent) felt that Jessye used a combination of drill and critical comment to achieve blend with her group. There were also written comments which mentioned that she demonstrated what she wanted the choir members to do and how to do it, for tone production and diction. Of course there were other factors which undoubtedly were at work, including Jessye's skills at group motivation, the development of the group's sensitivity to pitch, and her conducting skills. Many of Jessye's reviews comment on the precision of the attacks and releases of her group" ("The Life and Work of Eva Jessye," 126).

66. Souvenir Program for Eva Jessye's American Concert Ensemble, March 17, 1957.

67. Notes on "Three Tears," reproduced in Wilson, "Eva Jessye: Afro-American Choral Director," 187. The notes do not include the lyrics or music for this song, and I have not been able to locate any additional information about it except that Jessye wrote the arrangement her choir performed.

68. *Detroit News,* January 12, 1939, quoted in Black, "The Life and Work of Eva Jessye," 41.

69. A number of chapters in this collection pursue related questions about religion and embodiment that are useful for considering Jessye's approach to the way the body conveys theological commitments; see the editor's discussion in the introduction, as well as the essays by Lisa Gail Collins (chap. 10), Rachel Harding (chap. 1), and Carolyn Rouse (chap. 12).

70. Interviews with Jessye, September 11, 1982, and September 10, 1983, quoted in Wilson, "Eva Jessye: Afro-American Choral Director," 19, 20.

71. According to John Houseman, who directed the original production of *Four Saints in Three Acts,* the composer Virgil Thomson hired Jessye and her choir rather than Hall Johnson's choir because of Jessye's "high musical standard" and the choir's ability to learn

the music from reading the score. See John Houseman, *Run-Through: A Memoir* (New York: Simon and Schuster, 1972), 105, quoted in Wilson, "Eva Jessye: Afro-American Choral Director," 33–34.

72. Percy Goetschius to Eva Jessye, August 25, 1926; April 16, 1927; September 11, 1932; Eugene Ormandy to Eva Jessye, April 10, 1927; Leopold Stokowski to Eva Jessye, May 13, 1942; f. 11, Correspondence Series, Eva Jessye Collection. Quoted in Black, "The Life and Work of Eva Jessye," 135–37; *New York Times*, April 12, 1942. Jessye had the opportunity for her choir to appear in the premiere of Still's work but apparently required more money than the producers could afford. See Wayne D. Shirley, "William Grant Still's Choral Ballad *And They Lynched Him on a Tree*," *American Music*, 12, no. 4 (Winter 1994): 425–61.

73. Although in the early years the Jubilee Singers sometimes wore church robes, Jessye generally dressed her choirs in formal concert wear, with the men wearing tuxedos and the women full-length white dresses. This formal attire emphasized the choir's connections to the broader American concert scene.

74. Many of the performances of the Eva Jessye Choir took place at venues in New York City, but the choir also traveled frequently and appeared, e.g., in Buffalo; Chicago; Dallas; Detroit; Memphis; Washington, D.C.; Manhattan, Kansas; Boston and Lawrence, Massachusetts; Moorehead and Minneapolis, Minnesota; Fayetteville, Raleigh, Durham, and Greensboro, North Carolina; and Wheeling, West Virginia. See Black, "The Life and Work of Eva Jessye," 49–61.

75. The Eva Jessye Choir first performed *The Chronicle of Job* at Town Hall in New York City in 1948. The Eva Jessye Choir, Town Hall Program; *New York Times*, October 29, 1948.

76. I am relying upon the libretto/score from a 1979 production that Jessye directed at Pittsburg State University while she was the university's artist-in-residence, which indicates that she secured copyright in 1963; see *The Chronicle of Job (The Story of the Most Patient Man in Biblical History)*, September 30, 1979, McCray Hall, Pittsburg State University, Libretto and Choral Settings by Eva Jessye; Instrumental Music by Reginald Beane, f. 171, Scripts Series, Eva Jessye Collection.

77. Jessye, *The Chronicle of Job*, 5.

78. Beane's piano accompaniment for the piece differs considerably from Jessye's pared-down and simple compositional style. In his portions of the score Beane presents long sections of continuous eight notes, some in dramatic intervals and others in closer chromatic relation, which contrast with Jessye's economical approach.

79. "Simon, The Fisherman," for Mixed Voices (As Sung by the Eva Jessye Choir), transcribed by Eva Jessye (Summy-Birchard Co., 1947). In this *a capella* piece, Jessye alternates between a syncopated rhythmic recitation in unison and choral singing. With regard to the direction in *Job* to sing in "half tone," Jessye likely meant something similar to what Arnold Schoenberg termed *Sprechstimme*, a style of vocalization which lies between speaking and singing. Schoenberg used *Sprechstimme* in such pieces as *Pierrot Lunaire* (1912) and *A Survivor From Warsaw* (1947).

80. Jessye, *The Chronicle of Job*, 14.

81. Ibid., 6.

82. Ibid., 7.

83. In her survey of Jessye's secular and religious compositions, Wilson finds the use

of call-and-response and the variety in the voices leading the call to be notable characteristics of Jessye's work ("Eva Jessye: Afro-American Choral Director," 140).

84. See, e.g., Lawrence Levine, *Black Culture and Black Consciousness: Afro-American Folk Thought From Slavery to Freedom* (New York: Oxford University Press, 1977).

85. Jessye, *The Chronicle of Job*, 7.

86. An undated holiday greeting card from the Eva Jessye Choir "to friends throughout the world" advertises a Christmas day broadcast of "Baltasar, the Black Magus" on NBC radio and lists well-known stage (and, later, screen) actor Frank Wilson in the part of Baltasar (Clipping File, Schomburg Center for Research in Black Culture, New York). Jessye and Wilson appeared together in 1933 in the radio play of Octavus Roy Cohen's "The Townsend Murder Mystery," broadcast on WJZ; see *Chicago Defender*, April 21, 1933.

87. Eva Jessye, *The Story of Baltazar, The Black Magus* (1932), f. 182, Scripts Series, Eva Jessye Collection. In the title of the script Jessye spelled the name Baltazar, but it appears as Baltasar throughout the text.

88. Jessye wrote at least two other versions of the story: *The Story of the Black Wise Man* (1959), which also survives only as a fragment, and *Follow the Star of Bethlehem* (ca. 1954); see *The Story of the Black Wise Man* (1959), f. 183l; and *Follow the Star of Bethlehem* (n.d.), f. 172, Scripts Series, Eva Jessye Collection. *Follow the Star* was performed in 1954 by the Young Adult Group of the Lawrence, Massachusetts, Greater Council of Churches. *The Story of the Black Wise Man* was presented in 1959 at the Antioch Baptist Church of Brooklyn. See program for "The Story of the Black Wise Man," December 20, 1959, Clipping File, Schomburg Center for Research in Black Culture.

89. Jessye, *The Story of Baltazar*.

90. The group performed this piece at the Church of the Good Shepherd (Presbyterian), at Grace Chapel (Episcopal) in New York, and on Good Friday on NBC Radio (WJZ New York), in the spring of 1932. *New York Times*, April 4, 1932; May 8, 1932; *Pittsburgh Courier*, April 23, 1932. The script in the Eva Jessye Collection at Pittsburgh State University is undated but is likely a later version than that performed in 1932 since it contains a reference to Albert Hay Malotte's "The Beatitudes," published in 1938.

91. However, the Eva Jessye Choir did perform the oratorio again in 1955 and in 1959. See Black, "The Life and Work of Eva Jessye," 54–55.

92. Jessye wrote "Lucifer, Son of the Morning" and "That Ancient City on the Seven Hills."

93. There is no script for the original version of the oratorio in Jessye's papers at Pittsburg State University or in the catalogue of her papers at the University of Michigan. The script and score with which I am working date from a 1978 production that Jessye directed at Pittsburg State University (f. 141–45, Eva Jessye Collection). Other performances include one at Allen AME Church in Jamaica, New York, in 1935 and another in Manchester, New Hampshire, in 1955. Jessye's *Paradise Lost and Regained* was also televised in the 1950s on WBZ (Boston) in its "Our Believing World" series and was performed at the Washington Cathedral in 1972. Regarding the length of Jessye's concert presentations, her friend blues singer Victoria Spivey joked, "If I know Miss Jessye, her program is 10 hours and 15 minutes" (folder 13, Victoria Spivey Papers, Special Collections and Archives, Robert W. Woodruff Library, Emory University).

94. *Washington Post,* July 9, 1972, quoted in Wilson, "Eva Jessye: Afro-American Choral Director," 36. Jessye used the work of the American author Stephen Vincent Benét for her *Western Star,* which she described as "a panorama of American music" and "tonal pictures of the American scene." The Eva Jessye Collection at Pittsburg State University contains multiple fragments of scripts of this piece, one dated 1955, another 1976, and others undated. See *Western Star,* f. 187, Scripts Series, Eva Jessye Collection; and program for "The Eva Jessye Choir presents 'Western Star,'" November 11, 1966, reproduced in Wilson, "Eva Jessye: Afro-American Choral Director," 179–80.

95. *Paradise Lost and Regained, A Folk Oratorio* (John Milton/Eva Jessye), f. 141–45, Scripts Series, Eva Jessye Collection. The Antiguan-born author Jamaica Kincaid was also influenced by Milton's *Paradise Lost* but, unlike Jessye, found Milton's complex character Lucifer particularly compelling. She named the title character in her 1990 novel *Lucy* for Milton's Lucifer. See, e.g., Diane Simmons, "Jamaica Kincaid and the Canon: In Dialogue with *Paradise Lost* and *Jane Eyre,*" *MELUS* 23, no. 2 (Summer 1998): 65–85.

96. Joan Reinthaler, "Folk Oratorio at Cathedral," *Washington Post,* July 12, 1972, quoted in Wilson, "Eva Jessye: Afro-American Choral Director," 57. Jessye received honorary doctorate degrees from the University of Michigan and Wilberforce University.

97. Jessye, *Paradise Lost,* 7; book 3, lines 213–14, in Milton's *Paradise Lost.* Lucifer is a complex and active figure in Milton's work, but he appears almost exclusively in deflected ways in Jessye's oratorio. She introduces him through her own composition, "Lucifer, Son of the Morning," and he speaks for himself only near the oratorio's end when he tempts Jesus. Her song builds on Isaiah 14:12: "How art thou fallen from heaven, O Lucifer, son of the morning! how art thou cut down to the ground, which didst weaken the nations!" In this piece, Jessye does not simply declare Lucifer fallen, as in the biblical text, but, in the mournful key of D minor, has the singer inquire of Lucifer why he appears downcast and disquieted, thus preserving a bit of Milton's character.

98. Jessye, *Paradise Lost,* 7; book 3, lines 235–41, in Milton's *Paradise Lost.*

99. Jessye, *Paradise Lost,* 16; book 4, lines 595–99, 608, 613–614, in Milton's *Paradise Regained.*

100. Jacqueline Grant, *White Woman's Christ, Black Woman's Jesus* (Atlanta, GA: Scholar's Press, 1989), argues that this emphasis on Jesus' humanity and the resulting identification with the suffering of black people is characteristic of black women's theological perspectives.

101. "Comment on 'Paradise Lost and Regained,'" in program, n.d., Clipping File, Schomburg Center for Research in Black Culture.

102. The Eva Jessye Choir sang her composition "Freedom is a Thing Worth Talking About" (unpublished, 1944). The only other musical selection in the march's official program, aside from Marian Anderson's leading the national anthem, was offered by Mahalia Jackson.

103. In an interview late in her life, Jessye spoke of the sacrifices that her mother, her aunt, and her uncle made to send her to college. While in college, she recalled, her "Aunt May wrote, 'Eva, I'm sending you your class dues. Your uncle will do without shoes so you can get them paid.' There he was, only an uncle by marriage and a plain, laboring man

from Alabama who could hardly write his own name. When people have that much confidence in you, you can't fail them" (*New York Times,* October 7, 1979).

104. Jessye was interested in African American women's history, and among her scripts that did not deal with religious subjects is a tribute to Ida B. Wells. On black Baptist women and feminist theology, see Evelyn Brooks Higginbotham, *Righteous Discontent: The Women's Movement in the Black Baptist Church, 1880–1920* (Cambridge, MA: Harvard University Press, 1993).

105. Eva Jessye, "Chorus Girl Has Helped Glorify Modern Woman," *Pittsburgh Courier,* August 25, 1928. In many ways this piece reads as Jessye's defense of her own decision to go into stage work, and in it she labors to counter the image of the chorus girl as lacking in character. She tells the story of her experience working as a piano player in a small town in the Southwest and of the chorus girls who performed on the T.O.B.A. (Theater Owners' Booking Association) circuit. Their dances may have appeared risqué, she writes, but backstage, the women "spoke of church, books, [and] classics."

106. Wilson, "Eva Jessye: Afro-American Choral Director," 29.

107. Robert T. Kerlin, *Negro Poets and Their Poems* (Washington, DC: Associated Publishers, 1923), 69.

108. James A. Standifer, "Reminiscences of Black Musicians," *American Music,* 4, no. 2 (Summer 1986): 194–205.

Chapter 12. Shopping with Sister Zubayda

Epigraph: Hijab means a head covering and modest dress. *Hadith* is a record of the words and deeds of the Prophet Muhammad. Aisha was the Prophet Muhammad's youngest wife. Bukhari is an authoritative source for *hadith.* Zubayda is a pseudonym for one of the African American Sunni Muslim women whom I interviewed in depth during my research on black women and Islam in contemporary America. During the ten years I lived and worked in Los Angeles, I visited the homes of over 200 lower-middle-class African American Muslims. This essay features Zubayda, not because she is "typical" of the women I interviewed, but because she is an extremely articulate representative of this group and is widely respected among her peers. For a description of the fieldwork and methods, see Carolyn Rouse, *Engaged Surrender: African-American Women and Islam* (Berkeley: University of California Press, 2004).

1. See Michele Lamont and Virag Molnar, "How Blacks Use Consumption to Shape Their Collective Identity," Journal of Consumer Culture 1 (2001): 31–45; Gary S. Becker, *Accounting for Tastes* (Cambridge, MA: Harvard University Press, 1996); Mike Featherstone, *Consumer Culture and Postmodernism* (Newbury Park, CA: Sage, 1991); Stanley Lebergott, *Pursuing Happiness: American Consumers in the Twentieth Century* (Princeton: Princeton University

Press, 1993); Donald N. McCloskey, "The Economics of Choice," in *Economics for Historians*, ed. Thomas G. Rawski et al. (Berkeley: University of California Press, 1996).

2. Umberto Eco describes the symbolic function of goods as entailing "a posited correlation between content and expression"; see Eco, "On the contribution of film to semiotics," in *Film Theory and Criticism*, ed. Gerald Mast and Marshall Cohen (New York: Oxford University Press, 1985), 196. The second dimension to which I refer here is the material function of goods: how an object is produced, exchanged, and used, and thus how it authors social relations. See Pierre Bourdieu, *Distinction: A Social Critique of the Judgement of Taste*, ed. Richard Nice (Cambridge, MA: Harvard University Press, 1984); Wolfgang Haug, *Critique of Commodity Aesthetics: Appearance, Sexuality, and Advertising in Capitalist Society* (Minneapolis: University of Minnesota Press, 1986); Webb Keane, "Semiotics and the Social Analysis of Material Things," *Language and Communication* 23 (2003): 409–25; Karl Marx, *The Marx-Engels Reader*, ed. Robert C. Tucker (New York: W. W. Norton and Co., 1978), 302–29; Marilyn Strathern, *The Gender of the Gift: Problems with Women and Problems with Society in Melanesia* (Berkeley: University of California Press, 1988); and Thorstein Veblen, *The Theory of the Leisure Class* (New York: Macmillan, 1912).

3. Mike Davis, *City of Quartz: Excavating the Future in Los Angeles* (New York: Vintage, 1990), 257.

4. This is only one conceptualization and representation of Islam; Imam Saadiq, a prominent African American imam in Los Angeles, presented this interpretation at a masjid in Los Angeles in 2002.

5. Fatima Mernissi, *The Veil and the Male Elite: A Feminist Interpretation of Women's Rights in Islam*, trans. Mary Jo Lakeland (Reading, MA: Addison Wesley, 1991), 27–28.

6. Sura 4:34: "Men are the protectors and maintainers of women, because Allah has given the one more (strength) than the other, and because they support them from their means. Therefore the righteous women are devoutly obedient, and guard in (the husband's) absence what Allah would have them guard. As to those women on whose part ye fear disloyalty and ill-conduct, admonish them (first), (next), refuse to share their beds, (and last) beat them lightly; but if they return to obedience, seek not against them means (of annoyance): for Allah is Most High, Great (above you all)" (*The Holy Qur'an*, 1405 AH The Presidency of Islamic Researches, IFTA, ed. Al-Madinah Al-Munawarah [Saudi Arabia: King Fahd Holy Qur'an Printing Complex, 1405 AH]). Also see Maulana Muhammad Ali, *The Religion of Islam* (Lahore: Ahmadiyya Anjuman Isha'at Islam, 1990), 444–508. For more information on the role of women, see Mernissi, *The Veil and the Male Elite*, and Amina Wadud-Muhsin, *Qur'an and Woman* (Kuala Lumpur: Penerbit Fajar Bakti Snd. Bhd., 1995).

7. Elijah Muhammed, *Message to the Blackman in America* (Chicago: Muhammad's Mosque of Islam No. 2, 1965); Elijah Muhammad, *How to Eat to Live* (Chicago: Muhammad's Temple of Islam No. 2, 1967, and Muhammad's Mosque of Islam No. 2, 1972); and *Muhammad Speaks* (Muhammad's Mosque of Islam, No. 2 Chicago, IL, 1960–1975).

8. Talal Asad, *Formations of the Secular: Christianity, Islam, Modernity* (Stanford, CA: Stanford University Press, 2003); Mary Douglas and Baron Isherwood, *The World of Goods: Towards an Anthropology of Consumption* (New York: Routledge, 1996); and Carolyn Rouse and Janet Hoskins, "Purity, Soul Food, and Islam: Explorations at the Intersection of Consumption and Resistance," *Cultural Anthropology* 19, no. 2 (2004): 226–49.

9. Talal Asad, in *Formations of the Secular,* 13, asserts that secularism "employs prolif-erating technologies (of production, warfare, travel, entertainment, medicine) that gener-ate new experiences of space and time, of cruelty and health, of consumption and knowl-edge."

10. Many African American Muslims were never members of the Nation of Islam and therefore never made this transition. But the Sunni community in Los Angeles grew, to a large extent, out of the Nation of Islam, so when I paint a picture of the history of the com-munity using broad strokes, I refer to the Nation's history. See Aminah Beverly McCloud, *African American Islam* (New York: Routledge, 1995), and Claude Andrew Clegg, *An Orig-inal Man: The Life and Times of Elijah Muhammad* (New York: St. Martin's Griffin, 1997).

11. The Prophet Muhammad's last sermon is often used to clarify the community's po-sition on race: "All mankind is from Adam and Eve, an Arab has no superiority over a non-Arab nor a non-Arab has any superiority over an Arab; also a white has no superiority over a black nor a black has any superiority over a white—except by piety and good action." This quotation is found in a pamphlet distributed at the masjid where I conducted the majority of my research.

12. R. Marie Griffith, *God's Daughters: Evangelical Women and the Power of Submission* (Berkeley: University of California Press, 1997), 16.

13. Gary Peller, "Race Consciousness," in *Critical Race Theory,* ed. Kimberle Crenshaw, Neil Gotanda, Gary Peller, and Kendall Thomas (New York: The New Press, 1995), 127–58.

14. Clothing is different from food in this regard because most of the clothing manu-factured by multinational corporations and sold in chain stores is cut to reveal more than these women want to reveal. Most Muslim women buy from African and African Ameri-can designers and distributors who sell styles from South Asia, Africa, and the Middle East.

15. This is an old, and probably outdated, statistic that was used by black nationalists during the 1960s to promote race-conscious shopping.

16. Clegg, *An Original Man;* E. U. Essien-Udom, *Black Nationalism: A Search for Iden-tity in America* (Chicago: Chicago University Press, 1962); and Marla Frederick, *Between Sundays: Black Women and Everyday Struggles of Faith* (Berkeley: University of California Press, 2003).

17. Wolfgang Haug, *Critique of Commodity Aesthetics: Appearance, Sexuality, and Adver-tising in Capitalist Society* (Minneapolis: University of Minnesota Press, 1986), 7. Robin D. G. Kelley critiques the tyranny of the commodity aesthetic of the black power movement in *Yo' Mama's Disfunktional! Fighting the Culture Wars in Urban America* (Boston: Beacon, 1997).

18. From the products of local female entrepreneurs (Afrocentric skin-care products, gift baskets, African-inspired art objects and jewelry, and clothing), to the fashion design-ers featured, the fashion show was about consuming a female Muslim identity. For inter-esting discussions on consumption and black identity, see Tracy Poe, "The Origins of Soul Food in Black Urban Identity: Chicago, 1915–1947," *American Studies International* 37, no. 1 (1999): 4–33; and Doris Witt, *Black Hunger: Food and the Politics of U.S. Identity* (Oxford: Oxford University Press).

19. The distinction between what is secular and what is sacred is not always obvious. A strong belief in pluralism can seem more akin to an article of religious faith than to a

secular commitment. Pluralism encourages preserving the doctrine of a tolerant society over building exchange relationships with those who will reciprocate either directly or indirectly. Secular forms of exchange are contractual and stress economic efficiency and individualism over community. Reciprocation matters, but only with respect to supporting an abstract value. While one could argue that God is an abstract value, in the United States God is generally understood to be involved in the affairs of this world. According to most Americans, God wants marriages to succeed and communities to prosper. Thus my distinction between secular and religious forms of exchange applies only to the United States.

20. In *The Gift* (New York: W. W. Norton, 1950), Marcel Mauss noted that gift-giving and reciprocation are important parts of intergroup communication and that the failure to do either properly produces significant social consequences. Exchange communicates valuable social information, and one can extrapolate from Mauss's argument that all cultural modes of exchange—language, eating, aesthetics, etc.—are similarly entangled in moral discourses of obligation. In the 1970s, anthropologists reconsidered the social and moral embeddedness of symbolic culture and consumption. See Arjun Appadurai, "Commodities and the Politics of Value," in *The Social Life of Things: Commodities in Cultural Perspective* (Cambridge: Cambridge University Press, 1986); Pierre Bourdieu, *Outline of a Theory of Practice,* ed. Richard Nice (Cambridge: Cambridge University Press, 1977); Douglas and Isherwood, *The World of Goods;* and Marshall David Sahlins, *Culture and Practical Reason* (Chicago: University of Chicago Press, 1976). Bourdieu later elaborated on what he calls symbolic capital which is acquired primarily through exchange and consumption; see Bourdieu, *Distinction.* Deliberate choices about the cultural symbols with which one associates oneself and the exchange relationships one cultivates lead to greater or lesser access to material rewards. What one gives, how one reciprocates, and what one displays all communicate important cultural information, which is why Douglas and Isherwood argue that, contrary to neoliberal economic theory, consumption is not about rational economic self-interest but about defining social relationships. Douglas's thesis is patently evident in the discourse following the Muslim fashion show. For more on consumption and signification, see Jean Baudrillard, *For a Critique of the Political Economy of the Sign,* ed. Charles Levin (St. Louis, MO: Telos, 1981).

21. Dorinne Kondo, *About Face: Performing Race in Fashion and Theater* (New York: Routledge, 1997).

22. For an interesting discussion about the power of belief and faith to alter social dispositions, see Thomas Csordas, *The Sacred Self: A Cultural Phenomenology of Charismatic Healing* (Berkeley: University of California Press, 1994); Webb Keane, "Religious Language," *Annual Review of Anthropology* 26 (1997): 47–71; Webb Keane, "Semiotics and the Social Analysis of Material Things," *Language and Communication* 23 (2003): 409–25; and Saba Mahmood, "Rehearsed Spontaneity and the Conventionality of Ritual: Disciplines of Salat," *American Ethnologist* 28 (2001): 827–53.

23. Davis, *City of Quartz,* 87.

24. For a less dystopic vision of Los Angeles, see Peter Dreier, "America's Urban Crisis a Decade After the Los Angeles Riots," *National Civic Review* 92, no. 1 (2003): 35–55, which describes how poor Los Angelinos have organized interethnic alliances to support workers' rights.

25. For definitions and descriptions of the contested and complex concept of agency, see Carol J. Greenhouse, *A Moment's Notice: Time Politics across Cultures* (Ithaca, NY: Cornell University Press, 1996), and Laura Ahearn, "Language and Agency," *Annual Reviews of Anthropology* 30 (2001): 109–37.

Chapter 13. *"But, It's* Bible*"*

1. All names are pseudonyms, to protect the privacy of the women interviewed for this study.

2. See Jesus Martin-Barbero, "Mass Media as a Site of Resacralization of Contemporary Cultures," in *Rethinking Media, Religion and Culture*, ed. Stewart M. Hoover and Knut Lundby (Thousand Oaks, CA: Sage, 1997), 103. See also Wade Clark Roof, *Spiritual Marketplace: Baby Boomers and the Remaking of American Religion* (Princeton, NJ: Princeton University Press, 1999). According to sociologist Graham Murdock, at the height of modernity "spiritual authority had been undermined by science, and materialism and religion had retreated from the centers of institutional and imaginative life." People were struggling with what the classical German sociologist Max Weber called "the disenchantment of the world"; there was in essence an "absence of meaning." According to Murdock, "The resurgence of fundamentalism in the three great religions of the Book aims to intervene in the process of capitalist modernity and the existing social and moral order 'so as to bring it into line with the commands and values' of the holy texts." For Murdock three trends—"the loss of faith in 'progress', the intensified sense of meaningless at the heart of modernity, and the consumer system's increasing inability to compensate—have enlarged the space through which religion can reenter the mainstream of private and public life." The rise of religious fundamentalisms, however, is not only "a simple assertion of religious values" but also a "response to the crisis of late-arriving modernity that speaks to a range of anxieties through the rhetorics and rituals of faith . . . Religions absorb anxiety and feed upon it. In plain terms, this is the new magic, paradoxically brought about by the 'liberation from magic.'" See Graham Murdock, "The Re-enchantment of the World: Religion and the Transformations of Modernity," in *Rethinking Media, Religion and Culture*, 86, 95, 98.

3. While it is customary in today's political climate to consider those who talk openly about the Bible's influence upon their life as "conservative" Christians, this term often camouflages more than it illuminates. *Conservative* in some circles invites negative connotations of intolerance and bigotry, while in others the term conjures images of reverence for tradition and submission to God. In relation to African American women's commitments to scripture, such polarized views do not adequately illuminate the complexity of their faith commitments as they are expressed in personal life and partisan politics.

4. In this often-cited colloquial expression, "the Word," "the" stands alone as a definite article signifying the absolute and uncompromised authority of the biblical text. For those who use this phrase, its legitimacy is maintained through the belief that this very Word "became flesh" and "dwelt among us," as stated by the gospel of John in describing the birth of Jesus. This reading of "the Word" establishes it as divinely authoritative.

5. Bobby Alexander, in *Televangelism Reconsidered: Ritual in the Search for Human Community* (Atlanta: Scholars Press, 1994), 23, suggests that "at the outset it should be noted

that viewers are not converted to the television ministers' brand of religion. They are already committed to it . . . Viewers are already 'predisposed or self-selected to seek out the message of televangelism,' which reflects viewers' conservative Christian beliefs."

6. Lila Abu-Lughod, "The Interpretation of Culture(s) after Television," *Representations* 59 (Summer 1997): 120.

7. A growing body of literature considers the influence of religious television on communities throughout the African diaspora. In a thoughtful ethnographic account of the growth of religious television in Ghana, Marleen De Witte considers how the process of "making, broadcasting and watching" televangelism "creates charisma, informs ways of perception, and produces new kinds of religious subjectivity and spiritual experience." See Marleen De Witte, "Altar Media's *Living Word:* Televised Charismatic Christianity in Ghana," *Journal of Religion in Africa* 33, no. 2 (2003): 172.

8. Faye Ginsburg, Lila Abu-Lughod, and Brian Larkin, *Media Worlds: Anthropology on New Terrain* (Berkeley: University of California Press, 2002), 13.

9. Abu-Lughod, "The Interpretation of Culture(s) after Television," 127.

10. Ibid., 112.

11. Renita J. Weems, "Reading Her Way Through the Struggle: African American Women and the Bible," in *Stony the Road We Trod: African American Biblical Interpretation,* ed. Cain Hope Felder (Minneapolis, MN: Fortress, 1991), 62.

12. Ibid., 64.

13. Vincent L. Wimbush, ed., *African Americans and the Bible: Sacred Texts and Social Textures* (New York: Continuum, 2001), 9.

14. James Shopshire, Ida Rousseau Mukenge, Victoria Erickson, and Hans A. Baer, "The Bible and Contemporary African American Culture II: Report of a Preliminary Ethnographic Project," in *African Americans and the Bible,* 75.

15. Shaun Moores, *Interpreting Audiences: The Ethnography of Media Consumption* (Thousand Oaks, CA: Sage, 1993).

16. Ibid., 3.

17. While ministers reflect varying backgrounds, I use "evangelicals" throughout the article as an umbrella term to include Pentecostals, Charismatics, and conservative mainline Protestants. T. D. Jakes, who pastors a church of over 20,000 members in Dallas, Texas, and Creflo Dollar, who pastors a megachurch in Atlanta, Georgia, are two of the most popular contemporary African American television preachers among white and black viewers. While their ministries became noted in the early 1990s, Rev. Ike began broadcasting in the late 1960s and established the United Christian Evangelistic Association (UCEA) in 1962. Rev. Ike claimed over 1 million followers by 1972 and over 7 million by 1982.

18. Dennis N. Voskuil, "The Power of the Air," in *American Evangelicals and the Mass Media,* ed. Quentin Schultze (Grand Rapids, MI: Zondervan, 1990), 69.

19. Kimberly A. Neuendorf, "The Public Trust versus the Almighty Dollar," in *Religious Television: Controversies and Conclusions,* ed. Robert Abelman and Stewart M. Hoover (Norwood, NJ: Ablex, 1990), 71–72.

20. Peter Horsfield, *Religious Television: The American Experience* (New York: Longman, 1984), 40.

21. Stewart Hoover, *Mass Media Religion: The Social Sources of the Electronic Church* (Newbury Park, CA: Sage, 1988), 51.

22. Voskuil, "The Power of the Air," 85–86, cites James DeForest Murch, *Cooperation Without Compromise: A History of the National Association of Evangelicals* (Grand Rapids, MI: Eerdmans, 1956), 78–79.

23. Neuendorf, "The Public Trust versus the Almighty Dollar," 77.

24. Voskuil, "The Power of the Air," 90.

25. Mimi White, *Tele-Advising: Therapeutic Discourse in American Television* (Chapel Hill: University of North Carolina Press, 1992), 112.

26. See Jeffrey K. Hadden and Charles E. Swann, *Prime Time Preachers: The Rising Power of Televangelism* (Reading, MA: Addison-Wesley, 1981), and Jeffrey K. Hadden and Anson Shupe, *Televangelism: Power and Politics on God's Frontier* (New York: Henry Holt, 1988). Certainly the 2004 reelection of George W. Bush will inspire political scientists, media scholars, and other social scientists to explore how contemporary religious television, with its sermons encouraging parishioners and viewers to "vote the Bible" and "vote your values," challenged the populous to cast their ballots along the tenuous fault lines of presumably moral issues versus economic issues.

27. Many other critiques of television ministries weigh the influence of materialism and American culture on the types of messages that are preached by religious personalities to the larger public. See Quentin Schultze, *Televangelism and American Culture: The Business of Popular Religion* (Grand Rapids, MI: Baker Book House, 1991). More recent studies have gone beyond examining the medium to examining the influence of the medium on viewers across the United States and throughout the world. See Hoover, *Mass Media Religion;* Abelman and Hoover, *Religious Television;* Alexander, *Televangelism Reconsidered;* and Stewart M. Hoover and Lynn Schofield Clark, eds., *Practicing Religion in the Age of the Media: Explorations in Media, Religion and Culture* (New York: Columbia University Press, 2002).

28. Hoover, *Mass Media Religion,* 38.

29. Alexander, *Televangelism Reconsidered,* 50.

30. Schultze, *Televangelism and American Culture,* 55–56.

31. The now defunct Praise the Lord (PTL) ministry of Jim and Tammy Faye Bakker was the first satellite-transmitted religious broadcast to launch in the United States.

32. By using the term "black church tradition" I do not mean to suggest one monolithic and static black church. I take into consideration the assortment of churches and traditions that make up a composite of black church experiences. Regardless of denomination or origin, however, churches that emerge from historically black denominations must wrestle with how they will or will not address civil rights concerns.

33. See C. Eric Lincoln and Lawrence Mamiya, *The Black Church in the African American Experience* (Durham, NC: Duke University Press, 1990).

34. See Albert G. Miller, "The Construction of a Black Fundamentalist Worldview," in *African Americans and the Bible,* 724. The spiritual autobiographies of women like Jarena Lee, Zilpha Elaw, and Julia A. Foote point to a strong and viable evangelical history within African American religious practice. See William Andrews, *Sisters of the Spirit: Three Black Women's Autobiographies of the Nineteenth Century* (Bloomington: Indiana University Press,

1986). The emphasis that has prevailed in the scholarship of the last thirty years on the so-cial protest orientation of black religion often neglects to take into consideration the very real evangelical mission-oriented church that exists, perhaps because of an overreaction against past critiques of the church as escapist and otherworldly.

35. St. Clair Drake and Horace Cayton, *Black Metropolis: A Study of Negro Life in a North-ern City*, rev. ed. (New York: Harcourt, Brace, and World, 1970), 618–19, as quoted in Miller, "The Construction of a Black Fundamentalist Worldview," 712.

36. In *Between Sundays: Black Women and Everyday Struggles of Faith* (Berkeley: University of California Press, 2003), I explore the growth of televangelism in Halifax County and argue that its emergence shifts discourses of social justice, which are historically found in black churches, to discussions that attempt to alleviate suffering based upon notions of individualism, prosperity, and a naive multiculturalism.

37. Bart Laundry, *Black Working Wives: Pioneers of the American Family Revolution* (Berkeley: University of California Press, 2000).

38. Johnnetta Betsch Cole and Beverly Guy-Sheftall, *Gender Talk: The Struggle for Women's Equality in African American Communities* (New York: One World, 2003), 121.

39. See Frederick, *Between Sundays*, for an expanded discussion of how television ministries offer alternative visions of progress for African American communities.

40. Such messages not only inspire change in participants but also yield lucrative financial returns for ministers. The explosion of religious marketing tied to prosperity theologies has created a new niche market that is constantly expanding to include tapes, CDs, books, videos, magazines, conferences, Bibles, and gadgets aimed at helping viewers achieve prosperity. For further discussion of the intersection of religious media and the market, see Heather Hendershot, *Shaking the World for Jesus: Media and Conservative Evangelical Culture* (Chicago: University of Chicago Press, 2004).

41. On Joyce Meyer's website, listed immediately below the standard icons Home and About Us, and before her icons for Personal Ministry, World Outreach, or Help for the Hurting, viewers are invited to enter her page on "America," which is disturbingly similar to what scholars describe as the problematic linkage of Christian values to American values. This page invites the viewer to call her congressperson and support those members of congress and judicial nominees who are prolife and profamily, according to politically conservative understandings of family.

42. The flyer encouraged persons to "join the leadership of the conservative movement and grassroots activists from all over the country at Road to Victory 2002—the premier conference for pro-family conservatives in America today. Hear our nation's political and religious leaders talk about issues that impact you and your family. And learn how you can make a difference in your community and nation." Pictured on the cover of the flyer were Roberta Combs, President of Christian Coalition of America; Joyce Meyer; Pastor John Hagee of San Antonio, Texas; Rep. Tom DeLay; Pat Robertson; Rabbi Yeheil Eckstein; Rep. J. C. Watts; and Rev. James Robinson.

43. www.thepottershouse.org/BJ_faq.html.

44. Alexander, *Televangelism Reconsidered*, 71.

R. MARIE GRIFFITH is a professor of religion at Princeton University. She is the author of *God's Daughters: Evangelical Women and the Power of Submission* and *Born Again Bodies: Flesh and Spirit in American Christianity*, both published by the University of California Press. She is completing a documentary history of American religion for Oxford University Press and is also working on a book about the sexual beliefs and practices of American evangelicals.

BARBARA DIANNE SAVAGE is the Geraldine R. Segal Professor of American Social Thought and professor of history at the University of Pennsylvania. She is the author of *Broadcasting Freedom: Radio, War, and the Politics of Race, 1938–1948* (University of North Carolina Press, 1999). She is currently completing a book on the politics of African American religion, which examines the relationship between African American religion, politics, and culture in the twentieth century.

WALLACE BEST is an assistant professor of African American Religion at Harvard Divinity School. He is the author of *Passionately Human, No Less Divine: Religion and Culture in Black Chicago, 1915–1952* (Princeton University Press, 2005). He has received several research awards, including fellowships at Princeton University's Center for the Study of Religion and the W. E. B. Du Bois Institute at Harvard University.

ANTHEA D. BUTLER is an assistant professor of religion at the University of Rochester, teaching American and African American Religious History. Her publications include a forthcoming book, *Making a Sanctified World: Women in the Church of God in Christ* (University of North Carolina Press, 2006), and a chapter in *Religion and the South: Protestants and Others in History and in Culture,* also with UNC Press.

LISA GAIL COLLINS is the Associate Professor in Art and Africana Studies on the Class of 1951 Chair at Vassar College. She is the author of *The Art of History: African American Women Artists Engage the Past* (Rutgers University Press, 2002) and *Art by African-American Artists: Selections from the 20th Century* (Metropolitan Museum of Art, in association with Yale University Press, 2003). She is also coauthor of *African-American Artists, 1929–1945: Prints, Drawings, and Paintings in the Metropolitan Museum of Art* (Yale University Press, 2003) and coeditor of *New Thoughts on the Black Arts Movement* (Rutgers University Press, 2006).

DEIDRE HELEN CRUMBLEY is an associate professor of Africana Studies in Interdisciplinary Studies at North Carolina State University. Her book *Spirit, Structure and Flesh: Gender Practices in Three African Instituted Churches* is forthcoming from the University of Wisconsin Press. Her current research project focuses on the intersection of race, gender, migration, and religious innovation in the rise of an African American, female-founded storefront church. In addition to her terminal degree in anthropology, she holds a masters of theological studies.

MARLA FREDERICK-MCGLATHERY is an assistant professor of African and African American Studies and of the Study of Religion at Harvard University. An anthropologist by training, she is the author of *Between Sundays: Black Women and Everyday Struggles of Faith* (University of California Press, 2003). She is currently researching the influence of religious media, more specifically television ministries, on constructions of race and gender in the African diaspora.

CHERYL TOWNSEND GILKES is the John D. and Catherine T. MacArthur Professor of Sociology and African American Studies at Colby College and Director of the African American Studies Program. Her book, *"If It Wasn't For The Women . . .": Black Women's Experience And Womanist Culture In Church And Community* (Orbis Books, 2001), contains a selection of her essays on women and the Sanctified Church. She is currently working on *That Blessed Book: The Bible and the African American Cultural Imagination* (Orbis Books, in progress).

RACHEL ELIZABETH HARDING is an independent scholar, consultant, and writer living in Denver, Colorado. A Latin Americanist historian, Harding explores the intersections of religion, culture, and memory in the experience of the Afro-Atlantic diaspora. She is author of *A Refuge in Thunder: Candomblé and Alternative Spaces of Blackness* (Indiana University Press, 2000) and other essays on Afro-Brazilian religion. She is also a poet whose work has been widely published.

TRACEY E. HUCKS is an associate professor of religion at Haverford College. She is the author of several articles on Afro-Caribbean religion and the Black Church, as well as a piece on African American women in African-derived traditions. She will soon publish her first book, *Approaching the African God: African American Yoruba History in the United States* (Indiana University Press).

PAUL CHRISTOPHER JOHNSON is an associate professor in history at the Center for Afroamerican and African Studies at the University of Michigan–Ann Arbor. The author of *Secrets, Gossip and Gods: The Transformation of Brazilian Candomblé* (Oxford University Press, 2002), his second book, *Black Carib Religion: Ritual and Memory across Three Diasporic Horizons*, will soon be published by the University of California Press. Recent articles include "Three Paths to Legitimacy: African Diaspora Religions and the State," in *Culture and Religion* (2005).

MARTHA S. JONES is an assistant professor of history and Afroamerican and African Studies and visiting assistant professor of law at the University of Michigan. Her first book, *"All Bound Up Together": The "Woman Question" in African-American Public Culture, 1830–1900* (University of North Carolina Press, forthcoming), is an intellectual and cultural history of black women's public lives in the nineteenth-century United States. Her current work explores the relationship of black Americans to Atlantic World legal culture in the pre–Civil War period.

ISABEL (BELLA) MUKONYORA is an assistant professor of Global Christianity and Women and Religion in the Department of Philosophy and Religion at Western Kentucky University. She is a former British Commonwealth Scholar with a doctorate from the University of Oxford, a former Senior Fulbright Scholar and Carter G. Woodson Postdoctoral Fellow with a forthcoming book on gendered landscapes in Masowe spirituality. In addition, she has published a number of articles on Christianity in Africa today.

CAROLYN ROUSE is an associate professor of anthropology and also teaches in the African American Studies program at Princeton University. She is the author of *Engaged Surrender: African-American Women and Islam* (University of California Press, 2004) and is completing a book on racial health care disparities and sickle cell disease. In addition, she has produced, directed, and edited a number of documentaries.

JUDITH WEISENFELD is a professor of religion at Vassar College. She is the author of *African-American Women and Christian Activism: New York's Black YWCA, 1905–1945* (Harvard University Press, 1997), co-editor of *This Far By Faith: Readings in African American Women's Religious Biography* (Routledge, 1996), and author of the forthcoming *Hollywood Be Thy Name: African-American Religion in American Film, 1929–1950* (University of California Press, 2007).

Page numbers in *italics* refer to illustrations.